Design By Numbers

John Maeda

Design By Numbers

The MIT Press
Cambridge, Massachusetts
London, England

Designed by John Maeda.

Printed and bound in the United States of America.

Library of Congress Cataloging-in-Publication Data

Maeda, John.
Design By Numbers / John Maeda
p. cm.
Includes bibliographical references.
ISBN 0-262-13354-7 (hc : alk. paper)
1. Computer programming. 2. Computer Graphics. I. Title.
QA76.6.M336 1999
005.1—dc21 98-37583
CIP

To Kris

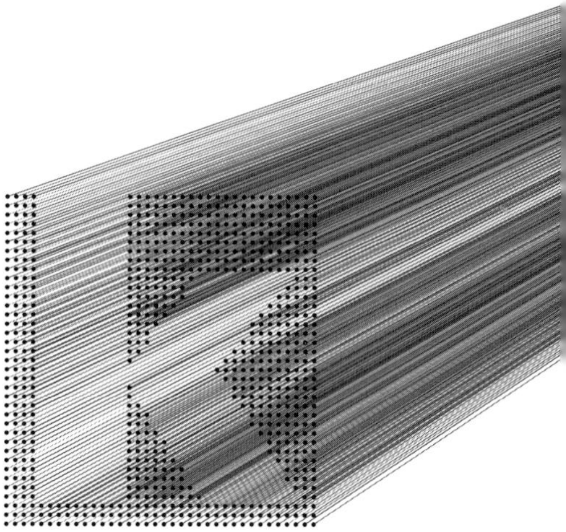

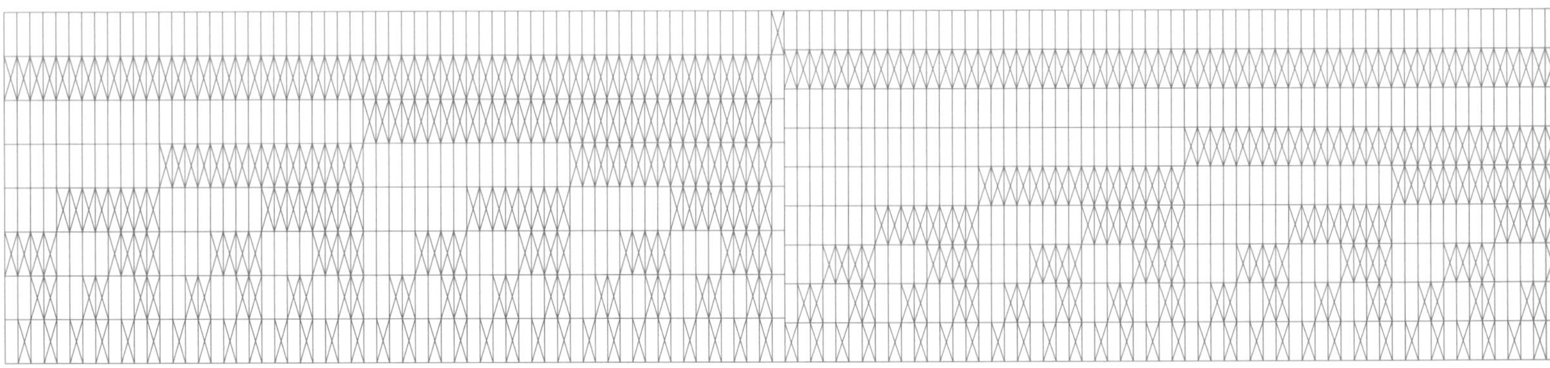

Design By Numbers Contents

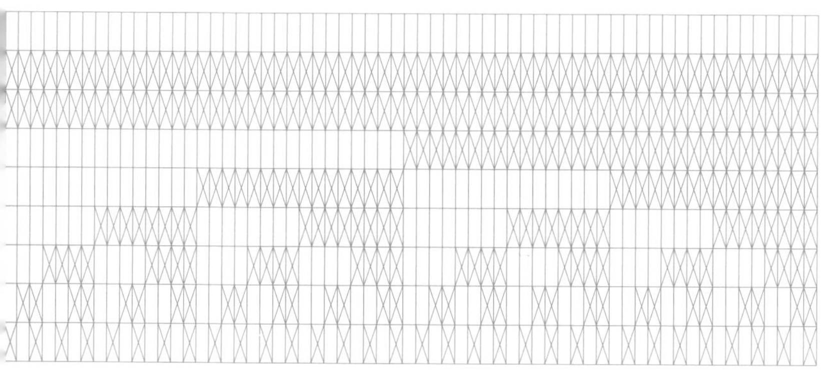

Paola Antonelli

Foreword

About fifteen years ago, the desktop computer entered the professional world. This fantastic brand-new medium demanded and deserved experimentation. Wherever it was implemented in the world of the arts, it changed not only the final product, but also the creative process itself. As always happens with disruptive innovations, the computer provoked much criticism. Self-discipline, its detractors said, was being abandoned in favor of less rigorous trial-and-error, cut-and-paste habits. The attraction of immediate results appeared to work against the strategic thought made necessary by earlier technologies. Thanks to the computer, writers could jot down concepts, and designers visual fragments, apparently at random and without a strong leading idea, rearranging them only at the end to form a finished text or design. Because of this apparently time-saving technology, its detractors concluded, texts, images, and objects would lose power and generate a world of diluted intensity and rigor.

In graphic design, in particular, the computer created a tidal wave whose impact was quick and massive. It quickly generated factions and ignited debate. On one side, against the computer, sat some of the best champions of hand-made modernism, like Paul Rand and Massimo Vignelli. On the other side sat many young talented designers and thinkers, like the group Emigre and Lorraine Wild, who were confident enough in their self-discipline and ability to exploit and ride the new medium. Modern design is about showing clarity of process and purpose, and the best among them relied on their post-modern flexibility to update the positive qualities of modern design and to express the most contemporary visual culture. As a matter of fact, modern design objects display in their function and form the process that generated them. Such objects are determined not by the process, but rather by the use that is made of it. When this characteristic is taken as a definition, modern design becomes timeless and styleless and can be found alike in ancient Greece, in 1938, and today.

The battle that is now history had many famous episodes and many less famous epilogues. Among the most emblematic is the encounter between Paul Rand, the idolized and cantankerous master who believed he rejected the new, and John Maeda, a younger designer who could play his computer like a violin, who happened to be a fervent fan of Rand. Maeda showed Rand that the computer is indeed a powerful tool that can be used to produce powerful designs, by generating with it brand new examples of historical modernism.

The most important part of Maeda's production, and the one he is most proud of, is not the final object, but rather the process. In his work, the process is the core that informs the final outcome. Maeda's fundamental idea is that to successfully design with a computer, one has to design, or at least understand, the program one uses. This position brings him close to post-modern pioneers like Rudy VanderLans and Zuzana Licko of Emigre, who in 1985 designed on their small Macintosh the low-resolution typefaces that they used in their graphics. It also brings Maeda close to the best contemporary industrial designers, who not only master the design process, but also influence the design of the materials they will use.

By stressing the necessity of knowing in depth the tools and methods of design, Maeda also responds to one of the major criticisms advanced by the detractors of the computer, the lack of self-discipline that it allegedly allows. Even though it is true that, in general, the new fields of design, like computer-based graphic design ten years ago and websites or wearable computing today, seem to attract many amateurs and to provoke in designers a short circuit that erases the school memory of a correct design process, it is also true that it always takes time. Graphic design is undergoing a postindustrial revolution similar to the industrial revolution that shook object design more than a century ago. It took some time and some polemic before design thinkers could give order to the exuberance of the hideous new objects, such as beflowered cast-iron toilets and chairs, that sang the praise of the industrial technology in the second half of the nineteenth century. It is still taking time for the graphic design profession as a whole to feel comfortable with this new and ever-improving technology.

With this book, Maeda teaches both professional and amateur designers a design process that paradoxically has a hands-on, almost Arts and Crafts feeling. His approach to computer graphic design is not different from an approach to wood carving. Aimed at exemplifying the basic design of a programming method that transforms itself into a visual design process, this book is an unmatched attempt to share precious knowledge. As awareness of the new medium continues to disseminate, the more designers will learn to incorporate the digital medium in their practice without being unsettled by it.

Paola Antonelli
Associate Curator
The Museum of Modern Art

Preface This book is meant for people who were too late for the computer design boom, those who hated the computer when it began to take control, or those who have just begun to take on the computer. I may have missed some people, but my intention is to write a book that reflects the positive aspects of the computer as it relates to design. I will introduce the concepts of computer programming in a language designed to engage you visually. By acquiring the skills necessary to write computer programs that are themselves visual expressions, you will come to appreciate the computer's unique role in the future of the arts and design.

My intent is to help build a basic understanding of the process behind creating a computer program. After reading this book, you probably won't be able to program the next competitor to Adobe's latest arsenal, but you will at least be able to appreciate the hidden alphanumeric chaos that underlies the digital design tools that many designers take for granted. Proceed slowly and, whenever possible, type each example into your computer. Although tedious, it is essential to your deeper awareness of the processes and structures described.

When I first mentioned this project to a senior colleague, her first response was disgust; "Design by numbers? Numbers can't design; only humans can!" At first I did not know what point she was trying to make. Then I was reminded about an area of research where the goal is to demonstrate computer systems that can design autonomously. To her, *Design By Numbers* implied that the numbers somehow do the designing. I have no intention to promote such systems, which would put us all out of business. Furthermore, as a designer, I would like to believe that such a goal is impossible. There is nothing that prevents the encoding of a designer's basic intelligence in digital form, but I subscribe to the belief that design is intuition, not intelligence. It is talent, not facts and rules. And if we can't teach humans how to be talented designers (I was told that they have to be born that way), I sincerely doubt that we can teach machines.

In designing this book, I realized that it would be insincere to take a straightforward, low-tech approach while espousing the unique benefits of the computational medium. However, the agreed-upon delivery date was only a few months away, which did not allow much time to be avant garde. But as I rummaged through my library for ideas and happened upon Paul Rand's brilliant *A Designer's Art,* I imagined Mr. Rand staring at me sternly and ever so disappointedly, and was reminded that there is no valor in being lazy. Consequently, *Design By Numbers* was developed using an intricate computational process developed specifically for it.

A New Language: DBN This book introduces a programming system available on the Web that can be freely downloaded or run directly within any Java-enabled Web browser. The name of the system is DBN, the acronym **D**esign **B**y **N**umbers. While DBN should work with any modern computer system, I recommend one that is post-1995. DBN has been tested to run on any Windows or MacOS-based system. Access the website at http://dbn.media.mit.edu.

The emphasis throughout the book is on building an understanding of the motivation behind computer programming and the many wonders that emerge from effectively written programs. I wrote it for the mathematically challenged people of the world, so there is minimal emphasis on mathematics in the first half. But because computation is inherently linked to mathematics, the latter half employs intermediate mathematical concepts that, wherever possible, do not go beyond secondary school algebra. There are twenty chapters. The first ten enable you to explore enough computational drawings to last several lifetimes. The remaining chapters cover successively advanced topics, ranging from interaction to artificial life, which you may find relevant in your future computational adventures.

The language introduced has been designed specifically for visual people—artists, designers, or anyone who can pick up a pencil and doodle. All numbers generally fall within the familiar range of 0 to 100, and are given some visual significance, such as position on the page or percentages of gray. The language itself has very few commands, and has been designed with elements that resemble many languages that I have used in the past such as Lisp, C, and Java. However such languages are very sophisticated. Do not assume that fluency in the system described in this book will guarantee an easy transition to mainstream languages. Nevertheless, you will find yourself well prepared to create in whichever language you ultimately choose.

Acknowledgments I wish to give my sincere thanks to Paola Antonelli for agreeing to write the foreword. Paola's unparalleled insight into the past, present, and future of design enables her to interpret technology in a playful manner that always retains the inherent joy of design.

Tom White and Peter Cho, two of my students at MIT, were instrumental in keeping this project going at a high level of quality, by playing an integral part in developing the language architecture and creating many entertaining examples to demonstrate the various merits and drawbacks of using DBN. Jared Schiffman, Elise Co, Ben Fry, Golan Levin, Richard DeVaul, Bill Keays, Phillip Tiongson, Nobuki Ueda, Jessica Wu, Jocelyn Lin, and Catherine Foo helped in the preparation of the book, and Matthew Grenby, Reed Kram, and Chloe Chao aided in its initial conception. David Small and Connie Van Rheenen kept my research group at MIT moving forward while I had temporarily lost my mind to DBN. Yasuyo Iguchi kept the design of the book on track by making sure I did not cut any corners. Ellen Hoffman provided editing aid with her signature small humor and other textual, flavor enhancements.

Bob Prior and Roger Conover, both of MIT Press, bought into this ambitious project, and I am grateful that they stayed with it throughout its development. Bob quickly realized the implications of this project and supported it all the way to the final details of the design.

Kris Maeda, my wife and work partner, never gave up encouraging, editing, and asking the questions that made me cringe. This book is dedicated to her and all the years she has lovingly supported me as I have tried to make sense of this dream.

```
/*** DBN VERSION 0, by John Maeda. An attempt to create a programming language that can teach the basics of computation to the non-mathematically inclined person. ***/ import java.awt.*; i
static int tMSG=0, tCMD=1; Image ic[]; Image ic2[]; String dir = “stuff/”; Image title; Image imp, ims; bufpanel bp; env app; Rectangle loadr = new Rectangle(); Rectangle saver = new Rectangle();
app.getImage(app.getDocumentBase(),dir+“play.GIF”); for(int i=0;i<=100;i+=10) { int v = 100-134*i*i/10000+34*i*i*i/1000000; System.out.println(i+“: ”+v); } } Graphics myg=null; int pw; public voi
setmsg(String s) { msg = s; repaint(); } public Dimension preferredSize() { return new Dimension(100,24); } public boolean mouseUp(Event ev, int x, int y) { if (x<24) { if (!playp) { app.goaheadandru
app.doload(); } else if (saver.inside(x,y)) { // System.out.println(“saver.......”); app.dosave(); } return true; } Font f = new Font(“Helvetica”,Font.PLAIN,10); public void paint(Graphics g) { Rectangle r =
24,0,24,r.height); g.setColor(Color.darkGray); g.fillRect(0,0,r.width,r.height); g.setColor(Color.white); g.setFont(f); pw = g.getFontMetrics().stringWidth(msg); g.drawString(msg,23,15); g.setColor(Co
g.fillRect(saver.x+4,saver.y+4,saver.width-8,saver.height-8); g.setColor(Color.white); g.drawString(“rd”,loadr.x+4+3,loadr.y+16); g.drawString(“wr”,saver.x+4+3,saver.y+16); } } } class StringTokeniz
return s.substring(start,i); } else { b=i+1; return s.substring(start,i+1); } } public String getuntilmatched(int start, char c1, char c2) { int i; int level = 0; for(i=start;i<len;i++) { if (s.charAt(i)==c1) level
for(i=b;i<len;i++) { char c = s.charAt(i); switch(c) { case ‘<’: return getuntilmatched(i,‘<’,‘>’); case ‘(’: // do balanced version return getuntilmatched(i,‘(’,‘)’); case ‘[’: return getuntilmatched(i,‘[’,‘
netinitp = false; boolean setting = false; int numgets; // hiresbuf int cbw, cbh; int pgcol = 0; int pencol = 100; int bw,bh; int [][]bits; byte [][]dbits; accessorypanel msg=null; long curt; Image bim=n
boolean stepp = false; // Image bimcp; public void createpage(int w, int h) { bw = w+1; bh = h+1; bits = new int[bw][bh]; dbits = new byte[bw][bh]; if (bim!=null) bim = null; bim = createImage(bw,b
= new Color[101]; for(i =0;i<101;i++) { int g = (int)((float)i*255f/100f+.5f); bitscol[i] = new Color(g,g,g); } for(i=0;i<26;i++) { keys[i] = false; keyt[i] = -1; } } int szw = 358, szh = 318; Font f = new Fo
bufpanel(String code, int sc) { doinits(); progstr = code; szw = 102; szh = 102; margx = margy = 4; runtimep = true; } int margx = 12, margy = 12; Image pat=null; Rectangle framer = new Rectangl
g.setColor(Color.white); g.fillRect(0,0,r.width,r.height); g.setColor(Color.black); g.drawRect(framer.x-1,framer.y-1,framer.width+1,framer.height+1); return; } if (pat == null) { pat = createImage(16,16
g.drawImage(pat,i*16,j*16,this); } g.setColor(Color.white); g.fillRect(framer.x-1,framer.y-1,framer.width+1,framer.height+1); g.setColor(Color.black); g.drawRect(framer.x-1,framer.y-1,framer.width+1,
step; if (sc==1) step = 50; else step = 10; for(i=0;i<=100;i+=step) { int x,y; y = framer.y+framer.height-framer.height*i/100-1; g.drawLine(framer.x-2,y,framer.x-4,y); g.drawString(“”+i,framer.x-4-g.ge
g.drawString(“”+i,framer.x+framer.width*i/100+1,framer.y+framer.height+12); } g.setColor(Color.darkGray); // g.drawLine(margx,0,margx,r.height); // g.drawLine(0,r.height-margy,r.width,r.height-ma
gpage(int val) { if (val>100) val = 100; if (val<0) val = 0; pgcol = 100-val; clearbits(); } public void gpen(int val) { pencol = 100-val;//100-val; } public void refreshbits() { int i,j; for(i=0;i<bw;i++) for(j=0
public void circpts(int x, int y, int x0, int y0, int v) { setbit(x+x0,y+y0,v); setbit(x+x0,-y+y0,v); setbit(-x+x0,y+y0,v); setbit(-x+x0,-y+y0,v); setbit(y+x0,x+y0,v); setbit(y+x0,-x+y0,v); setbit(-y+x0,x+y0,v)
r; int de = 3; int dse = -2*r+5; circpts(x,y,x0,y0,pencol); while(y>x) { if (d<0) { d+= de; de+=2; dse+=2; } else { d+= dse; de+=2; dse+=4; y—; } x++; circpts(x,y,x0,y0,pencol); } } public void grect(in
BresLine(x0,y0,x1,y1,pencol); if (true) return; if (dx == 0 && dy == 0) { setbit(x0,y0,pencol); } else if (dx == 0) { if (dy<0) { int dum = y0; y0 = y1; y1 = dum; } for(i=y0; i<y1;i++) setbit(x0,i,pencol); } el
bresen2(x0,y0,x1,y1,pencol); } else { if (dx>=-dy) bresen1(x0,y0,x1,y1,pencol); else { //System.out.println(“yell”); bresen2(x0,y0,x1,y1,pencol); } }*/ } } public void bresen1(int x0, int y0, int x1, int y
{ d+=incrNE; x++; y+=sny; } setbit(x,y,val); } } public void clearbits() { int i,j; for(i=0;i<bw;i++) for(j=0;j<bh;j++) { bits[i][j] = pgcol; dbits[i][j] = 1; } bimg.setColor(bitscol[pgcol]); bimg.fillRect(0,0,bw
int g = n; if (g<0) g = 0; if (g>100) g = 100; // System.out.println(“g is ”+g+“ n is ”+n); bimg.setColor(bitscol[g]); bimg.drawLine(i,j-1,i,j-1); /* myg = this.getGraphics(); myg.setColor(bitscol[g]); myg.
tx, ty; if (refreshp) { drawframe(g); refreshp = false; } // System.out.println(“predrawbits”); // if (!bdirtyp) return; g.translate(framer.x,framer.y);//tx=(margx+1),ty=(cb.height-margy-sc*bh)); orgx = fra
def_command(String s, Block b) { int i; Vector v = b.args; System.out.println(“def ” + s); cmdenv.put(s,b); } public void def_io(String s, Block b) { int i; Vector v = b.args; ioenv.put(s,b); } public Bloc
System.out.println(“set ”+s+“ to ”+n); if (s.startsWith(“[”)) { StringTokenizer2 st = new StringTokenizer2(trim2(s)); int x = evalarg(st.nextToken()); int y = evalarg(st.nextToken()); setbit(x,y,100-n);//t
String str = new String(st.nextToken() + “ ” + n); sendtoServer(str); } else { } } else curFrame().put(s,new Integer(n)); } Vector vframes = new Vector(); public void PushFrame() { // System.out.printl
return (Hashtable)vframes.elementAt(vframes.size()-1); } public int getvar(String s) throws lerr { { // need to search through all frames int i; Integer m = null; for(i=vframes.size()-1;i>=0;i—) { Hashta
char word[] = s.toCharArray(); for (int i = 0; i < s.length(); i++) { if (word[i] == c) { sp(“CONTAINS: ”+s.length()+“ ”+i); return i; } } return -1; } public String comesafter(String s, int n) { return s.subs
stack[] = new int[100]; int outc = 0; public int outputpop() throws lerr { if (outc == 0) throw new lerr(“out stack overflow”); outc—; return outstack[outc]; } public void outputpush(int v) { // System
//System.out.println(“new client”); client = new ClientConnection(hoster); netinitp = true; } public void settoServer(int place, int value) { //System.out.println(“set ” + place + “ ” + value); client.ou
//System.out.println(“gotfromserver ” + line + “ ” + numgets + “times”); return Integer.parseInt(line); } catch (IOException e) { System.out.println(e.toString()); } return -1; } public int evalarg(Strin
*/” s=s.trim(); // System.out.println(“EVAL ARG: >>”+s+“<<”); if (s.startsWith(“(”)) { // find the matching paren return evalarg(trim2(s)); } // does not work, needs to seek paren at this level and dec
v= 100-bits[x][y]; return v; } */else if (contains(s,‘(’)>0) { // got a paren up to bat // find out operator that occurs before int i; for(i=0;i<s.length();i++) { if (s.charAt(i)==‘(’) break; } i—; switch(s.charA
evalarg(s.substring(i+1,s.length())); case ‘/’: return evalarg(s.substring(0,i))/evalarg(s.substring(i+1,s.length())); default: System.out.println(“math: unknown operator”); return 0; } } else if (contai
StringTokenizer(s, “-”); return evalarg(st.nextToken())-evalarg(comesafter(s, contains(s, ‘-’)+1)); } else if (contains(s, ‘*’) > 0) { StringTokenizer st = new StringTokenizer(s, “*”); return evalarg(st.next
(s.startsWith(“[”)) { int v; StringTokenizer2 st = new StringTokenizer2(trim2(s)); int x = evalarg(st.nextToken()), y = evalarg(st.nextToken()); v= 100-bits[x][y]; // p(x+“/”+y+“: ”+bits[x][y]); return v; } e
num = evalarg(st.nextToken()); switch(num) { case 1: return mx; case 2: return my; case 3: return mb; default: throw new lerr(“Unknown <loc>: ”+num); } } else if (intype.equals(“key”)) { int
Date d = new Date(); switch(num) { case 1: return d.getHours(); case 2: return d.getMinutes(); case 3: return d.getSeconds(); case 4: return (int)(System.currentTimeMillis()/10; // break; defau
((gb = get_io(intype)) == null) throw new lerr(“Unknown input type: ‘”+s+“’”); else { Vector v = gb.args; if (v == null) { // no args doBlock(g,gb); return outputpop(); } else { // this should be a s
Integer.parseInt(s); } else { return getvar(s); } } // setvar A,2 // drawline A,A,10,20 final int mxstk = 10; Vector blockstk[] = new Vector[mxstk]; // public void pushblock(Vector Vector vect = null; pub
msgbox(“[”+mx+“/”+my+“]”); msgalive(); servicekeys(); // cmd = cmd.toLowerCase(); try { // System.out.println(“doline: ”+b.linenum); // while(!stepp); //System.out.println(“step”); if (cmd.equals(“l
gline(20,20+i,60,20+i); System.out.println(“line ”+(20)+“ ”+(20+i)+“ ”+60+“ ”+(20+i)); } System.out.println(“pen 25”); gpen(25); for(i=0;i<20;i++) { gline(20+i,60+i,60+i,60+i); System.out.println(“lin
(cmd.equals(“value”)) { outputpush(evalarg(st2.nextToken())); } else if (cmd.equals(“rectangle”)) { grect(evalarg(st2.nextToken()),evalarg(st2.nextToken()),evalarg(st2.nextToken()),evalarg(st2.nextTok
gcircle(evalarg(st2.nextToken()),evalarg(st2.nextToken()),Math.abs(evalarg(st2.nextToken()))); } else if (cmd.equals(“pause”)) { long wt= evalarg(st2.nextToken()); // in 100ths of seconds long t = Syst
gfield(evalarg(st2.nextToken()),evalarg(st2.nextToken()),evalarg(st2.nextToken()),evalarg(st2.nextToken()),evalarg(st2.nextToken())); } else if (cmd.equals(“set”)) { setvar(st2.nextToken(), evalarg(st2.n
//System.out.println(“cmd is: ” + cmd); Block bb = get_command(cmd); if (bb == null) { throw new lerr(“Unknown cmd: ”+cmd+“ at line ”+(b.linenum+1)); } else { // System.out.println(“Using name
PopFrame(); } } } } catch (lerr e) { if (e.lnum == -1) { e.lnum = b.linenum; throw e; } } stepp = false; drawbits(g); return false; } public void doStep(Graphics g, String a, int n, int t, int inc, Block b) th
doBlock(Graphics g, Block b) throws lerr { int i, j; // System.out.println(“Doing block: ”+b.getstr()); // b.pp(); msgalive(); //** SHOULD CHECK NARGS!!! if (b.type == Block.STR) { return doLine(g, b);
System.out.println(“Doing a stepone: ”); String line = a.s; StringTokenizer2 st = new StringTokenizer2(line); st.nextToken(); String arg = st.nextToken(); //A int inc = 1; Block nextb = (Block)v.ele
(Block)v.elementAt(i+1); i++; Graphics g2 = bufim.getGraphics(); drawframe(g2); for(;;) { // in a forever, should do automatic double buffering // but i think this would not work if we had nested
(doBlock(g2,nextb)) { // this dont work right because doblock has to be rewriten System.out.println(“ESCAPED”); break; } g.drawImage(bufim,0,0,this); } } else if (a.isa(“same?”)) { String line =
evalarg(arg2)) doBlock(g,nextb); } else if (a.isa(“notsame?”)) { String line = a.s; StringTokenizer2 st = new StringTokenizer2(line); st.nextToken(); String arg1 = st.nextToken(); String arg2 = st.ne
st.nextToken(); String arg1 = st.nextToken(); String arg2 = st.nextToken(); String arg3 = st.nextToken(); Block nextb = (Block)v.elementAt(i+1); i++; if (Math.abs(evalarg(arg1)-evalarg(arg2))<evala
nextb = (Block)v.elementAt(i+1); i++; if (evalarg(arg1) < evalarg(arg2)) doBlock(g,nextb); } else if (a.isa(“notsmaller?”)) { String line = a.s; StringTokenizer2 st = new StringTokenizer2(line); st.ne
= a.s; int nargs = cntargs(line); StringTokenizer2 st = new StringTokenizer2(line); st.nextToken(); String arg = st.nextToken(); Block nextb = (Block)v.elementAt(i+1); i++; if (nargs>2) { Vector nv
cntargs(line); StringTokenizer2 st = new StringTokenizer2(line); st.nextToken(); String arg = st.nextToken(); Block nextb = (Block)v.elementAt(i+1); i++; if (nargs>2) { Vector nv = new Vector(); fo
cntargs(String s) { int i, len = s.length(); int cnt = 0; boolean lst = true, st; for(i=0; i<len;i++) { st = s.charAt(i)!= ‘ ’; if (lst!=st && st) cnt++; lst = st; } return cnt+1; } Thread runner=null; public void st
(mousex-orgx)/sc; my = (orgy-mousey)/sc; mb = mouseb?100:0; //p(mx+“/”+my); } int mousex, mousey; boolean mouseb; public boolean mouseEnter(Event ev, int x, int y) { mousex = x; mousey = y;
y) { mousex = x; mousey = y;mouseb = true; if (zoomr.inside(x,y)) {sc++; if (sc == 4) sc = 1; refreshp = true; if (runner==null) repaint();} calcmouse(); if (runtimep&&((ev.modifiers)&(Event.SHIFT_MAS
false; calcmouse(); return true; } public boolean mouseDrag(Event ev, int x, int y) { mousex = x; mousey = y;mouseb = true; calcmouse(); return true; } public boolean mouseMove(Event ev, int x, in
msg.pulse(); } public void msgbox(lerr e) { System.out.println(“***MSG: ”+e.getMessage()+“ line: ”+e.lnum); if (msg == null) return; msg.setmsg(e.getMessage()); if (e.lnum>=0) { String s = ta.getTe
} } } if (end == -1) end = len; System.out.println(“st/end: ”+st+“/”+end); ta.select(st,end); //ta.replaceText(“AAAAAH”,st,end); // ta.selectAll(); ta.invalidate(); } } public boolean donep = true, errp = fa
runner.stop(); runner = null; } } public void stop() { if (runner !=null) { runner.stop(); runner = null; donep = true; if (netinitp == true) { client.out.flush(); netinitp = false; try {if (client.s != null) client
workaround: store when key comes down, allow valid for // certain amount of time, if exceed then flush. autokey // events come in as keydown so should refresh naturally public void servicekeys
System.currentTimeMillis(); keys[ind] = true; } else if (n>=‘A’&&n<=‘Z’) { int ind = n-‘A’; keyt[ind] = System.currentTimeMillis(); keys[ind] = true; } return true; } public synchronized boolean keyUp(E
stop(); // runp = true; progstr = s; start(); } public int executeprogram(String s) throws lerr { StringTokenizer st = new StringTokenizer(s,“\n”); Graphics g = getGraphics(); Rectangle bds = bounds();
(Exception e) { e.printStackTrace(); return 1; } gpage(0); gpen(100); clearbits(); for(int i = 0; i<keys.length;i++) { keys[i] = false; keyt[i] = -1; } vect = new Vector(); vframes = new Vector(); PushFrame(
public void paint(Graphics g) { Rectangle r = bounds(); cb = bounds(); if (bw == 0) { createpage(100,100); bufim = createImage(r.width,r.height); } zoomr.reshape(0,0,24,16); drawframe(g); myg = g; i
PrintStream out; public ClientConnection(String host) { try { s = new Socket(host, PORT); in = new DataInputStream(s.getInputStream()); out = new PrintStream(s.getOutputStream()); System.out.p
constraints = new GridBagConstraints(); String initcodestr = “{\n paper 50\n line 0 0 100 100\n}”; TextArea code; Button go = new Button(“run”); Button frame = new Button(“read files”); Button a
Button(“step”); String infilename = null; Button saveb = new Button(“save”); Button loadb = new Button(“load”); public void setupforrun() { System.out.println(“setup for run”); setLayout(new Bo
BorderLayout()); p.setLayout(new BorderLayout());//new GridLayout(1,2)); Panel p3 = new Panel(); p3.setLayout(new BorderLayout()); code = new TextArea(initcodestr); p3.add(“Center”,code); canva
FlowLayout(FlowLayout.LEFT)); p2.add(new Label(“Design by Numbers, Copyright 1998 John Maeda. All Rights Reserved.”)); /*cbg = new CheckboxGroup(); { Checkbox c; cb1=c = new Checkbox(“
”)); // p2.add(saveb); // p2.add(loadb); step.disable(); add(“Center”,p); // add(“North”,p2); // add(“North”,new accessorypanel(this,accessorypanel.tCMD)); p.add(“Center”,p3); p.add(“West”,canvas); }
true; } if (s!=null) { // run through and remove semicolons StringTokenizer f = new StringTokenizer(s,“;”); initcodestr = “”; while(f.hasMoreTokens()) { initcodestr = initcodestr+f.nextToken()+“\n”; }
name!=null) { try { initcodestr = readFile(infilename); } catch (Exception e) { initcodestr = “”; } if (runp) setupforrun(); else setupforedit(); } } public void autosemiprep() { String s = code.getText();
spc; int cnt = 0; StringTokenizer st = new StringTokenizer(s,“\n”); while(st.hasMoreTokens()) { String t = st.nextToken(); t = t.trim(); spc = nsp*lev; if (t.length()>0) { if (t.charAt(0) == ‘{’) { lev++; } e
s = code.getText(); canvas.runprogram(s); } public void doload() { Frame f = new Frame(); FileDialog fd = new FileDialog(f,“load”,FileDialog.LOAD); fd.show(); String fl = fd.getFile(); if (fl!=null) { try
msg.setmsg(“done.”); code.setText(new String(b,avail)); fp.close(); } catch (Exception e) { msg.setmsg(“Can’t load file ”+fl); } } } public void dosave() { Frame f = new Frame(); FileDialog fd = new
msg.setmsg(“Writing file: ”+fl); ds.writeBytes(code.getText()); msg.setmsg(“done.”); fp.close(); } catch (Exception e) { msg.setmsg(“Can’t save file ”+fl); } } } public boolean action(Event evt, Ob
else if (evt.target == loadb) { return true; } else if (evt.target == step) { canvas.step(); return true; } else if (evt.target == auto) { return true; } else if (evt.target == stop) { canvas.stop(); return true; } e
return true; } else return false; } public String picked() { String s = files.getSelectedItem(); String url = new String(); url = “http://acg.media.mit.edu/dbn/”+s+“.html”; return url; } public String readF
// InputStreamReader reader = new InputStreamReader(input); StreamTokenizer stream = new StreamTokenizer(input); int c; boolean first = false; stream.eolIsSignificant(true); stream.wordChars(0,
(int)stream.nval; String str2 = Integer.toString(number); yippee = yippee + str2 + “ ”; break; case StreamTokenizer.TT_EOL: yippee = yippee + “\n”; break; case StreamTokenizer.TT_EOF: break
{ e.printStackTrace(); } return yippee; } public void paint(Graphics g) { } } import java.awt.*; import java.applet.*; import java.util.*; import java.net.*; import java.io.*; import java.lang.*; class lerr e
return b<len; } public StringTokenizerNoSkip(String ss) { s = ss;//.trim(); len = s.length(); } public String nextToken() { // looking for parens first, then brace, then space int i; boolean capturingp = fa
// each block contains vector of either Strings or a bonafide Block public class Block { Vector v; String s; int linenum; Vector args=null; // ugly hack to hide args for a define static int STR = 0, BLK
aa.charAt(i); if (c == ‘{’) { lev++; res+=(c+“”+lev); } else if (c == ‘}’) { res+=(c+“”+lev); lev—; } else res+=c; } if (lev !=0) throw new lerr(“braces not balanced”); return res; } static int findstr(Vector
int i; Block b = new Block(); i = stind; b.setline(stind); // System.out.println(“sten: ”+stind+“/”+endind); while(i<endind) { String s = (String)v.elementAt(i); int len = s.length(); if (s!=null) { if (s.charA
else { Block bs = new Block(s); bs.setline(i); b.add(bs); i++; }} // else i++; } return b; } static Block parse(String aa) throws lerr { Block b = new Block(); Vector pre = new Vector(); // System.out.pri
StringTokenizerNoSkip(aa); while(st.hasMoreTokens()) { String s = st.nextToken(); s = s.trim(); if (!s.equals(“”)) { pre.addElement(s); // System.out.println(“add pre: ”+s); } else pre.addElement(“ ”);
s.startsWith(ss); } else return false; } public String getstr() { if (type==0) { return (“ [S: ”+s+“]”); } else { String a = “ [B: ”; int i; for(i=0;i<v.size();i++) { Block b = (Block)v.elementAt(i); a+=b.getstr(); }
```

```
pplet.*; import java.util.*; import java.net.*; import java.io.*; import java.lang.*; import Block; import lerr; class accessorypanel extends Panel { // does double duty as top panel and bottom panel
an playp = false; public accessorypanel(env ap, int type, bufpanel b) { super(); app = ap; bp = b; ty = type; ims = app.getImage(app.getDocumentBase(),dir+"stop.GIF"); imp =
ng t = System.currentTimeMillis(); if (myg==null) myg = this.getGraphics(); myg.setColor((t)>250?Color.gray:Color.darkGray); myg.drawLine(23,18,23+pw,18); } String msg="Hello."; public void
playp; } else { bp.stop(); playp = !playp; } if (myg==null) myg = this.getGraphics(); myg.drawImage(playp?ims:imp,4,4,this); } else if (loadr.inside(x,y)) { // System.out.println("loadr.......");
yg = null; playp = !(bp.errp||bp.donep); // System.out.println("errp: "+bp.errp+"/ donep: "+bp.donep); if (ty==tMSG) { loadr.reshape(r.width-48+4,0,24,r.height); saver.reshape(r.width-
drawRect(0,0,r.width-1,r.height-1); g.drawImage(playp?ims:imp,4,4,this); g.setColor(Color.gray); g.fillRect(loadr.x+4,loadr.y+4,loadr.width-8,loadr.height-8);
; int b = 0; int len; public StringTokenizer2(String ss) { s = ss.trim(); len = s.length(); } public String getuntil(int start, char c) { int i; for(i=start;i<len;i++) { if (s.charAt(i)==c) break; } if (c==' ') { b=i;
At(i)==c2) level—; if (level == 0) break; } b=i+1; return s.substring(start,i+1); } public String nextToken() { // looking for parens first, then brace, then space int i; boolean capturingp = false;
break; default: return getuntil(i,' '); } } return null; } } class bufpanel extends Panel implements Runnable { String hostname = "tschichold.media.mit.edu"; ClientConnection client; boolean
bimg; Rectangle cb; int sc = 1; Hashtable cmdenv = null, ioenv = null; Graphics myg; boolean runtimep= false; TextArea ta = null; boolean bdirtyp = false; Color ltgr = new Color(239,239,239);
createImage(bw,bh); bimg = bim.getGraphics(); p("buf size is: "+bw+" by "+bh); } boolean []keys = new boolean[26]; long []keyt = new long[26]; public void doinits() { int i; if(bitscol==null) { bitscol
a",Font.PLAIN,10); // store lines in dynamically allocated linebuf public bufpanel(TextArea t, accessorypanel m) { doinits(); ta = t; msg = m; margx=24;margy=16; bdirtyp = true; } public
id drawframe(Graphics g) { int i,j; Rectangle r = bounds(); cbw = bw*sc; cbh = sc*bh; framer.reshape((r.width-margx*2-cbw)/2+margx+2,(r.height-margy*2-cbh)/2+margy,cbw,cbh); if (runtimep) {
g = pat.getGraphics(); for(i=0;i<16;i++) for(j=0;j<16;j++) { pg.setColor(((i+j) ==0)?Color.gray:Color.darkGray); pg.drawLine(i,j,i,j); } } for(i=0;i<r.width/16+1;i++) for(j=0;j<r.height/16+1;j++)
t+1); g.setColor(Color.black); // g.drawRect(framer.x-1,framer.y-1,framer.width+1,framer.height); // g.drawRect(margx,r.height-margy-cbh-1,cbw+1,cbh+1); g.setColor(Color.white); g.setFont(f); int
().stringWidth(""+i),y); x=framer.x+framer.width*i/100; y = framer.y+framer.height+1; // g.setColor(Color.black); g.drawLine(x,y,x,y+2); g.setColor(Color.white);
 = true; // drawbits(g); { g.setColor(Color.black); g.fillRect(zoomr.x,zoomr.y,zoomr.width,zoomr.height); g.setColor(Color.white); g.drawString(sc+"x",zoomr.x+3,zoomr.y+12); } } public void
dbits[i][j] = 1; } bdirtyp = true; } public void setmode(int m) { if (m== 0) sc = 1; else sc = 3; stop(); System.out.println("sc is "+sc); refreshbits(); repaint(); // refreshlines(); // drawslate(getGraphics()); }
0,-x+y0,v); } public void gfield(int x0, int y0, int x1, int y1, int v) { int i,j; for(i=x0;i<=x1;i++) for(j=y0;j<=y1;j++) setbit(i,j,100-v); } public void gcircle(int x0, int y0, int r) { int x = 0; int y = r; int d = 1-
int x1, int y1) { gline(x0,y0,x1,y0); gline(x1,y0,x1,y1); gline(x1,y1,x0,y1); gline(x0,y1,x0,y0); } public void gline(int x0, int y0, int x1, int y1) { int dx = x1-x0; int dy = y1-y0; int i;
0) { if (dx<0) { int dum = x0; x0 = x1; x1 = dum; } for(i=x0; i<=x1;i++) setbit(i,y0,pencol); } else { BresLine(x0,y0,x1,y1,pencol); /* if (dy>0) { if (dx>dy) bresen1(x0,y0,x1,y1,pencol); else
nt dx = x1-x0; int sny = (y1>y0)?1:-1; int dy = (y1-y0)*sny; int d = 2*dy-dx; int incrE = 2*dy; int incrNE = 2*(dy-dx); int x = x0; int y = y0; setbit(x,y,val); while(x<x1) { if (d<=0) { d+=incrE; x++; } else
 = true; } public void setbit(int i, int j, int n) { if (i>bw-1) return; if (j>bh-1) return; if (j<0) return; if (i<0) return; // p("set: "+i+"/"+j+": "+n+" bds: "+bw+"/"+bh); bits[i][j] = n; dbits[i][j] = 1; j = bh-j;
er.x+i*sc-1,framer.y+j*sc,sc,sc); */ bdirtyp = true; } Color bitscol[] = null; boolean refreshp = false; Rectangle zoomr = new Rectangle(); public synchronized void drawbits(Graphics g) { int i,j; // int
 framer.y+sc*bh; // System.out.println("drawbits"); g.setColor(Color.black); g.drawImage(bim,0,0,bw*sc,bh*sc,this); g.translate(-framer.x,-framer.y); bdirtyp = false; } public void
and(String s) { System.out.println(s); return ((Block)cmdenv.get(s)); } public Block get_io(String s) { return ((Block)ioenv.get(s)); } public void setvar(String s, int n) throws lerr { //
 } else if (s.startsWith("<")) { StringTokenizer2 st = new StringTokenizer2(trim2(s)); String intype = st.nextToken(); if (intype.equals("net")) { if (netinitp == false) { connecttoServer(hostname); }
ne pushed"); vframes.addElement(new Hashtable()); } public void PopFrame() { // System.out.println("-new frame popped"); vframes.removeElement(vframes.lastElement()); } Hashtable curFrame() {
htable)vframes.elementAt(i); if ((m=(Integer)ht.get(s))!=null) break; } if (m == null) { throw new lerr("Unknown variable: "+s); } else return m.intValue(); } } public int contains(String s, char c) {
gth()); } public void sp(String s) { // System.out.println(s); } // this is the io stack, it is a temporary kludge until // we build a universal stack. String instackp[] = new String[100]; int inc = 0; int out-
"pushed: "+v); outstack[outc] = v; outc++; } public String trim2(String s) { // remove start and end return s.substring(1,s.length()-1); } public void connecttoServer(String hoster) {
 " + place + " " + value); } public void sendtoServer(String nums) { client.out.println(nums); client.out.flush(); } public int getfromServer() { try { String line; line = client.in.readLine(); numgets++;
err { // this is hard stuff // s = "A" // s = "A+1" // s = "(A+2)*B" // are there any operators? // if not, is it a number or symbol? // if yes, then stringtokenizer (evalarg(token1)+evalarg(token2)) // st "+-
se if (s.startsWith("[")) { int v; String ss = trim2(s); System.out.println("ss is: "+ss); StringTokenizer2 st = new StringTokenizer2(trim2(s)); int x = evalarg(st.nextToken()), y = evalarg(st.nextToken());
': return evalarg(s.substring(0,i))+evalarg(s.substring(i+1,s.length())); case '*': return evalarg(s.substring(0,i))*evalarg(s.substring(i+1,s.length())); case '-': return evalarg(s.substring(0,i))-
 { StringTokenizer st = new StringTokenizer(s, "+"); return evalarg(st.nextToken())+evalarg(comesafter(s, contains(s, '+')+1)); } else if (contains(s, '-') > 0) { StringTokenizer st = new
alarg(comesafter(s, contains(s, '*')+1)); } else if (contains(s, '/') > 0) { StringTokenizer st = new StringTokenizer(s, "/"); return evalarg(st.nextToken())/evalarg(comesafter(s, contains(s, '/')+1)); } else if
sWith("<")) { StringTokenizer2 st = new StringTokenizer2(trim2(s)); String intype = st.nextToken(); // System.out.println("THIS IS THE <>"); if (intype.equals("loc")||intype.equals("mouse")) { int
rg(st.nextToken()); if (num>=1 && num<=26) { return keys[num-1]?100:0; } else { throw new lerr("Unknown <key>: "+num); } } else if ( intype.equals("time")) { int num = evalarg(st.nextToken());
 } } else if (intype.equals("net")) { if (netinitp == false) { connecttoServer(hostname); } sendtoServer(st.nextToken()); return getfromServer(); } else { Block gb; Graphics g = this.getGraphics(); if
shFrame(); for(int i=0;i<v.size();i++) { setvar((String)v.elementAt(i),evalarg(st.nextToken())); } doBlock(g,gb); PopFrame(); return outputpop(); } } } } else if (Character.isDigit(s.charAt(0))) { return
doLine(Graphics g, Block b) throws lerr { String line = b.s; StringTokenizer2 st2 = new StringTokenizer2(line); String cmd = st2.nextToken(); int i; curt = System.currentTimeMillis(); //
(evalarg(st2.nextToken()),evalarg(st2.nextToken()),evalarg(st2.nextToken()),evalarg(st2.nextToken())); } else if (cmd.equals("cube")) { gpen(50); System.out.println("pen 50"); for(i=0;i<40;i++) {
 "+(60+i)+" "+(60+i)+" "+(60+i)); } System.out.println("pen 75"); gpen(75); for(i=0;i<40;i++) { gline(60,20+i,80,40+i); System.out.println("line "+(60)+" "+(20+i)+" "+(80)+" "+(40+i)); } } else if
 if (cmd.equals("circle")) { // for circle, should get absolute value of r, also rectangle // and field should be not order dependent.
imeMillis(); wt*=10; while (System.currentTimeMillis()-t<wt); } else if (cmd.equals("escape")) { return true; } else if (cmd.equals("field")) {
 } else if (cmd.equals("paper")) { gpage(evalarg(st2.nextToken())); } else if (cmd.equals("msg")) { System.out.println("**"+line); } else if (cmd.equals("pen")) { gpen(evalarg(st2.nextToken())); } else {
+cmd); Vector v = bb.args; if (v == null) { // no args doBlock(g,bb); } else { PushFrame(); for(i=0;i<v.size();i++) { setvar((String)v.elementAt(i),evalarg(st2.nextToken())); } doBlock(g,bb);
 if (inc <0) { for (int i=n; i>=t; i+=inc) { setvar(a, i); doBlock(g, b); } } else { for (int i=n; i<t+1; i+=inc) { setvar(a, i); doBlock(g, b); } } } // return 0 if normal // return 1 if get an 'escape' public boolean
ype == Block.BLK) { Vector v = b.v; for(i=0;i<v.size();i++) { Block a = (Block)v.elementAt(i); //System.out.println("DOING BLOCK: "+a.getstr()); if (a.isa("repeat")) { //stepone A, 1, 5 //
; i++; int start = evalarg(st.nextToken()); int end = evalarg(st.nextToken()); if (start>end) { inc = -1; } doStep(g, arg, start, end,inc,nextb); } else if (a.isa("forever")) { Block nextb =
ase, need robust image buffering? stack? // yes, this happpened. have to disable this cool // feature unfortunately // but i need it because it looks great so try to fix it tom // doBlock(g2,nextb); if
Tokenizer2 st = new StringTokenizer2(line); st.nextToken(); String arg1 = st.nextToken(); String arg2 = st.nextToken(); Block nextb = (Block)v.elementAt(i+1); i++; if (evalarg(arg1) ==
Block nextb = (Block)v.elementAt(i+1); i++; if (evalarg(arg1) != evalarg(arg2)) doBlock(g,nextb); } else if (a.isa("within?")) { String line = a.s; StringTokenizer2 st = new StringTokenizer2(line);
oBlock(g,nextb); } else if (a.isa("smaller?")) { String line = a.s; StringTokenizer2 st = new StringTokenizer2(line); st.nextToken(); String arg1 = st.nextToken(); String arg2 = st.nextToken(); Block
tring arg1 = st.nextToken(); String arg2 = st.nextToken(); Block nextb = (Block)v.elementAt(i+1); i++; if (evalarg(arg1) >= evalarg(arg2)) doBlock(g,nextb); } else if (a.isa("command")) { String line
or(); for(j=2;j<nargs;j++) { String s3 = st.nextToken(); nv.addElement(s3); } nextb.args = nv; } def_command(arg,nextb); //return false; } else if (a.isa("number")) { String line = a.s; int nargs =
s;j++) { String s3 = st.nextToken(); nv.addElement(s3); } nextb.args = nv; } def_io(arg,nextb); } else { doBlock(g, a); } } } } return false; } public String preprocess(String s) { return s; } public int
ner ==null) { runner = new Thread(this); runner.start(); } } String progstr = null; int mx, my, mb; int orgx, orgy; public void p(String s) { System.out.println(s);} public void calcmouse() { mx =
lse; calcmouse(); return true; } public boolean mouseExit(Event ev, int x, int y) { mousex = x; mousey = y;mouseb = false; calcmouse(); return true; } public boolean mouseDown(Event ev, int x, int
stem.out.println("runtime start/stop"); if (runner==null) start(); else stop();//runprogram(progstr); } return true; } public boolean mouseUp(Event ev, int x, int y) { mousex = x; mousey = y;mouseb =
 = x; mousey = y;mouseb = false; calcmouse(); return true; } public void step() { stepp = true; } public void msgbox(String s) { if (msg!=null) msg.setmsg(s); } public void msgalive() { if (msg!=null)
 s.length(); int lnum = e.lnum; int st=-1, end=-1; int lc = 0; if (lnum ==0) st = 0; for(int i=0;i<len;i++) { if (s.charAt(i) == '\n') { lc++; if (lc == lnum) st = i+1; else if (lc == lnum+1) { end = i; break;
void run() { errp = donep = false; try { msgbox("Running..."); executeprogram(progstr); donep = true; msgbox("Done."); runner.stop(); runner = null; } catch (lerr e) { errp = true; msgbox(e);
catch (IOException e2){}; } msgbox("Stopped."); //unp = false; } } // there is a bug in how key is trapped by win java (expect // worse in mac java). does not match keydowns with keyups //
(i=0;i<26;i++) { if (curt-keyt[i]>1000) { keyt[i] = -1; keys[i] = false; } } } } public synchronized boolean keyDown(Event ev, int n) { if (n>='a'&&n<='z') { int ind = n-'a'; keyt[ind] =
n) { if (n>='a'&&n<='z') { int ind = n-'a'; keyt[ind] = -1; keys[ind] = false; } else if (n>='A'&&n<='Z') { int ind = n-'A'; keyt[ind] = -1; keys[ind] = false;} return true; } public void runprogram(String s) {
1. run through and remove comments // s = preprocess(s); // currently absorbed by block.parse incorrectly // 2. do syntax check into blocks try { bb = Block.parse(s); } catch (lerr e) { throw e; } catch
 new Hashtable(); ioenv = new Hashtable(); // bb.pp(); // 4. do runblock try { doBlock(g,bb); } catch (lerr e) { throw e; } catch (Exception e) { e.printStackTrace(); return 1; } return -1; } Image bufim;
drawbits(g); } public Dimension preferredSize() { return new Dimension(szw,szh); } } class ClientConnection extends Object { public static final int PORT = 6800; Socket s; DataInputStream in;
nected to "+host+" on "+PORT); } catch (IOException e) { System.out.println(e.toString()); } } } public class env extends Applet { // GridBagLayout layout = new GridBagLayout(); // GridBagConstraints
Button("beautify"); Choice files = new Choice(); bufpanel canvas; int[] numb = new int[4]; CheckboxGroup cbg; Checkbox cb1,cb2; Button stop = new Button("stop"); Button step = new
); canvas = new bufpanel(initcodestr,1); add("Center",canvas); // bufpanel.set } accessorypanel msg; public void setupforedit() { Panel p = new Panel(); Panel p2 = new Panel(); setLayout(new
fpanel(code,msg); msg = new accessorypanel(this,accessorypanel.tMSG,canvas); canvas.msg = msg; p3.add("South",msg); code.setFont(new Font("Courier",Font.PLAIN,12)); p2.setLayout(new
g,true); p2.add(c); cb2=c = new Checkbox("zoom",cbg,false); p2.add(c); } */ // p2.add(go); // p2.add(step); // p2.add(stop); // p2.add(new Label("special: ")); // p2.add(auto); // p2.add(new Label(" i/o:
 init() { String s; boolean runp = false; Date d = new Date(); Date d2 = new Date(98,6,15); infilename = getParameter("url"); s = getParameter("initcode"); if (getParameter("run")!=null) { runp =
.println("CODE initted:"); System.out.println(initcodestr); System.out.println("done."); if (runp) { System.out.println("setting up for run"); setupforrun(); } else setupforedit(); } else if (infile-
 ""; if (s.startsWith("@")) s = s.substring(3,s.length()-1); ns = s.replace(';','\n'); code.setText(ns); } public void autotabbify() { String s = code.getText(); String ns = ""; int nsp = 2; int i; int lev = 0; int
rAt(0) == '}') { lev—; spc-=nsp; } } for(i=0;i<spc;i++) t=" "+t; if (cnt == 0) ns = t; else ns = ns+"\n"+t; cnt++; } code.setText(ns); } public void goaheadandrun() { autosemiprep(); autotabbify(); String
Stream fp = new FileInputStream(fl); DataInputStream ds = new DataInputStream(fp); msg.setmsg("Reading file: "+fl); int avail = ds.available(); byte b[] = new byte[avail]; ds.readFully(b);
f,"save",FileDialog.SAVE); fd.show(); String fl = fd.getFile(); if (fl!=null) { try { FileOutputStream fp = new FileOutputStream(fl); DataOutputStream ds = new DataOutputStream(fp);
System.out.println(""+code.getSelectionStart()); if (evt.target == go) { // here i do some insanely bad things // like autotab, each runcycle ... return true; } else if (evt.target == saveb) { return true; }
target == cb1) { // lines canvas.setmode(0); return true; } else if (evt.target == cb2) { // dots canvas.setmode(1); return true; } else if (evt.target == files) { readFile(picked()); //readFile(mainfr.picked());
 { String yippee = new String(""); try { URL u = new URL(s); URLConnection conn = u.openConnection(); InputStream input = u.openStream(); //DataInputStream data = new DataInputStream(input);
out: while (true) { switch (c = stream.nextToken()) { case StreamTokenizer.TT_WORD: yippee = yippee + stream.sval + " "; break; case StreamTokenizer.TT_NUMBER: int number; number =
code.setText(yippee); //code.replaceText(yippee, 0, 10000); } catch (IOException e) { e.printStackTrace(); } } catch (MalformedURLException e) { System.out.println("bad url"); } catch (IOException e)
ption { int lnum = -1; public lerr(String s) { super(s); } public lerr(String s, int a) { super(s); lnum = a; } } class StringTokenizerNoSkip { String s; int b = 0; int len; public boolean hasMoreTokens() {
2 = ""; if (b == len) return null; i = b; while(i<len) { char c = s.charAt(i); // System.out.println(i+"/"+c); if (c == '\n') { i++; break;} else { s2+=c; i++; } } b = i; return s2; } } // program is a bunch of blocks
 int type; // 0 is string, 1 is block. void setline(int l) { linenum = l; } static String labelled(String aa) throws lerr { int i, len = aa.length(); int lev = 0; String res = ""; for(i=0;i<len;i++) { char c =
 c) { int i; for(i=j;i<v.size();i++) { String s = (String)v.elementAt(i); if (s.charAt(1)==c) return i; } return v.size(); } static Block doparse(Vector v, int stind, int endind) throws lerr { // start with 1st line
 char c = s.charAt(1); i++; int targ = findstr(v,i,c); b.add(doparse(v,i,targ)); i = targ+1; } else if (s.charAt(0) == '/') { // comment if (s.charAt(1) == '/') // do nothing i++; } else if (s.length()<2) { i++; }
 am at\n"+aa+")"); aa = aa.toLowerCase(); // label blocks try { aa = labelled(aa); } catch(lerr l) { throw l; } //System.out.println("after labelled\n"+aa); StringTokenizerNoSkip st = new
addElement(null); } return doparse(pre,0,pre.size()); } public Block(String ss) { s=ss; type = STR; } public void sp(String s) { System.out.println(s); } boolean isa(String ss) { if (type == STR) { return
turn a; } } public void pp() { System.out.println(getstr()); } public Block() { v = new Vector(); type = BLK; } public void add(Block b) { v.addElement(b); } } // End. Let's hope this all works out somehow.
```

1 BEGIN Our forefathers at the Bauhaus, Ulm, and many other key centers for design education around the world labored to create a sense of order and method to their teaching. Thanks to their trailblazing work, teaching design at the university level gradually became accepted as a meaningful and constructive activity. A drawing board, small or large, became the stage for paper, pen, ink, and blade to interact in the disciplined activity that characterized the profession of visual design. Beginning in the early 1980s, however, affordable graphical computing systems emerged as the new drawing boards, forever disrupting the refined systems that had been carefully established over the previous decades. The page-description language PostScript was born, and the race for advanced software-based tools to aid a generation of computer-empowered youth began.

As could be expected by any sudden change in a field, the process of integrating computers into traditional design education has been akin to the proverbial mixing of oil and water. Understandably, the point-and-click ease of computers poses a threat to the painstakingly acquired skills of the precomputer design educator. The fact that each new generation of students clearly recognizes its technical advantage over their instructors only widens the gap that separates past and present. Digitally adept faculty members are hired at an alarming rate to try to tame the young gurus, but even those instructors who profess a lead over students quickly lose their nominal superiority with each new software release. Unfortunately, most of the parties involved do not realize that computers, as they are used today, have nothing to do with design skill, or design education for that matter, but the computer industry strives to convince us otherwise.

The skills and expertise of a designer are in question today, but this has not always been the case.

I recall the renowned Japanese art director Katsumi Asaba relating a story from his youth about the time he could draw 10 parallel lines within one millimeter using a bamboo pen that he had refined over many months, not to mention the fine motor skills that he had acquired over many years. This form of disciplined approach toward understanding one's medium is what we traditionally associated with *skill,* and at one time valued as one of many important steps to becoming a skilled designer. But today such superhuman skill is immediately trivialized by an amateur who, using a software tool, can effortlessly draw 50 perfect lines within the same millimeter. Due to the advent of the computer, mechanical skills have taken secondary importance to the skills required to use complex software tools. But what is the nature of these digital skills, and more importantly, are they really of any significance?

Most digital design skills are acquired by browsing through encyclopedic software manuals or other "how-to" books. Usually the methods discussed are described as a series of steps in complete detail, which can generally be reproduced verbatim with a few actions performed with the mouse. In contrast, any instructional material on traditional painting or drawing is usually vague and difficult to reproduce, even when the action is a simple stroke of the pencil. In both cases, the instructional exercise is building the *skill to see* together with the *skill to create.* The difference lies in the tremendous effort required to refine motor skills when working in traditional media, as in the story of Asaba, versus the ease of pushing buttons on a computer that launch a set of discrete actions, which render motor skills irrelevant. In place of motor skills, today's digital designer must develop an awareness of the many capabilities and sequences of interactions in the continuously growing set of pre-packaged digital tools. In other words, skill in the digital sense is nothing more than *knowledge,* and the reality is that we implicitly glorify rote memorization as the basis of skill for a digital designer.

The true skill of a digital designer is the practiced art of computer programming, or *computation,* as it is referenced in this book. I have reached this conclusion through my experimental studies across print and digital media, together with the recent worldwide emphasis in the field of design to reconcile the relevance of programming. This is reinforced by the countless young designers who ask me the same question, "How do you learn to program?" I have come to realize that the only correct answer is the same a painter might give when asked, "How do you paint?" My reply is, "You need a lot of practice, and most importantly, a lot of natural talent." Many are not satisfied with this answer and assume that there is a more definitive answer I am purposely hiding—a secret manual or book. I believe that this odd misconception of the difficulty involved in programming is related to the average person's experience with programming a video cassette recorder or a microwave oven. The perception is that while such programming can be disorienting initially, a well-written manual can carry you step by step through the process. So why shouldn't the same be true for a computer? If it were that easy, I would not have wasted 20 years trying to master the computational medium.

In the past, when new materials such as steel and glass, or mechanical advancements such as electricity and motors, first appeared, they seemed magical, but were nevertheless fathomable in a physical sense. Technology was either macroscopic or microscopic, and in either case you could build an analogue to something already existing in the physical world. Computation, on the other hand, is often misunderstood because the complexities of software and the process of creating it are invisible. For example, if I were to say, "I wrote a book," most people would have some idea of how to evaluate my work and the labor involved. On the other hand, if I were to say, "I wrote a digital paint program," the average person would have difficulty comprehending the amount of work involved. This ignorance is forgivable in the layperson, but has been oddly tolerated in a field like visual design, rooted in the craft of printing, where basic knowledge of ink and paper is requisite. The digital medium still remains only vaguely understood beyond the tools that are used.

Knowing how Photoshop works will not guarantee that you will win any new design awards. The goal of this book is not to push your interests in the direction of making or replicating any particular tool. Instead, by the time you complete the book you will have become aware of the many possibilities afforded by creating in the raw computational medium. With these basic skills, you will be able to go beyond the existing paradigms of digital media design that are reinforced by popular tools, and work with concepts that are closest to its true potential. Combine these skills with your enhanced creativity, and the result will be unique explorations of the digital medium that fully exploit its true character.

99
98
97
96
95
94
93
92
91
90
89
88
87
86
85
84
83
82
81
80
79
78
77
76
75
74
73
72
71
70
69
68
67
66
65
64
63
62
61
60
59
58
46
45
44
43
42
41
40
39
38
37
36
35
34
33
32
31
30
29
28
27
26
25
24
23
22
21
20
19
18
17
16
15
14
13
12
11
10
9
8
7
6
5
4
3
2

2 COMMANDS Writing programs requires you to assume a forceful personality. The computer will do anything within its abilities, but it will do absolutely nothing unless commanded to do so. A command must be issued clearly, in the strict format of a one-word action, followed by a set of descriptors which qualify the action. There is no need to add the formality of a "please" or even a "thank you." A command should not be confused with a request; you can fully expect that it will be obeyed. Of course, if you were to address a co-worker with similar bluntness there would be ensuing personal problems. The computer, however, is quite comfortable with this direct manner of communication. The only time that the computer will complain is when it cannot perform the command you requested because either (1) the command is unknown to the computer, or (2) the way in which the command's descriptors are presented is not in an acceptable form.

Whenever the computer fails to cooperate, the novice usually accuses the computer of stupidity. But the computer cannot think beyond anything you tell it. In contrast, a fellow human can cope with situations of incomplete information and usually recover. For example, "Go ahead and do it." "Do what?" "You know." And usually that person knows. The computer does not yet have this level of intuitive comprehension; therefore, we must address it in a specific manner.

Tell the computer exactly what you want and the computer will comply without error. But you must state specifically and completely the action that you wish to execute.

Specify a Paper The first step is to see the software system we will use in this book. Go to the DBN Web site and connect to the main system. You should see a display similar to what appears here. On the right is the program editing area. On the left is the main display area where the visual output of the program will always be shown. In the middle of the display area there is a small square called the *paper,* where all of your drawing will take place. When you enter a program and press the run button, any subsequent processing will be shown within the paper area.

Before you can draw in the display area, you must first specify the shade of paper using the **Paper** command. There is only one kind of paper in the DBN system. This paper can be any shade of gray you desire, specified by a number of 0 to 100, where 100 is 100 percent black (solid black) and 0 is 0 percent black (white). Into the editing area, type "Paper 100" and run the following program:

```
Paper 100
```

A new 100 percent black sheet of paper should appear in the display. Depending upon the type of computer monitor you are using, the sheet is about 100 points square, which translates to about a 1.5-inch or 35-mm square. You may be concerned about these cramped dimensions, but you will find that mastering this small swatch of space is not trivial. Note that there is a space character between the Paper command and the numerical descriptor 100. You must always separate the command and descriptors with at least one space. A few examples of this simple program are displayed on the facing page.

Unlike real paper, the Paper command can be run as many times as you wish because there is never a shortage of virtual paper. The choices are either black, white, or the 99 shades of gray in between, which adds up to 101 possibilities.

Never type anything like "10 Paper" or "Paper10." In either of these cases, the computer tries to reconcile "10" or "Paper10" as a command and is unsuccessful because such words are not in the basic DBN vocabulary and will signal an error. The computer always requires that the first word on a program line be a command, followed by a set of descriptors. In the case of Paper, there is only one descriptor.

You must be careful to obey the specified format or the computer will not respond.

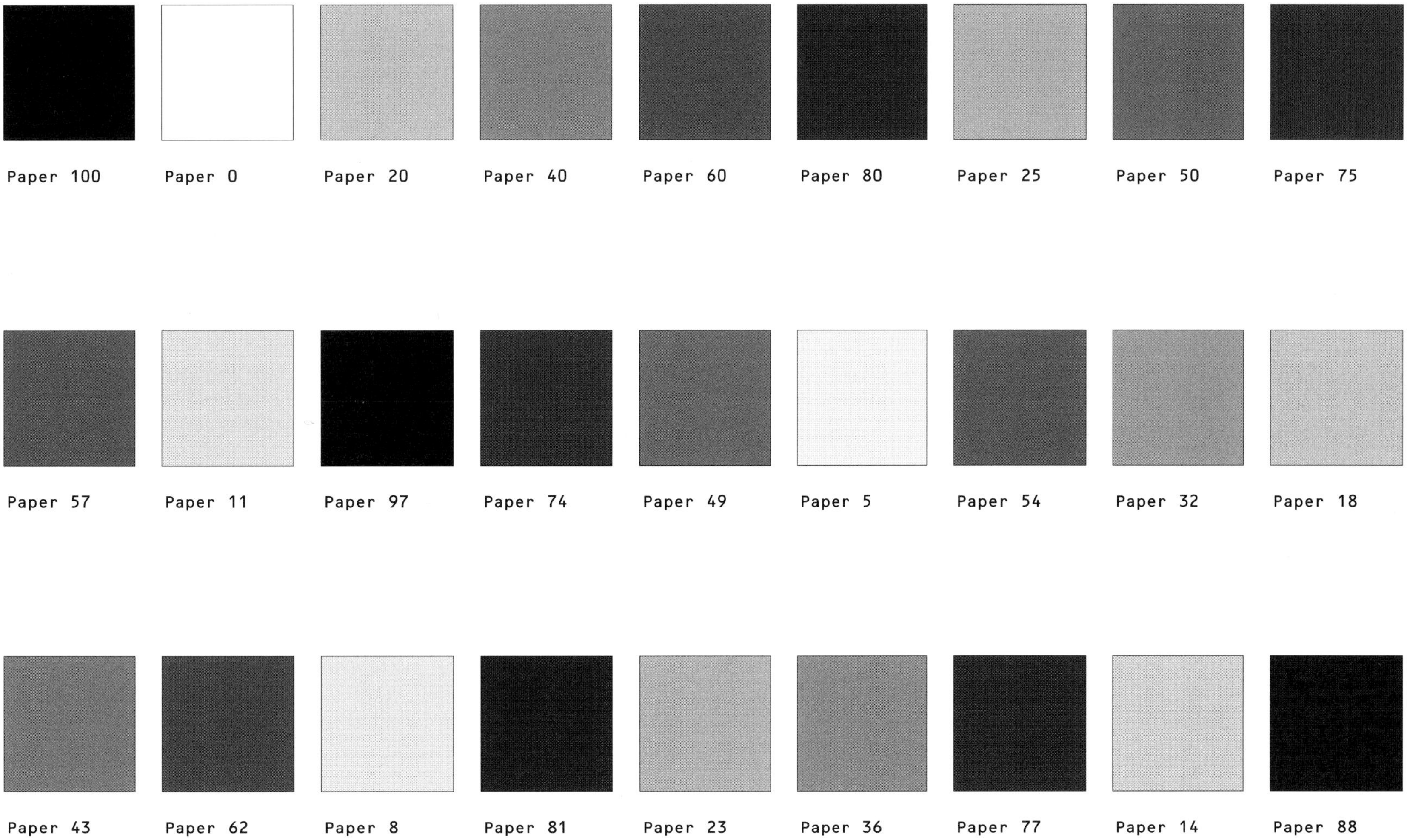
Paper 100
Paper 0
Paper 20
Paper 40
Paper 60
Paper 80
Paper 25
Paper 50
Paper 75
Paper 57
Paper 11
Paper 97
Paper 74
Paper 49
Paper 5
Paper 54
Paper 32
Paper 18
Paper 43
Paper 62
Paper 8
Paper 81
Paper 23
Paper 36
Paper 77
Paper 14
Paper 88

Selecting a Pen After choosing a paper to draw upon, you might guess that the second task to master is to select a pen. It might help to know it will be impossible to hold the pen.

When drawing, we tend to take for granted the natural reflex to extend our arm, grab a pen, and draw. This does not apply in the computational medium because the computer is both intermediary and medium. You instruct the computer to grab a pen, and then you instruct the computer what to draw upon itself.

The pen is selected with the **Pen** command and can draw in any shade of gray from 0 to 100, where 0 is white and 100 is solid black, for a total of 101 pens. Thus "Pen 100" selects a black pen.

```
Pen 100
```

When the program is run, there is no visible change to the paper because the Pen command only changes the internal state of the computer's readiness to draw. In contrast, the Paper command actually yielded a visible result, a new piece of paper in the requested shade.

You can specify a new sheet of paper and subsequently set the pen by issuing the two commands in sequence as the program:

```
Paper 100
Pen 0
```

As expected, there is no visible difference in the result, even though the pen is set. Notice that the commands are issued on separate lines of text. As a general rule, you should always enter commands on separate lines, not merely for legibility's sake, but because the syntax of the language requires you to do so.

Now that the paper is specified and pen is ready, all that is left is to draw something. But what? And how? For what purpose? The answers to the former two questions are revealed as this book progresses; the latter question is of utmost importance and can only be answered by you.

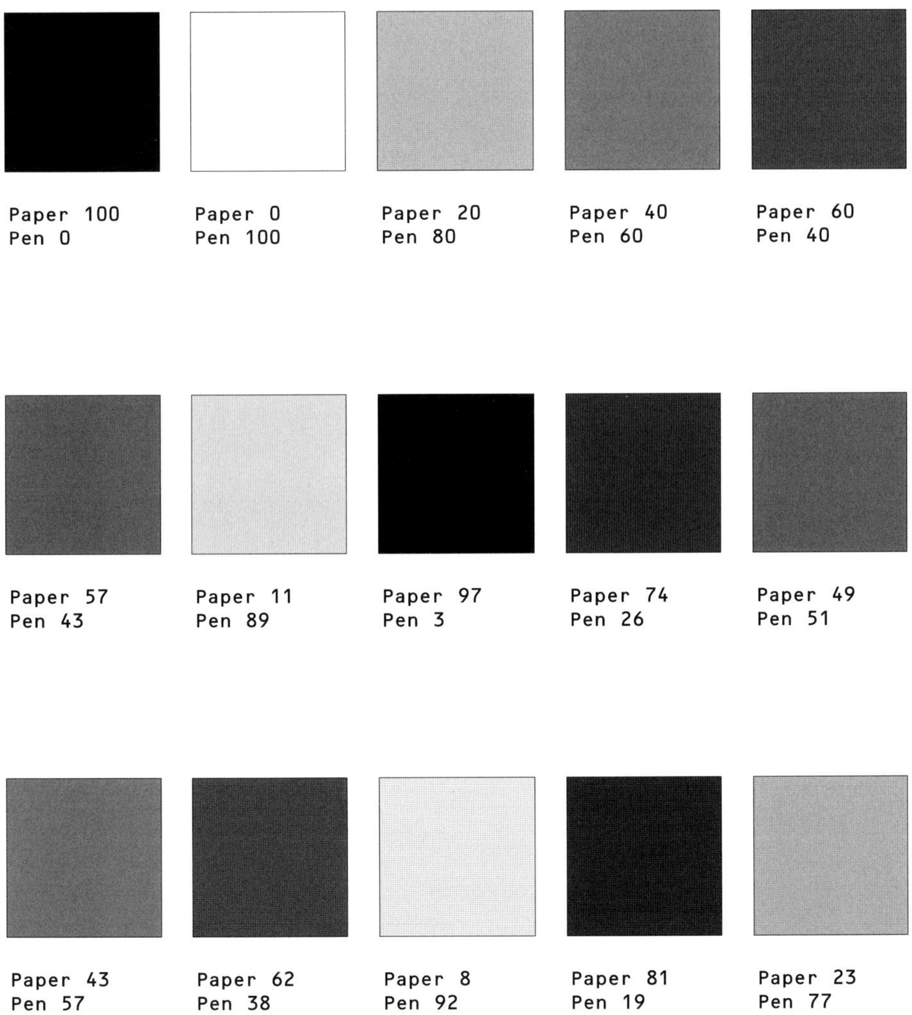

Summary There are two types of commands. One command changes what you see on the computer screen. The other appears to do nothing but actually changes the internal state in the computer. For example, “Paper 0” produces a visible result; “Pen 100” does not, but it does change the internal state of the pen. This should alert you to the fact that issuing a command does not necessarily produce a visual result.

Be sure to input commands to the computer in the specified format. The command comes first, followed by the description of how the command should be executed. Include a space between the command and the descriptor. When there is more than one command, enter each command on a separate line.

3 LINE Drawing a perfectly straight line usually requires a tool, such as a ruler. Although I have introduced analogues to physical implements such as paper and pen, there is no ruler. Instead there is the **Line** command for drawing a straight line that connects two points on the paper. Line will differ from Paper and Pen with respect to the quantity and type of descriptors needed. Paper and Pen require a single numerical value that specifies the percentage of black; Line requires a total of four numerical values that describe the locations of the two points to connect. Using numbers to specify tone or position should be familiar to professional visual creatives as part of their daily activity; however, even for those who are unfamiliar, the practice can be easily mastered.

By starting with a line instead of a freestyle stroke, you might guess that the drawings you create will be primarily of a geometric nature. Whenever you fail to see any beauty in these exercises and start to feel constrained, remember that the ideas presented are primarily of a structural nature and are mere building blocks to be formed into larger aspirations. All of the exercises have been designed to illustrate basic properties and skills related to computational media design which, given a great deal of determination, can be applied to realize any expressive intentions.

If you do not like what is being drawn, try to draw something else. Never let the computer suppress your will to freely express.

Describe a Line With Paper ready and Pen poised, the next step is to use the **Line** command. Specifying a line's starting and ending points is trivial if you point directly at the computer screen with your finger or indirectly using the mouse; however, these options are not available in this system. A line must be described as a corresponding line of text in the program editing area. Thus the format of that text needs to be clarified. Before revealing exactly how the Line command must be used, let us step back for a moment and think of how a line can be described.

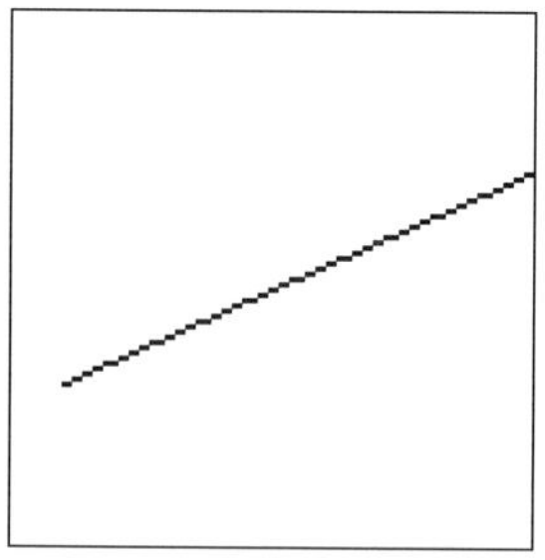

Given the line within the frame to the left, how would you describe it verbally? There are a variety of possible answers ranging from the extremely vague to the proper and precise.

1 *Line from the bottom left to the upper right.*

2 *Line from a little from the left and less than a half from the bottom, to less than a half from the top and on the right edge.*

3 *Line from a third from the bottom and close to the left, to a third from the top on the right edge.*

4 *Line from a third from the bottom and close to the left, to two-thirds from the bottom exactly on the right edge.*

5 *Line from about 3/8 inch from the left and about 7/16 inch from the bottom, to about 7/16 inch from the top on the right edge.*

6 *Line from about 3 millimeters from the left and about 10 millimeters from the bottom, to about 11 millimeters from the top on the right edge.*

7 *Line from 3 millimeters from the left and 30 points from the bottom, to about 7/16 inch from the top on the right edge.*

8 *Line from 10 points from the left and 30 points from the bottom, to about 11 millimeters from the top on the right edge.*

9 *Line from 10 points from the left and 30 points from the bottom, to about 7/16 inch from the top on the right edge.*

10 *Line from 90 points from the right and 30 points from the bottom, to 30 points from the top and 0 points from the right edge.*

11 *Line from 70 points from the top and 10 points from the left, to 70 points from the bottom and 100 points from the left edge.*

12 *Line from 10 points from the left and 30 points from the bottom, to 30 points from the top and 100 points from the left edge.*

In general, the computer is terrible at comprehending such a wide variety of descriptive formats, but excellent at understanding a single consistent format. Humans can be similar in this respect, so there should be some sympathy to the computer's needs for a standardized method of description.

Numerical specifications are clear when they are exact and in like units. The roman typographic convention of the point system is convenient for the purposes of this discussion. Narrowing the set of possibilities to descriptions in points reduces the list to a smaller subset.

1 *Line from 90 points from the right and 30 points from the bottom, to 30 points from the top and 0 points from the right edge.*

2 *Line from 70 points from the top and 10 points from the left, to 70 points from the bottom and 100 points from the left edge.*

3 *Line from 10 points from the left and 30 points from the bottom, to 30 points from the top and 100 points from the left edge.*

When making measurements, choosing a reference of a closest edge versus the opposite edge is a natural habit of efficiency. For example, "10 points from the left" is quicker to physically measure than "90 points from the right." This convention requires that the reference be stated explicitly. Imposing a standard reference of the left and bottom edges for any horizontal and vertical position, respectively, removes the need to specify a distinction of reference, at the slight expense of initially being counterintuitive.

1 *Line from 10 points horizontal and 30 points vertical, to 70 points vertical and 100 points horizontal.*

2 *Line from 30 points vertical and 10 points horizontal, to 70 points vertical and 100 points horizontal.*

3 *Line from 10 points horizontal and 30 points vertical, to 70 points vertical and 100 points horizontal.*

The next convention to remove is the need to distinguish between horizontal and vertical dimensions by enforcing that the horizontal always be written before vertical, and that the two points be listed one after the other. The reference to the unit system of points becomes unnecessary and the result is narrowed to only one possibility.

1 *Line from 10 30 to 100 70.*

Finally, the prepositions and punctuation are removed, and the true form of the Line command is at last revealed.

```
Line 10 30 100 70
```

This format will seem cryptic at first, but with practice you can adapt to this concise description of a line. To build familiarity, get into the habit of reading the statement out loud as, for example, "Line from 10 over and 30 up, to 100 over and 70 up." Note that this particular line, and for that matter any other line, can be redescribed as an alternative where the order of the two pairs of number is reversed.

```
Line 100 70 10 30
```

A line is described by two pairs of numbers that represent two positions on the paper. The order of the pairs has no significance, but the order within a pair does. Each pair of numbers represents a set of dimensions that are always referenced from the left and bottom edges of the paper, where the horizontal measure always precedes the vertical.

Draw a Line You can now write a three-line program, which is your first major graphics program, if only a single black line on white paper. (Note: all drawings are rendered at half their original scale for enhanced page balance.)

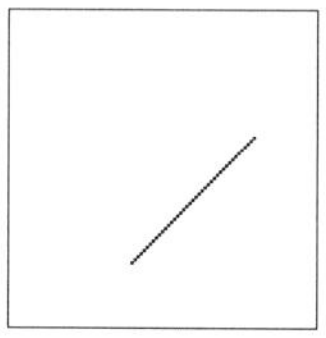

```
Paper 0
Pen 100
Line 40 20 80 60
```

The line is 40 over and 20 up, to 80 over and 60 up—not a particularly exciting line, aside from the similar lack of smoothness in the opening example. The reasons for this jaggy characteristic will be discussed in Chapter 8, but for now understand that the paper we draw upon (not to be confused with the actual paper used in this book) is coarse in a virtual sense. Therefore, any mark left on the paper will have a rough, textural flavor, the classic signature of digital artwork. In some cases, the texture will not be apparent, such as in a perfectly horizontal or vertical line. In these cases, the lines are smooth because they essentially fit into the perfect horizontal and vertical grooves in the texture of the page. But in general, the lines will be coarse.

You can now draw a variety of lines on different papers. The concept is best illustrated through practice. A good introductory exercise is to inspect the adjacent compositions by looking at the picture and imagining the corresponding program, or even better, looking at the program and imagining the corresponding picture.

```
Paper 100
Pen 1
Line 0 83 56 27
```

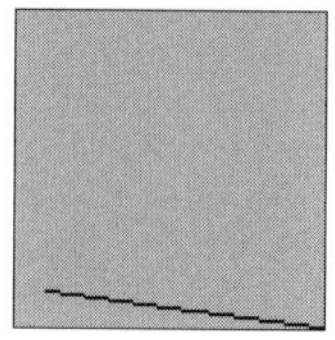

```
Paper 20
Pen 100
Line 100 0 10 11
```

```
Paper 50
Pen 0
Line 0 5 100 4
```

```
Paper 0
Pen 20
Line 40 40 90 90
```

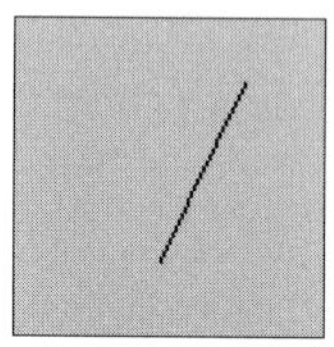

```
Paper 15
Pen 100
Line 48 23 75 80
```

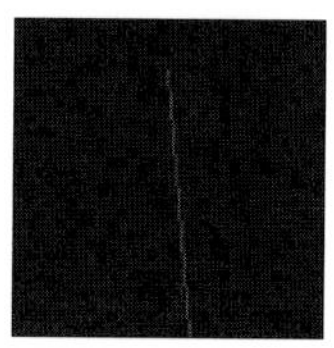

```
Paper 80
Pen 60
Line 58 0 50 84
```

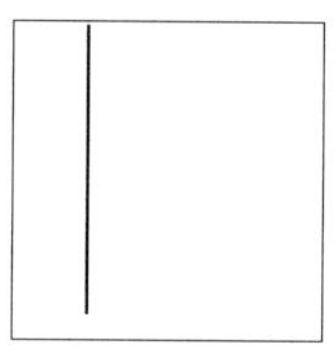

```
Paper 0
Pen 100
Line 24 99 24 8
```

Where Is the Line? There are some cases where you draw a line and do not see the intended result. For instance, imagine what happens when you draw outside the paper?

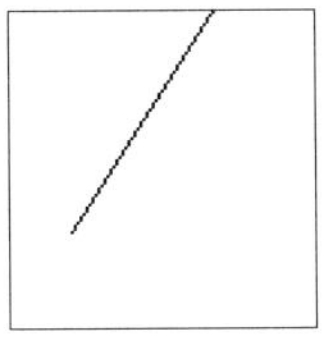

```
Paper 0
Pen 100
Line 20 30 200 300
```

The line starts from 20 left and 30 up to 200 left and 300 up, but you never see the line as it leaves the 101-point square. Any portion of a line drawn outside the space will be ignored and clipped to the edges in this fashion.

Also, what happens when you draw in the same shade as the paper?

```
Paper 66
Pen 66
Line 0 0 100 100
```

Since the digital medium is exact, drawing a diagonal line in the same shade as the underlying paper appears to produce nothing, even though you might expect to see some faint impression of the line as is common in a double hit of ink.

Another surprise occurs when you draw a line and then request a new sheet of paper.

```
Line 0 50 100 50
Paper 50
Pen 0
```

In this case, the intent is to draw a white horizontal line across the center of a gray sheet of paper, but the new sheet of paper is placed on top of the line. Thus the line is not visible.

Finally, there is the case where the Pen is not explicitly set and a Line is drawn.

```
Paper 100
Line 3 33 97 66
```

When the Pen is not set, the default setting is 100 percent black. As an additional convention, when the Paper is not set explicitly, the default setting is 0 percent black, meaning white.

With the exception of the first example, nothing appears to happen in the visual output. But be aware that something has indeed happened from the viewpoint of the computer. The computer has labored to create a line, just as if the line were visible. The computer does not know when it has done something completely useless, such as drawing a black line on black paper. Only you do.

Summary The process of drawing requires a means to establish where the pen is to be placed on the paper. Otherwise, the computer cannot know where to draw. Your hands usually serve as the means to locate points in space; however, in the computational model of drawing, the only purpose your hands serve is to type commands. The constraint of measuring horizontal and vertical dimensions from the lower-left corner was introduced as a way to make dimensions consistent. Dimensions are always in units of points.

The Line command is followed by two points, where each point is a pair of numbers, always horizontal then vertical, and separated by spaces.

4 LINES Drawing a solitary line on the computer is a uniquely satisfying activity. The program you write is short and incredibly easy to understand. With just six numbers, an entire scene is represented: four numbers for the line, one number for the shade of the line, and one number for the shade of the background. But you can easily get bored drawing a scene with only one line and will eventually want to seek the opportunity to draw another line and maybe even more lines.

If a drawing with one line is described by six numbers, then a drawing with two lines is described by 10 numbers when the four numbers for the extra line are added in, assuming that the line is the same shade of gray. In the case of 10 lines there are 42 numbers. In the case of 100 lines, there are 402 numbers. Therefore, you can say that a drawing with multiple lines will be composed of about four times as many numbers as there are lines. Although the resulting drawing may be visually compelling, the program that creates it will be long and tedious to input. The goal of this and the following three chapters is to show you that drawing multiple lines can be just as easy as drawing a single line using the basic concepts of computation.

Draw More Than One Line Drawing two lines is as simple as drawing a single line, only it's twice the work.

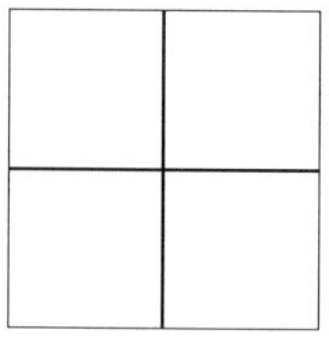

```
Paper 0
Pen 100
Line 50 0 50 100
Line 0 50 100 50
```

You can change the shade of the second Line by changing the pen value with another invocation of the Pen command.

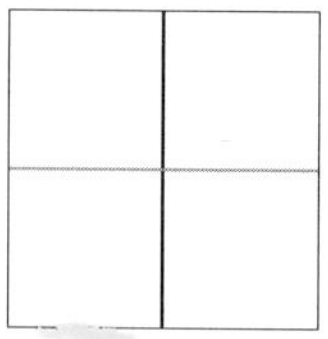

```
Paper 0
Pen 30
Line 0 50 100 50
Pen 100
Line 50 0 50 100
```

Lines are drawn in the order that the Line commands are issued, which you can verify when lines intersect. The difference is realized by simply rearranging the order in which Pen and Line commands are used.

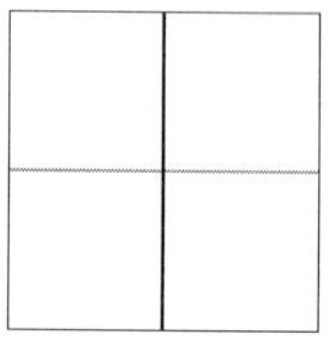

```
Paper 0
Pen 100
Line 50 0 50 100
Pen 30
Line 0 50 100 50
```

The gray line overlaps the black line at the center, whereas a change in the drawing order will cause the reverse to occur, shown here magnified:

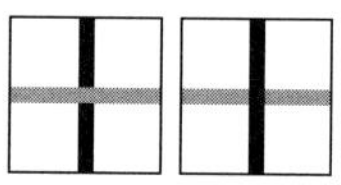

3x mag

Due to the effect of overlap, you can easily create the illusion of three lines from just two lines.

```
Paper 100
Pen 0
Line 30 30 100 30
Pen 50
Line 60 30 80 30
```

But it is also easy to mistakenly create one line from two lines.

```
Paper 0
Pen 50
Line 40 50 60 50
Pen 100
Line 30 50 70 50
```

Draw More Than Two Lines Three lines render the familiar shape of a triangle.

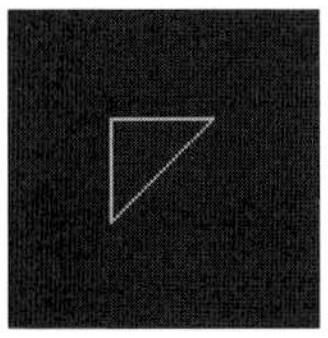

```
Paper 80
Pen 20
Line 33 33 33 66
Line 33 66 66 66
Line 66 66 33 33
```

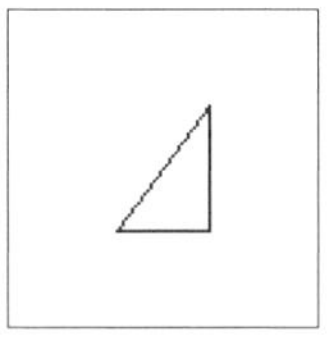

```
Paper 0
Pen 80
Line 35 30 65 30
Line 65 30 65 70
Line 65 70 35 30
```

```
Paper 100
Pen 0
Line 50 77 22 27
Line 22 27 78 27
Line 78 27 50 77
```

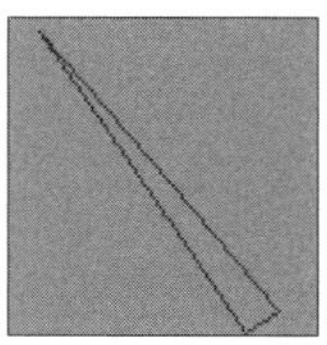

```
Paper 33
Pen 66
Line 77 0 88 7
Line 88 7 10 96
Line 10 96 77 0
```

Four lines compose a square, five a star, six a hexagon, and seven a floating pyramid.

```
Paper 20
Pen 50
Line 30 30 70 30
Line 70 30 70 70
Line 70 70 30 70
Line 30 70 30 30
```

```
Paper 33
Pen 78
Line 20 54 80 54
Line 80 54 32 20
Line 32 20 50 77
Line 50 77 68 20
Line 68 20 20 54
```

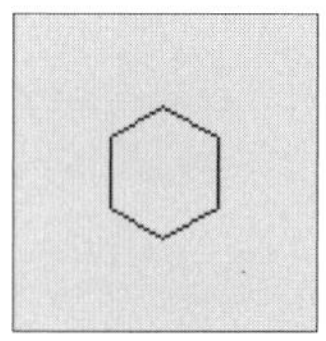

```
Paper 20
Pen 70
Line 32 61 32 39
Line 68 61 68 39
Line 68 61 50 71
Line 32 61 50 71
Line 32 39 50 29
Line 68 39 50 29
```

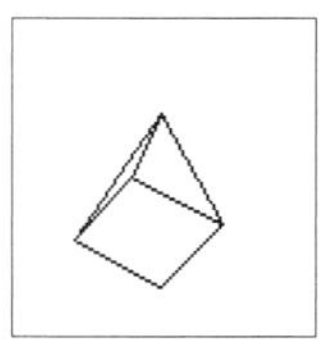

```
Paper 0
Pen 100
Line 40 50 70 35
Line 20 30 50 15
Line 70 35 50 15
Line 40 50 20 30
Line 40 50 50 70
Line 70 35 50 70
Line 20 30 50 70
```

An increased number of lines results in a transition from abstract to the representational.

```
Paper 0
Pen 100
Line 53 72 50 78
Line 50 78 54 82
Line 54 82 57 81
Line 57 81 59 77
Line 59 77 56 73
Line 56 73 53 72
Line 49 70 50 46
Line 58 69 60 45
Line 49 70 60 69
Line 49 70 42 63
Line 42 63 33 74
Line 60 69 64 57
Line 64 57 64 46
Line 50 46 60 45
Line 50 45 46 31
Line 46 31 49 13
Line 60 45 61 29
Line 61 29 63 11
```

```
Paper 0
Pen 100
Line 0 30 23 30
Line 23 30 23 40
Line 23 40 17 39
Line 17 39 12 46
Line 12 46 16 52
Line 16 52 15 57
Line 15 57 27 58
Line 27 58 34 52
Line 34 52 33 44
Line 33 44 26 40
Line 26 40 27 30
Line 27 30 40 30
Line 40 30 38 44
Line 36 43 55 58
Line 55 58 76 43
Line 73 45 72 30
Line 72 30 100 30
Line 46 30 47 30
Line 47 30 46 40
Line 46 40 53 40
Line 53 40 53 30
Line 53 30 55 30
Line 59 40 67 40
Line 67 40 66 35
Line 66 35 59 35
Line 59 35 59 40
```

```
Paper 20
Pen 100
Line 100 8 25 22
Line 20 25 50 36
Line 56 38 68 42
Line 20 25 20 18
Line 20 18 90 5
Line 44 14 44 0
Line 50 8 50 0
Line 54 11 54 0
Line 51 34 56 35
Line 50 35 35 60
Line 50 40 41 55
Line 54 40 41 60
Line 34 61 64 80
Line 41 60 61 75
Line 68 86 73 80
Line 68 86 65 84
Line 73 80 70 78
Line 63 83 67 75
Line 67 75 66 65
Line 66 65 82 75
```

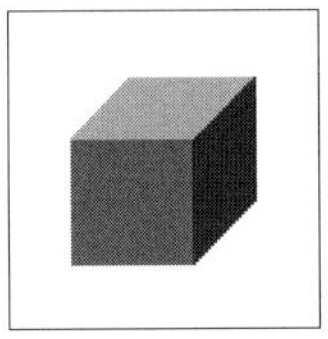

```
Paper 0
Pen 50
Line 20 20 60 20
Line 20 21 60 21
Line 20 22 60 22
Line 20 23 60 23
Line 20 24 60 24
Line 20 25 60 25
Line 20 26 60 26
Line 20 27 60 27
Line 20 28 60 28
Line 20 29 60 29
Line 20 30 60 30
Line 20 31 60 31
Line 20 32 60 32
Line 20 33 60 33
Line 20 34 60 34
Line 20 35 60 35
Line 20 36 60 36
Line 20 37 60 37
Line 20 38 60 38
Line 20 39 60 39
Line 20 40 60 40
Line 20 41 60 41
Line 20 42 60 42
Line 20 43 60 43
Line 20 44 60 44
Line 20 45 60 45
Line 20 46 60 46
Line 20 47 60 47
Line 20 48 60 48
Line 20 49 60 49
Line 20 50 60 50
Line 20 51 60 51
Line 20 52 60 52
Line 20 53 60 53
Line 20 54 60 54
Line 20 55 60 55
Line 20 56 60 56
Line 20 57 60 57
Line 20 58 60 58
Line 20 59 60 59
Pen 25
Line 20 60 60 60
Line 21 61 61 61
Line 22 62 62 62
Line 23 63 63 63
Line 24 64 64 64
Line 25 65 65 65
Line 26 66 66 66
Line 27 67 67 67
Line 28 68 68 68
Line 29 69 69 69
Line 30 70 70 70
Line 31 71 71 71
Line 32 72 72 72
Line 33 73 73 73
Line 34 74 74 74
Line 35 75 75 75
Line 36 76 76 76
Line 37 77 77 77
Line 38 78 78 78
Line 39 79 79 79
Pen 75
Line 60 20 80 40
Line 60 21 80 41
Line 60 22 80 42
Line 60 23 80 43
Line 60 24 80 44
Line 60 25 80 45
Line 60 26 80 46
Line 60 27 80 47
Line 60 28 80 48
Line 60 29 80 49
Line 60 30 80 50
Line 60 31 80 51
Line 60 32 80 52
Line 60 33 80 53
Line 60 34 80 54
Line 60 35 80 55
Line 60 36 80 56
Line 60 37 80 57
Line 60 38 80 58
Line 60 39 80 59
Line 60 40 80 60
Line 60 41 80 61
Line 60 42 80 62
Line 60 43 80 63
Line 60 44 80 64
Line 60 45 80 65
Line 60 46 80 66
Line 60 47 80 67
Line 60 48 80 68
Line 60 49 80 69
Line 60 50 80 70
Line 60 51 80 71
Line 60 52 80 72
Line 60 53 80 73
Line 60 54 80 74
Line 60 55 80 75
Line 60 56 80 76
Line 60 57 80 77
Line 60 58 80 78
Line 60 59 80 79
```

Because of the effort required to draw on the computer in this laborious way, where each line corresponds to four numbers that must be input, returning to conventional pen and paper would appear to be the more attractive option. Indeed, manually inputting a stream of numbers is insane when the same job could be done much better with regular pen and paper.
But there are superior methods of drawing on the computer that will demonstrate less emphasis on manual input and more emphasis on a style of *automatic* input.

Comments Before more advanced programs can be examined, the issue of program legibility must be addressed. When a program sequence is long, ensuring that the commands are executed in an order that matches your intentions is not a trivial task. While writing a program, you can usually remember which program line corresponds to which visual result; however, if you don't use the program for a few days, you might get lost trying to decipher your own code. It can also be difficult for another person to follow your programming intentions when facing many lines of opaquely defined code. Do the first 100 lines of code generate a tree or a house? Does the pen command mark the beginning of a new object? Although comments do nothing to affect the program, you can significantly increase the legibility of a program by interspersing textual comments.

Comments are added using the // command followed by an informative message. The message can be the title of your program, part of a step-by-step narrative of events in the program, or simply messages to yourself for the purpose of maintaining sanity during development of a long program. A comment is only valid on a line of its own, and cannot be combined with other programming statements.

```
// My First Clear Program
// Version 1
// This program makes a new,
// gorgeous sheet of black paper
Paper 100
```

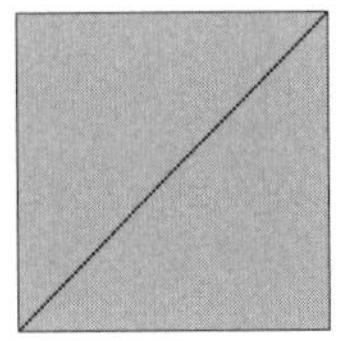

```
// Set the paper type
Paper 20
// Set the pen
Pen 80
// Draw a line from the lower left
// corner to the upper right corner
Line 0 0 100 100
```

```
// What follows is ten lines ...
Paper 0
Pen 100
Line 10 80 20 80
Line 10 81 20 81
Line 10 82 20 82
Line 10 83 20 83
Line 10 84 20 84
Line 10 85 20 85
Line 10 86 20 86
Line 10 87 20 87
Line 10 88 20 88
Line 10 89 20 89
Line 10 90 20 90
// I wish there were an easier way to
// draw a square, or other filled
// rectangular areas ...
```

All programming activity is enhanced with comments that clearly document the computational process. Consider the examples from the previous section, rewritten with comments.

```
Paper 0
Pen 100
// head
Line 53 72 50 78
Line 50 78 54 82
Line 54 82 57 81
Line 57 81 59 77
Line 59 77 56 73
Line 56 73 53 72
// spine lines
Line 49 70 50 46
Line 58 69 60 45
// shoulders
Line 49 70 60 69
// left arm
Line 49 70 42 63
Line 42 63 33 74
// right arm
Line 60 69 64 57
Line 64 57 64 46
// hips
Line 50 46 60 45
// left leg
Line 50 45 46 31
Line 46 31 49 13
// right leg
Line 60 45 61 29
Line 61 29 63 11
```

```
Paper 20
Pen 100
// table top
Line 100 8 25 22
Line 20 25 50 36
Line 56 38 68 42
Line 20 25 20 18
Line 20 18 90 5
Line 44 14 44 0
Line 50 8 50 0
Line 54 11 54 0
// lamp
Line 51 34 56 35
Line 50 35 35 60
Line 50 40 41 55
Line 54 40 41 60
Line 34 61 64 80
Line 41 60 61 75
Line 68 86 73 80
Line 68 86 65 84
Line 73 80 70 78
Line 63 83 67 75
Line 67 75 66 65
Line 66 65 82 75
```

```
Paper 0
Pen 100
// tree and horizon
Line 0 30 23 30
Line 23 30 23 40
Line 23 40 17 39
Line 17 39 12 46
Line 12 46 16 52
Line 16 52 15 57
Line 15 57 27 58
Line 27 58 34 52
Line 34 52 33 44
Line 33 44 26 40
Line 26 40 27 30
Line 27 30 40 30
// house and horizon
Line 40 30 38 44
Line 36 43 55 58
Line 55 58 76 43
Line 73 45 72 30
Line 72 30 100 30
// door
Line 46 30 47 30
Line 47 30 46 40
Line 46 40 53 40
Line 53 40 53 30
Line 53 30 55 30
// window
Line 59 40 67 40
Line 67 40 66 35
Line 66 35 59 35
Line 59 35 59 40
```

In addition to the use of comments, white space can visually segregate functionally different areas, or just give your eyes a rest.

```
// White space makes it all better...

Paper 37


// room to breathe... always nice ...
// why do we dirty this space?
```

Another common practice is using rows of characters such as % or # to mark out concrete lines of division in the program, or else to emphasize some important step.

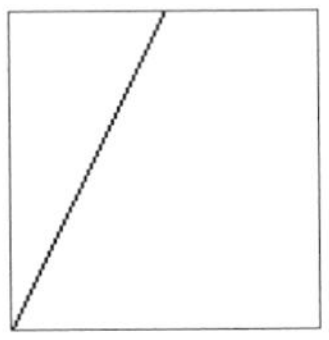

```
//
// A simple program
// *****************
// Prepare paper and pen
//
Paper 0
Pen 100
//
// ############################
// # This is a way to make an
// # emphatic comment even
// # though I am not doing
// # anything particularly
// # special ...
// ############################
//
Line 0 0 50 100
//
// ... my apologies to
//      the line of course.
```

You should exercise the same care with the graphics you draw and the programs you write. A program needs ample attention to legibility, which should be a combination of literate comments and a visual designer's attention to typography. Be consistent with the conventions you choose for writing comments and using white space, and the program will become a manageable endeavor.

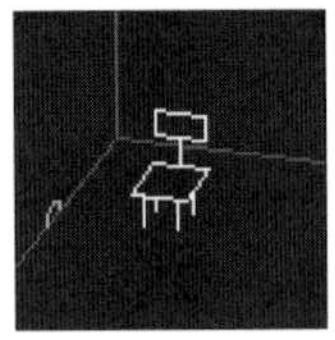

```
//
// %%%%%%%%%%%%%%%%%%%%%%%%
// %                      %
// %                      %
// %                      %
// %     A Small Scene    %
// %                      %
// %                      %
// %                      %
// %%%%%%%%%%%%%%%%%%%%%%%%

// Overview:

// First, a simple background is
// created, consisting of 3 lines
// on a gray backdrop. These lines
// imply the corner of some room.
// What room could this be? It
// could be any room of course.
// To say that it is *this* room
// over *that* room would surely
// be unjust. Thus, assume it
// stands for the representation
// of *any* room, for now.

// Second, a chair is rendered in
// order to establish the three-
// dimensional space better. Of
// course more chairs and other
// objects would help to concep-
// tually cement the depicted space.
// Alas, I am too far beyond the due
// date for this book and must
// suffer the fate of an empty room
// for now.

// Third, recognizing that the room
// does indeed look too visually
// impoverished to leave this
// example comfortably, I stare
// at my tabletop and the mouse
// looks back at me ... longing
// to belong to the scenery. And
// thus a small dab of virtual
// ink gives it that dose of hope.

// ********* setup backdrop
Paper 73

// ********* render the 'room'
Pen 50
Line 33 100 33 60
Line 0 20 33 60
Line 100 52 33 60
```

```
//
// Pause a bit to contemplate how
// nice an empty room looks, and
// consider how putting things into
// it might mess things up. But
// remember that you don't want
// you parents to worry, so you
// have to put something in there.

// ********* buy some furniture
// ********* paint it in white
Pen 0
// ********* a place to sit
Line 45 52 63 50
Line 45 52 38 42
Line 56 40 63 50
Line 38 42 56 40
// ********* needs some legs
Line 42 41 42 32
Line 53 39 53 31
Line 46 40 46 37
Line 58 42 58 36
// ********* something to lean against
Line 46 61 62 59
Line 46 61 46 69
Line 62 67 46 69
Line 62 67 62 59
// ********* have to support it
Line 54 51 54 59

//
// A tiny door in the wall (well,
// not really a door but a 'hole')
// is just big enough for a
// friend to come and go as he/she
// pleases.

// ********* a hole in the wall
Pen 20
Line 10 32 10 36
Line 10 36 12 40
Line 12 40 14 40
Line 14 40 14 38

//
// Comments aren't usually seen
// by other people, and thus you
// can ramble like this all you
// like. The fact that this will
// be published verbatim perhaps
// defeats the private nature of
// a good session of comments,
// but for the sake of education
// we must do all that we can.
```

Summary Because creating everyday drawings can involve hundreds of line commands, it may appear that writing programs to draw pictures is more suitable for simple subject matter. For five to ten lines, the advantage of numeric input is that the results are precise and are easy to edit to a high degree of satisfaction. Anything over ten lines can be difficult to manage. You would be better off drawing on regular paper with a regular pen instead of wrestling with a computerized Paper, Pen, and Line.

Then why write programs? First of all, programs make it possible to pinpoint position and tone to an exact specification. Second and most important, more advanced programs allow you to explore spaces of ten, one hundred, or one million lines with ease, which may seem unfathomable at this stage. Working toward an advanced goal usually implies greater complexity; however, in the case of programming, advancement is paradoxically in the direction of simplification.

Paper, Pen, and Line are the three commands that have been introduced thus far. You can use Line to effortlessly draw one, two, or many lines with unerring precision. Each line can be independently shaded to a specific percentage of black using the Pen command. You can also specify the background color with the Paper command. When there are many lines of code, interspersing comments for the reader or yourself is a useful technique in developing a clear program.

Comments are a means for the designer to leave a literal trail of thought as part of the process of creation on the computer.

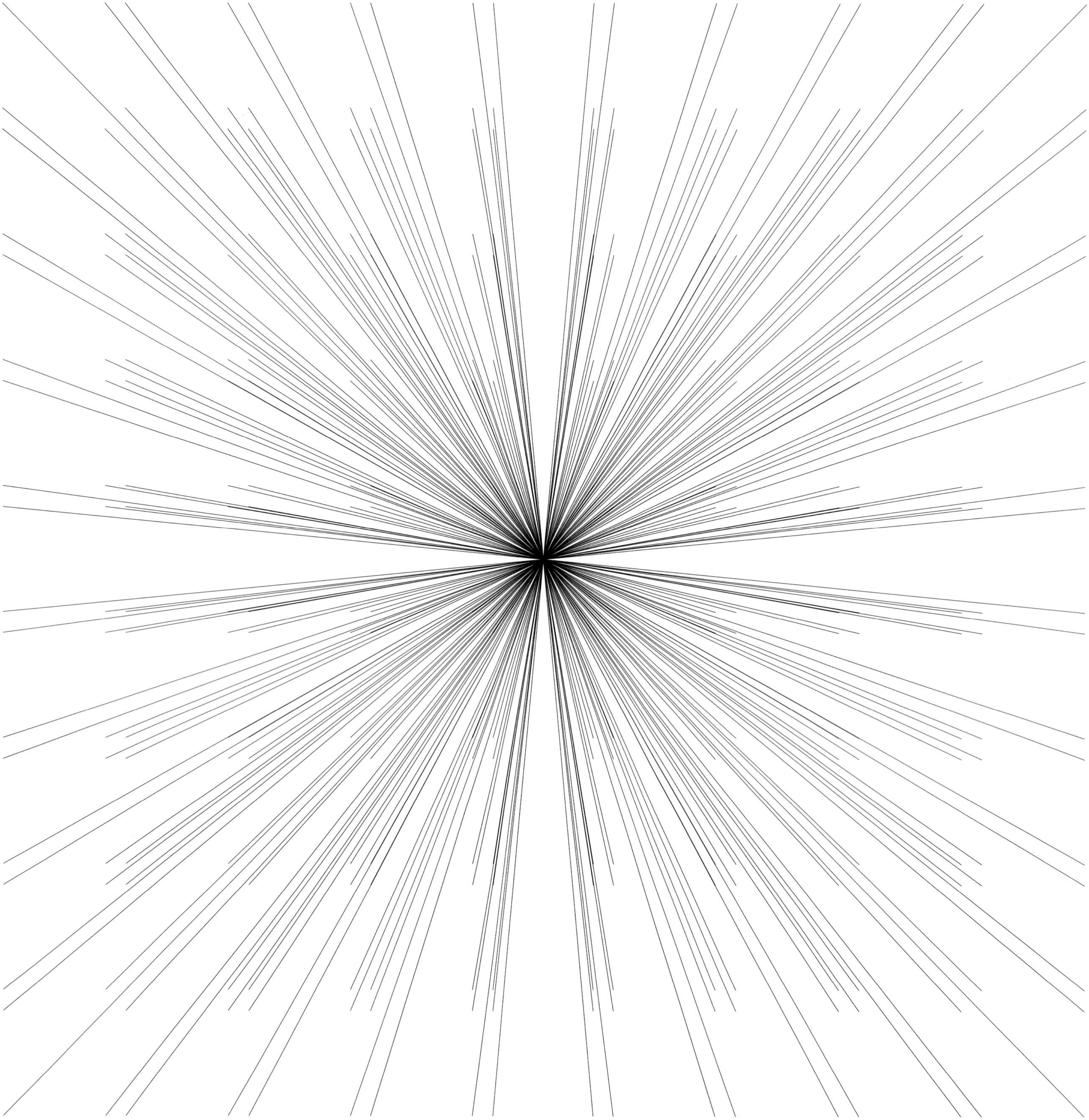

5 VARIABLES The first step in realizing the power of computational expression is learning how to recognize relations among numbers. And while there are many different types of relations that assume varying degrees of complexity, the canonical relation to identify is that of equality. As you write more programs, you will find that it is not uncommon to reuse a specific number that represents a relation among the objects you draw. For example, you may shade four lines with "Pen 50" and four lines with "Pen 75," or draw several lines that share a common starting or ending point. When there are such instances of using numbers with identical significance, applying a common symbol to represent the numbers in numerical relation yields profound advantages.

Gathering Like Numbers In this section, you will learn about a method for exploiting this natural tendency to use numerical quantities that relate to each other. Numbers can identify tone or dimension, but because they are quantitative, they can never signify a high-level meaning. For example, when discussing a structure, it is common practice to label specific dimensions as having some significance. "The fence height is always 5 meters," or "Keep the objects aligned at a 1-inch left margin." Labels like *height* or *margin* are associated with exact numerical values and labeling values helps to maintain a conceptual context when using numbers.

Thus, rather than refer to "5 meters" all the time, you can refer to *height.* Instead of specifying that all objects placed 1 inch from the left be moved to 2 inches from the left, you can ask that *margin* be moved to 2 inches. A carefully selected label keeps a numerical quantity in an intuitive frame of mind. You should, therefore, consciously label meaningful quantities. Conversely, attaching a label to every numeric quantity can have a distinctly negative effect because the key quantities are not obvious in the resulting sea of symbols. Use common sense when attempting to make sense of a program.

Consider the example of a horizontal line. You should immediately notice that 90 appears twice in the program.

```
Paper 0
Pen 100
// a horizontal line @90
Line 15 90 85 90
```

To change the vertical position of this line to 70, two instances of 90 must be replaced.

```
Paper 0
Pen 100
// a horizontal line @70
Line 15 70 85 70
```

The fact that the number occurs twice is no coincidence: the start and end points of a horizontal line obviously must share the same vertical position. You can assign a label to this quantity, such as V for the 'V'ertical.

```
Paper 0
Pen 100
Line 15 V 85 V
```

At a glance, the program identifies a line at the vertical position V drawn between 15 and 85.

However, the program is not complete until you specify the value of V with the **Set** command. The computer will otherwise assign a default value of 0 to any variables that are not Set, so you must be sure to explicitly Set them.

```
Paper 0
Pen 100
// V is the vertical position
Set V 70
Line 15 V 85 V
```

Set takes two qualifiers: the first is the label of the quantity to Set and the second is the value to assign to the symbol. Read in sequence, the Paper is specified as white, the Pen is specified as black, a quantity V is introduced and set to 70 pts, and then a Line is drawn from 15 V to 85 V, which translates to 15 70 to 85 70. In consideration of the labor involved in editing this program, the process of changing the vertical position is now reduced to the single edit.

```
Paper 0
Pen 100
// line is moved up with 1 edit
Set V 90
Line 15 V 85 V
```

```
Paper 0
Pen 100
// line is moved down with 1 edit
Set V 30
Line 15 V 85 V
```

Likewise, more indirect modifications occur when there are more instances of reusing the variable V.

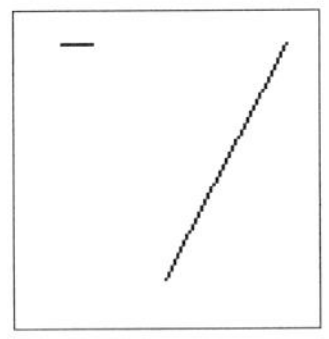

```
Paper 0
Pen 100
Set V 90
// draw 2 lines that use V
Line 15 V 25 V
Line 50 15 V V
```

Now a single change in V results in an indirect modification in four places in the program.

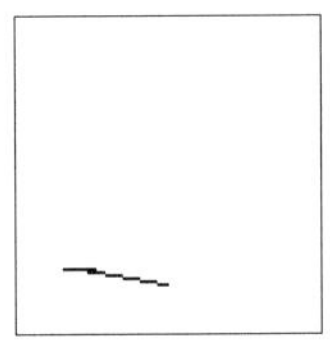

```
Paper 0
Pen 100
// the 2 lines are easily moved
// with one numerical edit
Set V 20
Line 15 V 25 V
Line 50 15 V V
```

The form thus becomes a graphical marionette, where numbers are the strings that are individually "pulled" to control it.

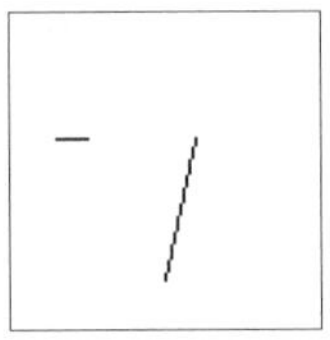

```
Paper 0
Pen 100
// 2 lines changed with 1 edit
Set V 60
Line 15 V 25 V
Line 50 15 V V
```

The slightest tug synthesizes a new posture.

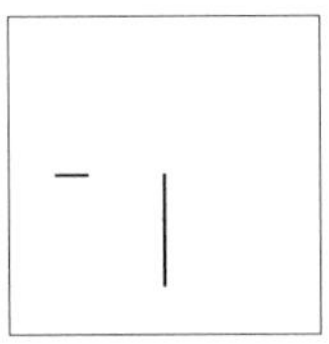

```
Paper 0
Pen 100
// slight tug
Set V 50
Line 15 V 25 V
Line 50 15 V V
```

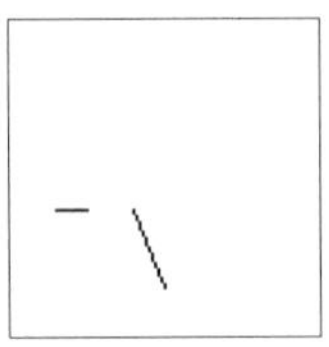

```
Paper 0
Pen 100
// again
Set V 40
Line 15 V 25 V
Line 50 15 V V
```

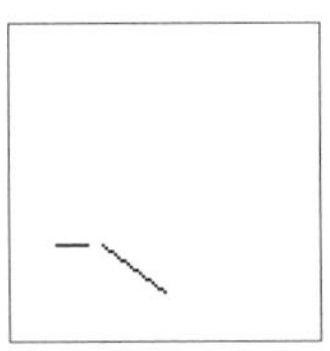

```
Paper 0
Pen 100
// and again
Set V 30
Line 15 V 25 V
Line 50 15 V V
```

You can also represent the gray value of the Pen with a label—for instance, G for gray.

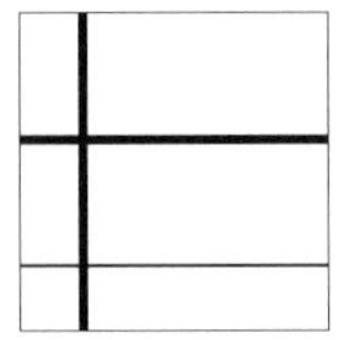

```
Paper 0
Set G 100
// G is used as a pen value
Pen G
// thick vertical
Line 19 0 19 100
Line 20 0 20 100
Line 21 0 21 100
Pen 100
Line 20 20 20 100
Pen G
// thick horizontal
Line 0 59 100 59
Line 0 60 100 60
Line 0 61 100 61
Pen 100
Line 0 20 100 20
```

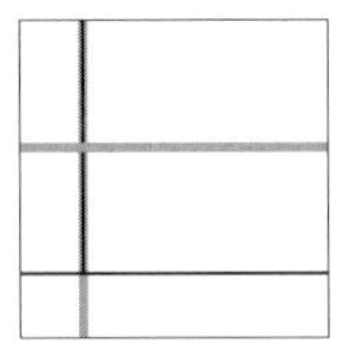

```
Paper 0
// a change in G changes the palette
// of the image, as well as its nature.
Set G 30
Pen G
// thick vertical
Line 19 0 19 100
Line 20 0 20 100
Line 21 0 21 100
Pen 100
Line 20 20 20 100
Pen G
// thick horizontal
Line 0 59 100 59
Line 0 60 100 60
Line 0 61 100 61
Pen 100
Line 0 20 100 20
```

Labeled quantities are commonly referred to as *variables* because they are often used when the numerical value of the quantity is to be varied. You will learn more about this technique in Chapter 6, but for now you will use variables for the purpose of abstracting numerical values that are reused throughout the program.

More Than One Variable With one variable, changing the numerical value in the Set command generates indirect changes throughout the program. In the case of two variables, changes in both of their corresponding Set commands would naturally generate two sets of indirect changes throughout the program. Depending on the intended drawing, one variable may be used in one set of lines, and the other may be used to control another set of lines.

For example, consider a horizontal and a vertical line where their respective positions are specified using variables. Changing one variable generates a change only in the respective line.

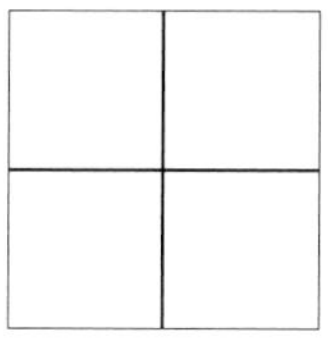

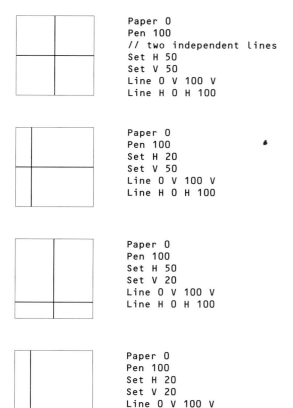

```
Paper 0
Pen 100
// two independent lines
Set H 50
Set V 50
Line 0 V 100 V
Line H 0 H 100
```

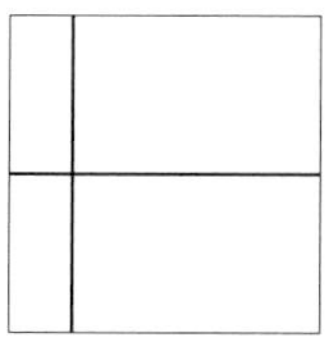

```
Paper 0
Pen 100
Set H 20
Set V 50
Line 0 V 100 V
Line H 0 H 100
```

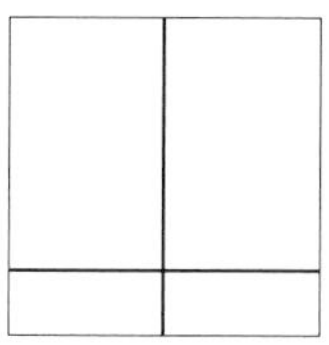

```
Paper 0
Pen 100
Set H 50
Set V 20
Line 0 V 100 V
Line H 0 H 100
```

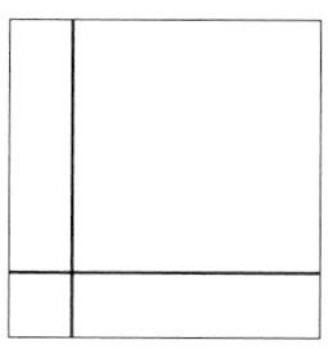

```
Paper 0
Pen 100
Set H 20
Set V 20
Line 0 V 100 V
Line H 0 H 100
```

Alternatively, you can define a system of relations between the two lines by sharing variables across drawing expressions.

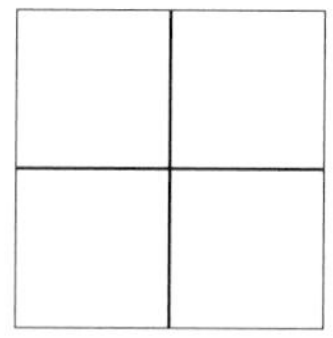

```
Paper 0
Pen 100
// two dependent lines
Set H 50
Set V 50
Line 0 V 100 H
Line H 0 V 100
```

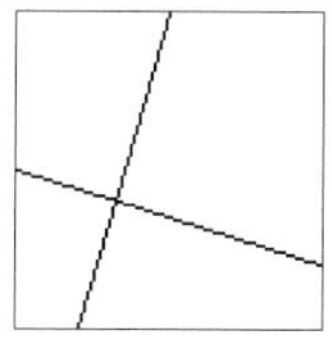

```
Paper 0
Pen 100
Set H 20
Set V 50
Line 0 V 100 H
Line H 0 V 100
```

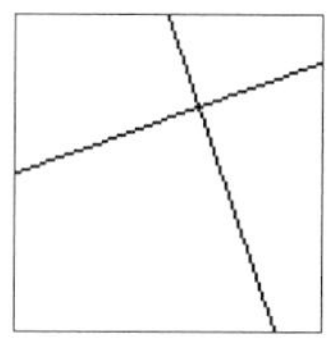

```
Paper 0
Pen 100
Set H 85
Set V 50
Line 0 V 100 H
Line H 0 V 100
```

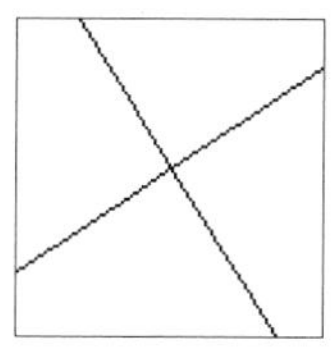

```
Paper 0
Pen 100
Set H 85
Set V 20
Line 0 V 100 H
Line H 0 V 100
```

Thus, changing either variable affects both lines simultaneously because they share variables. When lines are interrelated in this manner, a simple modification in the relation by switching variables can produce program results that will appear similar, but are fundamentally distinct.

When there are many lines involved, managing interrelationships between lines in a conscious fashion is difficult. However, systems of interdependent lines generally produce deep results, and are well worth the initial bout of confusion.

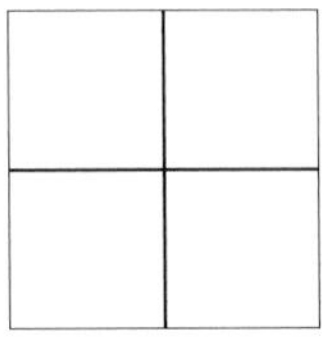

```
Paper 0
Pen 100
// two dependent lines
Set H 50
Set V 50
Line 0 V 100 H
Line V 0 H 100
```

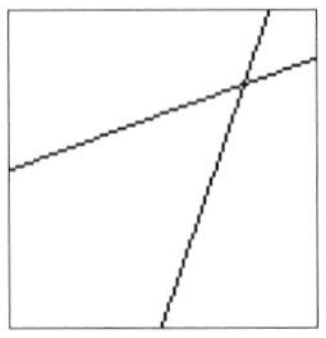

```
Paper 0
Pen 100
// a change in H
Set H 85
Set V 50
Line 0 V 100 H
Line V 0 H 100
```

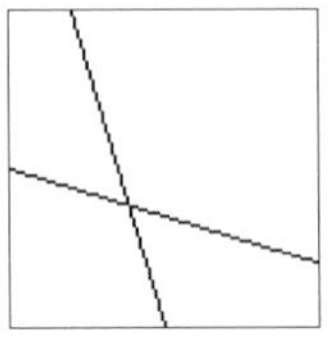

```
Paper 0
Pen 100
// a change in H
Set H 20
Set V 50
Line 0 V 100 H
Line V 0 H 100
```

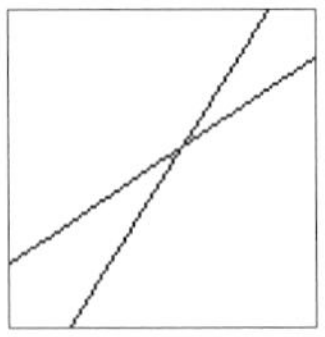

```
Paper 0
Pen 100
// a subsequent change in V
Set H 85
Set V 20
Line 0 V 100 H
Line V 0 H 100
```

The shade of a line can be directly related to its position because tone and scale both range from 0 to 100. For example, you can draw a 50 percent gray line at the horizontal position of 50 or a solid black line at position 100.

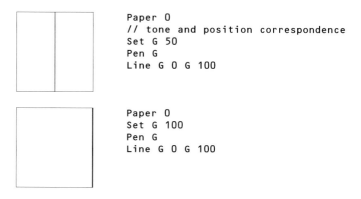

```
Paper 0
// tone and position correspondence
Set G 50
Pen G
Line G 0 G 100
```

```
Paper 0
Set G 100
Pen G
Line G 0 G 100
```

Adding a variable for the horizontal position breaks the relationship.

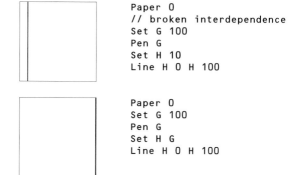

```
Paper 0
// broken interdependence
Set G 100
Pen G
Set H 10
Line H 0 H 100
```

```
Paper 0
Set G 100
Pen G
Set H G
Line H 0 H 100
```

The relationship is reestablished by Set-ing one variable relative to the other.

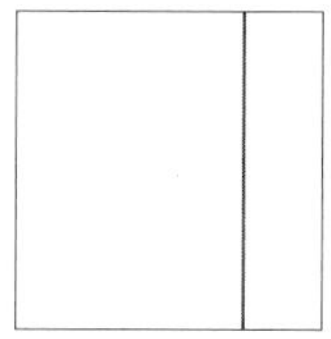

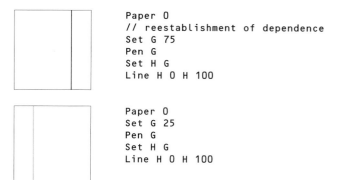

```
Paper 0
// reestablishment of dependence
Set G 75
Pen G
Set H G
Line H 0 H 100
```

```
Paper 0
Set G 25
Pen G
Set H G
Line H 0 H 100
```

This process is referred to as *copying* the contents of one variable to another. In this example, G is copied to H, so changing the value of G will effectively change all instances of H.

Rules Concerning Variables When using variables, there are several important rules that must be observed regarding legal naming of variables and general sequential issues.

Never use a variable before it has been defined with the Set command.

```
Paper 0
Pen 100
Line A A 100 A
Set A 30
```

```
Paper 0
Pen 100
Set A 30
Line A A 100 A
```

Remember that the computer reads the program in sequence; when A is referenced in this program, the computer does not know the value of A. Only after the Set command is processed does A actually signify 30. Thus, when the Line command is processed by the computer, A is unknown and the default value of zero is used.

When using variables, be aware that it is easy to misspell or misrepresent variables. For instance, when similar names are used in close proximity to each other, confusion occurs. The computer will strictly follow your instructions, but you or someone reading your program can easily become lost.

For instance, a simple misplacement of letters, in this case inadvertently switching AN and AM, can result in unintended variations.

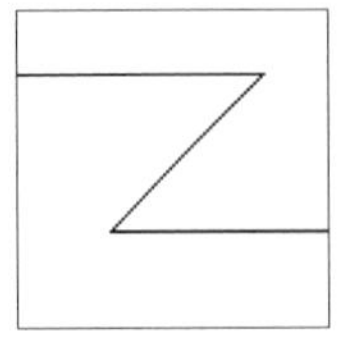

```
Paper 0
Pen 100
Set AN 30
Set AM 80
Line AN AN 100 AN
Line 0 AM AM AM
Line AN AN AM AM
```

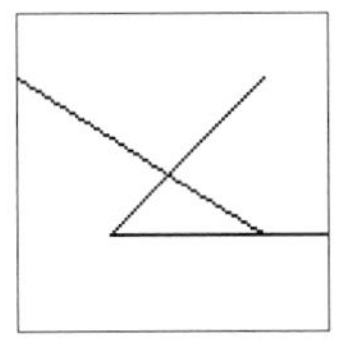

```
Paper 0
Pen 100
Set AN 30
Set AM 80
Line AN AN 100 AN
Line 0 AM AM AN
Line AN AN AM AM
```

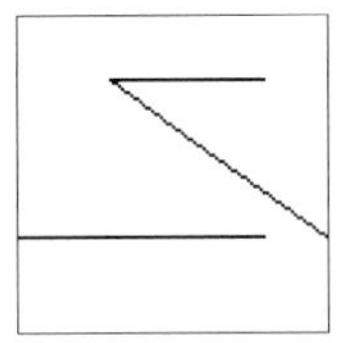

```
Paper 0
Pen 100
Set AN 30
Set AM 80
Line AN AM 100 AN
Line 0 AN AM AN
Line AN AM AM AM
```

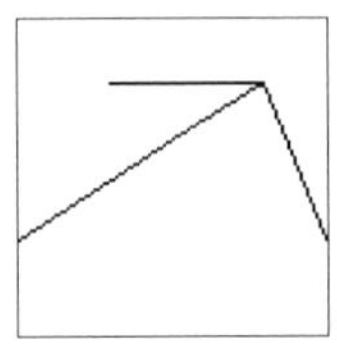

```
Paper 0
Pen 100
Set AN 30
Set AM 80
Line AM AM 100 AN
Line 0 AN AM AM
Line AM AM AN AM
```

Therefore, it is important to give clear, meaningful names to variables whenever possible.

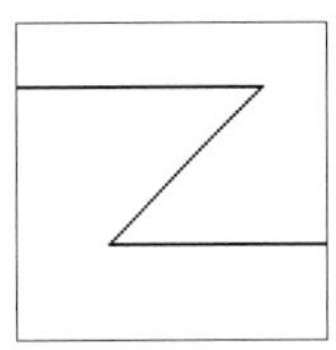

```
Paper 0
Pen 100
Set LEFT 30
Set RIGHT 80
Line LEFT LEFT 100 LEFT
Line 0 RIGHT RIGHT RIGHT
Line LEFT LEFT RIGHT RIGHT
```

A number is always a number and cannot be used as the name of a variable.

```
Paper 0
Pen 100
// set the variable "10" to 20
Set 10 20
```

Furthermore, the name of a variable must not start with a number.

```
Paper 0
Pen 100
// set the variable "753D" to 100
Set 753D 100
```

Finally, do not use the name of a command as a variable. The computer will not understand when command names are placed where descriptors should be, and as a result the program will not be processed and shall not run.

```
Paper 0
Pen 100
Set Set 50
Line Set 100 Set 50
```

Follow these simple rules when using variables, and variables will serve you well.

Summary A variable is a labeled numeric quantity. Variables can hold any type of number, whether it is a tone value, a position, or even another variable. When there is more than one instance of the same variable, changing the numerical value using the Set command will automatically change all subsequent instances of the variable. Using more than one variable results in drawings with elements that depend upon all, several, one, or no variables.

An element incorporating a variable is like a graphical form with a control dial attached. By turning the dial via changing the variable, the graphical form changes accordingly. For example, changing V in "Line 0 V 100 V" moves the line up or down. Using multiple variables allows more ways to control the variation of a form and thus allows more freedom. But it may cause difficulty when you have too many variables to maintain, so whenever possible keep it simple.

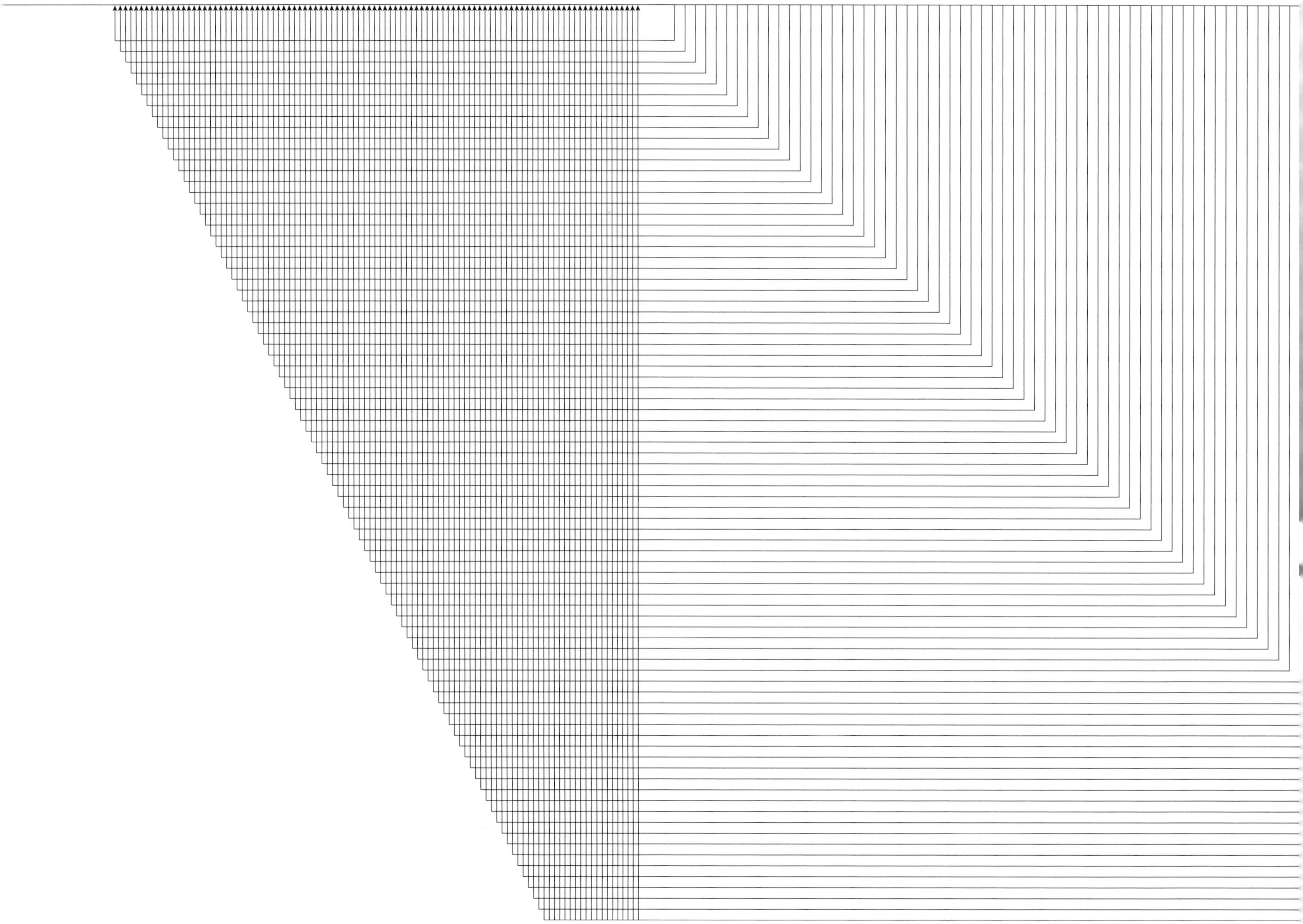

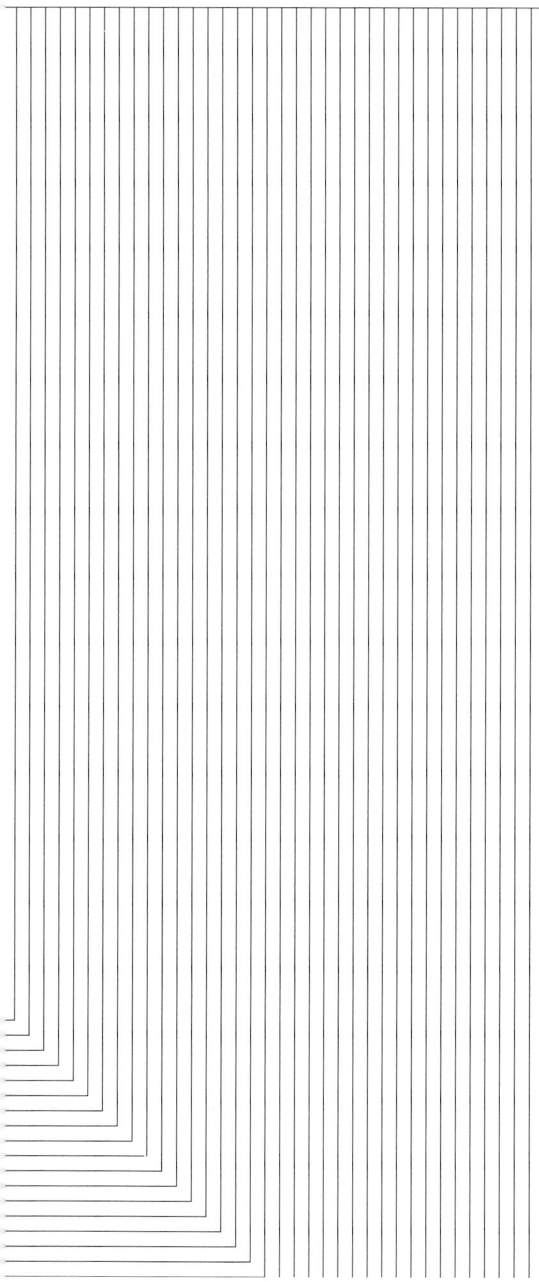

6 REPEAT The most elegant construct in computation is repetition, or a Repeat, as it is called in this book. We usually associate something repetitive as being anything but elegant. However, you will find that the manner in which you use repetition can, in fact, be very elegant, as can the way in which you instruct the computer to incorporate repetition. Both the resulting art work (form) and the expression of the program that produces it (structure) can represent the highest quality of design.

A Block of Code Before a Repeat can be introduced, the concept of a *block* of code must be discussed. Organizing your program into blocks serves a purpose similar to adding comments in the sense that blocks establish clarity within a program. The key difference is that a block is also a meaningful structural entity in a program. You can create a block by identifying a segment of code that pertains to a specific process and by marking the beginning and end of the block with special commands. The commands are easy to identify because they are a pair of symbols on the keyboard, namely the curly braces { and }. To begin a block, issue the command {, and to end the block, issue the command }.

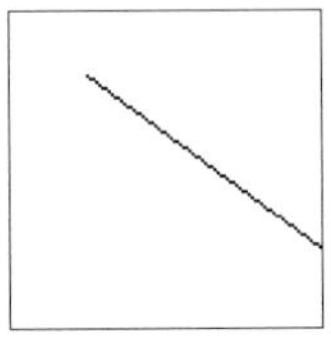

```
// plain
Paper 0
Pen 100
Line 25 80 100 25
```

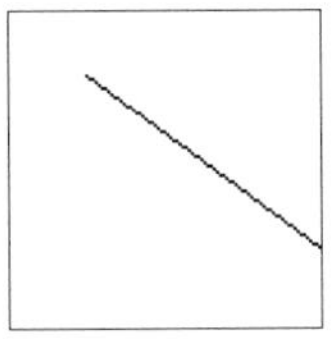

```
// with block
Paper 0
{
Pen 100
Line 25 80 100 25
}
```

A block does not change the way a program will run; a program will execute in the same top to bottom order regardless of the existence of a block. A single statement, several lines, even an entire program can be placed inside a block without affecting the final result.

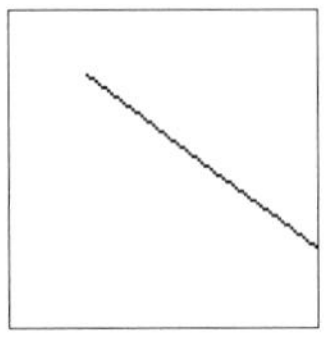

```
{
// entirety in block
Paper 0
Pen 100
Line 25 80 100 25
}
```

Although a block appears to accomplish no specific function, you can see from the program code that there is a distinct perceptual function performed by a block. The braces of a block visually bond the statements that lie within. A common convention used to emphasize this type of bond is to indent the statements by two or three spaces within a block in a consistent manner for neat left margins.

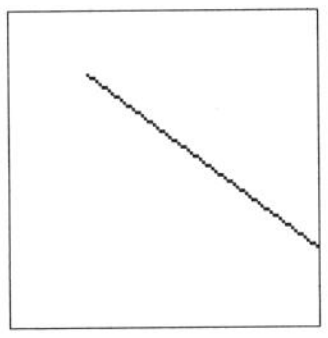

```
// with indention
{
   Paper 0
   Pen 100
   Line 25 80 100 25
}
```

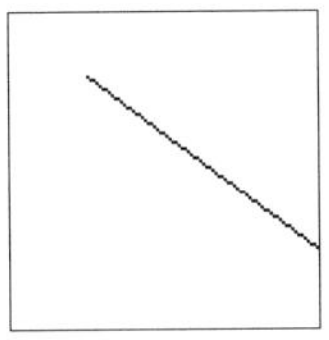

```
// with indention
Paper 0
Pen 100
{
   Line 25 80 100 25
}
```

The indention emphasizes that the lines of code are within a block. This organizing effect is the key characteristic of a block. It is a crucial factor when trying to comprehend long sequences of code. The block notation allows you to group actions of a sequence into smaller sequences that are more likely to be understood. An analogy would be the way in which conventional tasks are delegated to another person as a set of clear subtasks. With a set of smaller tasks defined, it is easy to create more complex tasks composed of combinations of the smaller tasks.

A block signifies a set of individual events that constitute a coherent program sequence. Within a complex block, you can expect that there are groups of actions that can be gathered into smaller blocks. In the previous section, such units were emphasized with comments, which was fine; blocks add a layer of structure that becomes relevant in the next section.

Note that the use of indention is extended when a block appears inside a block such that with each additional level, a block is indented accordingly. When blocks are distinctly identified in this manner, it is easier to make changes because the divisions in code are clear and meaningful.

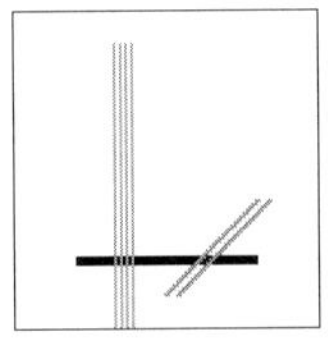

```
// beautifully indented blocks
Paper 0
{
   {
      // *A* draw black swatch
      Pen 100
      Line 20 20 80 20
      Line 20 21 80 21
      Line 20 22 80 22
   }
   {
      // *B* draw gray 25 swatch
      Pen 25
      Line 33 0 33 90
      Line 35 0 35 90
      Line 37 0 37 90
      Line 39 0 39 90
   }
   {
      // *C* draw gray 33 swatch
      Pen 33
      Line 50 10 80 40
      Line 51 10 81 40
      Line 54 10 84 40
      Line 55 10 85 40
   }
}
```

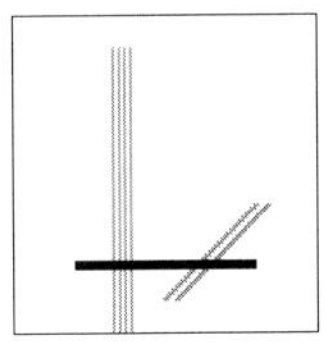

```
// changing the order of blocks
Paper 0
{
   {
      // *B* draw gray 25 swatch
      Pen 25
      Line 33 0 33 90
      Line 35 0 35 90
      Line 37 0 37 90
      Line 39 0 39 90
   }
   {
      // *C* draw gray 33 swatch
      Pen 33
      Line 50 10 80 40
      Line 51 10 81 40
      Line 54 10 84 40
      Line 55 10 85 40
   }
   {
      // *A* draw black swatch
      Pen 100
      Line 20 20 80 20
      Line 20 21 80 21
      Line 20 22 80 22
   }
}
```

Draw a Rectangle Once a block of code is understood, we can move on to encoding repetition. Repetition requires understanding the concept of blocks, which represent the particular portion of code you choose to highlight for repetition. Now that such a structure is in place, we will discuss how to apply the **Repeat** command.

As with a variable, finding a situation for Repeat depends upon identifying specific patterns of numbers in your code. A variable was shown to be useful when there is a pattern of reusing the same number. The characteristic pattern for a Repeat is in situations where a number increases in regular steps. Drawing a filled square is a good example that illustrates these patterns.

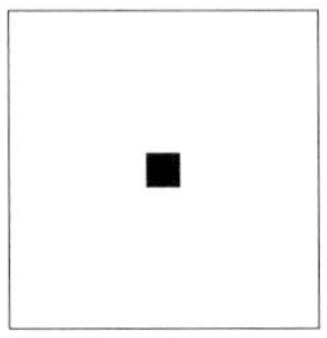

```
Paper 0
Pen 100
{
  // ten lines = 1 square
  Line 45 45 55 45
  Line 45 46 55 46
  Line 45 47 55 47
  Line 45 48 55 48
  Line 45 49 55 49
  Line 45 50 55 50
  Line 45 51 55 51
  Line 45 52 55 52
  Line 45 53 55 53
  Line 45 54 55 54
  Line 45 55 55 55
}
```

Notice that the vertical position of each Line drawn progresses from 45, to 46, to 47, and then all the way to 55 in a monotonic, repetitive manner. Were you to draw these ten lines manually with a ruler and pen, you would get a better sense of the repetitive nature as each line is swept out by your gestures. The action performed is essentially the same, except that with each new Line, the vertical position is moved one point vertically, for a total of eleven times.

Converting this process to a Repeat requires one more step. The task of drawing a line must be written in a general form by using a variable to represent the quantity that varies in the process.

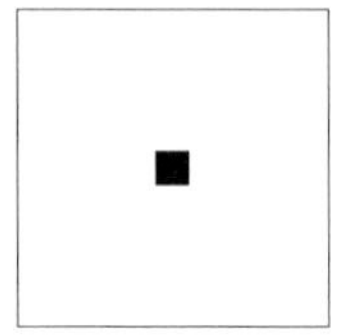

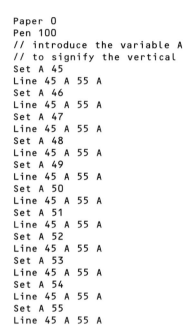

```
Paper 0
Pen 100
// introduce the variable A
// to signify the vertical
Set A 45
Line 45 A 55 A
Set A 46
Line 45 A 55 A
Set A 47
Line 45 A 55 A
Set A 48
Line 45 A 55 A
Set A 49
Line 45 A 55 A
Set A 50
Line 45 A 55 A
Set A 51
Line 45 A 55 A
Set A 52
Line 45 A 55 A
Set A 53
Line 45 A 55 A
Set A 54
Line 45 A 55 A
Set A 55
Line 45 A 55 A
```

The program is now twice as long, and the dream of being clear and concise seems far away.

Continuing in this direction, the task to be repeated must be clarified in a block.

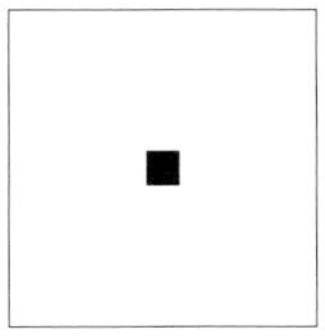

```
Paper 0
Pen 100
// block-ize it all
Set A 45
{
  Line 45 A 55 A
}
Set A 46
{
  Line 45 A 55 A
}
Set A 47
{
  Line 45 A 55 A
}
Set A 48
{
  Line 45 A 55 A
}
Set A 49
{
  Line 45 A 55 A
}
Set A 50
{
  Line 45 A 55 A
}
Set A 51
{
  Line 45 A 55 A
}
Set A 52
{
  Line 45 A 55 A
}
Set A 53
{
  Line 45 A 55 A
}
Set A 54
{
  Line 45 A 55 A
}
Set A 55
{
  Line 45 A 55 A
}
```

In this verbose form, the task of drawing "Line 45 A 55 A" is easily recognized as being repeated with respect to a variable A that ranges from 45 to 55. Once this fact is recognized, all that is left is to rewrite everything as a Repeat.

A Repeat is written by issuing the command Repeat, followed by the name of the variable that repeats, and then the starting and ending values of the variable. Repeat sets the variable to all of the numbers ranging from the specified start and end value. With each cycle, it executes the block that immediately follows the Repeat command.

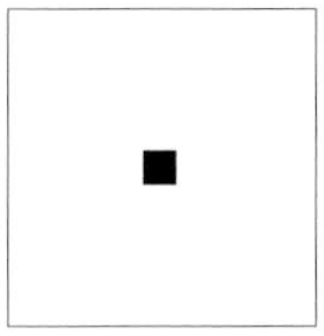

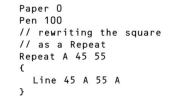

```
Paper 0
Pen 100
// rewriting the square
// as a Repeat
Repeat A 45 55
{
  Line 45 A 55 A
}
```

Many lines of code have now been reduced to very few by identifying a repeated task and using the Repeat construct.

A Repeat is a deceivingly compact computational structure that can reduce most repetitive tasks, irrespective of the number of cycles or the complexity of the task, to a concise set of statements. Because so much can happen in a small Repeat, when the program for a drawing is written in the form of a Repeat, a small change in the interval of the Repeat or in the actions that occur within the block to Repeat can result in a disproportionately large difference in the outcome.

```
Paper 0
Pen 100
// changing the start value
Repeat A 35 55
{
  Line 45 A 55 A
}
```

```
Paper 0
Pen 100
// changing the end value
Repeat A 45 85
{
  Line 45 A 55 A
}
```

```
Paper 0
Pen 100
// changing the action
Repeat A 45 65
{
  Line 25 A 85 A
}
```

```
Paper 0
Pen 100
// start and end are identical
Repeat A 50 50
{
  Line 45 A 55 A
}
```

Using a Repeat, drawing 1 line or 101 lines requires essentially the same amount of effort.

```
Paper 0
Pen 100
// one hundred lines
Repeat A 0 100
{
  Line 45 A 55 A
}
```

Add the rectangle to your vocabulary of forms to be expressed using computation.

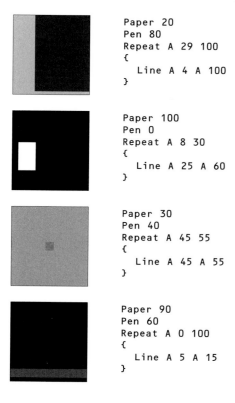

```
Paper 20
Pen 80
Repeat A 29 100
{
  Line A 4 A 100
}
```

```
Paper 100
Pen 0
Repeat A 8 30
{
  Line A 25 A 60
}
```

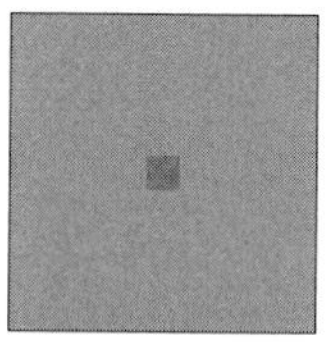

```
Paper 30
Pen 40
Repeat A 45 55
{
  Line A 45 A 55
}
```

```
Paper 90
Pen 60
Repeat A 0 100
{
  Line A 5 A 15
}
```

You can now see how the benefits of computation let you use an extremely compact set of instructions to accomplish a great deal of work with minimal effort. Even a relatively complex figure like the filled rectangle, which can be composed of as many as 101 lines, can be expressed in a compact form that aspires to the simplicity of the solitary line.

Triangles and More A set of standard shapes can be represented using Repeat. The first is the filled rectangle, which can be rendered in one of two ways—a series of horizontal or vertical lines.

```
Paper 0
Pen 100
// Repeat example in horizontal
Repeat A 40 70
{
   Line 20 A 80 A
}
```

```
Paper 0
Pen 100
// Repeat example in vertical
Repeat A 20 80
{
   Line A 40 A 70
}
```

The difference between the two is imperceivable in final visual form. However, the two cases can be made distinct by changing the Pen color based on the position of each line within the Repeat.

```
Paper 0
// lower lines are lighter
Repeat A 40 70
{
   Pen A
   Line 20 A 80 A
}
```

```
Paper 0
// lines to the left are lighter
Repeat A 20 80
{
   Pen A
   Line A 40 A 70
}
```

In addition to the rectangle there is the triangle, which you may have already accidentally discovered by mistyping the code for a rectangle. As with the rectangle, there are a variety of ways to draw a triangle, starting with a set of horizontal lines that become progressively shorter as they step in the upward direction.

```
Paper 0
Pen 100
// a triangle stepped in V
Repeat A 0 50
{
   Line A A 50 A
}
```

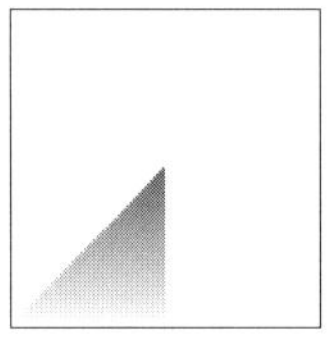

```
Paper 0
// shaded to mark direction
Repeat A 0 50
{
   Pen A
   Line A A 50 A
}
```

You can also render this triangle as a set of vertical lines that become progressively longer as they step to the right. Again, the difference is illustrated by redrawing the first triangle using the gradated Pen technique.

```
Paper 0
Pen 100
// a triangle stepped in V
Repeat A 0 50
{
   Line A A A 0
}
```

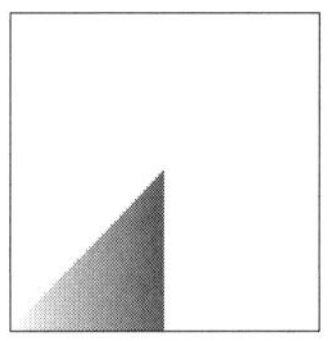

```
Paper 0
// shaded to mark direction
Repeat A 0 50
{
   Pen A
   Line A A A 0
}
```

Another type of triangle that can be rendered is a series of diagonal lines that become progressively longer as they move in the diagonal direction (northwesterly). Again, the nature of this form is made explicit by changing the respective intensities of the lines.

```
Paper 0
Pen 100
// triangle stepping in diagonal
Repeat A 0 50
{
  Line 0 A A 0
}
```

```
Paper 0
// shaded to mark direction
Repeat A 0 50
{
  Pen A
  Line 0 A A 0
}
```

A limitation of these triangles is that they all begin in the lower left corner and are all *right* triangles (i.e. there is one angle that is 90 degrees). It would be a sorry world if you could only draw right triangles that are constrained to the lower left corner. You can look forward to dropping this restriction in the next chapter. But there is one triangle that you can draw right now that is not trapped in the corner. By fixing one point anywhere in space, and drawing the lines that are traced out by a Repeat, a new free-spirited triangle unfolds.

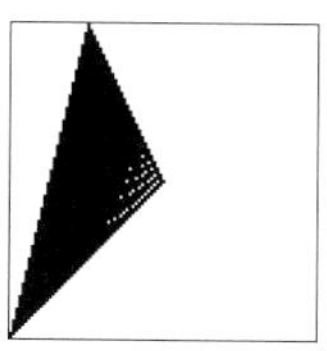

```
Paper 0
Pen 100
// one point fixed at 25 100
// and off we go ...
Repeat A 0 50
{
  Line 25 100 A A
}
```

The triangle's direction can be accentuated by the gradation effect. Notice that this triangle has a subtle textural imperfection. Because each rough line does not necessarily overlap, such triangles may be incompletely filled.

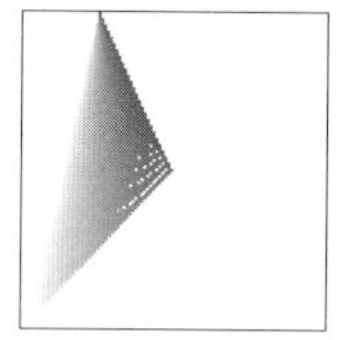

```
Paper 0
Pen 100
// shaded to mark direction
Repeat A 0 50
{
  Pen A
  Line 25 100 A A
}
```

Sometimes the textural defect is not noticeable, such as when drawing a small right triangle.

```
Paper 0
Pen 100
// another right triangle
Repeat A 0 50
{
  Line 50 50 A 0
}
```

Although this triangle looks familiar, it is drawn quite differently, as emphasized with individual shading of lines.

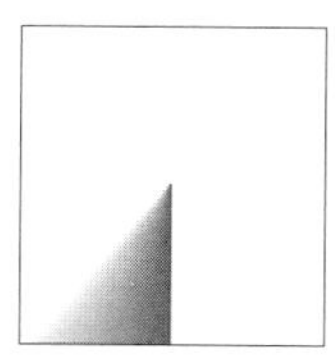

```
Paper 0
// shaded to mark direction
Repeat A 0 50
{
  Pen A
  Line 50 50 A 0
}
```

Additional varieties of forms can be constructed by simply combining any of the basic forms as a sequence of Repeats. For example, take any of the triangles and rectangles discussed so far and combine them in different ways.

Several triangles join to form anything from a square to the invisible man.

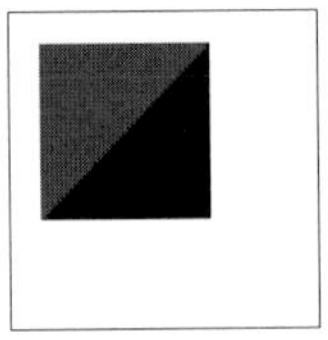

```
// square
Paper 0
Repeat A 10 65
{
  Pen 60
  Line 10 35 A 90
  Pen 100
  Line 65 90 A 35
}
```

```
// stack of triangles
Paper 0
Repeat A 20 80
{
  Pen A
  Line 50 75 A 20
}
Repeat A 36 64
{
  Pen 0
  Line 50 20 A 48
}
```

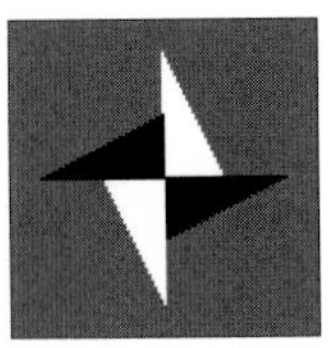

```
// a pinwheel
Paper 50
Pen 0
Repeat A 50 70
{
  Line 50 90 A 50
}
Repeat A 30 50
{
  Line 50 10 A 50
}
Pen 100
Repeat A 30 50
{
  Line 90 50 50 A
}
Repeat A 50 70
{
  Line 10 50 50 A
}
```

```
// lightning bolt
Paper 75
Pen 0
Repeat A 42 58
{
  Line 70 93 A 51
}
Repeat A 57 73
{
  Line 45 15 A 57
}
```

```
// paper airplane
Paper 30
Pen 0
Repeat A 20 85
{
  Line 75 55 A 25
}
Pen 40
Repeat A 20 85
{
  Line 95 45 A 25
}
```

```
// hi!
// you can't see me!
Paper 70
Pen 0
Repeat A 15 25
{
  Line 50 20 35 A
  Line 50 20 65 A
}
```

Combinations of triangles and rectangles create more variants of representative artwork.

```
// house
Paper 30
Pen 80
Repeat A 0 5
{
  Line 0 A 100 A
}
Pen 60
Repeat A 30 60
{
  Line A 6 A 26
}
Repeat A 27 63
{
  Line A 26 45 44
}
```

```
// cat
Paper 0
Pen 100
Repeat A 30 70
{
  Line A 35 A 60
}
Repeat A 30 40
{
  Line A 63 30 73
}
Repeat A 60 70
{
  Line A 63 70 73
}
Pen 0
Repeat A 44 56
{
  Line 50 44 A 50
}
```

```
// periscope
Paper 80
Pen 100
Repeat A 0 25
{
  Line 0 A 100 A
}
Pen 65
Repeat A 60 75
{
  Line A 26 A 75
}
Pen 55
Repeat A 63 87
{
  Line 76 75 58 A
}
Pen 45
Repeat A 49 58
{
  Line A 62 A 88
}
Pen 60
Repeat A 40 51
{
  Line 59 A 76 A
}
```

```
// loving trees
Paper 30
Pen 100
Repeat A 37 63
{
  Pen A
  Line 50 64 A 20
}
Repeat A 67 93
{
  Pen A
  Line 80 64 A 20
}
Pen 60
Repeat A 12 19
{
  Line 48 A 52 A
  Line 78 A 82 A
}
Pen 0
Repeat A 60 70
{
  Line 65 48 A 55
}
Pen 30
Repeat A 64 66
{
  Line 65 52 A 55
}
```

Rather than stringing together series of Repeats, you can combine all relevant commands into a single Repeat. This is superior from the perspective of writing elegant code but a bit more challenging to organize.

```
Paper 0
// packed repeat
Repeat A 0 100
{
  Pen 100
  Line A A 60 A
  Line A 62 29 78
  Line 63 70 70 A
  Line 1 A 3 A
  Pen 0
  Line 50 50 A A
}
```

```
Paper 0
Pen 100
// like the waves
Repeat A 0 50
{
  Line A 0 100 A
  Line A 50 0 A
}
```

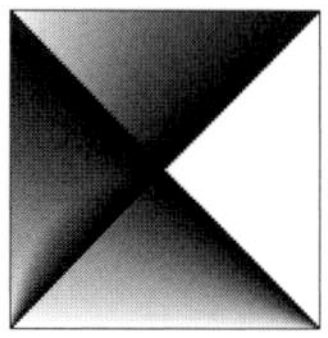

```
Paper 0
// gradated response
Repeat A 0 100
{
  Pen A
  Line 100 0 0 A
  Line 0 0 A 100
}
```

```
Paper 0
// surprisingly subtle
Repeat A 0 100
{
  Pen A
  Line 50 50 A 100
  Line 100 0 A 100
  Line 0 100 100 A
  Line 50 50 100 A
}
```

Even a single Repeat of one Line can hide more than one single shape.

```
Paper 0
Pen 100
// two triangles for the price of one
Repeat A 0 100
{
   Line A A 50 A
}
```

And hide a complex shape that would not seem possible from a single Repeat.

```
Paper 0
Pen 100
// quadrilateral for free
Repeat A 25 75
{
   Line A 0 0 A
}
```

Summary Repeat requires four pieces of information: (1) a variable to step with, (2) a beginning value for the variable, (3) an end value for the variable, and (4) a block of code that immediately follows the Repeat. This block of code is executed as many times as it takes to step from start to end value in increments of one. A block of code is a set of statements enclosed in braces { } that make up a coherent unit of work. When a block is defined that varies with respect to some variable, the block can be repeated over a range of values for that variable.

Using Repeat, drawing a filled triangle or rectangle is just a little more work than drawing a single line, which should seem counterintuitive from the perspective of drawing with your hand but completely natural when drawing on the computer. Many Repeats can encompass much work, but even a single Repeat can accomplish a great deal when its corresponding block of code is written effectively.

0+0=0, 0+1=1, 0+2=2, 0+3=3, 0+4=4, 0+5=5, 0+6=6, 0+7=7, 0+8=8, 0+9=9, 0+10=10,
1+6=7, 1+7=8, 1+8=9, 1+9=10, 1+10=11,
2+11=13, 2+12=14, 2+13=15, 2+14=16,
3+15=18, 3+16=19, 3+17=20, 3+18=21,
4+18=22, 4+19=23, 4+20=24, 4+21=25,
5+21=26, 5+22=27, 5+23=28,
6+24=30, 6+25=31, 6+26=32,
7+27=34, 7+28=35, 7+29=36,
8+29=37, 8+30=38, 8+31=39,
9+31=40, 9+32=41, 9+33=42,
10+29=39, 10+30=40, 10+31=41,
11+19=30, 11+20=31, 11+21=32,
12+9=21, 12+10=22, 12+11=23,
12+99=111, 12+100=112, 13+0=13, 13+1=14,
13+90=103, 13+91=104, 13+92=105,
14+80=94, 14+81=95, 14+82=96,
15+70=85, 15+71=86, 15+72=87,
16+60=76, 16+61=77, 16+62=78,
17+50=67, 17+51=68, 17+52=69,
18+40=58, 18+41=59, 18+42=60,
19+30=49, 19+31=50, 19+32=51,
20+19=39, 20+20=40, 20+21=41,
21+8=29, 21+9=30, 21+10=31,
21+98=119, 21+99=120, 21+100=121, 22+0=22,
22+88=110, 22+89=111, 22+90=112,
23+78=101, 23+79=102, 23+80=103,
24+67=91, 24+68=92, 24+69=93,
25+56=81, 25+57=82, 25+58=83,
26+45=71, 26+46=72, 26+47=73,
27+34=61, 27+35=62, 27+36=63,
28+23=51, 28+24=52, 28+25=53,
29+11=40, 29+12=41, 29+13=42,
29+99=128, 29+100=129, 30+0=30,
30+88=118, 30+89=119, 30+90=120,
31+77=108, 31+78=109, 31+79=110,
32+66=98, 32+67=99, 32+68=100,
33+54=87, 33+55=88, 33+56=89,
34+42=76, 34+43=77, 34+44=78,
35+30=65, 35+31=66, 35+32=67,
36+18=54, 36+19=55, 36+20=56,
37+5=42, 37+6=43, 37+7=44,
37+74=111, 37+75=112, 37+76=113,
38+41=79, 38+42=80, 38+43=81,
39+6=45, 39+7=46, 39+8=47,
39+75=114, 39+76=115, 39+77=116,
40+42=82, 40+43=83, 40+44=84,
41+7=48, 41+8=49, 41+9=50,
41+75=116, 41+76=117, 41+77=118,
42+42=84, 42+43=85, 42+44=86,
43+7=50, 43+8=51, 43+9=52,
43+75=118, 43+76=119, 43+77=120,
44+42=86, 44+43=87, 44+44=88,
45+6=51, 45+7=52, 45+8=53,
45+74=119, 45+75=120, 45+76=121,
46+41=87, 46+42=88, 46+43=89,
47+5=52, 47+6=53, 47+7=54,
47+73=120, 47+74=121, 47+75=122,
48+40=88, 48+41=89, 48+42=90,
49+4=53, 49+5=54, 49+6=55,
49+72=121, 49+73=122, 49+74=123,
50+39=89, 50+40=90, 50+41=91,
51+2=53, 51+3=54, 51+4=55,
51+70=121, 51+71=122, 51+72=123,
52+36=88, 52+37=89, 52+38=90,
52+100=152, 53+0=53, 53+1=54,
53+67=120, 53+68=121, 53+69=122,
54+33=87, 54+34=88, 54+35=89,
54+97=151, 54+98=152, 54+99=153,
55+64=119, 55+65=120,
56+30=86, 56+31=87,
56+94=150, 56+95=151,
57+61=118, 57+62=119,
58+26=84, 58+27=85,
58+90=148, 58+91=149,
59+57=116, 59+58=117,
60+22=82, 60+23=83,
60+87=147, 60+88=148,
61+54=115, 61+55=116,
62+19=81, 62+20=82,
62+84=146, 62+85=147,
63+50=113, 63+51=114,
64+14=78, 64+15=79,
64+79=143, 64+80=144,
65+45=110, 65+46=111,
66+8=74, 66+9=75,
66+74=140, 66+75=141,
67+40=107, 67+41=108,
68+2=70, 68+3=71,
68+69=137, 68+70=138,
69+35=104, 69+36=105,
70+19=89, 70+20=90,
71+2=73, 71+3=74,
71+88=159, 71+89=160,
72+73=145, 72+74=146,
73+58=131, 73+59=132,
74+43=117, 74+44=118,
75+28=103, 75+29=104,
76+12=88, 76+13=89,
76+96=172, 76+97=173,
77+81=158, 77+82=159,
78+66=144, 78+67=145,
79+50=129, 79+51=130,
80+34=114, 80+35=115,
81+18=99, 81+19=100,
81+100=181, 82+0=82,
82+84=166, 82+85=167,
83+68=151, 83+69=152,
84+52=136, 84+53=137,
85+36=121, 85+37=122,
86+20=106, 86+21=107,
87+2=89, 87+3=90,
87+86=173, 87+87=174,
88+70=158, 88+71=159,
89+53=142, 89+54=143,
90+36=126, 90+37=127,
91+19=110, 91+20=111,
92+1=93, 92+2=94,
92+85=177, 92+86=178,
93+68=161, 93+69=162,
94+51=145, 94+52=146,
95+34=129, 95+35=130,
96+17=113, 96+18=114,
96+99=195, 96+100=196, 97+0=97,
97+82=179, 97+83=180,
98+65=163, 98+66=164,
99+47=146, 99+48=147,
100+27=127, 100+28=128, 100+29=129, 100+30=130, 100+31=131, 100+32=132, 100+33=133, 100+34=134, 100+35=135, 100+36=136, 100+37=137, 100+38=138, 100+39=139, 100+40=140, 100+41=141, 100+42=142, 100+43=143, 100+44=144, 100+45=145, 100+46=146, 100+47=147, 100+48=148, 100+49=149, 100+50=150, 100+51=151, 100+52=152, 100+53=153, 100+54=154, 100+55=155, 100+56=156, 100+57=157, 100+58=158, 100+59=159, 100+60=160, 100+61=161, 100+62=162

7 CALCULATE Although the basic Repeat form has expanded the expressive range of a line into triangles and rectangles and has made perfect gradations trivial to realize, there is a subtle limitation to everything drawn. This limitation is most evident in a gradated rectangle. The range of grays is directly linked to a corresponding range of space; a small gradated square on white paper near the lower left corner is difficult to see because the grays are undiscernably close to white. There must be a way to shift the gray colors to a darker range to achieve better contrast without having to move the square to the upper right corner. In this chapter, you will find that the common mathematical operations of addition, multiplication, subtraction, and division will give us the increased flexibility we need.

The thought of mathematics might seem horrifying at first, but after you see how much more can be accomplished with a few simple calculations, you will surely be addicted for life. Think of addition as a way to move a quantity forward and subtraction as a way to move it back; multiplication as a way to magnify a quantity much faster and division as a way to reduce it very quickly. Manipulating numbers is much like sculpting in clay or mixing paints. The only difference is in the computer's speed and precision.

Add to Adjust Addition is primarily used to shift the position of a point either upward or to the right. For example, if a vertical line rests at 10 points from the bottom of the sheet, adding 10 to the vertical dimensions of the starting and ending points raises the line upward to 20 points.

```
Paper 0
Pen 100
// simple horizontal line
Line 30 50 70 50
```

Likewise, adding 10 to the horizontal dimensions shifts the line 10 points to the right. When lines are input with numerical dimensions and need to be shifted to the right or to the top, you are likely to mentally add the quantity to the existing dimensions and replace the original quantity with the new one. Given a horizontal line, shifting one of the points by 10 to the right is a trivial task.

```
Paper 0
Pen 100
//
// --> Line 30 50 70 50 is
// shifted by 10 to the right
//
Line 40 50 70 50
```

Alternatively, there is a way to shift the starting point to the right that requires absolutely no mathematical thought on your part. Instead of doing the addition in your head, you can have the computer do it for you. Calculations are always enclosed in parentheses **( )** and can be used in place of any numeric descriptor.

```
Paper 0
Pen 100
// enclose key quantity in parens
Line (30) 50 70 50
```

You can add 10 by inserting a "+10" into the parentheses of the calculation.

```
Paper 0
Pen 100
// voila! a calculation
Line (30+10) 50 70 50
```

Making a rightward shift is useful when encoding a general line that can be shifted horizontally. Labeling the amount of shift as A, and adding A to the end point's horizontal dimension, causes the line to translate in the horizontal direction by A.

```
Paper 0
Pen 100
Set A 10
// shifted a tiny bit
Line (30+A) 50 (70+A) 50
```

```
Paper 0
Pen 100
Set A 40
// hitting right edge
Line (30+A) 50 (70+A) 50
```

```
Paper 0
Pen 100
Set A 72
// push off edge of paper
Line (30+A) 50 (70+A) 50
```

Note that the program will not execute properly if a calculation is not enclosed inside a pair of parentheses.

```
Paper 0
Pen 100
Set A 10
// DOES *NOT* WORK
Line 30+A 50 70+A 50
```

If you try this example, you will find that it will not execute because the parentheses have been omitted. Although cumbersome to type, the parentheses provide much needed clarity for grouping quantities as a single unit, and thus they are a required convention.

Replacing the vertical dimension of 50 used in the previous expression, with the variable A, and placing the result within a Repeat yields the familiar shape of a parallelogram.

```
Paper 0
Pen 100
// introducing a slight skew
Repeat A 0 30
{
   Line (30+A) A (70+A) A
}
```

Each line can be drawn in a different shade to accent the Repeat.

```
Paper 0
// shaded to mark direction
Repeat A 0 30
{
   Pen A
   Line (30+A) A (70+A) A
}
```

However, the contrast of the figure is so low that the effect is not prominent. As mentioned in the introduction to this chapter, this is a subtle limitation of a Repeat. In addition to shifting position, addition can be used to adjust intensity by shifting gray values toward black.

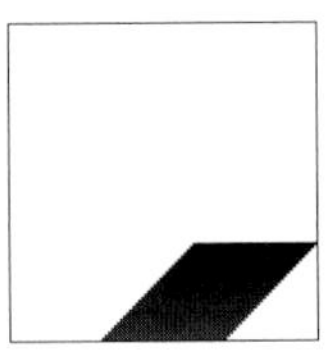

```
Paper 0
// adjusting the intensity by
// shifting the Pen tone
Repeat A 0 30
{
   Pen (A+70)
   Line (30+A) A (70+A) A
}
```

As expected, subtraction achieves the opposite effect of addition by shifting values either downward or to the left.

```
Paper 0
// skewing in the opposite direction
Repeat A 0 30
{
   Pen A
   Line (30-A) A (70-A) A
}
```

Subtraction is also useful for flipping the orientation of a figure across the horizontal or vertical.

```
Paper 0
// introducing a flip
Repeat A 0 30
{
   Pen A
   Line (30-A) (100-A) (70-A) (100-A)
}
```

And also for reversing the tone scale.

```
Paper 0
// inverting the intensity
Repeat A 0 30
{
   Pen (100-A)
   Line (30-A) A (70-A) A
}
```

The order of numbers does not matter in the case of addition but is very important in the case of subtraction. Consider all the combinations of ordered operations in a simple program.

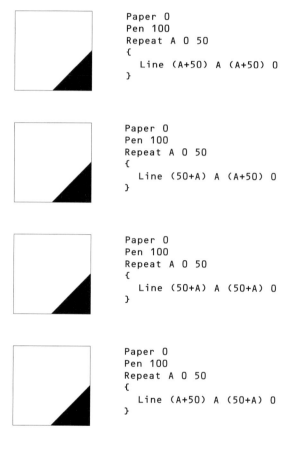

```
Paper 0
Pen 100
Repeat A 0 50
{
   Line (A+50) A (A+50) 0
}
```

```
Paper 0
Pen 100
Repeat A 0 50
{
   Line (50+A) A (A+50) 0
}
```

```
Paper 0
Pen 100
Repeat A 0 50
{
   Line (50+A) A (50+A) 0
}
```

```
Paper 0
Pen 100
Repeat A 0 50
{
   Line (A+50) A (50+A) 0
}
```

```
Paper 0
Pen 100
Repeat A 0 50
{
   Line (A-50) A (A-50) 0
}
```

```
Paper 0
Pen 100
Repeat A 0 50
{
   Line (50-A) A (A-50) 0
}
```

```
Paper 0
Pen 100
Repeat A 0 50
{
   Line (50-A) A (50-A) 0
}
```

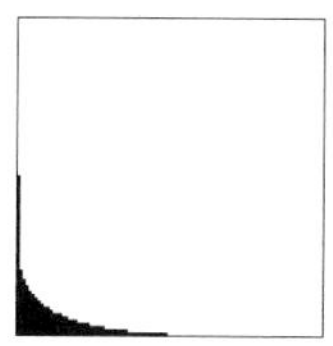

```
Paper 0
Pen 100
Repeat A 0 50
{
   Line (A-50) A (50-A) 0
}
```

As you can see, calculations involving addition are not order-dependent, while those involving subtraction are. This property is called *commutativity,* which you may remember from junior high school mathematics.

Enlarge or Reduce Multiplication allows you to increase values by discrete numerical factors. Magnifying or darkening an object by two or three times involves some form of multiplication. Consider using a calculation to draw a line two and three times as long as a reference line.

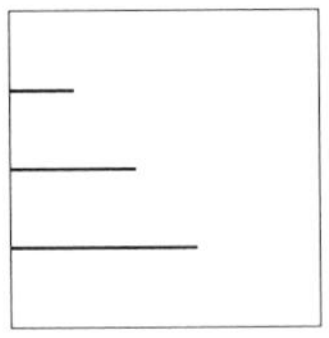

```
Paper 0
Pen 100
// increased length by 2x and 3x
Line 0 75 20 75
Line 0 50 (20*2) 50
Line 0 25 (20*3) 25
```

On the computer, the operator for multiply * has traditionally been the asterisk, probably because there wasn't a better symbol on the existing typewriter keyboard.

The darkness of a figure is dramatically changed with the incorporation of a multiplication factor in a style significantly different from that of addition, as demonstrated by comparison.

```
Paper 0
// no calculation
Repeat A 0 50
{
  Pen A
  Line A 0 A 100
}
```

```
Paper 0
// with addition
Repeat A 0 50
{
  Pen (A+50)
  Line A 0 A 100
}
```

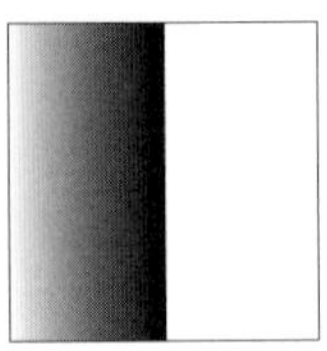

```
Paper 0
// with multiplication
Repeat A 0 50
{
  Pen (A*2)
  Line A 0 A 100
}
```

This difference arises because in the add calculation, the tonal range is shifted uniformly by 50 percent to a darker range of 50 to 100 percent; whereas in the multiply calculation the tonal range is expanded from 0 to 100 percent. This is better visualized in the spatial dimension.

```
Paper 0
Pen 100
// no calculation
Repeat A 0 50
{
  Line A 0 A 100
}
```

```
Paper 0
Pen 100
// with addition
Repeat A 0 50
{
  Line (A+50) 0 (A+50) 100
}
```

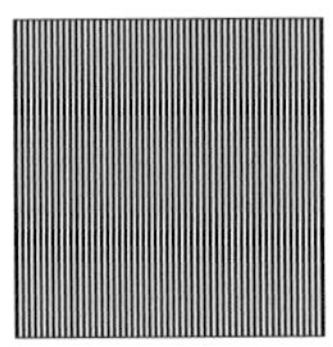

```
Paper 0
Pen 100
// with multiplication
Repeat A 0 50
{
  Line (A*2) 0 (A*2) 100
}
```

Division is performed with the / operator and is used when you want to reduce the range of a quantity by a given factor. Shrinking a shape with division can be a useful demonstration of its properties, starting with an equilateral triangle.

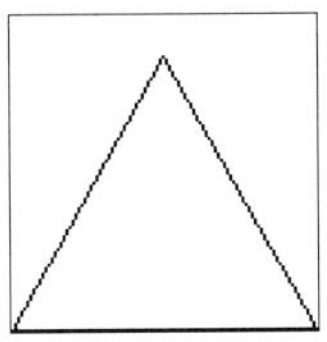

```
Paper 0
Pen 100
// equilateral triangle
Line 0 0 50 87
Line 50 87 100 0
Line 100 0 0 0
```

Each quantity is replaced with a calculation; the zeroes are left as is because zero divided by anything is still zero.

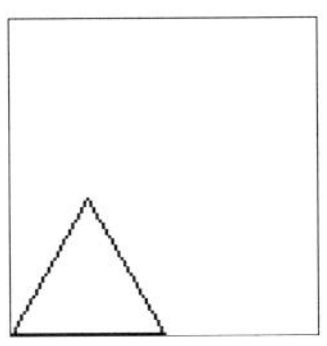

```
Paper 0
Pen 100
// reduced by 2
Line 0 0 (50/2) (87/2)
Line (50/2) (87/2) (100/2) 0
Line (100/2) 0 0 0
```

Halving the quantities produces a triangle that is half the original size. Dividing by 3, 4, and so forth produces a smaller triangle as the reduction factor increases. With the reduction factor labeled as R, the general form can be written and then rendered at different scales.

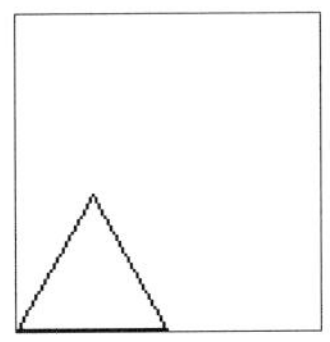

```
Paper 0
Pen 100
// reduce by 2 (50%)
Set R 2
Line 0 0 (50/R) (87/R)
Line (50/R) (87/R) (100/R) 0
Line (100/R) 0 0 0
```

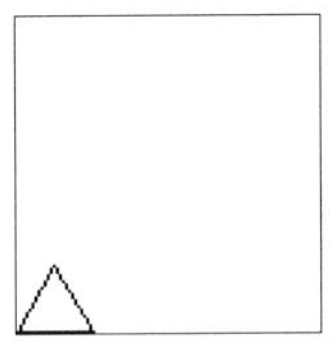

```
Paper 0
Pen 100
// reduce by 4 (25%)
Set R 4
Line 0 0 (50/R) (87/R)
Line (50/R) (87/R) (100/R) 0
```

```
Paper 0
Pen 100
// reduce by 8 (12.5%)
Set R 8
Line 0 0 (50/R) (87/R)
Line (50/R) (87/R) (100/R) 0
Line (100/R) 0 0 0
```

The tonal range of a figure can also be reduced by division in a manner that is clearly different from the lightening effect of a subtraction.

```
Paper 0
// base shading
Set R 1
Repeat A 0 100
{
  Pen (A/R)
  Line 0 A 100 A
}
```

```
Paper 0
// halved
Set R 2
Repeat A 0 100
{
  Pen (A/R)
  Line 0 A 100 A
}
```

```
Paper 0
// quartered
Set R 4
Repeat A 0 100
{
  Pen (A/R)
  Line 0 A 100 A
}
```

Spatial and tonal reduction can be demonstrated simultaneously in a single figure.

```
Paper 0
// base shading/size
Set R 1
Repeat A 0 100
{
  Pen (A/R)
  Line 0 (A/R) (100/R) (A/R)
}
```

```
Paper 0
// halved
Set R 2
Repeat A 0 100
{
  Pen (A/R)
  Line 0 (A/R) (100/R) (A/R)
}
```

```
Paper 0
// quartered
Set R 4
Repeat A 0 100
{
  Pen (A/R)
  Line 0 (A/R) (100/R) (A/R)
}
```

The order in which numbers are arranged in a calculation is irrelevant for multiplication because multiplication is commutative. Division does not commute and thus is order-dependent.

Combine Operations Complex calculations can easily be composed by creating chains of numbers and operators, such as (5*A+20*6/4+100) or (20+33*6-90+B*A). The computer can be used as a glorified calculator, and inflicting numerical punishment on the computer has its satisfying moments. However, there is a caveat to complex expressions with respect to the order in which different operations should be executed. With the exception of the convention of multiplication and division before addition and subtraction, a calculation is generally a left to right process unless more parentheses are used within a calculation to force a specific order of calculation. Compare the two cases of plain, straight calculation versus forced-order calculation.

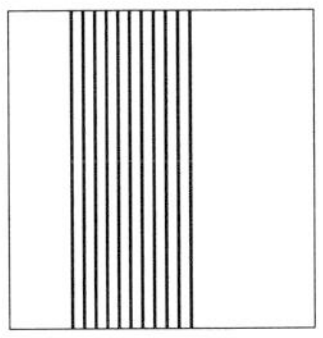

```
Paper 0
Pen 100
// multiply comes before add
Repeat A 0 10
{
  Line (20+A*4) 0 (20+A*4) 100
}
```

```
Paper 0
Pen 100
// force add to happen first
Repeat A 0 10
{
  Line ((20+A)*4) 0 ((20+A)*4) 100
}
```

In the former case, A*4 is calculated before adding 20. In the latter case, (20+A) is calculated, after which the result is multiplied by 4, arriving at a different result.

Returning to the example of the equilateral triangle, the issue of calculation order is significant when an object is sequentially translated and scaled. Depending upon the order of the addition and multiplication, the triangle is either magnified first, then translated, or else translated first, then magnified.

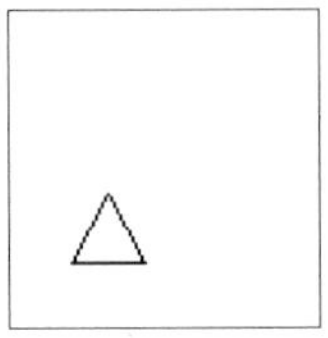

```
Paper 0
Pen 100
// horizontal and vertical position
Set H 10
Set V 10
// scale factor
Set S 1
//
// both triangles will overlap in this case
// because the scaling factor is '1'
//
// gray triangle: add first, then multiply
Pen 50
Line ((10+H)*S) ((10+V)*S) ((22+H)*S) ((32+V)*S)
Line ((22+H)*S) ((32+V)*S) ((34+H)*S) ((10+V)*S)
Line ((34+H)*S) ((10+V)*S) ((10+H)*S) ((10+V)*S)
// black triangle: multiply first, then add
Pen 100
Line (10+(H*S)) (10+(V*S)) (22+(H*S)) (32+(V*S))
Line (22+(H*S)) (32+(V*S)) (34+(H*S)) (10+(V*S))
Line (34+(H*S)) (10+(V*S)) (10+(H*S)) (10+(V*S))
```

Neither of the results listed to the right is more correct than the other, because it depends on what you intend to draw. You should give careful consideration to calculations that involve any numerical operations because a simple mistake in the order of execution can cause much lost sleep in trying to trace the error.

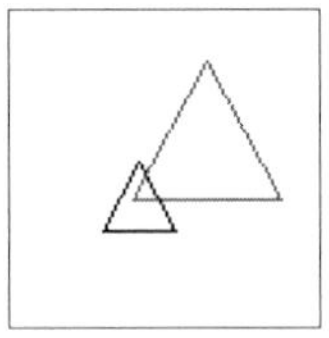

```
Paper 0
Pen 100
// horizontal and vertical position
Set H 10
Set V 10
// scale factor
Set S 2
...
```

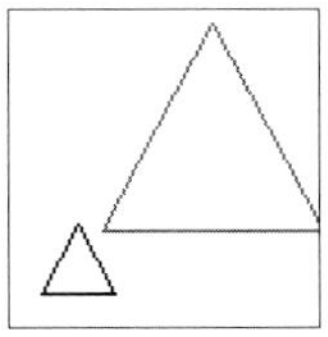

```
Paper 0
Pen 100
// horizontal and vertical position
Set H 0
Set V 0
// scale factor
Set S 3
...
```

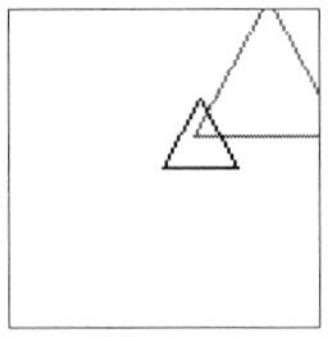

```
Paper 0
Pen 100
// horizontal and vertical position
Set H 20
Set V 20
// scale factor
Set S 2
...
```

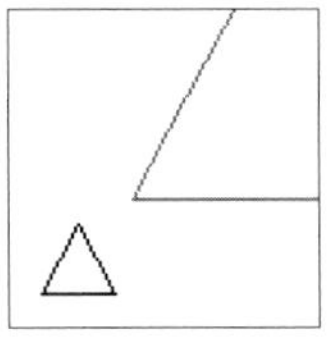

```
Paper 0
Pen 100
// horizontal and vertical position
Set H 0
Set V 0
// scale factor
Set S 4
...
```

When complex calculations require many levels of parentheses to be specific about order of calculation, confusion naturally arises. A common problem is balancing parentheses. In an expression like (4+(20*(3+20*(40+2)/(12/3*(33-8)))), making sure that all pairs of parentheses balance can be a traumatic experience. Modern program editing software alleviates the problem by graphically denoting the matched parenthesis of the pair you are entering. A more effective technique is to write simpler expressions by storing intermediate calculations in appropriately named variables.

In the case of a tonal adjustment where shifting the range before expanding, or vice-versa, is sensitive to order, making the sequence of calculations explicit with an intermediate variable clarifies the program's operation.

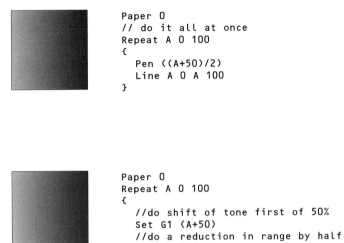

```
Paper 0
// do it all at once
Repeat A 0 100
{
  Pen ((A+50)/2)
  Line A 0 A 100
}
```

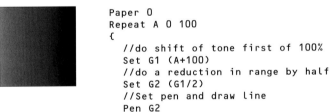

```
Paper 0
Repeat A 0 100
{
  //do shift of tone first of 50%
  Set G1 (A+50)
  //do a reduction in range by half
  Set G2 (G1/2)
  //Set pen and draw line
  Pen G2
  Line A 0 A 100
}
```

```
Paper 0
Repeat A 0 100
{
  //do shift of tone first of 100%
  Set G1 (A+100)
  //do a reduction in range by half
  Set G2 (G1/2)
  //Set pen and draw line
  Pen G2
  Line A 0 A 100
}
```

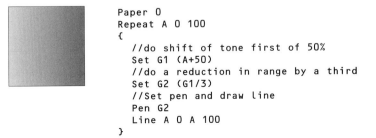

```
Paper 0
Repeat A 0 100
{
  //do shift of tone first of 50%
  Set G1 (A+50)
  //do a reduction in range by a third
  Set G2 (G1/3)
  //Set pen and draw line
  Pen G2
  Line A 0 A 100
}
```

Composing many mathematical calculations on a solitary program line can be confusing. When lost, rewriting an expression with intermediate variables can improve legibility.

```
Paper 0
Pen 100
// a simple dense expression
Repeat A 0 100
{
   Line (A+0) (A+0) (100-A) (A+0)
}
```

By naming the respective components of the start point as H1 and V1 and the end point as H2 and V2, manipulating the expression can become more manageable.

```
Paper 0
Pen 100
// taking out the first horizontal
// component and naming it H1
Repeat A 0 100
{
   Set H1 (A+0)
   Line H1 (A+0) (100-A) (A+0)
}
```

```
Paper 0
Pen 100
// taking out both horizontal *and*
// the vertical component (H1,V1)
Repeat A 0 100
{
   Set H1 (A+0)
   Set V1 (A+0)
   Line H1 V1 (100-A) (A+0)
}
```

```
Paper 0
Pen 100
Repeat A 0 100
{
   // the first point (H1,V1)
   Set H1 (A+0)
   Set V1 (A+0)
   // the second point (H2,V2)
   Set H2 (100-A)
   Set V2 (A+0)
   Line H1 V1 H2 V2
}
```

With the expression's sub-components clearly extracted, the form can be tweaked in a way that lends to greater control.

```
Paper 0
Pen 100
Repeat A 0 100
{
   // scale horizontal-1 to 25%
   Set H1 (A/4)
   Set V1 (A+0)
   Set H2 (100-A)
   Set V2 (A+0)
   Line H1 V1 H2 V2
}
```

```
Paper 0
Pen 100
Repeat A 0 100
{
   // shift vertical-2 up by 50,
   // move vertical-1 significantly down
   Set H1 (A/4)
   Set V1 (A-300)
   Set H2 (100-A)
   Set V2 (A+50)
   Line H1 V1 H2 V2
}
```

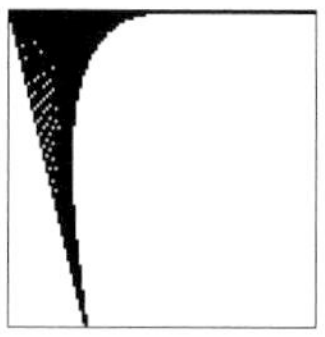

```
Paper 0
Pen 100
Repeat A 0 100
{
  // invert vertical-1,
  // raise vertical-2 by 100
  Set H1 (A/4)
  Set V1 (100-A)
  Set H2 (100-A)
  Set V2 (A+100)
  Line H1 V1 H2 V2
}
```

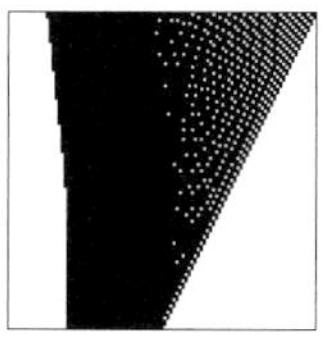

```
Paper 0
Pen 100
Repeat A 0 100
{
  // invert vertical-1 again
  // in opposite direction
  Set H1 (A/4)
  Set V1 (A-100)
  Set H2 (100-A)
  Set V2 (A+100)
  Line H1 V1 H2 V2
}
```

Just as you gradually learned to add without using your fingers, you will gradually learn how to program without writing intermediate steps, making the program shorter and more concise. But the numerical medium can often distort your senses. In such moments, nothing works better than explicitly writing out all intermediate steps. Do not hesitate to alternate between using compact and expanded expressions when developing your programs.

Summary Calculations are a way to transform numerical quantities into other quantities that are either larger or smaller. Addition and subtraction increase or decrease the quantity by some set value; multiplication and division reduce or magnify the quantity by some set factor. All calculated expressions must be enclosed in parentheses, and you can place calculations within calculations to make the order of execution explicit.

Numbers are a kind of raw material that require mathematical processing to refine the material into a usable state. Addition, subtraction, multiplication, and division are distinctive tools applied to the material to achieve the desired result. Like any process of craft, spirited practice that leads to a mature sense of experience is the natural path to mastering the numerical medium.

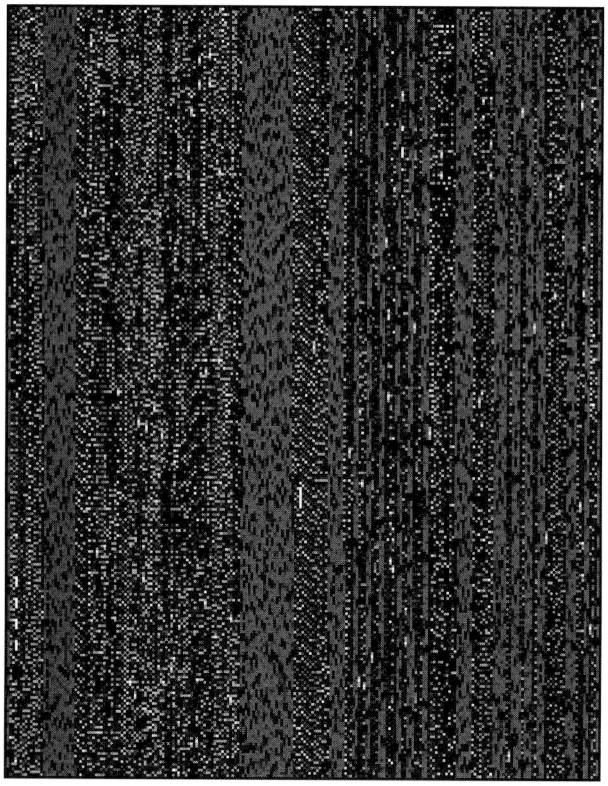

8 DOT The realm of visual expression described thus far rests upon a single primitive: the line. Starting with a single line and adding more lines along the way, the rectangle and triangle emerged as elements upon which more complex shapes could be built. Imagine if you spent your whole life with a ruler in one hand and a pen in the other. Over time you would inevitably come to create squares, triangles, and other Constructivist compositions, and always be forced to think only in terms of lines.

The tool or technique used to draw usually governs the final outcome. Therefore, it is useful to describe an alternative method for line drawings that can lead to new expressive possibilities. The analogy would be to cast aside pen and ruler, pick up a stick, dip the stick in ink, and paint with dots. Since you are free to paint individual dots without being constrained to a line, you naturally have the potential to explore a different world of drawing.

In the same manner you learned that there really is no pen to hold, there is no stick to hold for painting with dots. Dots are painted by specifying positions on the page as a pair of horizontal and vertical positions. To be more precise, you do not paint with dots. Rather, the paper, which is made up of dots, paints itself.

There are a total of 101 by 101 dots to address in this manner, making a total of 10,201 dots from which to choose. You might wonder why there are 101 dots instead of 100, which would seem more natural. The leftmost dot is at 0 points, the rightmost dot is at 100 points, and there is a total of 99 points in between. There are 101 points in each dimension, in the same way that there are many shades of gray by including the 0th shade, which is pure white.

Draw a Dot Each dot in the grid can be individually set to a desired intensity. A dot on the page corresponds to a discrete location on the paper. With lines, you specified the endpoints on a grid that begins in the lower left corner extending to the right and upward. To specify a dot to paint, you specify the point in the same manner as Line, with the special convention of enclosing the pair of dimensions between square brackets **[ ]**. For example, [0 0] corresponds to the dot in the lower left corner, and [1 0] corresponds to the dot horizontally adjacent to [0 0].

A specific dot enclosed in [ ] can be used in a manner identical to a variable. In essence, a dot on the grid is a variable with a specific value and location, with the difference that the value of the variable is visible at all times. You can Set the dot in the lower-left corner to black (100).

```
Paper 0
// set dot at horizontal 0, vertical 0
// to be 100 (black)
Set [0 0] 100
```

Similarly, you can set the adjacent dot to 50 percent gray with another Set.

```
Paper 0
// set the dot at [1,0] to 50% gray
Set [1 0] 50
```

Notice how selecting a Pen of 100 percent black does not affect the Set-ing of the dot to 50.

```
Paper 0
Pen 100
// setting the Pen does not matter
Set [1 0] 50
```

The selection of Pen only applies to a Line command. The equivalent of setting a dot can be realized with a Line by specifying an identical start and end point, in which case setting the Pen does determine the shade of the dot-like line.

```
Paper 0
Pen 100
// the effect of a dot, from a line
Line 50 50 50 50
```

However, from a conceptual perspective, drawing a line and setting a dot are two distinct tasks because a line involves a pen and two points and a dot involves a reference to a location and a value to Set.

Draw Dots Drawing more than one shaded dot is no different from drawing more than one line. The program sequence just gets longer.

```
Paper 100
// 6 dots
Set [50 0] 0
Set [51 0] 30
Set [52 0] 0
Set [53 0] 30
Set [54 0] 0
Set [55 0] 30
```

Notice that the length of the program does not increase as much as with an increase in shaded lines because a Pen/Line combination requires two lines of program code (one to set the shade of the line, and the other to draw the line versus the one line of program code to shade a dot).

A few placed dots are simple yet captivating.

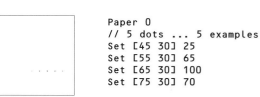

```
Paper 0
// 5 dots ... 5 examples
Set [45 30] 25
Set [55 30] 65
Set [65 30] 100
Set [75 30] 70
```

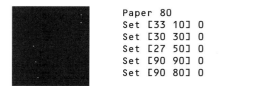

```
Paper 80
Set [33 10] 0
Set [30 30] 0
Set [27 50] 0
Set [90 90] 0
Set [90 80] 0
```

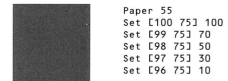

```
Paper 55
Set [100 75] 100
Set [99 75] 70
Set [98 75] 50
Set [97 75] 30
Set [96 75] 10
```

```
Paper 100
Set [88 20] 0
Set [98 20] 0
Set [98 30] 0
Set [88 30] 0
Set [12 85] 40
```

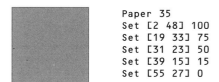

```
Paper 35
Set [2 48] 100
Set [19 33] 75
Set [31 23] 50
Set [39 15] 15
Set [55 27] 0
```

By adding more lines, you get a greater level of detail in a figure with many dots. Dots are most useful when the subject is rendered in a natural, freehand style. Consider the classic example of a flower vase.

```
// begin vase
Set [52 83] 100
Set [53 83] 100
Set [54 83] 100
Set [55 83] 100
Set [56 83] 100
Set [57 83] 100
Set [58 83] 100
Set [60 83] 100
Set [45 82] 100
Set [48 82] 100
Set [49 82] 100
Set [51 82] 100
Set [52 82] 100
Set [53 82] 100
Set [58 82] 100
Set [61 82] 100
Set [62 82] 100
Set [63 82] 100
Set [64 82] 100
Set [65 82] 100
Set [41 81] 100
Set [45 81] 100
Set [46 81] 100
Set [59 81] 100
Set [60 81] 100
Set [62 81] 100
Set [66 81] 100
Set [67 81] 100
Set [39 80] 100
Set [40 80] 100
Set [41 80] 100
Set [42 80] 100
Set [48 80] 100
Set [51 80] 100
Set [54 80] 100
Set [56 80] 100
Set [60 80] 100
Set [62 80] 100
Set [65 80] 100
Set [67 80] 100
Set [68 80] 100
Set [69 80] 100
Set [37 79] 100
Set [38 79] 100
Set [40 79] 100
Set [42 79] 100
Set [46 79] 100
Set [49 79] 100
Set [50 79] 100
Set [53 79] 100
Set [54 79] 100
Set [55 79] 100
Set [59 79] 100
Set [61 79] 100
Set [64 79] 100
Set [67 79] 100
Set [68 79] 100
Set [69 79] 100
Set [37 78] 100
Set [38 78] 100
Set [39 78] 100
Set [44 78] 100
Set [50 78] 100
Set [51 78] 100
Set [62 78] 100
Set [63 78] 100
Set [65 78] 100
Set [66 78] 100
Set [67 78] 100
Set [68 78] 100
Set [38 77] 100
Set [39 77] 100
Set [40 77] 100
Set [42 77] 100
Set [50 77] 100
Set [52 77] 100
Set [54 77] 100
Set [55 77] 100
Set [56 77] 100
Set [58 77] 100
Set [60 77] 100
Set [61 77] 100
Set [63 77] 100
Set [64 77] 100
Set [66 77] 100
Set [67 77] 100
Set [39 76] 100
Set [40 76] 100
Set [41 76] 100
Set [42 76] 100
Set [43 76] 100
Set [44 76] 100
Set [46 76] 100
Set [47 76] 100
Set [48 76] 100
Set [51 76] 100
Set [52 76] 100
Set [54 76] 100
Set [56 76] 100
Set [58 76] 100
Set [59 76] 100
Set [62 76] 100
Set [67 76] 100
Set [40 75] 100
Set [42 75] 100
Set [44 75] 100
Set [49 75] 100
Set [50 75] 100
Set [51 75] 100
Set [53 75] 100
Set [54 75] 100
Set [55 75] 100
Set [56 75] 100
Set [57 75] 100
Set [60 75] 100
Set [67 75] 100
Set [40 74] 100
Set [41 74] 100
Set [42 74] 100
Set [43 74] 100
Set [45 74] 100
Set [41 73] 100
Set [44 73] 100
Set [45 73] 100
Set [46 73] 100
Set [47 73] 100
Set [48 73] 100
Set [66 73] 100
Set [41 72] 100
Set [43 72] 100
Set [44 72] 100
Set [45 72] 100
Set [46 72] 100
Set [47 72] 100
Set [41 71] 100
Set [43 71] 100
Set [45 71] 100
Set [65 71] 100
Set [41 70] 100
Set [42 70] 100
Set [43 70] 100
Set [44 70] 100
Set [45 70] 100
Set [49 70] 100
Set [50 70] 100
Set [59 70] 100
Set [65 70] 100
Set [66 70] 100
Set [41 69] 100
Set [42 69] 100
Set [43 69] 100
Set [44 69] 100
Set [46 69] 100
Set [47 69] 100
Set [48 69] 100
Set [65 69] 100
Set [41 68] 100
Set [45 68] 100
Set [51 68] 100
Set [41 67] 100
Set [42 67] 100
Set [45 67] 100
Set [46 67] 100
Set [63 67] 100
Set [66 67] 100
Set [40 66] 100
Set [41 66] 100
Set [43 66] 100
Set [45 66] 100
Set [47 66] 100
Set [41 65] 100
Set [42 65] 100
Set [43 65] 100
Set [46 65] 100
Set [48 65] 100
Set [49 65] 100
Set [50 65] 100
Set [67 65] 100
Set [39 64] 100
Set [40 64] 100
Set [42 64] 100
Set [44 64] 100
Set [45 64] 100
Set [51 64] 100
Set [53 64] 100
Set [68 64] 100
Set [39 63] 100
Set [40 63] 100
Set [41 63] 100
Set [43 63] 100
Set [45 63] 100
Set [46 63] 100
Set [49 63] 100
Set [50 63] 100
Set [54 63] 100
Set [56 63] 100
Set [69 63] 100
Set [38 62] 100
Set [39 62] 100
Set [41 62] 100
Set [43 62] 100
Set [44 62] 100
Set [51 62] 100
Set [37 61] 100
Set [38 61] 100
Set [39 61] 100
Set [40 61] 100
Set [42 61] 100
Set [70 61] 100
Set [37 60] 100
Set [40 60] 100
Set [43 60] 100
Set [45 60] 100
Set [46 60] 100
Set [51 60] 100
Set [71 60] 100
Set [35 59] 100
Set [36 59] 100
Set [38 59] 100
Set [34 58] 100
Set [39 58] 100
Set [40 58] 100
Set [41 58] 100
Set [65 58] 100
Set [66 58] 100
Set [73 58] 100
Set [34 57] 100
Set [36 57] 100
Set [37 57] 100
Set [38 57] 100
Set [39 57] 100
Set [43 57] 100
Set [45 57] 100
Set [33 56] 100
Set [36 56] 100
Set [37 56] 100
Set [38 56] 100
Set [39 56] 100
Set [41 56] 100
Set [43 56] 100
Set [45 56] 100
Set [49 56] 100
Set [51 56] 100
Set [57 56] 100
Set [74 56] 100
Set [33 55] 100
Set [34 55] 100
Set [36 55] 100
Set [37 55] 100
Set [41 55] 100
Set [51 55] 100
Set [75 55] 100
Set [32 54] 100
Set [35 54] 100
Set [39 54] 100
Set [40 54] 100
Set [42 54] 100
Set [46 54] 100
Set [47 54] 100
Set [34 53] 100
Set [35 53] 100
Set [37 53] 100
Set [44 53] 100
Set [75 53] 100
Set [32 52] 100
Set [34 52] 100
Set [36 52] 100
Set [39 52] 100
Set [47 52] 100
Set [51 52] 100
Set [32 51] 100
Set [33 51] 100
Set [34 51] 100
Set [35 51] 100
Set [37 51] 100
Set [39 51] 100
Set [42 51] 100
Set [75 51] 100
Set [32 50] 100
Set [33 50] 100
Set [35 50] 100
Set [37 50] 100
Set [38 50] 100
Set [42 50] 100
Set [74 50] 100
Set [32 49] 100
Set [33 49] 100
Set [34 49] 100
Set [35 49] 100
Set [36 49] 100
Set [37 49] 100
Set [38 49] 100
Set [39 49] 100
Set [40 49] 100
Set [41 49] 100
Set [75 49] 100
Set [32 48] 100
Set [33 48] 100
Set [34 48] 100
Set [36 48] 100
Set [38 48] 100
Set [40 48] 100
Set [42 48] 100
Set [43 48] 100
Set [46 48] 100
Set [74 48] 100
Set [33 47] 100
Set [35 47] 100
Set [36 47] 100
```

```
Set [39 47] 100
Set [41 47] 100
Set [42 47] 100
Set [44 47] 100
Set [72 47] 100
Set [33 46] 100
Set [34 46] 100
Set [35 46] 100
Set [37 46] 100
Set [38 46] 100
Set [40 46] 100
Set [42 46] 100
Set [43 46] 100
Set [45 46] 100
Set [33 45] 100
Set [34 45] 100
Set [35 45] 100
Set [36 45] 100
Set [38 45] 100
Set [39 45] 100
Set [40 45] 100
Set [41 45] 100
Set [74 45] 100
Set [33 44] 100
Set [34 44] 100
Set [36 44] 100
Set [37 44] 100
Set [39 44] 100
Set [40 44] 100
Set [42 44] 100
Set [44 44] 100
Set [45 44] 100
Set [72 44] 100
Set [34 43] 100
Set [35 43] 100
Set [38 43] 100
Set [39 43] 100
Set [43 43] 100
Set [73 43] 100
Set [34 42] 100
Set [35 42] 100
Set [37 42] 100
Set [38 42] 100
Set [41 42] 100
Set [50 42] 100
Set [35 41] 100
Set [36 41] 100
Set [38 41] 100
Set [40 41] 100
Set [41 41] 100
Set [42 41] 100
Set [45 41] 100
Set [51 41] 100
Set [72 41] 100
Set [35 40] 100
Set [36 40] 100
Set [37 40] 100
Set [40 40] 100
Set [43 40] 100
Set [44 40] 100
Set [45 40] 100
Set [46 40] 100
Set [36 39] 100
Set [37 39] 100
Set [38 39] 100
Set [39 39] 100
Set [40 39] 100
Set [42 39] 100
Set [47 39] 100
Set [49 39] 100
Set [71 39] 100
Set [36 38] 100
Set [37 38] 100
Set [38 38] 100
Set [40 38] 100
Set [42 38] 100
Set [43 38] 100
Set [69 38] 100
Set [37 37] 100
Set [38 37] 100
Set [39 37] 100
Set [41 37] 100
Set [42 37] 100
Set [48 37] 100
Set [49 37] 100
Set [51 37] 100
Set [38 36] 100
Set [40 36] 100
Set [42 36] 100
Set [44 36] 100
Set [46 36] 100
Set [47 36] 100
Set [70 36] 100
Set [38 35] 100
Set [39 35] 100
Set [49 35] 100
Set [39 34] 100
Set [40 34] 100
Set [41 34] 100
Set [43 34] 100
Set [45 34] 100
Set [46 34] 100
Set [47 34] 100
Set [64 34] 100
Set [69 34] 100
Set [40 33] 100
Set [41 33] 100
Set [42 33] 100
Set [40 32] 100
Set [41 32] 100
Set [44 32] 100
Set [45 32] 100
Set [46 32] 100
Set [47 32] 100
Set [49 32] 100
Set [50 32] 100
Set [54 32] 100
Set [65 32] 100
Set [68 32] 100
Set [41 31] 100
Set [42 31] 100
Set [43 31] 100
Set [44 31] 100
Set [48 31] 100
Set [50 31] 100
Set [52 31] 100
Set [41 30] 100
Set [42 30] 100
Set [45 30] 100
Set [47 30] 100
Set [51 30] 100
Set [57 30] 100
Set [41 29] 100
Set [42 29] 100
Set [43 29] 100
Set [44 29] 100
Set [46 29] 100
Set [49 29] 100
Set [53 29] 100
Set [63 29] 100
Set [66 29] 100
Set [42 28] 100
Set [44 28] 100
Set [45 28] 100
Set [47 28] 100
Set [49 28] 100
Set [51 28] 100
Set [52 28] 100
Set [55 28] 100
Set [42 27] 100
Set [43 27] 100
Set [44 27] 100
Set [45 27] 100
Set [46 27] 100
Set [57 27] 100
Set [42 26] 100
Set [43 26] 100
Set [44 26] 100
Set [46 26] 100
Set [49 26] 100
Set [50 26] 100
Set [52 26] 100
Set [53 26] 100
Set [56 26] 100
Set [59 26] 100
Set [65 26] 100
Set [42 25] 100
Set [43 25] 100
Set [44 25] 100
Set [45 25] 100
Set [46 25] 100
Set [47 25] 100
Set [48 25] 100
Set [49 25] 100
Set [51 25] 100
Set [53 25] 100
Set [55 25] 100
Set [57 25] 100
Set [65 25] 100
Set [26 24] 100
Set [42 24] 100
Set [43 24] 100
Set [44 24] 100
Set [45 24] 100
Set [46 24] 100
Set [48 24] 100
Set [49 24] 100
Set [50 24] 100
Set [52 24] 100
Set [54 24] 100
Set [55 24] 100
Set [63 24] 100
Set [64 24] 100
Set [65 24] 100
Set [15 23] 100
Set [21 23] 100
Set [22 23] 100
Set [24 23] 100
Set [25 23] 100
Set [27 23] 100
Set [28 23] 100
Set [30 23] 100
Set [33 23] 100
Set [35 23] 100
Set [36 23] 100
Set [38 23] 100
Set [39 23] 100
Set [41 23] 100
Set [42 23] 100
Set [43 23] 100
Set [44 23] 100
Set [45 23] 100
Set [48 23] 100
Set [50 23] 100
Set [54 23] 100
Set [61 23] 100
Set [66 23] 100
Set [14 22] 100
Set [18 22] 100
Set [22 22] 100
Set [23 22] 100
Set [24 22] 100
Set [25 22] 100
Set [26 22] 100
Set [27 22] 100
Set [28 22] 100
Set [29 22] 100
Set [30 22] 100
Set [31 22] 100
Set [32 22] 100
Set [34 22] 100
Set [35 22] 100
Set [37 22] 100
Set [39 22] 100
Set [40 22] 100
Set [41 22] 100
Set [42 22] 100
Set [43 22] 100
Set [44 22] 100
Set [45 22] 100
Set [46 22] 100
Set [47 22] 100
Set [48 22] 100
Set [49 22] 100
Set [51 22] 100
Set [52 22] 100
Set [53 22] 100
Set [55 22] 100
Set [60 22] 100
Set [63 22] 100
Set [65 22] 100
Set [66 22] 100
Set [67 22] 100
Set [10 21] 100
Set [13 21] 100
Set [15 21] 100
Set [16 21] 100
Set [18 21] 100
Set [21 21] 100
Set [22 21] 100
Set [23 21] 100
Set [24 21] 100
Set [25 21] 100
Set [26 21] 100
Set [29 21] 100
Set [30 21] 100
Set [31 21] 100
Set [33 21] 100
Set [34 21] 100
Set [36 21] 100
Set [37 21] 100
Set [38 21] 100
Set [40 21] 100
Set [41 21] 100
Set [42 21] 100
Set [43 21] 100
Set [44 21] 100
Set [46 21] 100
Set [47 21] 100
Set [48 21] 100
Set [50 21] 100
Set [51 21] 100
Set [53 21] 100
Set [54 21] 100
Set [56 21] 100
Set [59 21] 100
Set [62 21] 100
Set [67 21] 100
Set [15 20] 100
Set [16 20] 100
Set [17 20] 100
Set [18 20] 100
Set [19 20] 100
Set [20 20] 100
Set [23 20] 100
Set [24 20] 100
Set [25 20] 100
Set [26 20] 100
Set [27 20] 100
Set [28 20] 100
Set [29 20] 100
Set [32 20] 100
Set [33 20] 100
Set [34 20] 100
Set [35 20] 100
Set [37 20] 100
Set [38 20] 100
Set [41 20] 100
Set [42 20] 100
Set [43 20] 100
```

```
Set [44 20] 100
Set [45 20] 100
Set [47 20] 100
Set [50 20] 100
Set [51 20] 100
Set [53 20] 100
Set [55 20] 100
Set [57 20] 100
Set [60 20] 100
Set [61 20] 100
Set [62 20] 100
Set [63 20] 100
Set [64 20] 100
Set [65 20] 100
Set [66 20] 100
Set [7 19] 100
Set [14 19] 100
Set [16 19] 100
Set [18 19] 100
Set [19 19] 100
Set [20 19] 100
Set [21 19] 100
Set [23 19] 100
Set [24 19] 100
Set [25 19] 100
Set [26 19] 100
Set [28 19] 100
Set [29 19] 100
Set [30 19] 100
Set [31 19] 100
Set [33 19] 100
Set [35 19] 100
Set [36 19] 100
Set [37 19] 100
Set [39 19] 100
Set [40 19] 100
Set [41 19] 100
Set [43 19] 100
Set [44 19] 100
Set [45 19] 100
Set [46 19] 100
Set [47 19] 100
Set [48 19] 100
Set [49 19] 100
Set [50 19] 100
Set [51 19] 100
Set [52 19] 100
Set [53 19] 100
Set [54 19] 100
Set [56 19] 100
Set [57 19] 100
Set [58 19] 100
Set [62 19] 100
Set [63 19] 100
Set [65 19] 100
Set [11 18] 100
Set [12 18] 100
Set [14 18] 100
Set [15 18] 100
Set [20 18] 100
Set [21 18] 100
Set [23 18] 100
Set [25 18] 100
Set [26 18] 100
Set [27 18] 100
Set [28 18] 100
Set [29 18] 100
Set [30 18] 100
Set [32 18] 100
Set [33 18] 100
Set [36 18] 100
Set [38 18] 100
Set [39 18] 100
Set [41 18] 100
Set [42 18] 100
Set [43 18] 100
Set [44 18] 100
Set [45 18] 100
Set [46 18] 100
Set [47 18] 100
Set [48 18] 100
Set [49 18] 100
Set [50 18] 100
Set [51 18] 100
Set [52 18] 100
Set [53 18] 100
Set [54 18] 100
Set [55 18] 100
Set [56 18] 100
Set [58 18] 100
Set [59 18] 100
Set [60 18] 100
Set [61 18] 100
Set [62 18] 100
Set [16 17] 100
Set [17 17] 100
Set [18 17] 100
Set [19 17] 100
Set [20 17] 100
Set [21 17] 100
Set [23 17] 100
Set [25 17] 100
Set [27 17] 100
Set [28 17] 100
Set [29 17] 100
Set [30 17] 100
Set [31 17] 100
Set [32 17] 100
Set [33 17] 100
Set [34 17] 100
Set [35 17] 100
Set [37 17] 100
Set [38 17] 100
Set [40 17] 100
Set [41 17] 100
Set [43 17] 100
Set [45 17] 100
Set [46 17] 100
Set [47 17] 100
Set [49 17] 100
Set [51 17] 100
Set [52 17] 100
Set [57 17] 100
Set [8 16] 100
Set [12 16] 100
Set [13 16] 100
Set [15 16] 100
Set [18 16] 100
Set [19 16] 100
Set [20 16] 100
Set [21 16] 100
Set [22 16] 100
Set [23 16] 100
Set [24 16] 100
Set [25 16] 100
Set [26 16] 100
Set [28 16] 100
Set [29 16] 100
Set [30 16] 100
Set [32 16] 100
Set [34 16] 100
Set [36 16] 100
Set [37 16] 100
Set [38 16] 100
Set [39 16] 100
Set [40 16] 100
Set [41 16] 100
Set [42 16] 100
Set [43 16] 100
Set [44 16] 100
Set [45 16] 100
Set [46 16] 100
Set [47 16] 100
Set [48 16] 100
Set [49 16] 100
Set [50 16] 100
Set [54 16] 100
Set [6 15] 100
Set [13 15] 100
Set [14 15] 100
Set [15 15] 100
Set [16 15] 100
Set [19 15] 100
Set [22 15] 100
Set [25 15] 100
Set [26 15] 100
Set [27 15] 100
Set [28 15] 100
Set [29 15] 100
Set [32 15] 100
Set [33 15] 100
Set [34 15] 100
Set [35 15] 100
Set [36 15] 100
Set [37 15] 100
Set [40 15] 100
Set [42 15] 100
Set [44 15] 100
Set [45 15] 100
Set [48 15] 100
Set [51 15] 100
Set [52 15] 100
Set [10 14] 100
Set [13 14] 100
Set [23 14] 100
Set [24 14] 100
Set [28 14] 100
Set [29 14] 100
Set [30 14] 100
Set [32 14] 100
Set [36 14] 100
Set [38 14] 100
Set [43 14] 100
Set [18 13] 100
Set [20 13] 100
Set [21 13] 100
Set [30 13] 100
Set [32 13] 100
Set [33 13] 100
Set [36 13] 100
Set [37 13] 100
Set [40 13] 100
Set [45 13] 100
Set [12 12] 100
Set [16 12] 100
Set [24 11] 100
Set [29 11] 100
Set [41 11] 100
Set [44 11] 100
// end vase
```

In addition to a natural appearance, Set-ing dots can result in close approximations to reality.

```
Set [3 100] 100
Set [5 100] 100
Set [10 100] 100
Set [13 100] 100
Set [15 100] 100
Set [17 100] 100
Set [19 100] 100
Set [21 100] 100
Set [23 100] 100
Set [24 100] 100
Set [26 100] 100
Set [28 100] 100
Set [29 100] 100
Set [31 100] 100
Set [32 100] 100
Set [34 100] 100
Set [36 100] 100
Set [38 100] 100
Set [40 100] 100
Set [42 100] 100
Set [44 100] 100
Set [46 100] 100
Set [49 100] 100
Set [53 100] 100
Set [56 100] 100
Set [63 100] 100
Set [67 100] 100
Set [69 100] 100
Set [72 100] 100
Set [74 100] 100
Set [76 100] 100
Set [79 100] 100
Set [0 99] 100
Set [1 99] 100
Set [5 99] 100
Set [7 99] 100
Set [8 99] 100
Set [10 99] 100
Set [12 99] 100
Set [14 99] 100
Set [16 99] 100
Set [18 99] 100
Set [20 99] 100
Set [22 99] 100
Set [24 99] 100
Set [26 99] 100
Set [27 99] 100
Set [29 99] 100
Set [30 99] 100
Set [32 99] 100
Set [33 99] 100
Set [35 99] 100
Set [36 99] 100
Set [37 99] 100
Set [39 99] 100
Set [41 99] 100
Set [43 99] 100
Set [46 99] 100
Set [48 99] 100
Set [50 99] 100
Set [51 99] 100
Set [54 99] 100
Set [57 99] 100
Set [58 99] 100
Set [60 99] 100
Set [61 99] 100
Set [64 99] 100
Set [65 99] 100
Set [68 99] 100
Set [70 99] 100
Set [73 99] 100
Set [75 99] 100
Set [77 99] 100
Set [80 99] 100
Set [82 99] 100
Set [83 99] 100
Set [85 99] 100
Set [86 99] 100
Set [88 99] 100
Set [91 99] 100
Set [99 99] 100
Set [3 98] 100
Set [4 98] 100
Set [6 98] 100
Set [9 98] 100
Set [11 98] 100
Set [13 98] 100
Set [15 98] 100
Set [17 98] 100
Set [19 98] 100
Set [20 98] 100
Set [22 98] 100
Set [24 98] 100
Set [25 98] 100
Set [27 98] 100
Set [28 98] 100
Set [31 98] 100
Set [33 98] 100
Set [34 98] 100
Set [36 98] 100
Set [38 98] 100
Set [40 98] 100
Set [42 98] 100
Set [44 98] 100
Set [45 98] 100
Set [48 98] 100
Set [52 98] 100
Set [55 98] 100
Set [59 98] 100
Set [62 98] 100
Set [67 98] 100
Set [69 98] 100
Set [71 98] 100
Set [72 98] 100
Set [73 98] 100
Set [76 98] 100
Set [78 98] 100
Set [79 98] 100
Set [81 98] 100
Set [84 98] 100
Set [89 98] 100
Set [94 98] 100
Set [97 98] 100
Set [0 97] 100
Set [1 97] 100
Set [4 97] 100
Set [7 97] 100
Set [8 97] 100
Set [10 97] 100
Set [11 97] 100
Set [12 97] 100
Set [13 97] 100
Set [15 97] 100
Set [17 97] 100
Set [18 97] 100
Set [20 97] 100
Set [21 97] 100
Set [22 97] 100
Set [23 97] 100
Set [25 97] 100
Set [26 97] 100
Set [28 97] 100
Set [29 97] 100
Set [30 97] 100
Set [32 97] 100
Set [34 97] 100
Set [36 97] 100
Set [37 97] 100
Set [39 97] 100
Set [41 97] 100
Set [43 97] 100
Set [45 97] 100
Set [46 97] 100
Set [49 97] 100
Set [53 97] 100
Set [55 97] 100
Set [57 97] 100
Set [60 97] 100
Set [63 97] 100
Set [64 97] 100
Set [65 97] 100
Set [67 97] 100
Set [69 97] 100
Set [71 97] 100
Set [73 97] 100
Set [74 97] 100
Set [75 97] 100
Set [76 97] 100
Set [77 97] 100
Set [79 97] 100
Set [80 97] 100
Set [81 97] 100
Set [82 97] 100
Set [84 97] 100
Set [85 97] 100
Set [87 97] 100
Set [90 97] 100
Set [92 97] 100
Set [98 97] 100
Set [1 96] 100
Set [3 96] 100
Set [5 96] 100
Set [7 96] 100
Set [9 96] 100
Set [11 96] 100
Set [12 96] 100
Set [13 96] 100
Set [14 96] 100
Set [15 96] 100
Set [16 96] 100
Set [18 96] 100
Set [19 96] 100
Set [21 96] 100
Set [23 96] 100
Set [24 96] 100
Set [26 96] 100
Set [27 96] 100
Set [28 96] 100
Set [30 96] 100
Set [31 96] 100
Set [33 96] 100
Set [35 96] 100
Set [37 96] 100
Set [39 96] 100
Set [41 96] 100
Set [46 96] 100
Set [47 96] 100
Set [49 96] 100
Set [51 96] 100
Set [58 96] 100
Set [61 96] 100
Set [65 96] 100
Set [67 96] 100
Set [68 96] 100
Set [69 96] 100
Set [70 96] 100
Set [71 96] 100
Set [72 96] 100
Set [74 96] 100
Set [76 96] 100
Set [77 96] 100
Set [79 96] 100
Set [81 96] 100
Set [82 96] 100
Set [84 96] 100
Set [85 96] 100
Set [87 96] 100
Set [90 96] 100
Set [94 96] 100
Set [99 96] 100
Set [1 95] 100
Set [4 95] 100
Set [5 95] 100
Set [7 95] 100
Set [8 95] 100
Set [9 95] 100
Set [10 95] 100
Set [12 95] 100
Set [13 95] 100
Set [15 95] 100
Set [16 95] 100
Set [17 95] 100
Set [18 95] 100
Set [20 95] 100
Set [21 95] 100
Set [22 95] 100
Set [23 95] 100
Set [24 95] 100
Set [25 95] 100
Set [26 95] 100
Set [27 95] 100
Set [29 95] 100
Set [30 95] 100
Set [31 95] 100
Set [33 95] 100
Set [34 95] 100
Set [36 95] 100
Set [38 95] 100
Set [40 95] 100
Set [42 95] 100
Set [43 95] 100
Set [45 95] 100
Set [48 95] 100
Set [50 95] 100
Set [53 95] 100
Set [55 95] 100
Set [57 95] 100
Set [59 95] 100
Set [62 95] 100
Set [64 95] 100
Set [66 95] 100
Set [68 95] 100
Set [69 95] 100
Set [71 95] 100
Set [72 95] 100
Set [73 95] 100
Set [74 95] 100
Set [75 95] 100
Set [77 95] 100
Set [78 95] 100
Set [79 95] 100
Set [80 95] 100
Set [82 95] 100
Set [83 95] 100
Set [85 95] 100
Set [86 95] 100
Set [88 95] 100
Set [92 95] 100
Set [95 95] 100
Set [98 95] 100
Set [0 94] 100
Set [2 94] 100
Set [4 94] 100
Set [6 94] 100
Set [8 94] 100
Set [10 94] 100
Set [11 94] 100
Set [13 94] 100
Set [14 94] 100
Set [16 94] 100
Set [18 94] 100
Set [19 94] 100
Set [20 94] 100
Set [21 94] 100
Set [22 94] 100
Set [23 94] 100
Set [25 94] 100
Set [27 94] 100
Set [28 94] 100
Set [29 94] 100
```

```
Set [79 95] 100
Set [80 95] 100
Set [82 95] 100
Set [83 95] 100
Set [85 95] 100
Set [86 95] 100
Set [88 95] 100
Set [92 95] 100
Set [95 95] 100
Set [98 95] 100
Set [0 94] 100
Set [2 94] 100
Set [4 94] 100
Set [6 94] 100
Set [8 94] 100
Set [10 94] 100
Set [11 94] 100
Set [13 94] 100
Set [14 94] 100
Set [16 94] 100
Set [18 94] 100
Set [19 94] 100
Set [20 94] 100
Set [21 94] 100
Set [22 94] 100
Set [23 94] 100
Set [25 94] 100
Set [27 94] 100
Set [28 94] 100
Set [29 94] 100
Set [31 94] 100
Set [32 94] 100
Set [34 94] 100
Set [36 94] 100
Set [37 94] 100
Set [39 94] 100
Set [41 94] 100
Set [44 94] 100
Set [46 94] 100
Set [51 94] 100
Set [54 94] 100
Set [57 94] 100
Set [60 94] 100
Set [61 94] 100
Set [65 94] 100
Set [67 94] 100
Set [68 94] 100
Set [70 94] 100
Set [71 94] 100
Set [73 94] 100
Set [75 94] 100
Set [76 94] 100
Set [78 94] 100
Set [80 94] 100
Set [81 94] 100
Set [83 94] 100
Set [84 94] 100
Set [87 94] 100
Set [88 94] 100
Set [90 94] 100
Set [91 94] 100
Set [93 94] 100
Set [96 94] 100
Set [0 93] 100
Set [2 93] 100
Set [3 93] 100
Set [5 93] 100
Set [6 93] 100
Set [7 93] 100
Set [9 93] 100
Set [10 93] 100
Set [11 93] 100
Set [12 93] 100
Set [13 93] 100
Set [14 93] 100
Set [15 93] 100
Set [16 93] 100
Set [17 93] 100
Set [18 93] 100
Set [20 93] 100
Set [22 93] 100
Set [23 93] 100
Set [24 93] 100
Set [25 93] 100
Set [26 93] 100
Set [27 93] 100
Set [29 93] 100
Set [31 93] 100
Set [32 93] 100
Set [34 93] 100
Set [35 93] 100
Set [37 93] 100
Set [39 93] 100
Set [41 93] 100
Set [43 93] 100
Set [47 93] 100
Set [48 93] 100
Set [51 93] 100
Set [55 93] 100
Set [58 93] 100
Set [62 93] 100
Set [63 93] 100
Set [66 93] 100
Set [68 93] 100
Set [69 93] 100
Set [71 93] 100
Set [72 93] 100
Set [73 93] 100
Set [74 93] 100
Set [75 93] 100
Set [76 93] 100
Set [77 93] 100
Set [78 93] 100
Set [79 93] 100
Set [81 93] 100
Set [82 93] 100
Set [84 93] 100
Set [85 93] 100
Set [86 93] 100
Set [88 93] 100
Set [93 93] 100
Set [97 93] 100
Set [99 93] 100
Set [0 92] 100
Set [3 92] 100
Set [5 92] 100
Set [7 92] 100
Set [8 92] 100
Set [11 92] 100
Set [14 92] 100
Set [16 92] 100
Set [18 92] 100
Set [20 92] 100
Set [21 92] 100
Set [23 92] 100
Set [26 92] 100
Set [27 92] 100
Set [28 92] 100
Set [29 92] 100
Set [31 92] 100
Set [32 92] 100
Set [35 92] 100
Set [37 92] 100
Set [39 92] 100
Set [41 92] 100
Set [44 92] 100
Set [48 92] 100
Set [52 92] 100
Set [58 92] 100
Set [60 92] 100
Set [63 92] 100
Set [64 92] 100
Set [66 92] 100
Set [68 92] 100
Set [69 92] 100
Set [71 92] 100
Set [73 92] 100
Set [75 92] 100
Set [78 92] 100
Set [79 92] 100
Set [81 92] 100
Set [82 92] 100
Set [86 92] 100
Set [88 92] 100
Set [89 92] 100
Set [91 92] 100
Set [94 92] 100
Set [98 92] 100
Set [1 91] 100
Set [2 91] 100
Set [4 91] 100
Set [6 91] 100
Set [9 91] 100
Set [10 91] 100
Set [12 91] 100
Set [13 91] 100
Set [15 91] 100
Set [17 91] 100
Set [18 91] 100
Set [19 91] 100
Set [21 91] 100
Set [22 91] 100
Set [24 91] 100
Set [25 91] 100
Set [27 91] 100
Set [29 91] 100
Set [30 91] 100
Set [32 91] 100
Set [33 91] 100
Set [34 91] 100
Set [36 91] 100
Set [37 91] 100
Set [40 91] 100
Set [42 91] 100
Set [43 91] 100
Set [45 91] 100
Set [47 91] 100
Set [50 91] 100
Set [53 91] 100
Set [55 91] 100
Set [57 91] 100
Set [61 91] 100
Set [64 91] 100
Set [66 91] 100
Set [67 91] 100
Set [69 91] 100
Set [70 91] 100
Set [72 91] 100
Set [74 91] 100
Set [76 91] 100
Set [77 91] 100
Set [80 91] 100
Set [83 91] 100
Set [84 91] 100
Set [86 91] 100
Set [89 91] 100
Set [96 91] 100
Set [100 91] 100
Set [3 90] 100
Set [5 90] 100
Set [7 90] 100
Set [8 90] 100
Set [11 90] 100
Set [14 90] 100
Set [17 90] 100
Set [20 90] 100
Set [22 90] 100
Set [23 90] 100
Set [25 90] 100
Set [26 90] 100
Set [27 90] 100
Set [28 90] 100
Set [31 90] 100
Set [33 90] 100
Set [35 90] 100
Set [37 90] 100
Set [39 90] 100
Set [46 90] 100
Set [48 90] 100
Set [51 90] 100
Set [55 90] 100
Set [58 90] 100
Set [59 90] 100
Set [62 90] 100
Set [65 90] 100
Set [68 90] 100
Set [69 90] 100
Set [71 90] 100
Set [72 90] 100
Set [73 90] 100
Set [75 90] 100
Set [76 90] 100
Set [78 90] 100
Set [80 90] 100
Set [82 90] 100
Set [85 90] 100
Set [87 90] 100
Set [90 90] 100
Set [92 90] 100
Set [94 90] 100
Set [98 90] 100
Set [0 89] 100
Set [1 89] 100
Set [4 89] 100
Set [8 89] 100
Set [9 89] 100
Set [12 89] 100
Set [14 89] 100
Set [15 89] 100
Set [18 89] 100
Set [19 89] 100
Set [21 89] 100
Set [23 89] 100
Set [24 89] 100
Set [27 89] 100
Set [28 89] 100
Set [29 89] 100
Set [31 89] 100
Set [34 89] 100
Set [36 89] 100
Set [38 89] 100
Set [40 89] 100
Set [41 89] 100
Set [43 89] 100
Set [44 89] 100
Set [48 89] 100
Set [51 89] 100
Set [56 89] 100
Set [59 89] 100
Set [64 89] 100
Set [66 89] 100
Set [67 89] 100
Set [69 89] 100
Set [73 89] 100
Set [76 89] 100
Set [78 89] 100
Set [79 89] 100
Set [81 89] 100
Set [83 89] 100
Set [85 89] 100
Set [88 89] 100
Set [90 89] 100
Set [92 89] 100
Set [99 89] 100
Set [2 88] 100
Set [4 88] 100
Set [5 88] 100
Set [9 88] 100
Set [10 88] 100
Set [12 88] 100
Set [15 88] 100
Set [16 88] 100
Set [19 88] 100
Set [21 88] 100
Set [22 88] 100
Set [24 88] 100
Set [25 88] 100
Set [27 88] 100
Set [29 88] 100
Set [31 88] 100
Set [32 88] 100
Set [35 88] 100
Set [37 88] 100
Set [41 88] 100
Set [45 88] 100
Set [48 88] 100
Set [52 88] 100
Set [59 88] 100
Set [61 88] 100
Set [64 88] 100
Set [67 88] 100
Set [68 88] 100
Set [69 88] 100
Set [70 88] 100
Set [71 88] 100
Set [72 88] 100
Set [74 88] 100
Set [76 88] 100
Set [79 88] 100
Set [81 88] 100
Set [83 88] 100
Set [85 88] 100
Set [87 88] 100
Set [92 88] 100
Set [94 88] 100
Set [1 87] 100
Set [3 87] 100
Set [6 87] 100
Set [7 87] 100
Set [10 87] 100
Set [13 87] 100
Set [14 87] 100
Set [16 87] 100
Set [17 87] 100
Set [18 87] 100
Set [19 87] 100
Set [20 87] 100
Set [22 87] 100
Set [23 87] 100
Set [25 87] 100
Set [26 87] 100
Set [28 87] 100
Set [29 87] 100
Set [30 87] 100
Set [32 87] 100
Set [33 87] 100
Set [36 87] 100
Set [38 87] 100
Set [43 87] 100
Set [46 87] 100
Set [49 87] 100
Set [53 87] 100
Set [56 87] 100
Set [59 87] 100
Set [62 87] 100
Set [65 87] 100
Set [66 87] 100
Set [68 87] 100
Set [71 87] 100
Set [73 87] 100
Set [74 87] 100
Set [75 87] 100
Set [76 87] 100
Set [77 87] 100
Set [78 87] 100
Set [80 87] 100
Set [81 87] 100
Set [82 87] 100
Set [84 87] 100
Set [86 87] 100
Set [88 87] 100
Set [89 87] 100
Set [93 87] 100
Set [95 87] 100
Set [97 87] 100
Set [99 87] 100
Set [0 86] 100
Set [4 86] 100
Set [8 86] 100
Set [9 86] 100
Set [11 86] 100
Set [12 86] 100
Set [14 86] 100
Set [15 86] 100
Set [16 86] 100
Set [18 86] 100
Set [19 86] 100
Set [20 86] 100
Set [21 86] 100
Set [22 86] 100
Set [23 86] 100
Set [24 86] 100
Set [25 86] 100
Set [26 86] 100
Set [27 86] 100
Set [28 86] 100
Set [29 86] 100
Set [31 86] 100
Set [33 86] 100
Set [34 86] 100
Set [37 86] 100
Set [39 86] 100
Set [41 86] 100
Set [42 86] 100
Set [44 86] 100
Set [51 86] 100
Set [55 86] 100
Set [61 86] 100
Set [64 86] 100
Set [66 86] 100
Set [67 86] 100
Set [69 86] 100
Set [71 86] 100
Set [72 86] 100
Set [73 86] 100
Set [74 86] 100
Set [75 86] 100
Set [76 86] 100
Set [77 86] 100
Set [78 86] 100
Set [79 86] 100
Set [80 86] 100
Set [82 86] 100
Set [83 86] 100
Set [84 86] 100
Set [85 86] 100
Set [87 86] 100
Set [90 86] 100
Set [91 86] 100
Set [93 86] 100
Set [0 85] 100
Set [2 85] 100
Set [4 85] 100
Set [5 85] 100
Set [6 85] 100
Set [7 85] 100
Set [9 85] 100
Set [10 85] 100
Set [11 85] 100
Set [12 85] 100
Set [13 85] 100
Set [15 85] 100
Set [16 85] 100
Set [17 85] 100
Set [18 85] 100
Set [19 85] 100
Set [20 85] 100
Set [21 85] 100
Set [22 85] 100
Set [23 85] 100
Set [24 85] 100
Set [25 85] 100
Set [26 85] 100
Set [27 85] 100
Set [28 85] 100
Set [29 85] 100
Set [30 85] 100
Set [32 85] 100
Set [34 85] 100
Set [35 85] 100
Set [38 85] 100
Set [45 85] 100
Set [47 85] 100
Set [49 85] 100
Set [52 85] 100
Set [56 85] 100
Set [59 85] 100
Set [62 85] 100
Set [64 85] 100
Set [67 85] 100
Set [68 85] 100
Set [69 85] 100
Set [70 85] 100
Set [71 85] 100
Set [72 85] 100
Set [74 85] 100
Set [75 85] 100
Set [76 85] 100
Set [77 85] 100
Set [78 85] 100
Set [79 85] 100
Set [80 85] 100
Set [81 85] 100
Set [82 85] 100
Set [83 85] 100
Set [84 85] 100
Set [85 85] 100
Set [86 85] 100
Set [87 85] 100
Set [88 85] 100
Set [89 85] 100
Set [91 85] 100
Set [94 85] 100
Set [95 85] 100
Set [96 85] 100
Set [97 85] 100
Set [99 85] 100
Set [1 84] 100
Set [6 84] 100
Set [8 84] 100
Set [9 84] 100
Set [11 84] 100
Set [12 84] 100
Set [13 84] 100
Set [14 84] 100
Set [15 84] 100
Set [16 84] 100
Set [17 84] 100
Set [18 84] 100
Set [19 84] 100
Set [20 84] 100
Set [21 84] 100
Set [22 84] 100
Set [23 84] 100
Set [24 84] 100
Set [25 84] 100
Set [26 84] 100
Set [27 84] 100
Set [28 84] 100
Set [29 84] 100
Set [30 84] 100
Set [31 84] 100
Set [32 84] 100
Set [35 84] 100
Set [36 84] 100
Set [39 84] 100
Set [41 84] 100
Set [43 84] 100
Set [52 84] 100
Set [56 84] 100
Set [60 84] 100
Set [62 84] 100
Set [65 84] 100
Set [66 84] 100
Set [67 84] 100
Set [69 84] 100
Set [70 84] 100
Set [71 84] 100
Set [72 84] 100
Set [73 84] 100
Set [74 84] 100
Set [75 84] 100
Set [76 84] 100
Set [77 84] 100
Set [78 84] 100
Set [79 84] 100
Set [80 84] 100
Set [81 84] 100
Set [82 84] 100
Set [83 84] 100
Set [84 84] 100
Set [85 84] 100
Set [86 84] 100
Set [87 84] 100
Set [88 84] 100
Set [89 84] 100
Set [90 84] 100
Set [91 84] 100
Set [92 84] 100
Set [2 83] 100
Set [3 83] 100
Set [4 83] 100
Set [5 83] 100
Set [6 83] 100
Set [7 83] 100
Set [8 83] 100
Set [9 83] 100
Set [10 83] 100
Set [11 83] 100
Set [12 83] 100
Set [13 83] 100
Set [14 83] 100
Set [15 83] 100
Set [16 83] 100
Set [17 83] 100
Set [18 83] 100
Set [19 83] 100
Set [20 83] 100
Set [21 83] 100
Set [22 83] 100
Set [23 83] 100
Set [24 83] 100
Set [25 83] 100
Set [26 83] 100
Set [27 83] 100
Set [28 83] 100
Set [29 83] 100
Set [30 83] 100
Set [31 83] 100
Set [32 83] 100
Set [33 83] 100
Set [34 83] 100
Set [37 83] 100
Set [39 83] 100
Set [42 83] 100
Set [45 83] 100
Set [47 83] 100
Set [49 83] 100
Set [53 83] 100
Set [58 83] 100
Set [63 83] 100
Set [64 83] 100
Set [66 83] 100
Set [67 83] 100
Set [68 83] 100
Set [69 83] 100
Set [71 83] 100
Set [72 83] 100
Set [73 83] 100
Set [74 83] 100
Set [75 83] 100
Set [76 83] 100
Set [77 83] 100
Set [78 83] 100
Set [79 83] 100
Set [80 83] 100
Set [81 83] 100
Set [82 83] 100
Set [83 83] 100
Set [84 83] 100
Set [85 83] 100
Set [86 83] 100
Set [87 83] 100
Set [88 83] 100
Set [89 83] 100
Set [90 83] 100
Set [92 83] 100
Set [93 83] 100
Set [94 83] 100
Set [96 83] 100
Set [97 83] 100
Set [99 83] 100
Set [0 82] 100
Set [1 82] 100
Set [3 82] 100
Set [5 82] 100
Set [6 82] 100
Set [7 82] 100
Set [8 82] 100
Set [9 82] 100
Set [10 82] 100
Set [11 82] 100
Set [12 82] 100
Set [13 82] 100
Set [14 82] 100
Set [15 82] 100
Set [16 82] 100
Set [18 82] 100
Set [19 82] 100
Set [21 82] 100
Set [22 82] 100
Set [23 82] 100
Set [24 82] 100
Set [25 82] 100
Set [26 82] 100
Set [27 82] 100
Set [28 82] 100
Set [29 82] 100
Set [30 82] 100
Set [31 82] 100
Set [32 82] 100
Set [34 82] 100
Set [35 82] 100
Set [38 82] 100
Set [40 82] 100
Set [44 82] 100
Set [51 82] 100
Set [54 82] 100
Set [56 82] 100
Set [61 82] 100
Set [64 82] 100
Set [66 82] 100
Set [68 82] 100
Set [69 82] 100
Set [70 82] 100
Set [71 82] 100
Set [72 82] 100
Set [73 82] 100
Set [74 82] 100
Set [76 82] 100
Set [77 82] 100
Set [78 82] 100
Set [79 82] 100
Set [80 82] 100
Set [81 82] 100
Set [82 82] 100
Set [83 82] 100
Set [84 82] 100
Set [86 82] 100
Set [87 82] 100
Set [88 82] 100
Set [89 82] 100
Set [90 82] 100
Set [91 82] 100
Set [92 82] 100
Set [93 82] 100
Set [94 82] 100
Set [95 82] 100
Set [98 82] 100
Set [1 81] 100
Set [3 81] 100
Set [4 81] 100
Set [5 81] 100
Set [6 81] 100
Set [7 81] 100
Set [8 81] 100
Set [10 81] 100
Set [12 81] 100
Set [16 81] 100
Set [19 81] 100
Set [21 81] 100
Set [24 81] 100
Set [26 81] 100
Set [28 81] 100
Set [29 81] 100
Set [30 81] 100
Set [31 81] 100
Set [32 81] 100
Set [33 81] 100
Set [35 81] 100
Set [36 81] 100
Set [39 81] 100
Set [41 81] 100
Set [45 81] 100
Set [47 81] 100
Set [49 81] 100
Set [58 81] 100
Set [62 81] 100
Set [64 81] 100
Set [66 81] 100
Set [67 81] 100
Set [68 81] 100
Set [69 81] 100
Set [70 81] 100
Set [72 81] 100
Set [74 81] 100
Set [75 81] 100
Set [77 81] 100
Set [79 81] 100
Set [82 81] 100
Set [84 81] 100
Set [85 81] 100
Set [90 81] 100
Set [91 81] 100
Set [93 81] 100
Set [94 81] 100
Set [95 81] 100
Set [96 81] 100
Set [97 81] 100
Set [99 81] 100
Set [1 80] 100
Set [2 80] 100
Set [4 80] 100
Set [8 80] 100
Set [12 80] 100
Set [14 80] 100
Set [17 80] 100
Set [19 80] 100
Set [21 80] 100
Set [24 80] 100
Set [26 80] 100
Set [27 80] 100
Set [29 80] 100
Set [31 80] 100
Set [33 80] 100
Set [36 80] 100
Set [39 80] 100
Set [41 80] 100
Set [43 80] 100
Set [50 80] 100
Set [52 80] 100
Set [55 80] 100
Set [59 80] 100
Set [63 80] 100
Set [65 80] 100
Set [67 80] 100
Set [69 80] 100
Set [70 80] 100
Set [71 80] 100
Set [73 80] 100
Set [75 80] 100
Set [77 80] 100
Set [79 80] 100
Set [80 80] 100
Set [83 80] 100
Set [86 80] 100
Set [88 80] 100
Set [91 80] 100
Set [93 80] 100
Set [94 80] 100
Set [96 80] 100
Set [98 80] 100
Set [0 79] 100
Set [3 79] 100
Set [5 79] 100
Set [6 79] 100
Set [9 79] 100
Set [10 79] 100
Set [15 79] 100
Set [18 79] 100
Set [22 79] 100
Set [24 79] 100
Set [27 79] 100
Set [29 79] 100
Set [30 79] 100
Set [32 79] 100
Set [34 79] 100
Set [35 79] 100
Set [37 79] 100
Set [41 79] 100
Set [45 79] 100
Set [47 79] 100
Set [60 79] 100
Set [62 79] 100
Set [66 79] 100
Set [67 79] 100
Set [71 79] 100
Set [73 79] 100
Set [76 79] 100
Set [85 79] 100
Set [95 79] 100
Set [96 79] 100
Set [99 79] 100
Set [2 78] 100
Set [13 78] 100
Set [16 78] 100
Set [20 78] 100
Set [21 78] 100
Set [23 78] 100
Set [25 78] 100
Set [28 78] 100
Set [31 78] 100
Set [33 78] 100
Set [36 78] 100
Set [39 78] 100
Set [43 78] 100
Set [48 78] 100
Set [52 78] 100
Set [56 78] 100
Set [58 78] 100
Set [64 78] 100
Set [65 78] 100
Set [68 78] 100
Set [69 78] 100
Set [70 78] 100
Set [74 78] 100
Set [77 78] 100
Set [79 78] 100
Set [81 78] 100
Set [82 78] 100
Set [88 78] 100
Set [90 78] 100
Set [92 78] 100
Set [94 78] 100
Set [98 78] 100
Set [0 77] 100
Set [3 77] 100
Set [5 77] 100
Set [7 77] 100
Set [10 77] 100
Set [11 77] 100
Set [14 77] 100
Set [16 77] 100
Set [18 77] 100
Set [23 77] 100
Set [25 77] 100
Set [26 77] 100
Set [28 77] 100
Set [29 77] 100
Set [31 77] 100
Set [33 77] 100
Set [35 77] 100
Set [37 77] 100
Set [41 77] 100
Set [44 77] 100
Set [49 77] 100
Set [53 77] 100
Set [60 77] 100
Set [62 77] 100
Set [66 77] 100
Set [71 77] 100
Set [72 77] 100
Set [74 77] 100
Set [77 77] 100
Set [82 77] 100
Set [84 77] 100
Set [86 77] 100
Set [12 76] 100
Set [18 76] 100
Set [20 76] 100
Set [21 76] 100
Set [23 76] 100
Set [25 76] 100
Set [26 76] 100
Set [28 76] 100
Set [29 76] 100
Set [30 76] 100
Set [32 76] 100
Set [37 76] 100
Set [39 76] 100
Set [45 76] 100
Set [57 76] 100
Set [63 76] 100
Set [66 76] 100
Set [68 76] 100
Set [69 76] 100
Set [72 76] 100
Set [74 76] 100
Set [75 76] 100
Set [78 76] 100
Set [80 76] 100
Set [3 75] 100
Set [6 75] 100
Set [8 75] 100
Set [10 75] 100
Set [14 75] 100
Set [16 75] 100
Set [19 75] 100
Set [22 75] 100
Set [24 75] 100
Set [27 75] 100
Set [30 75] 100
Set [32 75] 100
Set [34 75] 100
Set [35 75] 100
Set [38 75] 100
Set [42 75] 100
Set [46 75] 100
```

```
Set [49 75] 100
Set [55 75] 100
Set [64 75] 100
Set [67 75] 100
Set [70 75] 100
Set [71 75] 100
Set [73 75] 100
Set [76 75] 100
Set [77 75] 100
Set [81 75] 100
Set [83 75] 100
Set [85 75] 100
Set [87 75] 100
Set [94 75] 100
Set [0 74] 100
Set [12 74] 100
Set [15 74] 100
Set [17 74] 100
Set [18 74] 100
Set [20 74] 100
Set [21 74] 100
Set [23 74] 100
Set [25 74] 100
Set [26 74] 100
Set [28 74] 100
Set [29 74] 100
Set [31 74] 100
Set [40 74] 100
Set [44 74] 100
Set [51 74] 100
Set [61 74] 100
Set [67 74] 100
Set [69 74] 100
Set [72 74] 100
Set [75 74] 100
Set [78 74] 100
Set [79 74] 100
Set [81 74] 100
Set [84 74] 100
Set [88 74] 100
Set [90 74] 100
Set [3 73] 100
Set [8 73] 100
Set [13 73] 100
Set [15 73] 100
Set [18 73] 100
Set [22 73] 100
Set [24 73] 100
Set [26 73] 100
Set [27 73] 100
Set [29 73] 100
Set [32 73] 100
Set [33 73] 100
Set [35 73] 100
Set [37 73] 100
Set [46 73] 100
Set [52 73] 100
Set [64 73] 100
Set [69 73] 100
Set [71 73] 100
Set [73 73] 100
Set [75 73] 100
Set [77 73] 100
Set [80 73] 100
Set [82 73] 100
Set [85 73] 100
Set [91 73] 100
Set [97 73] 100
Set [4 72] 100
Set [9 72] 100
Set [16 72] 100
Set [18 72] 100
Set [20 72] 100
Set [22 72] 100
Set [24 72] 100
Set [30 72] 100
Set [35 72] 100
Set [39 72] 100
Set [41 72] 100
Set [48 72] 100
Set [57 72] 100
Set [66 72] 100
Set [71 72] 100
Set [73 72] 100
Set [75 72] 100
Set [77 72] 100
Set [78 72] 100
Set [80 72] 100
Set [82 72] 100
Set [85 72] 100
Set [87 72] 100
Set [10 71] 100
Set [12 71] 100
Set [19 71] 100
Set [21 71] 100
Set [25 71] 100
Set [27 71] 100
Set [29 71] 100
Set [33 71] 100
Set [43 71] 100
Set [46 71] 100
Set [68 71] 100
Set [72 71] 100
Set [76 71] 100
Set [83 71] 100
Set [6 70] 100
Set [14 70] 100
Set [16 70] 100
Set [18 70] 100
Set [23 70] 100
Set [31 70] 100
Set [35 70] 100
Set [38 70] 100
Set [53 70] 100
Set [70 70] 100
Set [74 70] 100
Set [79 70] 100
Set [81 70] 100
Set [2 69] 100
Set [7 69] 100
Set [19 69] 100
Set [21 69] 100
Set [25 69] 100
Set [27 69] 100
Set [31 69] 100
Set [39 69] 100
Set [41 69] 100
Set [75 69] 100
Set [77 69] 100
Set [81 69] 100
Set [84 69] 100
Set [87 69] 100
Set [93 69] 100
Set [96 69] 100
Set [10 68] 100
Set [14 68] 100
Set [22 68] 100
Set [28 68] 100
Set [32 68] 100
Set [34 68] 100
Set [46 68] 100
Set [59 68] 100
Set [3 67] 100
Set [8 67] 100
Set [17 67] 100
Set [35 67] 100
Set [42 67] 100
Set [53 67] 100
Set [72 67] 100
Set [81 67] 100
Set [11 66] 100
Set [19 66] 100
Set [25 66] 100
Set [27 66] 100
Set [30 66] 100
Set [36 66] 100
Set [39 66] 100
Set [44 66] 100
Set [49 66] 100
Set [77 66] 100
Set [87 66] 100
Set [90 66] 100
Set [13 65] 100
Set [20 65] 100
Set [22 65] 100
Set [31 65] 100
Set [36 65] 100
Set [40 65] 100
Set [62 65] 100
Set [65 65] 100
Set [69 65] 100
Set [82 65] 100
Set [2 64] 100
Set [14 64] 100
Set [27 64] 100
Set [32 64] 100
Set [44 64] 100
Set [72 64] 100
Set [4 63] 100
Set [8 63] 100
Set [23 63] 100
Set [25 63] 100
Set [28 63] 100
Set [33 63] 100
Set [36 63] 100
Set [40 63] 100
Set [49 63] 100
Set [11 62] 100
Set [17 62] 100
Set [19 62] 100
Set [31 62] 100
Set [35 62] 100
Set [38 62] 100
Set [42 62] 100
Set [66 62] 100
Set [76 62] 100
Set [79 62] 100
Set [91 62] 100
Set [0 61] 100
Set [14 61] 100
Set [21 61] 100
Set [24 61] 100
Set [27 61] 100
Set [29 61] 100
Set [31 61] 100
Set [33 61] 100
Set [45 61] 100
Set [66 61] 100
Set [69 61] 100
Set [82 61] 100
Set [2 60] 100
Set [7 60] 100
Set [12 60] 100
Set [18 60] 100
Set [25 60] 100
Set [31 60] 100
Set [34 60] 100
Set [36 60] 100
Set [43 60] 100
Set [51 60] 100
Set [61 60] 100
Set [67 60] 100
Set [70 60] 100
Set [83 60] 100
Set [5 59] 100
Set [16 59] 100
Set [21 59] 100
Set [23 59] 100
Set [28 59] 100
Set [30 59] 100
Set [32 59] 100
Set [38 59] 100
Set [41 59] 100
Set [46 59] 100
Set [49 59] 100
Set [72 59] 100
Set [75 59] 100
Set [78 59] 100
Set [86 59] 100
Set [10 58] 100
Set [14 58] 100
Set [19 58] 100
Set [25 58] 100
Set [27 58] 100
Set [29 58] 100
Set [30 58] 100
Set [33 58] 100
Set [39 58] 100
Set [55 58] 100
Set [68 58] 100
Set [70 58] 100
Set [91 58] 100
Set [96 58] 100
Set [0 57] 100
Set [3 57] 100
Set [21 57] 100
Set [23 57] 100
Set [26 57] 100
Set [30 57] 100
Set [34 57] 100
Set [56 57] 100
Set [65 57] 100
Set [69 57] 100
Set [72 57] 100
Set [78 57] 100
Set [80 57] 100
Set [83 57] 100
Set [87 57] 100
Set [5 56] 100
Set [7 56] 100
Set [10 56] 100
Set [15 56] 100
Set [18 56] 100
Set [24 56] 100
Set [26 56] 100
Set [27 56] 100
Set [29 56] 100
Set [31 56] 100
Set [35 56] 100
Set [40 56] 100
Set [44 56] 100
Set [48 56] 100
Set [70 56] 100
Set [72 56] 100
Set [73 56] 100
Set [75 56] 100
Set [81 56] 100
Set [3 55] 100
Set [12 55] 100
Set [20 55] 100
Set [22 55] 100
Set [25 55] 100
Set [28 55] 100
Set [30 55] 100
Set [37 55] 100
Set [42 55] 100
Set [46 55] 100
Set [68 55] 100
Set [70 55] 100
Set [79 55] 100
Set [88 55] 100
Set [92 55] 100
Set [0 54] 100
Set [9 54] 100
Set [13 54] 100
Set [16 54] 100
Set [19 54] 100
Set [23 54] 100
Set [26 54] 100
Set [27 54] 100
Set [29 54] 100
Set [34 54] 100
Set [39 54] 100
Set [43 54] 100
Set [50 54] 100
Set [52 54] 100
Set [71 54] 100
Set [73 54] 100
Set [75 54] 100
Set [77 54] 100
Set [83 54] 100
Set [86 54] 100
Set [89 54] 100
Set [4 53] 100
Set [6 53] 100
Set [14 53] 100
Set [20 53] 100
Set [21 53] 100
Set [24 53] 100
Set [27 53] 100
Set [30 53] 100
Set [40 53] 100
Set [45 53] 100
Set [47 53] 100
Set [53 53] 100
Set [57 53] 100
Set [69 53] 100
Set [72 53] 100
Set [77 53] 100
Set [80 53] 100
Set [90 53] 100
Set [93 53] 100
Set [1 52] 100
Set [7 52] 100
Set [9 52] 100
Set [15 52] 100
Set [17 52] 100
Set [21 52] 100
Set [22 52] 100
Set [24 52] 100
Set [25 52] 100
Set [27 52] 100
Set [30 52] 100
Set [32 52] 100
Set [34 52] 100
Set [35 52] 100
Set [37 52] 100
Set [40 52] 100
Set [42 52] 100
Set [46 52] 100
Set [48 52] 100
Set [50 52] 100
Set [54 52] 100
Set [59 52] 100
Set [72 52] 100
Set [73 52] 100
Set [75 52] 100
Set [78 52] 100
Set [81 52] 100
Set [83 52] 100
Set [4 51] 100
Set [11 51] 100
Set [18 51] 100
Set [19 51] 100
Set [22 51] 100
Set [24 51] 100
Set [26 51] 100
Set [28 51] 100
Set [35 51] 100
Set [37 51] 100
Set [39 51] 100
Set [41 51] 100
Set [43 51] 100
Set [44 51] 100
Set [46 51] 100
Set [49 51] 100
Set [52 51] 100
Set [55 51] 100
Set [57 51] 100
Set [60 51] 100
Set [62 51] 100
Set [70 51] 100
Set [72 51] 100
Set [74 51] 100
Set [76 51] 100
Set [85 51] 100
Set [91 51] 100
Set [94 51] 100
Set [2 50] 100
Set [6 50] 100
Set [9 50] 100
Set [13 50] 100
Set [15 50] 100
Set [17 50] 100
Set [20 50] 100
Set [21 50] 100
Set [23 50] 100
Set [25 50] 100
Set [28 50] 100
Set [30 50] 100
Set [32 50] 100
Set [33 50] 100
Set [34 50] 100
Set [36 50] 100
Set [38 50] 100
Set [39 50] 100
Set [42 50] 100
Set [45 50] 100
Set [47 50] 100
Set [48 50] 100
Set [51 50] 100
Set [53 50] 100
Set [54 50] 100
Set [58 50] 100
Set [62 50] 100
Set [64 50] 100
Set [65 50] 100
Set [66 50] 100
Set [69 50] 100
Set [73 50] 100
Set [76 50] 100
Set [78 50] 100
Set [80 50] 100
Set [83 50] 100
Set [87 50] 100
Set [3 49] 100
Set [7 49] 100
Set [11 49] 100
Set [15 49] 100
Set [18 49] 100
Set [21 49] 100
Set [23 49] 100
Set [25 49] 100
Set [26 49] 100
Set [30 49] 100
Set [32 49] 100
Set [34 49] 100
Set [35 49] 100
Set [36 49] 100
Set [37 49] 100
Set [39 49] 100
Set [40 49] 100
Set [42 49] 100
Set [43 49] 100
Set [45 49] 100
Set [49 49] 100
Set [50 49] 100
Set [54 49] 100
Set [55 49] 100
Set [56 49] 100
Set [58 49] 100
Set [60 49] 100
Set [62 49] 100
Set [63 49] 100
Set [66 49] 100
Set [70 49] 100
Set [73 49] 100
Set [75 49] 100
Set [78 49] 100
Set [81 49] 100
Set [88 49] 100
Set [96 49] 100
Set [3 48] 100
Set [9 48] 100
Set [50 44] 100
Set [52 44] 100
Set [54 44] 100
Set [56 44] 100
Set [60 44] 100
Set [73 44] 100
Set [77 44] 100
Set [79 44] 100
Set [81 44] 100
Set [83 44] 100
Set [86 44] 100
Set [90 44] 100
Set [98 44] 100
Set [1 43] 100
Set [3 43] 100
Set [5 43] 100
Set [9 43] 100
Set [11 43] 100
Set [13 43] 100
Set [14 43] 100
Set [16 43] 100
Set [17 43] 100
Set [18 43] 100
Set [20 43] 100
Set [21 43] 100
Set [23 43] 100
Set [26 43] 100
Set [29 43] 100
Set [35 43] 100
Set [37 43] 100
Set [41 43] 100
Set [43 43] 100
Set [44 43] 100
Set [47 43] 100
Set [49 43] 100
Set [51 43] 100
Set [52 43] 100
Set [54 43] 100
Set [56 43] 100
Set [58 43] 100
Set [67 43] 100
Set [70 43] 100
Set [74 43] 100
Set [76 43] 100
Set [78 43] 100
Set [80 43] 100
Set [82 43] 100
Set [84 43] 100
Set [87 43] 100
Set [89 43] 100
Set [93 43] 100
Set [97 43] 100
Set [2 42] 100
Set [6 42] 100
Set [8 42] 100
Set [10 42] 100
Set [12 42] 100
Set [15 42] 100
Set [19 42] 100
Set [21 42] 100
Set [24 42] 100
Set [33 42] 100
Set [38 42] 100
Set [40 42] 100
Set [46 42] 100
Set [48 42] 100
Set [50 42] 100
Set [53 42] 100
Set [55 42] 100
Set [62 42] 100
Set [65 42] 100
Set [78 42] 100
Set [80 42] 100
Set [82 42] 100
Set [84 42] 100
Set [86 42] 100
Set [91 42] 100
Set [95 42] 100
Set [0 41] 100
Set [4 41] 100
Set [13 41] 100
Set [15 41] 100
Set [16 41] 100
Set [17 41] 100
Set [18 41] 100
Set [19 41] 100
Set [20 41] 100
Set [22 41] 100
Set [28 41] 100
Set [30 41] 100
Set [35 41] 100
Set [41 41] 100
Set [43 41] 100
Set [45 41] 100
Set [48 41] 100
Set [51 41] 100
Set [55 41] 100
Set [57 41] 100
Set [59 41] 100
Set [71 41] 100
Set [74 41] 100
Set [76 41] 100
Set [80 41] 100
Set [82 41] 100
Set [84 41] 100
Set [87 41] 100
Set [89 41] 100
Set [98 41] 100
Set [1 40] 100
Set [5 40] 100
Set [6 40] 100
Set [8 40] 100
Set [9 40] 100
Set [10 40] 100
Set [11 40] 100
Set [13 40] 100
Set [16 40] 100
Set [20 40] 100
Set [22 40] 100
Set [24 40] 100
Set [25 40] 100
Set [31 40] 100
Set [36 40] 100
Set [38 40] 100
Set [43 40] 100
Set [46 40] 100
Set [48 40] 100
Set [52 40] 100
Set [55 40] 100
Set [72 40] 100
Set [77 40] 100
Set [78 40] 100
Set [80 40] 100
Set [82 40] 100
Set [84 40] 100
Set [85 40] 100
Set [87 40] 100
Set [90 40] 100
Set [91 40] 100
Set [92 40] 100
Set [95 40] 100
Set [2 39] 100
Set [3 39] 100
Set [6 39] 100
Set [11 39] 100
Set [13 39] 100
Set [14 39] 100
Set [16 39] 100
Set [17 39] 100
Set [18 39] 100
Set [20 39] 100
Set [29 39] 100
Set [33 39] 100
Set [40 39] 100
Set [41 39] 100
Set [45 39] 100
Set [49 39] 100
Set [50 39] 100
Set [53 39] 100
Set [57 39] 100
Set [61 39] 100
Set [67 39] 100
Set [75 39] 100
Set [79 39] 100
Set [81 39] 100
Set [83 39] 100
Set [86 39] 100
Set [88 39] 100
Set [93 39] 100
Set [99 39] 100
Set [1 38] 100
Set [5 38] 100
Set [8 38] 100
Set [9 38] 100
Set [12 38] 100
Set [15 38] 100
Set [16 38] 100
Set [18 38] 100
Set [19 38] 100
Set [22 38] 100
Set [24 38] 100
Set [27 38] 100
Set [30 38] 100
Set [35 38] 100
Set [38 38] 100
Set [43 38] 100
Set [46 38] 100
Set [48 38] 100
Set [51 38] 100
Set [54 38] 100
Set [59 38] 100
Set [65 38] 100
Set [69 38] 100
Set [77 38] 100
Set [80 38] 100
Set [82 38] 100
Set [84 38] 100
Set [86 38] 100
Set [89 38] 100
Set [91 38] 100
Set [96 38] 100
Set [1 37] 100
Set [3 37] 100
Set [6 37] 100
Set [7 37] 100
Set [9 37] 100
Set [11 37] 100
Set [13 37] 100
Set [14 37] 100
Set [16 37] 100
Set [17 37] 100
Set [20 37] 100
Set [22 37] 100
Set [25 37] 100
Set [32 37] 100
Set [36 37] 100
Set [39 37] 100
Set [49 37] 100
Set [55 37] 100
Set [71 37] 100
Set [78 37] 100
Set [81 37] 100
Set [82 37] 100
Set [84 37] 100
Set [86 37] 100
Set [87 37] 100
Set [89 37] 100
Set [91 37] 100
Set [93 37] 100
Set [97 37] 100
Set [2 36] 100
Set [4 36] 100
Set [7 36] 100
Set [9 36] 100
Set [11 36] 100
Set [14 36] 100
Set [16 36] 100
Set [18 36] 100
Set [23 36] 100
Set [27 36] 100
Set [30 36] 100
Set [33 36] 100
Set [40 36] 100
Set [42 36] 100
Set [44 36] 100
Set [47 36] 100
Set [50 36] 100
Set [53 36] 100
Set [56 36] 100
Set [59 36] 100
Set [74 36] 100
Set [79 36] 100
Set [82 36] 100
Set [83 36] 100
Set [87 36] 100
Set [89 36] 100
Set [91 36] 100
Set [93 36] 100
Set [95 36] 100
Set [1 35] 100
Set [3 35] 100
Set [5 35] 100
Set [7 35] 100
Set [10 35] 100
Set [12 35] 100
Set [13 35] 100
Set [14 35] 100
Set [15 35] 100
Set [16 35] 100
Set [17 35] 100
Set [19 35] 100
Set [20 35] 100
Set [28 35] 100
Set [37 35] 100
Set [45 35] 100
Set [51 35] 100
Set [72 35] 100
Set [76 35] 100
Set [78 35] 100
Set [80 35] 100
Set [81 35] 100
Set [83 35] 100
Set [84 35] 100
Set [85 35] 100
Set [86 35] 100
Set [88 35] 100
Set [92 35] 100
Set [97 35] 100
Set [4 34] 100
Set [8 34] 100
Set [9 34] 100
Set [11 34] 100
Set [13 34] 100
Set [15 34] 100
Set [18 34] 100
Set [21 34] 100
Set [24 34] 100
Set [26 34] 100
Set [32 34] 100
Set [35 34] 100
Set [39 34] 100
Set [42 34] 100
Set [49 34] 100
Set [54 34] 100
Set [79 34] 100
Set [82 34] 100
Set [84 34] 100
Set [87 34] 100
Set [89 34] 100
Set [90 34] 100
Set [93 34] 100
Set [95 34] 100
Set [99 34] 100
Set [1 33] 100
Set [5 33] 100
Set [6 33] 100
Set [9 33] 100
Set [11 33] 100
Set [13 33] 100
Set [15 33] 100
Set [16 33] 100
Set [17 33] 100
Set [19 33] 100
Set [22 33] 100
Set [27 33] 100
Set [29 33] 100
Set [36 33] 100
Set [40 33] 100
Set [43 33] 100
Set [45 33] 100
Set [47 33] 100
Set [50 33] 100
Set [55 33] 100
Set [57 33] 100
Set [60 33] 100
Set [63 33] 100
Set [73 33] 100
Set [75 33] 100
Set [80 33] 100
Set [82 33] 100
Set [84 33] 100
Set [85 33] 100
Set [87 33] 100
Set [90 33] 100
Set [92 33] 100
Set [95 33] 100
Set [1 32] 100
Set [6 32] 100
Set [8 32] 100
Set [10 32] 100
Set [12 32] 100
Set [13 32] 100
Set [14 32] 100
Set [17 32] 100
Set [19 32] 100
Set [20 32] 100
Set [22 32] 100
Set [24 32] 100
Set [30 32] 100
Set [32 32] 100
Set [37 32] 100
Set [40 32] 100
Set [43 32] 100
Set [50 32] 100
Set [57 32] 100
Set [60 32] 100
Set [64 32] 100
Set [66 32] 100
Set [76 32] 100
Set [78 32] 100
Set [81 32] 100
Set [82 32] 100
Set [84 32] 100
Set [85 32] 100
Set [87 32] 100
Set [88 32] 100
Set [90 32] 100
Set [93 32] 100
Set [95 32] 100
Set [97 32] 100
Set [2 31] 100
Set [3 31] 100
Set [7 31] 100
Set [9 31] 100
Set [11 31] 100
Set [13 31] 100
Set [15 31] 100
Set [16 31] 100
Set [18 31] 100
Set [23 31] 100
Set [25 31] 100
Set [28 31] 100
Set [33 31] 100
Set [35 31] 100
Set [37 31] 100
Set [38 31] 100
Set [40 31] 100
Set [41 31] 100
Set [43 31] 100
Set [44 31] 100
Set [45 31] 100
Set [46 31] 100
Set [47 31] 100
Set [48 31] 100
Set [51 31] 100
Set [52 31] 100
Set [53 31] 100
Set [54 31] 100
Set [55 31] 100
Set [57 31] 100
Set [58 31] 100
Set [61 31] 100
Set [68 31] 100
Set [74 31] 100
Set [79 31] 100
Set [82 31] 100
Set [83 31] 100
Set [85 31] 100
Set [86 31] 100
Set [88 31] 100
Set [91 31] 100
Set [92 31] 100
Set [99 31] 100
Set [0 30] 100
Set [4 30] 100
Set [5 30] 100
Set [6 30] 100
Set [10 30] 100
Set [12 30] 100
Set [13 30] 100
Set [14 30] 100
Set [16 30] 100
Set [17 30] 100
Set [19 30] 100
Set [20 30] 100
Set [22 30] 100
Set [26 30] 100
Set [29 30] 100
Set [30 30] 100
Set [31 30] 100
Set [32 30] 100
Set [34 30] 100
Set [35 30] 100
Set [36 30] 100
Set [39 30] 100
Set [40 30] 100
Set [42 30] 100
Set [43 30] 100
Set [46 30] 100
Set [49 30] 100
Set [50 30] 100
Set [52 30] 100
Set [54 30] 100
Set [56 30] 100
Set [57 30] 100
Set [59 30] 100
Set [60 30] 100
Set [62 30] 100
Set [63 30] 100
Set [65 30] 100
Set [66 30] 100
Set [70 30] 100
Set [72 30] 100
Set [76 30] 100
Set [78 30] 100
Set [80 30] 100
Set [81 30] 100
Set [84 30] 100
Set [85 30] 100
Set [87 30] 100
Set [89 30] 100
Set [90 30] 100
Set [93 30] 100
Set [95 30] 100
```

```
Set [12 48] 100
Set [15 48] 100
Set [18 48] 100
Set [20 48] 100
Set [21 48] 100
Set [23 48] 100
Set [26 48] 100
Set [28 48] 100
Set [33 48] 100
Set [37 48] 100
Set [38 48] 100
Set [40 48] 100
Set [42 48] 100
Set [45 48] 100
Set [46 48] 100
Set [47 48] 100
Set [50 48] 100
Set [51 48] 100
Set [52 48] 100
Set [56 48] 100
Set [58 48] 100
Set [59 48] 100
Set [61 48] 100
Set [63 48] 100
Set [64 48] 100
Set [71 48] 100
Set [75 48] 100
Set [76 48] 100
Set [78 48] 100
Set [81 48] 100
Set [83 48] 100
Set [85 48] 100
Set [89 48] 100
Set [93 48] 100
Set [97 48] 100
Set [0 47] 100
Set [4 47] 100
Set [6 47] 100
Set [10 47] 100
Set [13 47] 100
Set [15 47] 100
Set [17 47] 100
Set [19 47] 100
Set [22 47] 100
Set [23 47] 100
Set [25 47] 100
Set [31 47] 100
Set [34 47] 100
Set [35 47] 100
Set [38 47] 100
Set [40 47] 100
Set [41 47] 100
Set [43 47] 100
Set [44 47] 100
Set [47 47] 100
Set [48 47] 100
Set [50 47] 100
Set [53 47] 100
Set [54 47] 100
Set [56 47] 100
Set [57 47] 100
Set [59 47] 100
Set [60 47] 100
Set [62 47] 100
Set [65 47] 100
Set [67 47] 100
Set [69 47] 100
Set [73 47] 100
Set [76 47] 100
Set [79 47] 100
Set [83 47] 100
Set [92 47] 100
Set [1 46] 100
Set [7 46] 100
Set [9 46] 100
Set [12 46] 100
Set [16 46] 100
Set [18 46] 100
Set [20 46] 100
Set [21 46] 100
Set [23 46] 100
Set [26 46] 100
Set [29 46] 100
Set [32 46] 100
Set [35 46] 100
Set [37 46] 100
Set [39 46] 100
Set [42 46] 100
Set [43 46] 100
Set [45 46] 100
Set [46 46] 100
Set [48 46] 100
Set [49 46] 100
Set [51 46] 100
Set [52 46] 100
Set [54 46] 100
Set [55 46] 100
Set [56 46] 100
Set [58 46] 100
Set [61 46] 100
Set [63 46] 100
Set [74 46] 100
Set [76 46] 100
Set [78 46] 100
Set [79 46] 100
Set [81 46] 100
Set [84 46] 100
Set [86 46] 100
Set [89 46] 100
Set [3 45] 100
Set [5 45] 100
Set [10 45] 100
Set [12 45] 100
Set [14 45] 100
Set [16 45] 100
Set [19 45] 100
Set [21 45] 100
Set [22 45] 100
Set [24 45] 100
Set [27 45] 100
Set [35 45] 100
Set [37 45] 100
Set [39 45] 100
Set [41 45] 100
Set [43 45] 100
Set [45 45] 100
Set [48 45] 100
Set [50 45] 100
Set [52 45] 100
Set [54 45] 100
Set [56 45] 100
Set [58 45] 100
Set [59 45] 100
Set [63 45] 100
Set [71 45] 100
Set [76 45] 100
Set [79 45] 100
Set [81 45] 100
Set [86 45] 100
Set [89 45] 100
Set [93 45] 100
Set [96 45] 100
Set [0 44] 100
Set [6 44] 100
Set [8 44] 100
Set [12 44] 100
Set [15 44] 100
Set [17 44] 100
Set [19 44] 100
Set [22 44] 100
Set [25 44] 100
Set [28 44] 100
Set [31 44] 100
Set [39 44] 100
Set [42 44] 100
Set [45 44] 100
Set [46 44] 100
Set [48 44] 100
Set [97 30] 100
Set [1 29] 100
Set [7 29] 100
Set [8 29] 100
Set [11 29] 100
Set [13 29] 100
Set [14 29] 100
Set [16 29] 100
Set [18 29] 100
Set [20 29] 100
Set [21 29] 100
Set [23 29] 100
Set [24 29] 100
Set [26 29] 100
Set [27 29] 100
Set [30 29] 100
Set [32 29] 100
Set [33 29] 100
Set [35 29] 100
Set [36 29] 100
Set [37 29] 100
Set [39 29] 100
Set [41 29] 100
Set [43 29] 100
Set [44 29] 100
Set [45 29] 100
Set [46 29] 100
Set [47 29] 100
Set [48 29] 100
Set [50 29] 100
Set [52 29] 100
Set [54 29] 100
Set [55 29] 100
Set [57 29] 100
Set [58 29] 100
Set [60 29] 100
Set [61 29] 100
Set [63 29] 100
Set [64 29] 100
Set [66 29] 100
Set [67 29] 100
Set [68 29] 100
Set [70 29] 100
Set [73 29] 100
Set [74 29] 100
Set [77 29] 100
Set [81 29] 100
Set [82 29] 100
Set [83 29] 100
Set [85 29] 100
Set [87 29] 100
Set [89 29] 100
Set [92 29] 100
Set [2 28] 100
Set [4 28] 100
Set [6 28] 100
Set [8 28] 100
Set [9 28] 100
Set [11 28] 100
Set [12 28] 100
Set [14 28] 100
Set [15 28] 100
Set [16 28] 100
Set [18 28] 100
Set [21 28] 100
Set [23 28] 100
Set [25 28] 100
Set [26 28] 100
Set [27 28] 100
Set [28 28] 100
Set [30 28] 100
Set [31 28] 100
Set [33 28] 100
Set [35 28] 100
Set [36 28] 100
Set [37 28] 100
Set [38 28] 100
Set [39 28] 100
Set [41 28] 100
Set [42 28] 100
Set [45 28] 100
Set [47 28] 100
Set [48 28] 100
Set [49 28] 100
Set [50 28] 100
Set [51 28] 100
Set [52 28] 100
Set [54 28] 100
Set [56 28] 100
Set [58 28] 100
Set [60 28] 100
Set [61 28] 100
Set [62 28] 100
Set [64 28] 100
Set [66 28] 100
Set [68 28] 100
Set [70 28] 100
Set [71 28] 100
Set [73 28] 100
Set [74 28] 100
Set [75 28] 100
Set [77 28] 100
Set [78 28] 100
Set [79 28] 100
Set [82 28] 100
Set [83 28] 100
Set [84 28] 100
Set [85 28] 100
Set [87 28] 100
Set [89 28] 100
Set [90 28] 100
Set [92 28] 100
Set [94 28] 100
Set [98 28] 100
Set [1 27] 100
Set [4 27] 100
Set [10 27] 100
Set [12 27] 100
Set [13 27] 100
Set [14 27] 100
Set [16 27] 100
Set [18 27] 100
Set [19 27] 100
Set [20 27] 100
Set [22 27] 100
Set [23 27] 100
Set [24 27] 100
Set [26 27] 100
Set [28 27] 100
Set [29 27] 100
Set [31 27] 100
Set [32 27] 100
Set [33 27] 100
Set [34 27] 100
Set [39 27] 100
Set [41 27] 100
Set [43 27] 100
Set [45 27] 100
Set [46 27] 100
Set [49 27] 100
Set [52 27] 100
Set [54 27] 100
Set [56 27] 100
Set [59 27] 100
Set [63 27] 100
Set [65 27] 100
Set [66 27] 100
Set [67 27] 100
Set [68 27] 100
Set [69 27] 100
Set [71 27] 100
Set [72 27] 100
Set [74 27] 100
Set [75 27] 100
Set [77 27] 100
Set [80 27] 100
Set [81 27] 100
Set [84 27] 100
Set [86 27] 100
Set [88 27] 100
Set [91 27] 100
Set [96 27] 100
Set [0 26] 100
Set [5 26] 100
Set [7 26] 100
Set [8 26] 100
Set [9 26] 100
Set [12 26] 100
Set [14 26] 100
Set [15 26] 100
Set [16 26] 100
Set [17 26] 100
Set [18 26] 100
Set [20 26] 100
Set [21 26] 100
Set [22 26] 100
Set [24 26] 100
Set [25 26] 100
Set [26 26] 100
Set [27 26] 100
Set [29 26] 100
Set [30 26] 100
Set [32 26] 100
Set [35 26] 100
Set [36 26] 100
Set [38 26] 100
Set [40 26] 100
Set [43 26] 100
Set [45 26] 100
Set [47 26] 100
Set [48 26] 100
Set [50 26] 100
Set [51 26] 100
Set [53 26] 100
Set [55 26] 100
Set [59 26] 100
Set [61 26] 100
Set [63 26] 100
Set [65 26] 100
Set [67 26] 100
Set [69 26] 100
Set [70 26] 100
Set [72 26] 100
Set [73 26] 100
Set [75 26] 100
Set [76 26] 100
Set [77 26] 100
Set [78 26] 100
Set [79 26] 100
Set [81 26] 100
Set [82 26] 100
Set [83 26] 100
Set [85 26] 100
Set [86 26] 100
Set [87 26] 100
Set [89 26] 100
Set [90 26] 100
Set [93 26] 100
Set [94 26] 100
Set [1 25] 100
Set [2 25] 100
Set [8 25] 100
Set [10 25] 100
Set [12 25] 100
Set [14 25] 100
Set [16 25] 100
Set [18 25] 100
Set [19 25] 100
Set [20 25] 100
Set [21 25] 100
Set [22 25] 100
Set [23 25] 100
Set [24 25] 100
Set [25 25] 100
Set [27 25] 100
Set [28 25] 100
Set [30 25] 100
Set [32 25] 100
Set [34 25] 100
Set [39 25] 100
Set [41 25] 100
Set [43 25] 100
Set [47 25] 100
Set [49 25] 100
Set [51 25] 100
Set [53 25] 100
Set [56 25] 100
Set [57 25] 100
Set [60 25] 100
Set [67 25] 100
Set [70 25] 100
Set [72 25] 100
Set [73 25] 100
Set [75 25] 100
Set [76 25] 100
Set [77 25] 100
Set [78 25] 100
Set [79 25] 100
Set [81 25] 100
Set [82 25] 100
Set [83 25] 100
Set [84 25] 100
Set [87 25] 100
Set [90 25] 100
Set [92 25] 100
Set [95 25] 100
Set [98 25] 100
Set [2 24] 100
Set [4 24] 100
Set [6 24] 100
Set [8 24] 100
Set [10 24] 100
Set [12 24] 100
Set [13 24] 100
Set [14 24] 100
Set [16 24] 100
Set [17 24] 100
Set [19 24] 100
Set [20 24] 100
Set [21 24] 100
Set [22 24] 100
Set [23 24] 100
Set [24 24] 100
Set [25 24] 100
Set [26 24] 100
Set [28 24] 100
Set [30 24] 100
Set [32 24] 100
Set [34 24] 100
Set [36 24] 100
Set [39 24] 100
Set [44 24] 100
Set [47 24] 100
Set [49 24] 100
Set [53 24] 100
Set [58 24] 100
Set [61 24] 100
Set [63 24] 100
Set [65 24] 100
Set [67 24] 100
Set [71 24] 100
Set [73 24] 100
Set [74 24] 100
Set [75 24] 100
Set [76 24] 100
Set [77 24] 100
Set [78 24] 100
Set [79 24] 100
Set [80 24] 100
Set [82 24] 100
Set [84 24] 100
Set [85 24] 100
Set [87 24] 100
Set [90 24] 100
Set [92 24] 100
Set [95 24] 100
Set [4 23] 100
Set [9 23] 100
Set [11 23] 100
Set [14 23] 100
Set [15 23] 100
Set [16 23] 100
Set [17 23] 100
Set [18 23] 100
Set [19 23] 100
Set [20 23] 100
Set [21 23] 100
Set [22 23] 100
Set [23 23] 100
Set [24 23] 100
Set [25 23] 100
Set [27 23] 100
Set [31 23] 100
Set [33 23] 100
Set [37 23] 100
Set [40 23] 100
Set [42 23] 100
Set [50 23] 100
Set [51 23] 100
Set [56 23] 100
Set [59 23] 100
Set [65 23] 100
Set [66 23] 100
Set [68 23] 100
Set [69 23] 100
Set [72 23] 100
Set [73 23] 100
Set [75 23] 100
Set [76 23] 100
Set [77 23] 100
Set [78 23] 100
Set [79 23] 100
Set [80 23] 100
Set [81 23] 100
Set [82 23] 100
Set [83 23] 100
Set [84 23] 100
Set [85 23] 100
Set [87 23] 100
Set [88 23] 100
Set [93 23] 100
Set [96 23] 100
Set [99 23] 100
Set [1 22] 100
Set [3 22] 100
Set [6 22] 100
Set [8 22] 100
Set [10 22] 100
Set [12 22] 100
Set [13 22] 100
Set [14 22] 100
Set [15 22] 100
Set [18 22] 100
Set [20 22] 100
Set [22 22] 100
Set [23 22] 100
Set [24 22] 100
Set [25 22] 100
Set [26 22] 100
Set [27 22] 100
Set [29 22] 100
Set [32 22] 100
Set [35 22] 100
Set [39 22] 100
Set [46 22] 100
Set [48 22] 100
Set [57 22] 100
Set [63 22] 100
Set [66 22] 100
Set [71 22] 100
Set [72 22] 100
Set [73 22] 100
Set [74 22] 100
Set [75 22] 100
Set [76 22] 100
Set [77 22] 100
Set [78 22] 100
Set [79 22] 100
Set [80 22] 100
Set [83 22] 100
Set [85 22] 100
Set [88 22] 100
Set [90 22] 100
Set [92 22] 100
Set [94 22] 100
Set [1 21] 100
Set [5 21] 100
Set [7 21] 100
Set [10 21] 100
Set [13 21] 100
Set [15 21] 100
Set [16 21] 100
Set [18 21] 100
Set [20 21] 100
Set [21 21] 100
Set [22 21] 100
Set [23 21] 100
Set [24 21] 100
Set [25 21] 100
Set [26 21] 100
Set [27 21] 100
Set [30 21] 100
Set [32 21] 100
Set [33 21] 100
Set [35 21] 100
Set [40 21] 100
Set [42 21] 100
Set [49 21] 100
Set [51 21] 100
Set [58 21] 100
Set [60 21] 100
Set [66 21] 100
Set [68 21] 100
Set [70 21] 100
Set [72 21] 100
Set [73 21] 100
Set [74 21] 100
Set [75 21] 100
Set [76 21] 100
Set [78 21] 100
Set [80 21] 100
Set [81 21] 100
Set [83 21] 100
Set [85 21] 100
Set [86 21] 100
Set [88 21] 100
Set [90 21] 100
Set [94 21] 100
Set [96 21] 100
Set [2 20] 100
Set [3 20] 100
Set [7 20] 100
Set [8 20] 100
Set [10 20] 100
Set [12 20] 100
Set [13 20] 100
Set [14 20] 100
Set [15 20] 100
Set [16 20] 100
Set [17 20] 100
Set [18 20] 100
Set [19 20] 100
Set [21 20] 100
Set [22 20] 100
Set [23 20] 100
Set [24 20] 100
Set [25 20] 100
Set [26 20] 100
Set [27 20] 100
Set [32 20] 100
Set [36 20] 100
Set [38 20] 100
Set [44 20] 100
Set [53 20] 100
Set [64 20] 100
Set [66 20] 100
Set [70 20] 100
Set [72 20] 100
Set [73 20] 100
Set [74 20] 100
Set [75 20] 100
Set [76 20] 100
Set [77 20] 100
Set [78 20] 100
Set [80 20] 100
Set [81 20] 100
Set [83 20] 100
Set [84 20] 100
Set [86 20] 100
Set [90 20] 100
Set [92 20] 100
Set [96 20] 100
Set [1 19] 100
Set [5 19] 100
Set [9 19] 100
Set [11 19] 100
Set [14 19] 100
Set [19 19] 100
Set [22 19] 100
Set [23 19] 100
Set [25 19] 100
Set [27 19] 100
Set [28 19] 100
Set [30 19] 100
Set [33 19] 100
Set [46 19] 100
Set [48 19] 100
Set [65 19] 100
Set [71 19] 100
Set [72 19] 100
Set [73 19] 100
Set [74 19] 100
Set [76 19] 100
Set [78 19] 100
Set [82 19] 100
Set [84 19] 100
Set [86 19] 100
Set [88 19] 100
Set [91 19] 100
Set [94 19] 100
Set [97 19] 100
Set [4 18] 100
Set [7 18] 100
Set [10 18] 100
Set [12 18] 100
Set [13 18] 100
Set [15 18] 100
Set [16 18] 100
Set [17 18] 100
Set [18 18] 100
Set [20 18] 100
Set [21 18] 100
Set [23 18] 100
Set [24 18] 100
Set [25 18] 100
Set [26 18] 100
Set [29 18] 100
Set [32 18] 100
Set [33 18] 100
Set [35 18] 100
Set [37 18] 100
Set [39 18] 100
Set [40 18] 100
Set [42 18] 100
Set [44 18] 100
Set [47 18] 100
Set [50 18] 100
Set [52 18] 100
Set [56 18] 100
Set [58 18] 100
Set [60 18] 100
Set [62 18] 100
Set [65 18] 100
Set [67 18] 100
Set [68 18] 100
Set [70 18] 100
Set [72 18] 100
Set [73 18] 100
Set [75 18] 100
Set [76 18] 100
Set [77 18] 100
Set [78 18] 100
Set [80 18] 100
Set [82 18] 100
Set [83 18] 100
Set [85 18] 100
Set [87 18] 100
Set [89 18] 100
Set [90 18] 100
Set [93 18] 100
Set [98 18] 100
Set [1 17] 100
Set [2 17] 100
Set [5 17] 100
Set [7 17] 100
Set [8 17] 100
Set [11 17] 100
Set [13 17] 100
Set [14 17] 100
Set [15 17] 100
Set [18 17] 100
Set [21 17] 100
Set [22 17] 100
Set [24 17] 100
Set [25 17] 100
Set [26 17] 100
Set [27 17] 100
Set [30 17] 100
Set [33 17] 100
Set [40 17] 100
Set [45 17] 100
Set [48 17] 100
Set [49 17] 100
Set [51 17] 100
Set [54 17] 100
Set [58 17] 100
Set [62 17] 100
Set [66 17] 100
Set [70 17] 100
Set [73 17] 100
Set [74 17] 100
Set [75 17] 100
Set [79 17] 100
Set [83 17] 100
Set [84 17] 100
Set [86 17] 100
Set [91 17] 100
Set [95 17] 100
Set [3 16] 100
Set [5 16] 100
Set [8 16] 100
Set [9 16] 100
Set [11 16] 100
Set [13 16] 100
Set [15 16] 100
Set [16 16] 100
Set [18 16] 100
Set [22 16] 100
Set [25 16] 100
Set [27 16] 100
Set [30 16] 100
Set [33 16] 100
Set [35 16] 100
Set [37 16] 100
Set [41 16] 100
Set [43 16] 100
Set [45 16] 100
Set [47 16] 100
Set [49 16] 100
Set [51 16] 100
Set [52 16] 100
Set [55 16] 100
Set [59 16] 100
Set [62 16] 100
Set [67 16] 100
Set [70 16] 100
Set [71 16] 100
Set [72 16] 100
Set [75 16] 100
Set [76 16] 100
Set [77 16] 100
Set [79 16] 100
Set [81 16] 100
Set [84 16] 100
Set [86 16] 100
Set [87 16] 100
Set [88 16] 100
Set [91 16] 100
Set [92 16] 100
Set [97 16] 100
Set [0 15] 100
Set [2 15] 100
Set [7 15] 100
Set [10 15] 100
Set [12 15] 100
Set [14 15] 100
Set [17 15] 100
Set [19 15] 100
Set [21 15] 100
Set [23 15] 100
Set [24 15] 100
Set [26 15] 100
Set [27 15] 100
Set [28 15] 100
Set [30 15] 100
Set [31 15] 100
Set [38 15] 100
Set [42 15] 100
Set [48 15] 100
Set [53 15] 100
Set [55 15] 100
Set [57 15] 100
Set [64 15] 100
Set [67 15] 100
Set [68 15] 100
Set [72 15] 100
Set [73 15] 100
Set [80 15] 100
Set [83 15] 100
Set [85 15] 100
Set [89 15] 100
Set [93 15] 100
Set [99 15] 100
Set [1 14] 100
Set [4 14] 100
Set [5 14] 100
Set [7 14] 100
Set [9 14] 100
Set [11 14] 100
Set [13 14] 100
Set [15 14] 100
Set [16 14] 100
Set [20 14] 100
Set [24 14] 100
Set [26 14] 100
Set [29 14] 100
Set [31 14] 100
Set [33 14] 100
Set [36 14] 100
Set [40 14] 100
Set [44 14] 100
Set [46 14] 100
Set [47 14] 100
Set [49 14] 100
Set [50 14] 100
Set [52 14] 100
Set [55 14] 100
Set [60 14] 100
Set [62 14] 100
Set [66 14] 100
Set [69 14] 100
Set [70 14] 100
Set [71 14] 100
Set [75 14] 100
Set [76 14] 100
Set [78 14] 100
Set [82 14] 100
Set [86 14] 100
Set [88 14] 100
Set [90 14] 100
Set [91 14] 100
Set [94 14] 100
Set [96 14] 100
Set [2 13] 100
Set [5 13] 100
Set [7 13] 100
Set [9 13] 100
Set [11 13] 100
Set [13 13] 100
Set [14 13] 100
Set [17 13] 100
Set [18 13] 100
Set [21 13] 100
Set [22 13] 100
Set [25 13] 100
Set [27 13] 100
Set [28 13] 100
Set [30 13] 100
Set [34 13] 100
Set [37 13] 100
Set [39 13] 100
Set [42 13] 100
Set [44 13] 100
Set [48 13] 100
Set [50 13] 100
Set [53 13] 100
Set [56 13] 100
Set [63 13] 100
Set [67 13] 100
Set [71 13] 100
Set [73 13] 100
Set [80 13] 100
Set [83 13] 100
Set [84 13] 100
Set [87 13] 100
Set [92 13] 100
Set [94 13] 100
Set [1 12] 100
Set [3 12] 100
Set [7 12] 100
Set [9 12] 100
Set [11 12] 100
Set [14 12] 100
Set [15 12] 100
Set [18 12] 100
Set [22 12] 100
Set [25 12] 100
Set [28 12] 100
Set [30 12] 100
Set [31 12] 100
Set [32 12] 100
Set [34 12] 100
Set [36 12] 100
Set [39 12] 100
Set [42 12] 100
Set [44 12] 100
Set [46 12] 100
Set [48 12] 100
Set [50 12] 100
Set [51 12] 100
Set [53 12] 100
Set [56 12] 100
Set [58 12] 100
Set [61 12] 100
Set [63 12] 100
Set [65 12] 100
Set [67 12] 100
Set [68 12] 100
Set [75 12] 100
Set [77 12] 100
```

```
Set [81 12] 100
Set [84 12] 100
Set [85 12] 100
Set [87 12] 100
Set [89 12] 100
Set [91 12] 100
Set [95 12] 100
Set [4 11] 100
Set [6 11] 100
Set [8 11] 100
Set [10 11] 100
Set [12 11] 100
Set [15 11] 100
Set [19 11] 100
Set [23 11] 100
Set [25 11] 100
Set [27 11] 100
Set [32 11] 100
Set [34 11] 100
Set [35 11] 100
Set [37 11] 100
Set [39 11] 100
Set [40 11] 100
Set [42 11] 100
Set [44 11] 100
Set [45 11] 100
Set [47 11] 100
Set [49 11] 100
Set [51 11] 100
Set [53 11] 100
Set [54 11] 100
Set [56 11] 100
Set [59 11] 100
Set [61 11] 100
Set [64 11] 100
Set [66 11] 100
Set [73 11] 100
Set [79 11] 100
Set [82 11] 100
Set [86 11] 100
Set [88 11] 100
Set [90 11] 100
Set [93 11] 100
Set [97 11] 100
Set [0 10] 100
Set [1 10] 100
Set [3 10] 100
Set [5 10] 100
Set [6 10] 100
Set [9 10] 100
Set [11 10] 100
Set [13 10] 100
Set [16 10] 100
Set [17 10] 100
Set [20 10] 100
Set [22 10] 100
Set [28 10] 100
Set [30 10] 100
Set [31 10] 100
Set [33 10] 100
Set [36 10] 100
Set [38 10] 100
Set [41 10] 100
Set [43 10] 100
Set [46 10] 100
Set [48 10] 100
Set [50 10] 100
Set [52 10] 100
Set [55 10] 100
Set [57 10] 100
Set [60 10] 100
Set [63 10] 100
Set [80 10] 100
Set [84 10] 100
Set [88 10] 100
Set [91 10] 100
Set [92 10] 100
Set [96 10] 100
Set [99 10] 100
Set [2 9] 100
Set [7 9] 100
Set [9 9] 100
Set [11 9] 100
Set [12 9] 100
Set [14 9] 100
Set [18 9] 100
Set [22 9] 100
Set [24 9] 100
Set [26 9] 100
Set [28 9] 100
Set [31 9] 100
Set [34 9] 100
Set [35 9] 100
Set [37 9] 100
Set [39 9] 100
Set [41 9] 100
Set [43 9] 100
Set [44 9] 100
Set [46 9] 100
Set [48 9] 100
Set [50 9] 100
Set [51 9] 100
Set [53 9] 100
Set [54 9] 100
Set [56 9] 100
Set [58 9] 100
Set [61 9] 100
Set [62 9] 100
Set [64 9] 100
Set [68 9] 100
Set [70 9] 100
Set [75 9] 100
Set [77 9] 100
Set [82 9] 100
Set [85 9] 100
Set [86 9] 100
Set [89 9] 100
Set [92 9] 100
Set [94 9] 100
Set [97 9] 100
Set [0 8] 100
Set [2 8] 100
Set [3 8] 100
Set [5 8] 100
Set [7 8] 100
Set [9 8] 100
Set [12 8] 100
Set [15 8] 100
Set [19 8] 100
Set [24 8] 100
Set [28 8] 100
Set [32 8] 100
Set [37 8] 100
Set [39 8] 100
Set [44 8] 100
Set [46 8] 100
Set [48 8] 100
Set [51 8] 100
Set [54 8] 100
Set [56 8] 100
Set [59 8] 100
Set [64 8] 100
Set [66 8] 100
Set [79 8] 100
Set [83 8] 100
Set [87 8] 100
Set [90 8] 100
Set [4 7] 100
Set [5 7] 100
Set [8 7] 100
Set [10 7] 100
Set [13 7] 100
Set [14 7] 100
Set [16 7] 100
Set [20 7] 100
Set [22 7] 100
Set [26 7] 100
Set [29 7] 100
Set [31 7] 100
Set [34 7] 100
Set [36 7] 100
Set [40 7] 100
Set [41 7] 100
Set [43 7] 100
Set [46 7] 100
Set [48 7] 100
Set [50 7] 100
Set [52 7] 100
Set [55 7] 100
Set [57 7] 100
Set [60 7] 100
Set [62 7] 100
Set [71 7] 100
Set [81 7] 100
Set [84 7] 100
Set [86 7] 100
Set [88 7] 100
Set [91 7] 100
Set [92 7] 100
Set [94 7] 100
Set [97 7] 100
Set [0 6] 100
Set [2 6] 100
Set [3 6] 100
Set [6 6] 100
Set [8 6] 100
Set [11 6] 100
Set [12 6] 100
Set [16 6] 100
Set [18 6] 100
Set [23 6] 100
Set [25 6] 100
Set [27 6] 100
Set [29 6] 100
Set [32 6] 100
Set [34 6] 100
Set [39 6] 100
Set [42 6] 100
Set [44 6] 100
Set [45 6] 100
Set [47 6] 100
Set [51 6] 100
Set [53 6] 100
Set [59 6] 100
Set [64 6] 100
Set [67 6] 100
Set [69 6] 100
Set [77 6] 100
Set [79 6] 100
Set [85 6] 100
Set [89 6] 100
Set [93 6] 100
Set [95 6] 100
Set [99 6] 100
Set [0 5] 100
Set [4 5] 100
Set [6 5] 100
Set [8 5] 100
Set [10 5] 100
Set [13 5] 100
Set [14 5] 100
Set [18 5] 100
Set [20 5] 100
Set [28 5] 100
Set [30 5] 100
Set [33 5] 100
Set [35 5] 100
Set [36 5] 100
Set [37 5] 100
Set [41 5] 100
Set [46 5] 100
Set [48 5] 100
Set [49 5] 100
Set [52 5] 100
Set [54 5] 100
Set [56 5] 100
Set [57 5] 100
Set [60 5] 100
Set [62 5] 100
Set [65 5] 100
Set [72 5] 100
Set [80 5] 100
Set [82 5] 100
Set [87 5] 100
Set [89 5] 100
Set [91 5] 100
Set [97 5] 100
Set [1 4] 100
Set [2 4] 100
Set [4 4] 100
Set [6 4] 100
Set [8 4] 100
Set [10 4] 100
Set [11 4] 100
Set [14 4] 100
Set [16 4] 100
Set [21 4] 100
Set [23 4] 100
Set [25 4] 100
Set [29 4] 100
Set [31 4] 100
Set [33 4] 100
Set [37 4] 100
Set [38 4] 100
Set [39 4] 100
Set [41 4] 100
Set [42 4] 100
Set [43 4] 100
Set [45 4] 100
Set [49 4] 100
Set [50 4] 100
Set [52 4] 100
Set [54 4] 100
Set [57 4] 100
Set [58 4] 100
Set [60 4] 100
Set [62 4] 100
Set [66 4] 100
Set [68 4] 100
Set [83 4] 100
Set [85 4] 100
Set [89 4] 100
Set [92 4] 100
Set [94 4] 100
Set [98 4] 100
Set [1 3] 100
Set [4 3] 100
Set [7 3] 100
Set [9 3] 100
Set [12 3] 100
Set [17 3] 100
Set [19 3] 100
Set [24 3] 100
Set [26 3] 100
Set [30 3] 100
Set [34 3] 100
Set [35 3] 100
Set [40 3] 100
Set [43 3] 100
Set [45 3] 100
Set [46 3] 100
Set [47 3] 100
Set [49 3] 100
Set [51 3] 100
Set [53 3] 100
Set [55 3] 100
Set [56 3] 100
Set [58 3] 100
Set [60 3] 100
Set [62 3] 100
Set [63 3] 100
Set [73 3] 100
Set [86 3] 100
Set [88 3] 100
Set [90 3] 100
Set [93 3] 100
Set [95 3] 100
Set [0 2] 100
Set [3 2] 100
Set [5 2] 100
Set [6 2] 100
Set [8 2] 100
Set [10 2] 100
Set [13 2] 100
Set [14 2] 100
Set [16 2] 100
Set [21 2] 100
Set [23 2] 100
Set [28 2] 100
Set [29 2] 100
Set [31 2] 100
Set [32 2] 100
Set [33 2] 100
Set [36 2] 100
Set [37 2] 100
Set [38 2] 100
Set [39 2] 100
Set [41 2] 100
Set [42 2] 100
Set [44 2] 100
Set [48 2] 100
Set [52 2] 100
Set [54 2] 100
Set [57 2] 100
Set [60 2] 100
Set [63 2] 100
Set [65 2] 100
Set [66 2] 100
Set [69 2] 100
Set [74 2] 100
Set [76 2] 100
Set [79 2] 100
Set [87 2] 100
Set [90 2] 100
Set [92 2] 100
Set [97 2] 100
Set [99 2] 100
Set [0 1] 100
Set [1 1] 100
Set [3 1] 100
Set [6 1] 100
Set [8 1] 100
Set [11 1] 100
Set [14 1] 100
Set [18 1] 100
Set [24 1] 100
Set [26 1] 100
Set [34 1] 100
Set [39 1] 100
Set [42 1] 100
Set [44 1] 100
Set [45 1] 100
Set [46 1] 100
Set [48 1] 100
Set [49 1] 100
Set [50 1] 100
Set [52 1] 100
Set [53 1] 100
Set [55 1] 100
Set [56 1] 100
Set [58 1] 100
Set [59 1] 100
Set [61 1] 100
Set [66 1] 100
Set [70 1] 100
Set [80 1] 100
Set [82 1] 100
Set [84 1] 100
Set [87 1] 100
Set [91 1] 100
Set [93 1] 100
Set [95 1] 100
Set [1 0] 100
Set [3 0] 100
Set [4 0] 100
Set [7 0] 100
Set [9 0] 100
Set [11 0] 100
Set [14 0] 100
Set [16 0] 100
Set [19 0] 100
Set [22 0] 100
Set [26 0] 100
Set [28 0] 100
Set [30 0] 100
Set [32 0] 100
Set [34 0] 100
Set [36 0] 100
Set [37 0] 100
Set [40 0] 100
Set [43 0] 100
Set [46 0] 100
Set [49 0] 100
Set [53 0] 100
Set [56 0] 100
Set [60 0] 100
Set [62 0] 100
Set [67 0] 100
Set [88 0] 100
Set [92 0] 100
Set [96 0] 100
Set [98 0] 100
// done rie face
```

Individually assigning each dot on the grid is a natural task for the super-realist painter, but you could probably make better use of your time. Creating carefully shaded graphics out of dots can result in an image of superior quality, but requires a disproportionate amount of time and labor. As you learned in Chapters 6 and 7, the right computational construct can help you avoid repeating tedious commands. Chapter 9 discusses a more sophisticated form of repetition.

Copy Dots I mentioned earlier that setting a dot fundamentally differs from drawing a Line that starts and ends at the same point. A reference to a dot is equivalent to a variable. You can use the value stored at a dot in the same manner that you set a dot. For example, you can place the gray value at [0 0] into a variable A. If nothing is drawn, this value will just be the numerical shade of the paper.

```
Paper 100
// A is acquired from what is displayed
// which is in this case, 'black'
Set A [0 0]
```

The value of variable A is 100, which you can verify by drawing a line that incorporates A.

```
Paper 100
Set A [0 0]
Pen 0
// a line determined by paper tone
Line 50 0 50 A
```

The line extends from 0 to 100 vertically. A modification to the shade of the paper shade now indirectly changes the line's height.

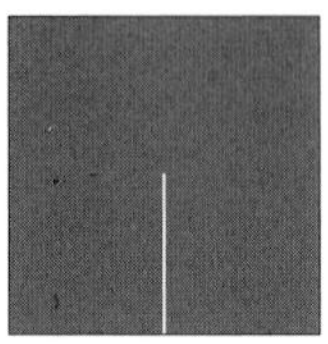

```
Paper 50
Set A [0 0]
Pen 0
// line is shortened by lightening
// the tone of the paper
Line 50 0 50 A
```

The variable A can be removed by simply relating the line directly to the dot on the paper.

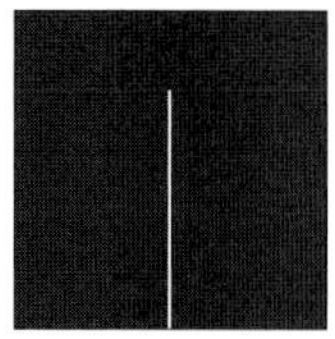

```
Paper 75
Pen 0
// removing one intermediate step
Line 50 0 50 [0 0]
```

A dot can be the object of a calculation.

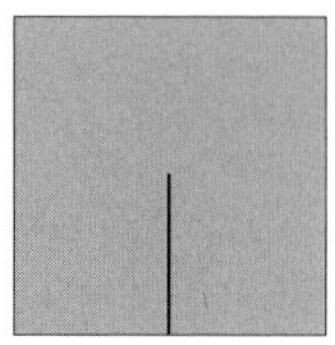

```
Paper 25
Pen 100
// calculation using dot value
Line 50 0 50 ([0 0]*2)
```

And it can also include calculations.

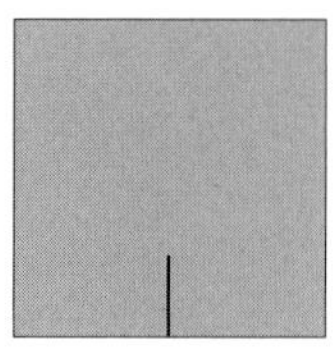

```
Paper 25
Pen 100
// dot position by calculation
Line 50 0 50 ([([0 0]*2) 0])
```

Dots are variables that express their values in a visual manner. For instance, a process like copying a stream of variables is easily visualized.

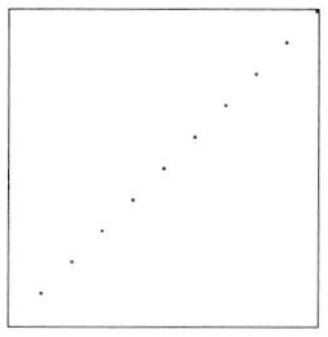

```
Paper 0
Set [10 10] 100
// pass the dot value on ...
Set [20 20] [10 10]
Set [30 30] [20 20]
Set [40 40] [30 30]
Set [50 50] [40 40]
Set [60 60] [50 50]
Set [70 70] [60 60]
Set [80 80] [70 70]
Set [90 90] [80 80]
Set [100 100] [90 90]
```

Successively decreasing the copied value results in a subtle effect.

```
Paper 0
Set [10 10] 100
// decrease by 10 each copy step
Set [20 20] ([10 10]-10)
Set [30 30] ([20 20]-10)
Set [40 40] ([30 30]-10)
Set [50 50] ([40 40]-10)
Set [60 60] ([50 50]-10)
Set [70 70] ([60 60]-10)
Set [80 80] ([70 70]-10)
Set [90 90] ([80 80]-10)
Set [100 100] ([90 90]-10)
```

Again, changing the initial value of the copy directly affects the rest of the variables.

```
Paper 0
// change the starting value to 50
Set [10 10] 50
Set [20 20] ([10 10]-10)
Set [30 30] ([20 20]-10)
Set [40 40] ([30 30]-10)
Set [50 50] ([40 40]-10)
Set [60 60] ([50 50]-10)
Set [70 70] ([60 60]-10)
Set [80 80] ([70 70]-10)
Set [90 90] ([80 80]-10)
Set [100 100] ([90 90]-10)
```

Numbers can flow through a program in many roundabout ways, flitting behind conventional variables and appearing in the shade of a dot. A more visual (versus textual) language would show this flow much clearer; however, your imagination should be more than sufficient to visualize the flow of numbers through a code.

```
Paper 0
// copy the dot at 50 50 to A
Set A [50 50]
// Set a dot in relation to A
Set [(A/2) 100] 50
Set [100 (A/2)] 0
Set [(A/4) (A/4)] 25
// copy the dot at 25 25 to B
Set B [25 25]
// Set a dot in relation to B
Set [(B*2) 75] 50
Set [75 (B*2)] 0
// Set a dot in relation to A and B
Set [(A/2) (B*2)] 0
```

```
Paper 25
// copy the dot at 50 50 to A
Set A [50 50]
// Set a dot in relation to A
Set [(A/2) 100] 50
Set [100 (A/2)] 0
Set [(A/4) (A/4)] 25
// copy the dot at 25 25 to B
Set B [25 25]
// Set a dot in relation to B
Set [(B*2) 75] 50
Set [75 (B*2)] 0
// Set a dot in relation to A and B
Set [(A/2) (B*2)] 0
```

```
Paper 50
// copy the dot at 50 50 to A
Set A [50 50]
// Set a dot in relation to A
Set [(A/2) 100] 50
Set [100 (A/2)] 0
Set [(A/4) (A/4)] 25
// copy the dot at 25 25 to B
Set B [25 25]
// Set a dot in relation to B
Set [(B*2) 75] 50
Set [75 (B*2)] 0
// Set a dot in relation to A and B
Set [(A/2) (B*2)] 0
```

```
Paper 75
// copy the dot at 50 50 to A
Set A [50 50]
// Set a dot in relation to A
Set [(A/2) 100] 50
Set [100 (A/2)] 0
Set [(A/4) (A/4)] 25
// copy the dot at 25 25 to B
Set B [25 25]
// Set a dot in relation to B
Set [(B*2) 75] 50
Set [75 (B*2)] 0
// Set a dot in relation to A and B
Set [(A/2) (B*2)] 0
```

Sometimes all of the numbers line up, and a hidden process is revealed.

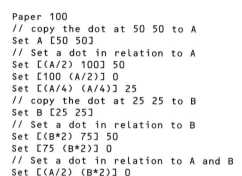

```
Paper 100
// copy the dot at 50 50 to A
Set A [50 50]
// Set a dot in relation to A
Set [(A/2) 100] 50
Set [100 (A/2)] 0
Set [(A/4) (A/4)] 25
// copy the dot at 25 25 to B
Set B [25 25]
// Set a dot in relation to B
Set [(B*2) 75] 50
Set [75 (B*2)] 0
// Set a dot in relation to A and B
Set [(A/2) (B*2)] 0
```

Summary Dots make up the basic fabric of any visible computational expression. Each dot is a variable with visible properties that, when set to a number between 0 and 100, will assume a corresponding shade of gray. A dot represents the smallest mark that can be left on a page, composed of a precise grid of 101 by 101 individual dots. Thus our paper is occasionally described as a set of neatly arranged, adjustable lightbulbs rather than a weave of absorptive fibers, as with actual paper.

9 DOTS As we have seen, visual expression with many dots produces images with a distinctly different character than those produced using the Line command. Because Set-ing one dot corresponds to one line of program code, Set-ing many dots would imply the necessity for many lines of code. Computation is the process of reducing labor-intensive, repetitive processes into simple expressions of code so it should seem logical that the need to manipulate systems of many dots could be efficiently addressed with a well-designed program.

A graphical form created by a computational process begins as a core system of numerical constraints that are either fixed, or left to vary. When left to vary, the form can be placed within a Repeat that endows the form with malleability over a specified range. Incorporating numerical operations permits refinement of position and tone, which can also be fixed or left to vary. A dot is the purest manifestation of all three numerical parameters of visual inquiry: horizontal position, vertical position, and the tone value at that position. Collections of dots, when left to vary within a Repeat, reveal the visual breadth of computational drawing.

Dots in Repeat A line that varies in one dimension may form a rectangle or a triangle when placed within a Repeat. A dot that varies in one dimension when placed into a Repeat produces a horizontal or vertical line.

```
Paper 0
// horizontal left to vary
Repeat A 0 100
{
  Set [A 50] 100
}
```

```
Paper 0
// vertical left to vary
Repeat A 0 100
{
  Set [50 A] 100
}
```

Allowing variation in two dimensions produces a diagonal line.

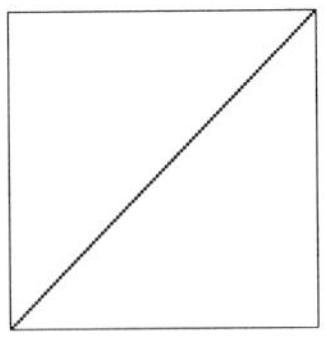

```
Paper 0
// horizontal & vertical left to vary
Repeat A 0 100
{
   Set [A A] 100
}
```

The Repeat is emphasized by individually Set-ing the shade of each dot.

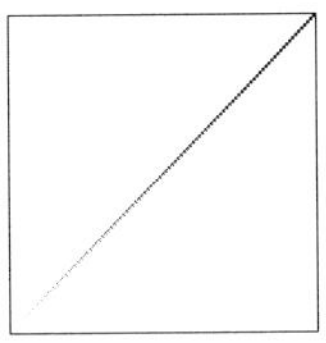

```
Paper 0
// value left to vary
Repeat A 0 100
{
   Set [A A] A
}
```

The angle at which the diagonal rises can be modified by changing the ratio of the horizontal to the vertical dimensions. You can draw a steeper line by decreasing the horizontal dimension, as in the following example.

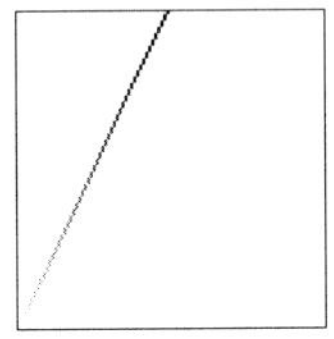

```
Paper 0
// horizontal step scaled by 50%
Repeat A 0 100
{
   Set [(A/2) A] A
}
```

Accordingly, the position of the line can be adjusted by adding a constant to the horizontal or vertical dimension.

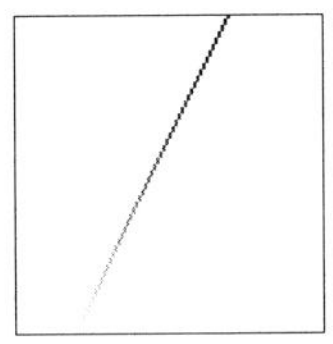

```
Paper 0
// shited horizontally
Repeat A 0 100
{
   Set [((A/2)+20) A] A
}
```

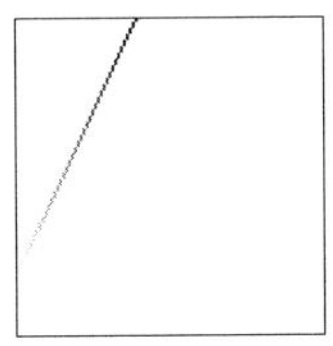

```
Paper 0
// shifted vertically
Repeat A 0 100
{
   Set [(A/2) (A+20)] A
}
```

A simple adjustment of the domain of the Repeat over the calculations performed produces a variety of lines.

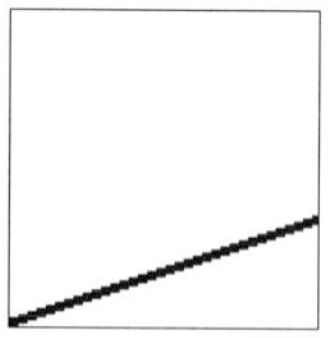

```
Paper 0
// thick Line
Repeat A 0 100
{
   Set [A (A/3)] 100
   Set [A (1+(A/3))] 100
   Set [A (2+(A/3))] 100
}
```

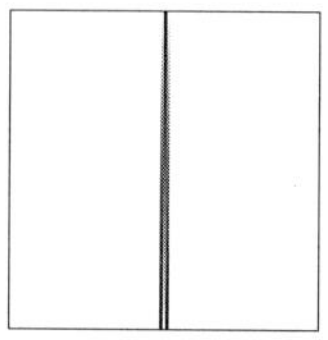

```
Paper 0
// sharp needle
Repeat A 0 100
{
   Set [50 A] A
   Set [51 A] (100-A)
   Set [49 A] (100-A)
}
```

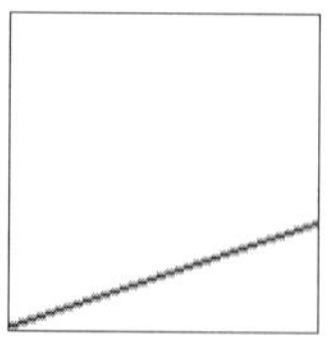

```
Paper 0
// anti-aliased style Line
Repeat A 0 100
{
   Set [A (2+(A/3))] 20
   Set [A (1+(A/3))] 70
   Set [A (A/3)] 20
}
```

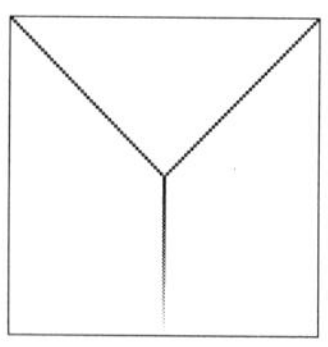

```
Paper 0
// why?
Repeat A 0 50
{
   Set [A (100-A)] 100
   Set [(100-A) (100-A)] 100
   Set [50 A] (A*2)
}
```

How do these lines differ from those created with Line? While they are similar, Line is significantly more clever because it has been programmed with a more sophisticated technique, or algorithm, for drawing a line than just a Repeat of the Set command for a dot. Compare the two lines.

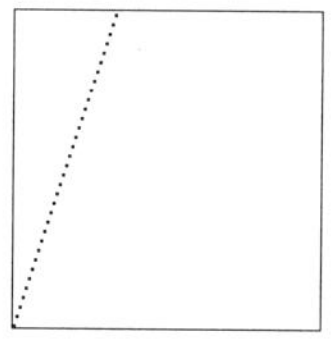

```
Paper 0
// dotted Lines
Repeat A 0 33
{
   Set [A (A*3)] 100
}
```

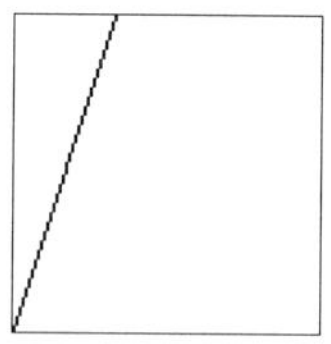

```
Paper 0
Pen 100
// a real line
Line 0 0 33 100
```

Before we lament the primitive state of our method of drawing a line versus the superior Line command, we should celebrate the addition of the dotted line to our vocabulary by drawing a few more variations of the dotted line.

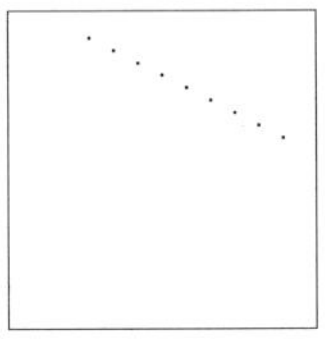

```
Paper 0
// flaunting the dots
Repeat A 2 10
{
  Set [(10+A*8) (100-A*4)] 100
}
```

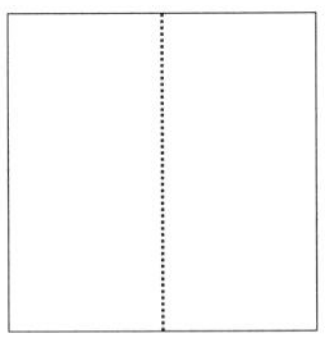

```
Paper 0
// basic vertical dotted line
Repeat A 0 50
{
  Set [50 (A*2)] 100
}
```

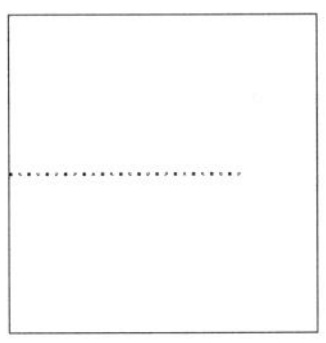

```
Paper 0
// subtle patterning
Repeat A 0 12
{
  Set [(3+A*6) 50] 50
  Set [(A*6) 50] 100
}
```

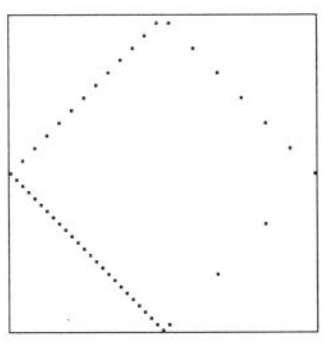

```
Paper 0
// multiple dot frequencies
Repeat A 0 25
{
  Set [(A*4) (50+A*4)] 100
  Set [(A*2) (50-A*2)] 100
  Set [(100-A*8) (50+A*8)] 100
  Set [(100-A*16) (50-A*16)] 100
}
```

When working within the constraints of the Line command, it probably never occurred to you to draw a dotted line. Reliance on an existing high-level primitive such as Line creates a certain model of thinking. Understanding the medium and speaking to it at its innermost level always results in discovery of new possibilities. But there is always a misguided use for a good tool; patching those unsightly holes connecting the dots is an example of overkill.

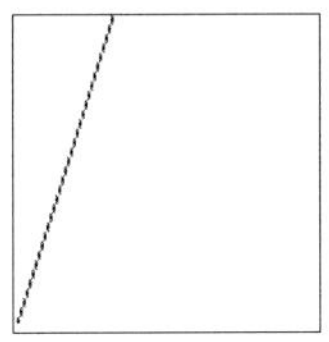

```
Paper 0
// connect the dots
Repeat A 1 33
{
  Pen 50
  Line A (A*3) (A+1) ((A+1)*3)
  Set [A (A*3)] 100
}
```

Draw a Curve A variety of lines can be rendered with a Repeat construct and by the Set of dots within the Repeat. Although some deviations from a plain linear form have been shown with gradated and dotted lines, there appears to be a conflict in my promise at the start of Chapter 8 that drawing with dots should always lead you away from the Line primitive. You may suspect that you are just back to drawing lines again. To confuse matters, much more work is required to draw a line using dots.

Line is a tool that knows how to draw a line in the medium. Repeat is an abstract tool for constructing processes that repeat. Dots, which store the values for a location and the tonal value there, are neither tool nor process but the medium itself. Therefore, you can deduce that Line is a tool that must be built on top of an abstract computational tool like Repeat that interacts with the medium of dots. In other words, if you could open up the box that holds the magic of the Line command, you would see familiar parts like a Repeat and manipulations of dots. But a line is not the only artifact of a Repeat of dots.

In the previous section, the horizontal and vertical position of the dot that is set within the Repeat was translated or scaled by some constant factor. When one of the dimensions is multiplied by itself, the results can be intriguing.

```
Paper 0
// no longer just a dotted line
Repeat A 0 100
{
   Set [A (A*A)] 100
}
```

The line is no longer straight but appears to be a bent, dotted line. A scaling factor can make the shape more evident.

```
Paper 0
// zooming in ...
Repeat A 0 100
{
   Set [A (A*A/200)] 100
}
```

Now what you see is not a line but a curve. Applying more calculations places more of the curve in view.

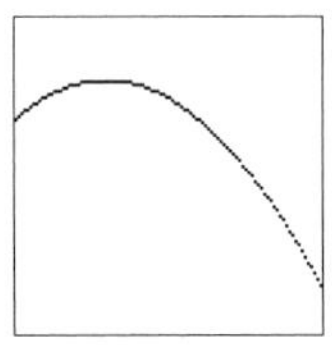

```
Paper 0
// adjusting the focus ...
Repeat A 0 100
{
   Set B (30-A)
   Set [A (80-B*B/75)] 100
}
```

Adjusting the various scale and translation factors changes the shape of the curve. If there were a curve in your mind that you wished to draw, you could eventually fit the curve with the right team of numbers. This is the general idea behind adjusting the points on the ubiquitous Bezier curve found in digital illustration software.

A distribution of values on a curve, when displayed in the tonal dimension, creates an effect that is subtly different from a line.

```
Paper 0
// showing nonlinear tonal gradation
Repeat A 0 100
{
  Set [A 55]  (A*A/100)
  Set [A 45] A
}
```

The difference is more pronounced when the visual density is expanded.

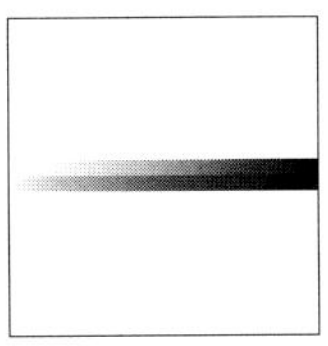

```
Paper 0
// increasing line density
Repeat A 0 100
{
  Set [A 55] (A*A/100)
  Set [A 54] [A 55]
  Set [A 53] [A 55]
  Set [A 52] [A 55]
  Set [A 51] [A 55]
  Set [A 50] A
  Set [A 49] A
  Set [A 48] A
  Set [A 47] A
  Set [A 46] A
}
```

Line is nothing more than a quick way to set a series of many dots. Distinguishing between a drawing composed of lines as opposed to dots does not make any sense because you are essentially comparing dots to dots.

Beware of Zero Playing with numbers as pure abstractions can be a rather forgiving exercise. Programming, on the other hand, can be quite hazardous when numbers are treated without proper respect. You may have already stumbled upon this when trying to execute a carefully crafted Repeat: numbers, for example, do not respond well when divided by zero.
In daily life, you rarely make the effort to divide something into zero parts; the situation never arises. On the computer, though, you can easily stumble into this common trap when innocently constructing a simple calculation. Consider drawing a line.

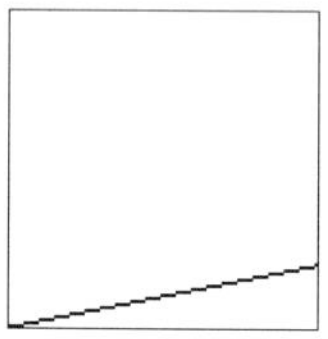

```
Paper 0
// draw a line
Repeat A 0 100
{
  Set [A (A/5)] 100
}
```

Curiosity forces you to change the divide to multiply, revealing a dotted line.

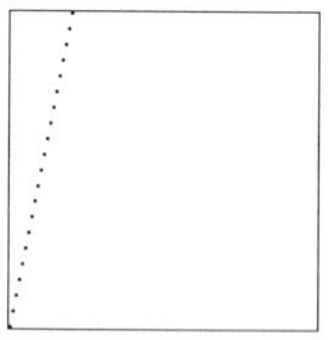

```
Paper 0
// draw a dotted line
Repeat A 0 100
{
  Set [A (A*5)] 100
}
```

Charged by this small success, you go back to the original and move quantities around.

```
Paper 0
// exchange position for value
Repeat A 0 100
{
  Set [100 (A/5)] A
}
```

Then before you know it, you experiment.

```
Paper 0
// wonder what this does ... ?
Repeat A 0 100
{
  Set [A (5/A)] 100
}
```

And the program does not execute.

In the old days, computers would crash while attempting to execute the above program. But today's computers are a bit more forgiving and will only give you an error message. Where is the problem? The computer attempted to divide by zero. This act is obscured by the Repeat, but when A assumes the value 0, the Set becomes "Set [0 (5/0)] 100." Why is it wrong to divide by zero? Plotting the rest of the values helps to illustrate why. The Repeat is fixed by starting from 1 instead of 0.

Expanding the range clarifies the situation.

```
Paper 0
// some detective work
Repeat A 1 100
{
  Set [A (5/A)] 100
}
```

```
Paper 0
// zoom in
Repeat A 1 100
{
  Set [A (50/A)] 100
}
```

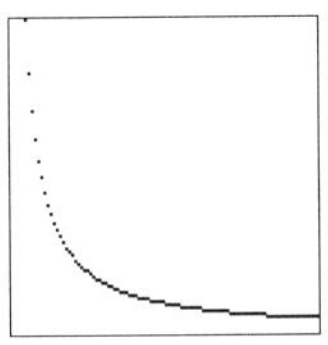

```
Paper 0
// even further
Repeat A 1 100
{
  Set [A (500/A)] 100
}
```

When you mentally project upward where the curve should be heading, the answer, you can guess, is somewhere quite high. In fact, the curve extends to infinity. We humans can at least cope with the concept of infinity in a vague sense. Computers, on the other hand, are usually not programmed to handle infinity.

Summary Either a line or a curve is traced out by a dot that is set in a Repeat. The position, orientation, and, in the case of a curve, shape, are adjusted with pertinent calculations. An occasional by-product of the process is a dotted effect where the line or curve is not continuous. In such cases, you can either correct the situation by connecting the dots with the Line command or you can choose to take advantage of the unique qualities of a dotted form.

The fact that a dotted line can be created using a Repeat distinguishes the resulting line from the result of using the Line command. You now know the general computational process that underlies Line but there are finer details to learn.

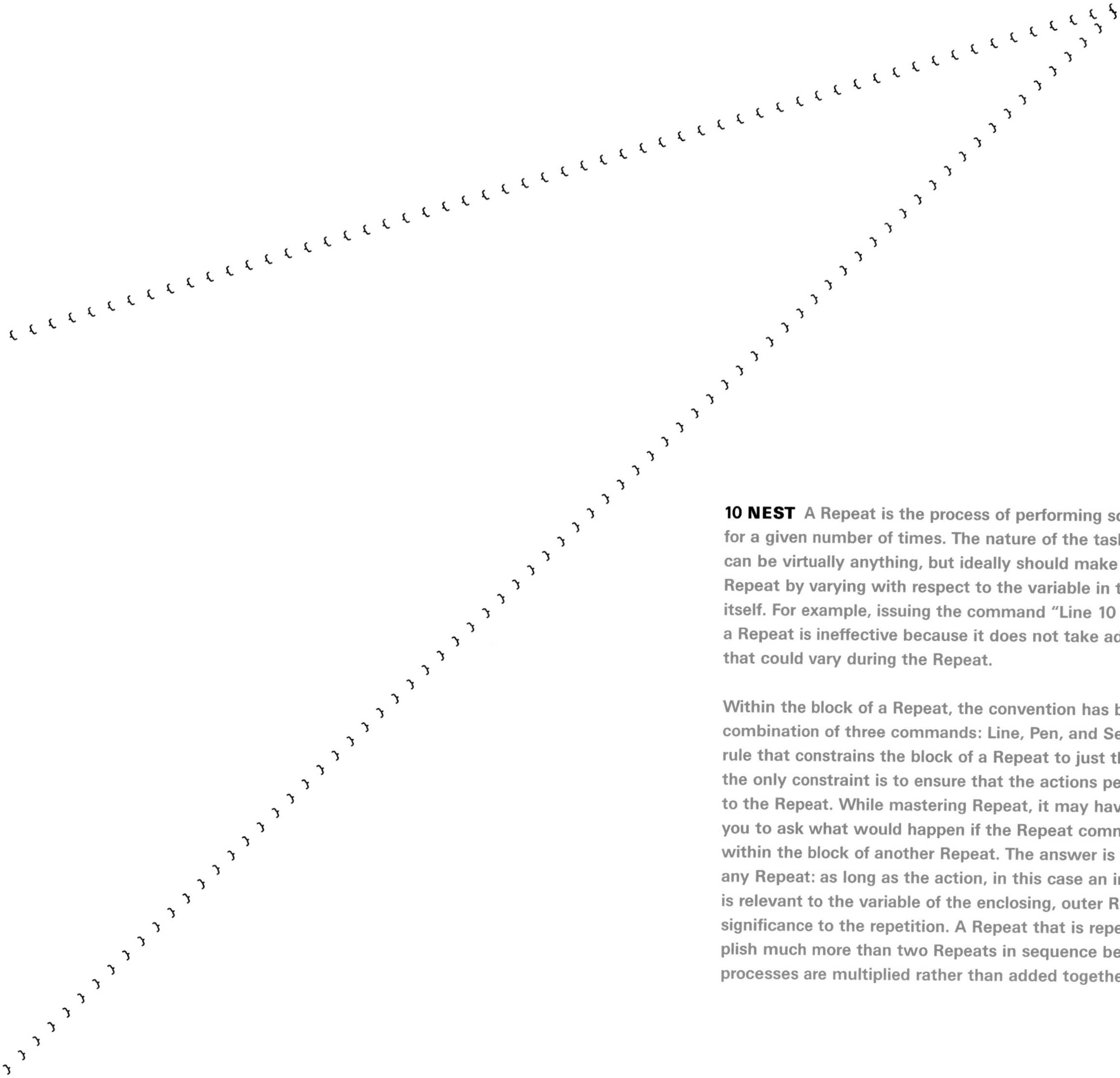

10 NEST A Repeat is the process of performing some task repeatedly for a given number of times. The nature of the task to be repeated can be virtually anything, but ideally should make good use of the Repeat by varying with respect to the variable in the Repeat command itself. For example, issuing the command "Line 10 20 70 80" within a Repeat is ineffective because it does not take advantage of quantity that could vary during the Repeat.

Within the block of a Repeat, the convention has been to use some combination of three commands: Line, Pen, and Set. There is no rule that constrains the block of a Repeat to just these three commands; the only constraint is to ensure that the actions performed are relevant to the Repeat. While mastering Repeat, it may have occurred to you to ask what would happen if the Repeat command were used within the block of another Repeat. The answer is the same with any Repeat: as long as the action, in this case an inner Repeat, is relevant to the variable of the enclosing, outer Repeat, there will be significance to the repetition. A Repeat that is repeated can accomplish much more than two Repeats in sequence because the two processes are multiplied rather than added together.

Repeat in Repeat Using the Repeat command, a great deal of drawing activity can be expressed in a counterintuitively small textual form. With just four lines of code, a row or column of a hundred dots can easily be set to black or white. And with a few additional lines of code, several rows can be set accordingly, implying the straightforward manipulation of hundreds or even thousands of dots. Consider setting a total of 303 dots in a single Repeat.

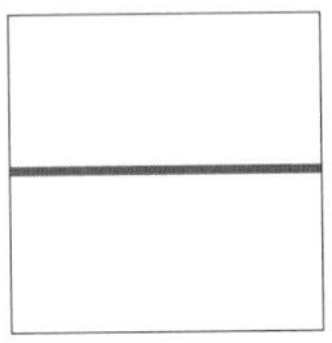

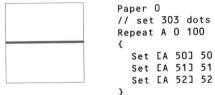

```
Paper 0
// set 303 dots
Repeat A 0 100
{
  Set [A 50] 50
  Set [A 51] 51
  Set [A 52] 52
}
```

And to set 606 dots, add 3 more statements.

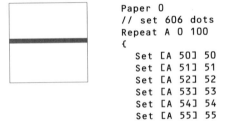

```
Paper 0
// set 606 dots
Repeat A 0 100
{
  Set [A 50] 50
  Set [A 51] 51
  Set [A 52] 52
  Set [A 53] 53
  Set [A 54] 54
  Set [A 55] 55
}
```

Naturally, setting progressively more rows of dots requires more code. However, you should recognize this as a case where a Repeat can be useful. You can verify this by identifying the variable to Repeat over, in this case called B.

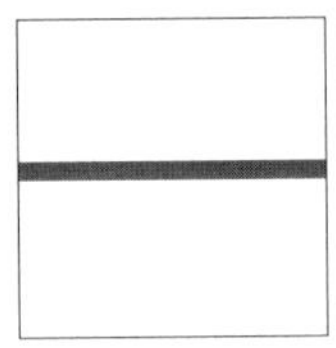

```
Paper 0
// rewrite the dot setting
Repeat A 0 100
{
  Set B 50
  Set [A B] B
  Set B 51
  Set [A B] B
  Set B 52
  Set [A B] B
  Set B 53
  Set [A B] B
  Set B 54
  Set [A B] B
  Set B 55
  Set [A B] B
}
```

But oddly, there already is a Repeat involved in stepping through the individual columns of dots as A, and thus cannot be incorporated in stepping through the rows B at the same time. Therefore, a Repeat is introduced inside the body of a Repeat, where the outer Repeat steps over the columns and the inner Repeat steps over the rows and gray values to be Set.

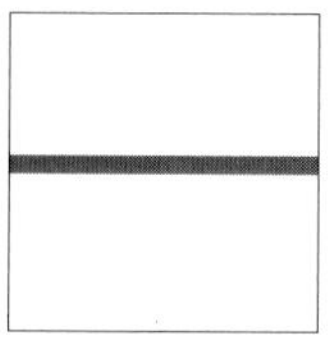

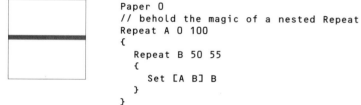

```
Paper 0
// behold the magic of a nested Repeat
Repeat A 0 100
{
  Repeat B 50 55
  {
    Set [A B] B
  }
}
```

This form can be read as a Repeat over the variable A, from 0 to 100, applied to the process of a Repeat over the variable B, from 50 to 55. The process concerning B is setting [A B] to the gray value B. The outer Repeat repeats a sequence of inner Repeats. Because there is this distinction between the outer and inner Repeats, this type of coded form is referred to as a *nested* form because one form nests within another. Notice that the additional indention of the inner block greatly enhances the legibility of the code.

You can verify the nested Repeat's spectrum by reducing the limits of B to 50 through 52, which you recognize as equivalent to the starting point for this example.

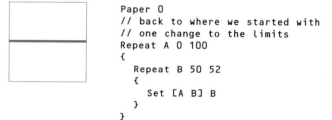

```
Paper 0
// back to where we started with
// one change to the limits
Repeat A 0 100
{
  Repeat B 50 52
  {
    Set [A B] B
  }
}
```

The power of a nested Repeat can be demonstrated by increasing the limits of A and B from 0 to 100, where over 10,000 dots are set in only seven lines of code.

```
Paper 0
// 10201 dots set
Repeat A 0 100
{
  Repeat B 0 100
  {
    Set [A B] B
  }
}
```

You might have noticed that there is an easier way to do all of this without the nested Repeat by using just a single Repeat and Line.

```
Paper 0
// using line instead
Repeat A 0 100
{
  Pen A
  Line 0 A 100 A
}
```

But as you might recall from Chapter 9, a Line command actually conceals an underlying Repeat process. Therefore, although this short form appears dramatically simpler, the same amount of work is being performed. In other words, the two forms are equivalent.

Consider another process that can reduce in a similar manner, like Set-ing all dots on the paper to a certain value of 50.

```
Paper 0
// use Set
Repeat A 0 100
{
  Repeat B 0 100
  {
    Set [A B] 50
  }
}
```

This process can be written as a single Repeat over variably positioned Line.

```
Paper 0
// use Line
Pen 50
Repeat A 0 100
{
  Line A 0 A 100
}
```

Furthermore, the process can be reduced to the single command we started from.

```
// use brain
Paper 50
```

One conclusion we can now draw is that Paper is a nested Repeat of Set-ing dots. Not only Line, but also Paper involves the computational processing of Set-ing dots in the more sophisticated form of a nested Repeat. Paper and Line are primitives that represent computational processes that have been abstracted into a single command.

Two Dimensions in Repeat The nested Repeat allows you to encode complex relations between the horizontal and vertical dimensions. By using the basic construct of stepping over all dots on the 101 by 101 grid with the dimensions coded as A and B, interesting results can be obtained by Set-ing each dot as [A B] to some calculation that involves both A and B. Set-ing [A B] to a constant value, like 50, is equivalent to making a new sheet of paper as demonstrated previously; equating [A B] to one of the dimensions A or B results in a simple horizontal or vertical gradation pattern. A greater variety of interactions between the horizontal and vertical are possible by coding more complex relations, for instance (A+B).

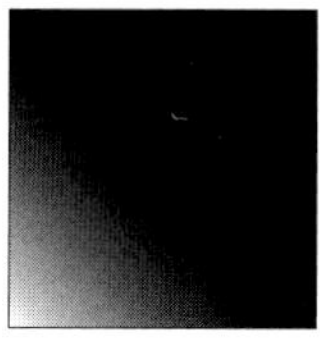

```
Paper 0
Repeat A 0 100
{
  Repeat B 0 100
  {
    Set [A B] (A+B)
  }
}
```

A less familiar relationship is described by (A*B).

```
Paper 0
Repeat A 0 100
{
  Repeat B 0 100
  {
    Set [A B] (A*B)
  }
}
```

Expanding the tonal range of this figure reveals more of the detail in this pattern, reminiscent of the mysterious *hyperbola* from high school mathematics.

```
Paper 0
Repeat A 0 100
{
  Repeat B 0 100
  {
    Set [A B] ((A*B)/10)
  }
}
```

You can always find comfort in a circle.

```
Paper 0
// circle defined by a^2 + b^2
Repeat A 0 100
{
   Repeat B 0 100
   {
      Set [A B] (A*A+B*B)
   }
}
```

The center of the circle can be adjusted by introducing a shift of H and V.

```
Paper 0
// center at (H,V)
Set H 50
Set V 30
Repeat A 0 100
{
   Repeat B 0 100
   {
      Set [A B] ((A-H)*(A-H)+(B-V)*(B-V))
   }
}
```

The size can also be adjusted by incorporating a scaling factor of R.

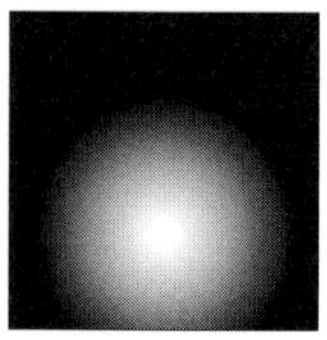

```
Paper 0
Set H 50
Set V 30
// bigger ...
Set R 20
Repeat A 0 100
{
   Repeat B 0 100
   {
      Set [A B] (((A-H)*(A-H)+(B-V)*(B-V))/R)
   }
}
```

One pattern that may be less familiar to you is a circle taken two powers higher, which bears a striking resemblance to a square.

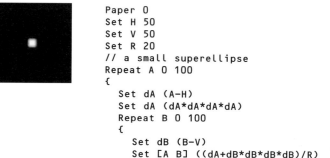

```
Paper 0
Set H 50
Set V 50
Set R 20
// a small superellipse
Repeat A 0 100
{
   Set dA (A-H)
   Set dA (dA*dA*dA*dA)
   Repeat B 0 100
   {
      Set dB (B-V)
      Set [A B] ((dA+dB*dB*dB*dB)/R)
   }
}
```

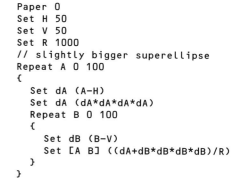

```
Paper 0
Set H 50
Set V 50
Set R 1000
// slightly bigger superellipse
Repeat A 0 100
{
   Set dA (A-H)
   Set dA (dA*dA*dA*dA)
   Repeat B 0 100
   {
      Set dB (B-V)
      Set [A B] ((dA+dB*dB*dB*dB)/R)
   }
}
```

A few more examples demonstrate the variety of forms that can be rendered in this manner.

```
Paper 0
Repeat A 0 100
{
  Repeat B 0 100
  {
    Set [A B] ((A*100-66)/(B+1))
  }
}
```

```
Paper 0
Repeat A 0 100
{
  Repeat B 0 100
  {
    Set [A B] (((A-25)+(100-B))/2+B)
  }
}
```

```
Paper 0
Repeat A 0 100
{
  Set dA (A-50)
  Set dA (dA*dA*dA*dA)
  Repeat B 0 100
  {
    Set [A B] (dA/2000+B/2)
  }
}
```

This activity is the exploration of mathematical relations between two dimensions, which would seem uninteresting if posed as a mathematics problem but is more engaging when expressed visually. I urge you to experiment, and most important, to develop intuition for the phenomena you observe.

Patterns from Repeat Painting each individual dot in an entire image is a standard technique for creating synthetic imagery on the computer. The nested Repeat enables you to pursue this activity with grace. Instead of Set-ing all dots, why not select a few? You can choose to address half of the dots instead of all of them by skipping the odd-numbered ones.

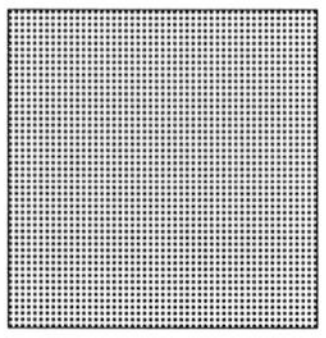

```
Paper 0
// a pattern
Repeat A 0 50
{
   Repeat B 0 50
   {
      Set [(A*2) (B*2)] 100
   }
}
```

Notice that the limits have been reduced to 0 through 50 in both dimensions and the dot that is set is always a multiple of 2. A regular pattern of step-size 2 is created within the Repeat. The visual character of these patterns is easily changed through adjustment of either the background Paper value or the value that is being Set.

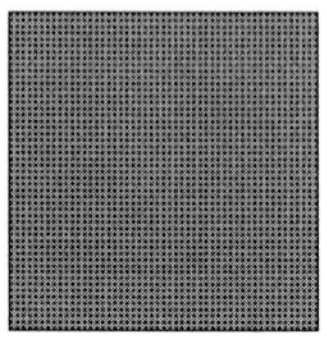

```
Paper 25
// foreground & background adjusted
Repeat B 0 50
{
   Repeat A 0 50
   {
      Set [(A*2) (B*2)] 75
   }
}
```

```
Paper 50
// again ...
Repeat B 0 50
{
   Repeat A 0 50
   {
      Set [(A*2) (B*2)] 75
   }
}
```

The density of the pattern can be modified by adjusting the magnitude of the step-size.

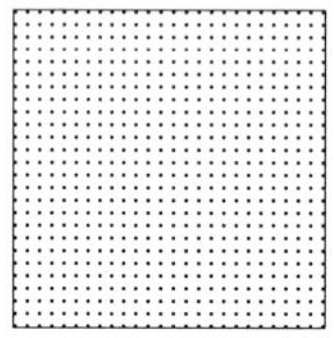

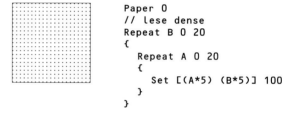

```
Paper 0
// dense
Repeat B 0 25
{
   Repeat A 0 25
   {
      Set [(A*4) (B*4)] 100
   }
}
```

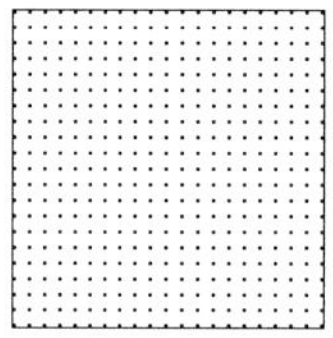

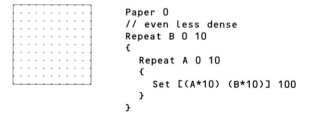

```
Paper 0
// lese dense
Repeat B 0 20
{
   Repeat A 0 20
   {
      Set [(A*5) (B*5)] 100
   }
}
```

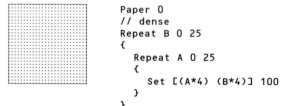

```
Paper 0
// even less dense
Repeat B 0 10
{
   Repeat A 0 10
   {
      Set [(A*10) (B*10)] 100
   }
}
```

When you manipulate a form in this manner, it is good practice to write a general description of the process whenever possible. In this case, if the step-size is C, then the process can be generalized.

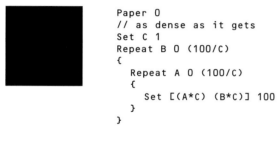

```
Paper 0
// as dense as it gets
Set C 1
Repeat B 0 (100/C)
{
  Repeat A 0 (100/C)
  {
    Set [(A*C) (B*C)] 100
  }
}
```

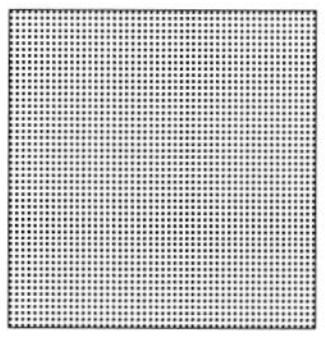

```
Paper 0
Set C 2
// less dense
Repeat B 0 (100/C)
{
  Repeat A 0 (100/C)
  {
    Set [(A*C) (B*C)] 100
  }
}
```

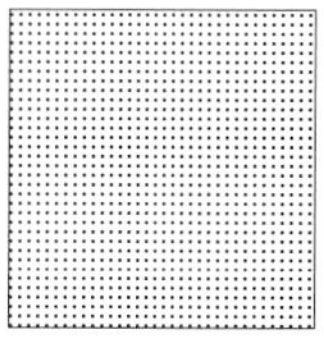

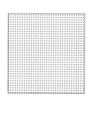

```
Paper 0
Set C 3
// even less dense
Repeat B 0 (100/C)
{
  Repeat A 0 (100/C)
  {
    Set [(A*C) (B*C)] 100
  }
}
```

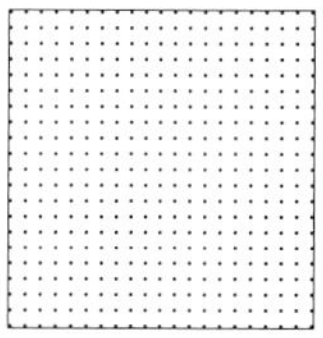

```
Paper 0
Set C 4
// what we started with
Repeat B 0 (100/C)
{
  Repeat A 0 (100/C)
  {
    Set [(A*C) (B*C)] 100
  }
}
```

The pattern can be skewed in horizontal, vertical, or both dimensions at the same time.

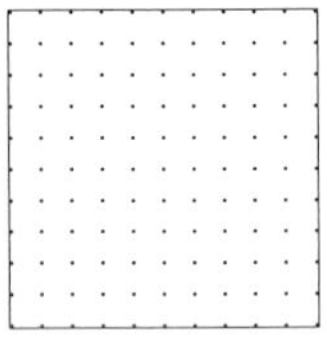

```
Paper 0
// plain
Repeat B 0 10
{
  Repeat A 0 10
  {
    Set [(A*10) (B*10)] 100
  }
}
```

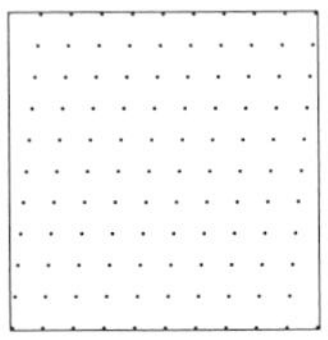

```
Paper 0
// horizontal skew
Repeat B 0 10
{
  Repeat A 0 10
  {
    Set [(B+(A*10)) (B*10)] 100
  }
}
```

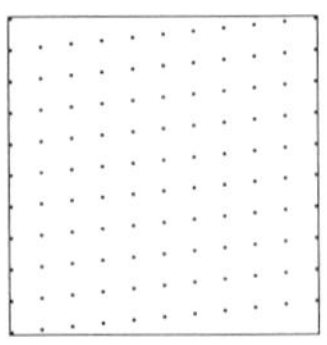

```
Paper 0
// vertical skew
Repeat B 0 10
{
  Repeat A 0 10
  {
    Set [(A*10) (A+(B*10))] 100
  }
}
```

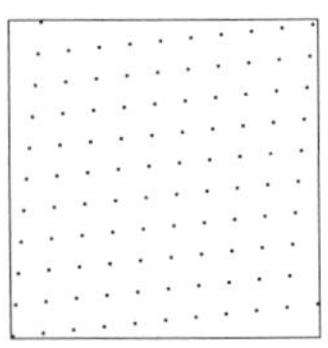

```
Paper 0
// both
Repeat B 0 10
{
  Repeat A 0 10
  {
    Set [(B+(A*10)) (A+(B*10))] 100
  }
}
```

Another area to explore is the pattern density, which can be deepened by overlaying an offset pattern on top.

```
Paper 0
// layered examples ...
Repeat B 0 50
{
  Repeat A 0 50
  {
    Set [(A*2) (B*2)] 100
    Set [((A*2)+1) ((B*2)+1)] 100
  }
}
```

```
Paper 0
Repeat B 0 50
{
  Repeat A 0 50
  {
    Set [(A*2) (B*2)] 70
    Set [((A*2)+1) ((B*2)+1)] 45
  }
}
```

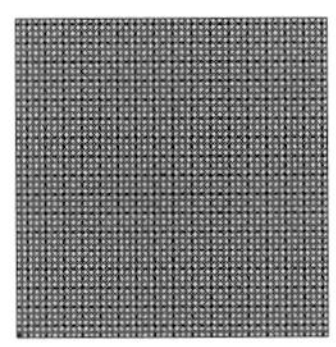

```
Paper 50
// different kind of offset
Repeat B 0 50
{
  Repeat A 0 50
  {
    Set [(A*2) (B*2)] 0
    Set [(A*3) (B*3)] 100
  }
}
```

A variety of these types of patterns, called *stippled* patterns, can be generated in this manner. Before computers could display many shades of gray or a wide spectrum of color, these patterns were a common sight on computer screens. You do not see them often today because they are generally considered less favorable compared to pure, flat tones. It is just another instance where technology governs what is to be deemed better. I personally find these patterns lovely. They lend a richness of texture that is often needed on the bland computer screen.

We close with a few triply-nested loops.

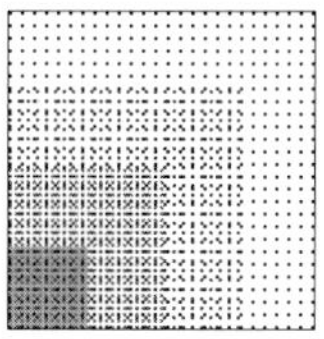

```
Paper 0
// plain triple nesting
Repeat C 1 4
{
  Repeat B 0 25
  {
    Repeat A 0 25
    {
      Set [(A*C) (B*C)] (C*25)
    }
  }
}
```

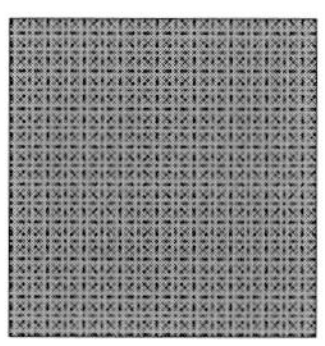

```
Paper 0
// triple nesting with fancy
// limit adjusting
Repeat C 1 4
{
  Repeat B 0 (100/C)
  {
    Repeat A 0 (100/C)
    {
      Set [(A*C) (B*C)] (C*25)
    }
  }
}
```

Summary Thus far we have seen lines, gradated lines, filled triangles and rectangles, curves, photograph-like images, and now a rich series of images that illustrates a tiny fraction of the possibilities of computational expression. A nested Repeat is a special kind of construct that not only doubles the handling of complexity by a Repeat, but also can increase the level of complexity in a single Repeat by many times. The reason the complexity of the process can increase so dramatically is that computational structures can be multiplicatively structured in addition to being arranged in a series.

For instance, two Repeat processes placed in a sequence represent twice the processing of a single Repeat, three Repeats represent three times, and so forth. The effect of Repeats in sequence is additive in terms of process. On the other hand, a Repeat nested inside a Repeat is not additive because each cycle of the outer Repeat represents an entire inner Repeat process and is thus multiplicative. To further illustrate, a Repeat of 100 cycles, plus another Repeat of 100 cycles, equals a total of 200 cycles. An outer Repeat of 100 cycles and an inner Repeat of 100 cycles implies 100 inner cycles per outer cycle, totaling 100 times 100 or 10,000 cycles.

Try to imagine a Repeat of a Repeat of a Repeat, which could result in a process of 1 million cycles, given that each Repeat lasts 100 cycles. A quadruply nested Repeat would run for 100 million cycles, all within 15 or so lines of code. The implications should be obvious, but are nonetheless daunting.

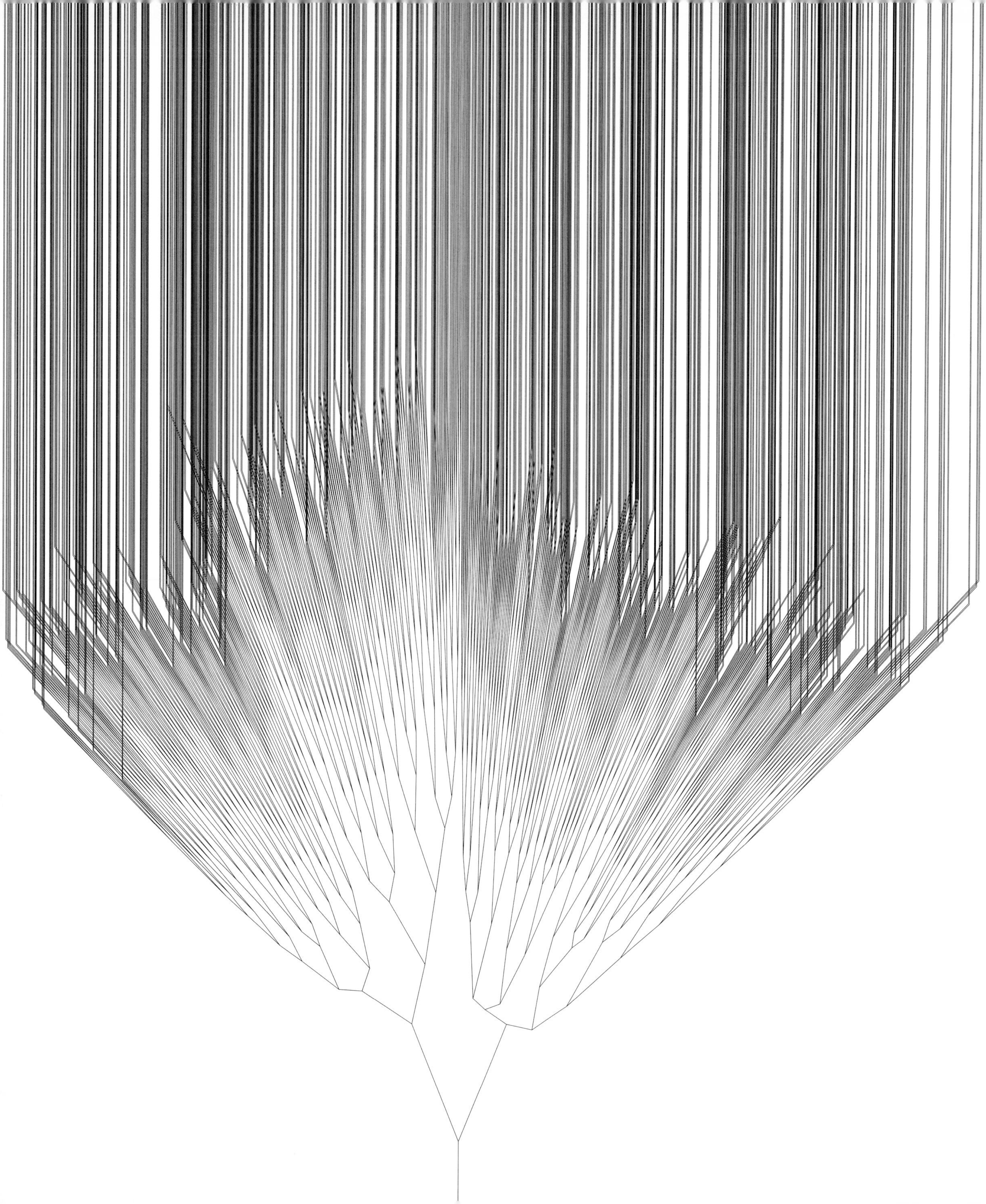

11 QUESTION As we have discussed so far, a program proceeds one step at a time from the beginning until the ending statement is reached. Regardless of how many Repeats, Lines, or Dots need to be processed, the mighty computer trudges through the program the same way every time. If you or I were somehow cast in such a position, we would surely go insane. The computer, on the other hand, finds this lifestyle quite comfortable because it never has to make any decisions. In other words, the computer never has to think about what it is doing—it just follows the directions in the program.

The analogy would be a toy train on a track; the computer is the train, the program is the track. Anyone who has played with a train knows that a single track quickly fails to entertain. The standard method for improvement is to build a more complex track where the train can travel on different subroutes. Switches on the track activate and deactivate the various subroutes so the track remains as one large track without having to be disassembled. In a computer program, you can accomplish a similar function by declaring specific blocks within your program that can be either activated or deactivated, depending upon a given condition. A condition is imposed by asking a simple question. There are a variety of questions that will be asked, instead of answered, in this chapter.

Ask a Question Suppose the computer were to ask you the following question:

Do you want a square or a line? Make a choice.

Today, on a conventional computer, you would most likely select icons on a menu. However, before mice and graphical user interfaces emerged, the common method for answering the question was with a number, so you needed to pose the question differently:

Do you want (1) a square, or (2) a line? Make a choice by entering either a '1' or a '2.'

The computer knows how to draw both a square, and, of course, a Line, so given the user's preference of 1 or 2, it delivers the requested result as one of two programs.

```
Paper 0
Pen 100
// a square
Line 5 5 95 5
Line 95 5 95 95
Line 95 95 5 95
Line 5 95 5 5
```

```
Paper 0
Pen 100
// a Line
Line 10 50 90 50
```

But the computer cannot automatically type the desired program into itself upon demand. There must be a way to access these two programs from within a single program—and there is, namely by asking a *question.*

A question command can control the flow of processing in a program. Each question compares two numbers. Depending upon the specific question asked, if the answer is *yes,* then the block immediately following the question is processed. If the answer is *no,* then the action block is skipped and processing resumes immediately after the block. For our example of choosing an object to draw, a variable, C, is declared to hold the choice of a square versus a line.

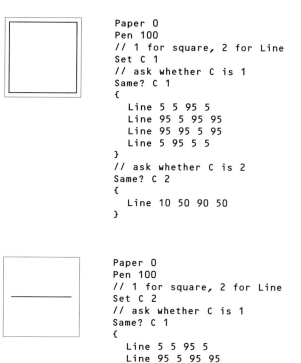

```
Paper 0
Pen 100
// 1 for square, 2 for Line
Set C 1
// ask whether C is 1
Same? C 1
{
  Line 5 5 95 5
  Line 95 5 95 95
  Line 95 95 5 95
  Line 5 95 5 5
}
// ask whether C is 2
Same? C 2
{
  Line 10 50 90 50
}
```

```
Paper 0
Pen 100
// 1 for square, 2 for Line
Set C 2
// ask whether C is 1
Same? C 1
{
  Line 5 5 95 5
  Line 95 5 95 95
  Line 95 95 5 95
  Line 5 95 5 5
}
// ask whether C is 2
Same? C 2
{
  Line 10 50 90 50
}
```

As you can see in the question **Same?**, a characteristic of the question command is the question mark at the end. In the first example, C was 1, and the square was drawn; since C was not 2, the line was not drawn. But when C is 2, the line gets drawn and the square does not.

Returning to the train analogy, you can imagine that when C is 1, the train passes the first test and enters the four-line sequence. When it exits, it does not pass the second test and proceeds directly to the end of the program. The set of choices can easily be extended by adding more Same? clauses.

```
Paper 0
Pen 100
// 1 for square,
// 2 for Line,
// 3 for single dot,
// 4 for gray Paper,
// 5 for gray pattern
//
// this is the setting
Set C 3
// ask whether C is 1
Same? C 1
{
  Line 5 5 95 5
  Line 95 5 95 95
  Line 95 95 5 95
  Line 5 95 5 5
}
// ask whether C is 2
Same? C 2
{
  Line 10 50 90 50
}
// ask whether C is 3
Same? C 3
{
  Set [50 50] 100
}
// ask whether C is 4
Same? C 4
{
  Paper 50
}
// ask whether C is 5
Same? C 5
{
  Repeat A 0 50
  {
    Repeat B 0 50
    {
      Set [(A*2) (B*2)] 50
    }
  }
}
```

```
Paper 0
Pen 100
// this is the setting
Set C 4
// ask whether C is 1
Same? C 1
{
  Line 5 5 95 5
  Line 95 5 95 95
  Line 95 95 5 95
  Line 5 95 5 5
}
// ask whether C is 2
Same? C 2
{
  Line 10 50 90 50
}
// ask whether C is 3
Same? C 3
{
  Set [50 50] 100
}
// ask whether C is 4
Same? C 4
{
  Paper 50
}
// ask whether C is 5
Same? C 5
{
  Repeat A 0 50
  {
    Repeat B 0 50
    {
      Set [(A*2) (B*2)] 50
    }
  }
}
```

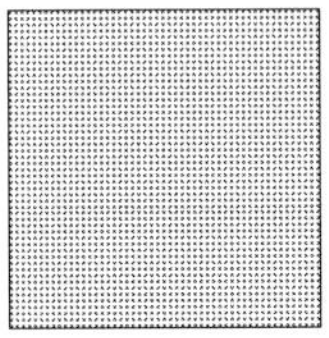

```
Paper 0
Pen 100
// this is the setting
Set C 5
// ask whether C is 1
Same? C 1
{
  Line 5 5 95 5
  Line 95 5 95 95
  Line 95 95 5 95
  Line 5 95 5 5
}
// ask whether C is 2
Same? C 2
{
  Line 10 50 90 50
}
// ask whether C is 3
Same? C 3
{
  Set [50 50] 100
}
// ask whether C is 4
Same? C 4
{
  Paper 50
}
// ask whether C is 5
Same? C 5
{
  Repeat A 0 50
  {
    Repeat B 0 50
    {
      Set [(A*2) (B*2)] 50
    }
  }
}
```

Notice that C has to be Set to 1, 2, 3, 4, or 5; otherwise the page is blank.

More Questions In addition to Same? there is **NotSame?** As you can guess by the name, NotSame? asks if two quantities are *not* the same. Although you might think Same? and NotSame? are similar because they both deal with the property of equality, they have strikingly different behaviors. Consider asking a question within the body of a Repeat.

```
Paper 0
// ask a question within a repeat
Repeat A 0 100
{
  Pen A
  Same? A 50
  {
    Line A 0 A 100
  }
}
```

A single gray line is rendered at the horizontal position of 50 because only when the value of A is 50 is the question "Same? A 50" answered *yes.* Now replace NotSame? with Same?

```
Paper 0
// ask another question
Repeat A 0 100
{
  Pen A
  NotSame? A 50
  {
    Line A 0 A 100
  }
}
```

There is only one position, 50, where the condition "NotSame? A 50" is not satisfied, so a line is missing at 50. Every other position satisfied the condition, as evidenced by the gap at the center.

From the viewpoint of program flow, Same? is extremely selective about when it is activated, whereas NotSame? less selective. NotSame? satisfies many more cases than Same? so their respective uses can differ significantly. Usually Same? and NotSame? are used in conjunction as a way to construct a brief forking in the process flow. If a condition is satisfied, then one path is taken; if the condition is not satisfied, then the other path is taken.

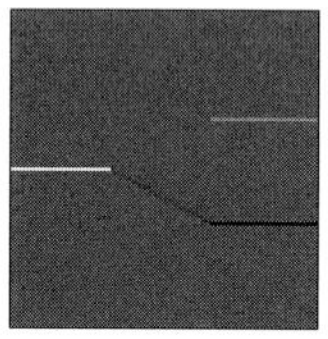

```
Paper 50
Pen 0
Set C 0
Line 0 50 33 50
Same? C 100
{
  Pen 60
  Line 33 50 66 33
}
// if C is not 100 then link downwards
NotSame? C 100
{
  Pen 40
  Line 33 50 66 66
}
Pen 100
Line 66 33 100 33
Pen 30
Line 66 66 100 66
```

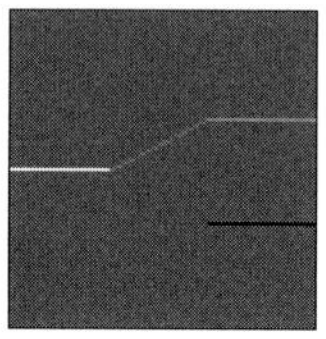

```
Paper 50
Pen 0
Set C 100
Line 0 50 33 50
// if C is 100 then link upwards
Same? C 100
{
  Pen 60
  Line 33 50 66 33
}
NotSame? C 100
{
  Pen 40
  Line 33 50 66 66
}
Pen 100
Line 66 33 100 33
Pen 30
Line 66 66 100 66
```

The Same? and NotSame? pair is often used within the block of a Repeat.

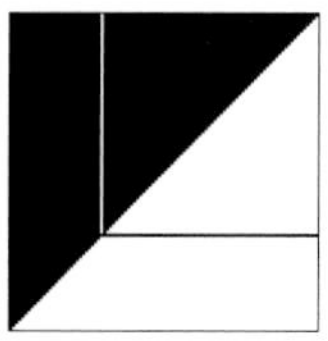

```
Paper 0
Pen 100
// ask 202 questions
Repeat A 0 100
{
  Same? A 30
  {
    Line 100 A A A
  }
  NotSame? A 30
  {
    Line A A A 100
  }
}
```

A question can be posed with calculations in either, or both, of the descriptors.

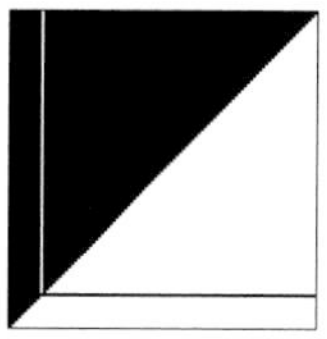

```
Paper 0
Pen 100
// throw in a calculation
Repeat A 0 100
{
  Same? (A+20) 30
  {
    Line 100 A A A
  }
  NotSame? (A+20) 30
  {
    Line A A A 100
  }
}
```

Also, both descriptors can use variables.

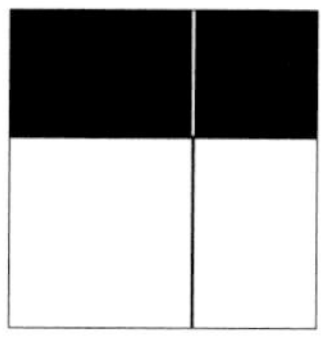

```
Paper 0
Pen 100
// be multivariate
Set B 60
Repeat A 0 100
{
  Same? A B
  {
    Line A 0 A B
  }
  NotSame? A B
  {
    Line A 100 A B
  }
}
```

In addition, there are the question commands of **Smaller?** and **NotSmaller?** The former compares two quantities and asks if the first quantity is smaller than the second quantity; the latter asks if the first quantity is not smaller than the second. Whereas Same? and NotSame? look for either very specific or very broad conditions, Smaller? and NotSmaller? specialize in handling ranges of numbers. Rewriting the opening example with Smaller? and NotSmaller? demonstrates this striking difference in properties.

```
Paper 0
// range less than 50
Repeat A 0 100
{
  Pen A
  Smaller? A 50
  {
    Line A 0 A 100
  }
}
```

```
Paper 0
// range larger or equal to 50
Repeat A 0 100
{
  Pen A
  NotSmaller? A 50
  {
    Line A 0 A 100
  }
}
```

Thus Smaller? and NotSmaller? are useful for specifying a general condition over numbers. In this example, all numbers that are less than 50 satisfy Smaller? Those larger satisfy Not-Smaller? When the number is equal to 50, it satisfies NotSmaller? but fails to satisfy Smaller?

As with Same? and NotSame?, Smaller? and NotSmaller? are also commonly used in pairs.

```
Paper 0
// both ranges incorporated
Repeat A 0 100
{
  Smaller? A 51
  {
    Repeat B 0 100
    {
      Set [A B] (B*2)
    }
  }
  NotSmaller? A 51
  {
    Repeat B 0 100
    {
      Set [A B] A
    }
  }
}
```

```
Paper 0
// displayed with different content
Repeat A 0 100
{
  Smaller? A 51
  {
    Repeat B 0 100
    {
      Set [A B] (A*2)
    }
  }
  NotSmaller? A 51
  {
    Repeat B 0 100
    {
      Set [A B] B
    }
  }
}
```

```
Paper 0
// more variations ...
Repeat A 0 100
{
  Repeat B 0 100
  {
    Smaller? A B
    {
      Set [A B] A
    }
    NotSmaller? A B
    {
      Set [A B] B
    }
  }
}
```

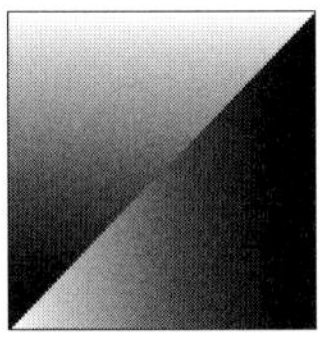

```
Paper 0
Repeat A 0 100
{
  Repeat B 0 100
  {
    Smaller? B A
    {
      Set [A B] A
    }
    NotSmaller? B A
    {
      Set [A B] (100-B)
    }
  }
}
```

```
Paper 0
Repeat A 0 100
{
  Repeat B 0 100
  {
    Smaller? (B*2) A
    {
      Set [A B] B
    }
    NotSmaller? (B*2) A
    {
      Set [A B] A
    }
  }
}
```

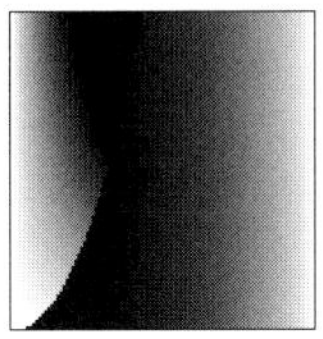

```
Paper 0
// something a bit more decorative
Repeat A 0 100
{
  Repeat B 0 100
  {
    Smaller? B (A*A/20)
    {
      Set [A B] (100-A*A/100)
    }
    NotSmaller? B (A*A/20)
    {
      Set [A B] (A*B/20)
    }
  }
}
```

Deeper Questions In the same manner that it is possible to construct a nested Repeat, you can also create a nested question by placing a question inside the action block of a question. The benefit of such an arrangement is the ability to define more specific conditions after an overall condition has been satisfied. This arises when ranges within ranges must be defined.

With a Smaller? and NotSmaller? pair there are two ranges of numbers separated in a Repeat. If within the Smaller? action block there is another Smaller? and NotSmaller? pair, there could be a total of three ranges. With another pair, there could be four distinct ranges. Dividing the horizontal dimension into four distinct areas is illustrated in the following example.

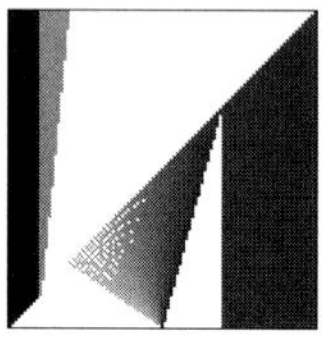

```
Paper 0
// four distinct divisions of paper
Repeat A 0 100
{
  Smaller? A 20
  {
    Smaller? A 10
    {
      Pen 100
      Line A 100 A A
    }
    NotSmaller? A 10
    {
      Pen 33
      Line 10 10 A 100
    }
  }
  NotSmaller? A 20
  {
    Smaller? A 70
    {
      Pen A
      Line 50 0 A A
    }
    NotSmaller? A 70
    {
      Pen 66
      Line A 0 A A
    }
  }
}
```

Another illustration of this zoning of the sheet is to divide the sheet into four quadrants by repeating over A and B, and defining an A cutoff of C, and a B cutoff of D. By simply changing the cutoff values C and D, the four different sub-actions assume different degrees of relevance.

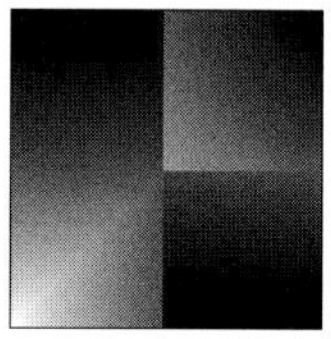

```
Paper 0
// as quadrants
Set C 50
Set D 50
Repeat A 0 100
{
  Repeat B 0 100
  {
    Smaller? A C
    {
      Smaller? B D
      {
        Smaller? A B
        {
          Set [A B] B
        }
        NotSmaller? A B
        {
          Set [A B] A
        }
      }
      NotSmaller? B D
      {
        Set [A B] B
      }
    }
    NotSmaller? A C
    {
      Smaller? B D
      {
        Set [A B] (100-B)
      }
      NotSmaller? B D
      {
        Set F (A*B)
        Set [A B] (F/100)
      }
    }
  }
}
```

```
Paper 0
// off-center
Set C 20
Set D 20
Repeat A 0 100
{
  Repeat B 0 100
  {
    Smaller? A C
    {
      Smaller? B D
      {
        Smaller? A B
        {
          Set [A B] B
        }
        NotSmaller? A B
        {
          Set [A B] A
        }
      }
      NotSmaller? B D
      {
        Set [A B] B
      }
    }
    NotSmaller? A C
    {
      Smaller? B D
      {
        Set [A B] (100-B)
      }
      NotSmaller? B D
      {
        Set F (A*B)
        Set [A B] (F/100)
      }
    }
  }
}
```

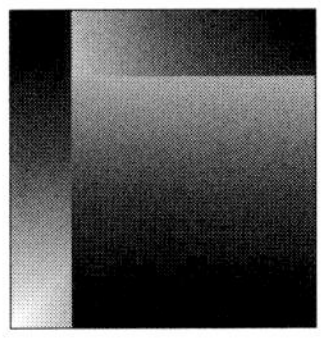

```
Paper 0
// center moved vertically
Set C 20
Set D 80
Repeat A 0 100
{
  Repeat B 0 100
  {
    Smaller? A C
    {
      Smaller? B D
      {
        Smaller? A B
        {
          Set [A B] B
        }
        NotSmaller? A B
        {
          Set [A B] A
        }
      }
      NotSmaller? B D
      {
        Set [A B] B
      }
    }
    NotSmaller? A C
    {
      Smaller? B D
      {
        Set [A B] (100-B)
      }
      NotSmaller? B D
      {
        Set F (A*B)
        Set [A B] (F/100)
      }
    }
  }
}
```

Same? and NotSame? can also be placed in a nested fashion in the context of a two-dimensional Repeat. The result is similar in that it separates the sheet into four distinct areas. However, in the case of Smaller? and NotSmaller? there are quadrants; Same? and NotSame? produce a less obvious division system.

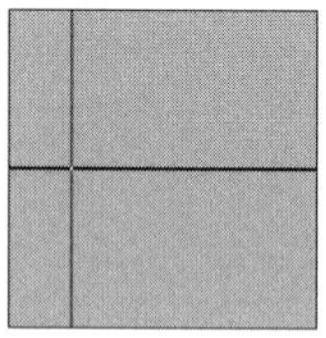

```
Paper 0
// four tiny areas
Repeat B 0 100
{
   Repeat A 0 100
   {
      Same? A 20
      {
         Same? B 50
         {
            Set [A B] 0
         }
         NotSame? B 50
         {
            Set [A B] 50
         }
      }
      NotSame? A 20
      {
         Same? B 50
         {
            Set [A B] 100
         }
         NotSame? B 50
         {
            Set [A B] 20
         }
      }
   }
}
```

The four areas can be identified as (1) the point of intersection between the horizontal and vertical lines, (2) the area of the horizontal line excluding the point of intersection, (3) the area of the vertical line excluding the point of intersection, and (4) the area not included in the first three areas.

Mixing the two types of questions together in the framework of the new program illustrates the ability to create complex nested questions.

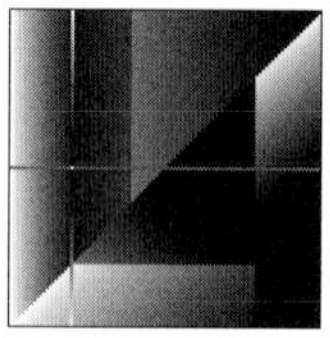

```
Paper 0
// an abundancy of subdivisions
Repeat B 0 100
{
   Repeat A 0 100
   {
      Same? A 20
      {
         Same? B 50
         {
            Set [A B] 0
         }
         NotSame? B 50
         {
            Smaller? B 50
            {
               Set [A B] (B*2)
            }
            NotSmaller? B 50
            {
               Set [A B] (2*(100-B))
            }
         }
      }
      NotSame? A 20
      {
         Same? B 50
         {
            Set [A B] 50
         }
         NotSame? B 50
         {
            Smaller? (B-A) 0
            {
               Smaller? A 80
               {
                  Smaller? B 20
                  {
```

```
              Set [A B] (A-B)
            }
            NotSmaller? B 20
            {
              Set [A B] (A+B)
            }
          }
          NotSmaller? A 80
          {
            Set [A B] (2*(A-B))
          }
        }
        NotSmaller? (B-A) 0
        {
          Smaller? A 40
          {
            Smaller? A 20
            {
              Set [A B] (A*4)
            }
            NotSmaller? A 20
            {
              Set [A B] (100-A)
            }
          }
          NotSmaller? A 40
          {
            Set [A B] A
          }
        }
      }
    }
  }
}
```

Summary A block of code can be defined to activate depending upon the numerical circumstance of a variable, a set of variables, numbers, or any calculation expression. When a question is answered with *yes,* the block is activated and the flow of the program is routed into the block. When the question is answered with *no,* the program flow is routed past the block. Questions can be nested as deeply as required, with the effect of fine-tuning a circumstance with precision.

Without conditions, programs are simple to trace because they flow in a strictly top-to-bottom order. Incorporating questions makes a program considerably more difficult to read because the processing flow is not always obvious. If you do not feel comfortable using questions, do not be concerned, because you can easily avoid using them for quite a while. But eventually you will start to ask questions, as we all do.

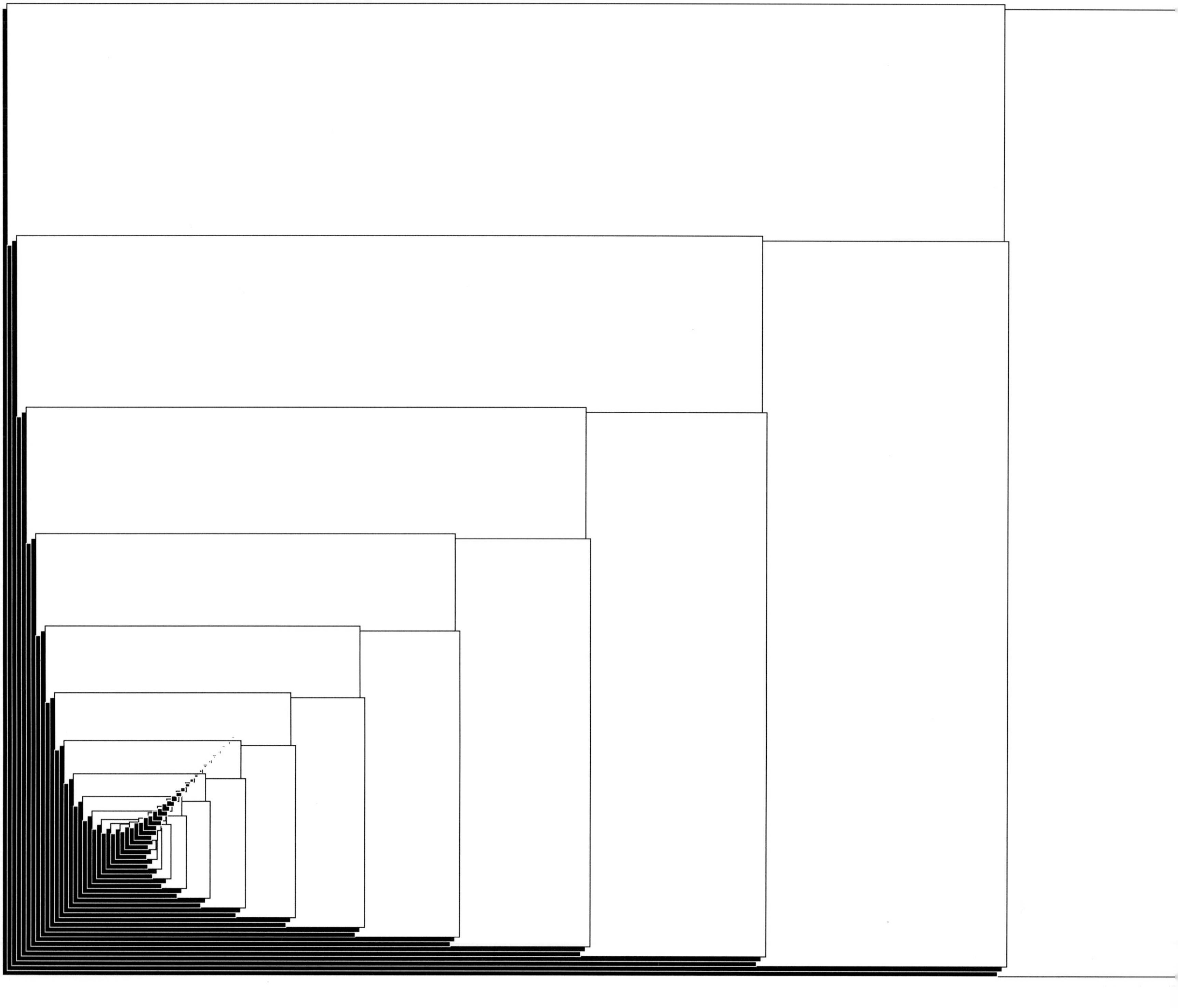

12 COMMANDS Repeats, variables, dots, calculations, and questions are essentially all that you need to explore computational illustration. There are many other methods and structures of computation that you can spend your entire lifetime trying to learn; if you are eager to do so, you should seriously pursue the field of computer science. I have found, however, that this basic set of concepts is sufficient for taking the first step toward understanding the nature of computer programming for visual expression.

As you continue to build more complex codes for drawing, there is one last technique you should be aware of which, although clearly useful, requires a great deal of effort to put into practice. It assumes a level of programming fluency that you may not have yet. I recall it took me at least a year before I began to feel comfortable using this technique, which is the signature of organized programming. Until now, all the commands you have used, such as Paper and Line, have been given to you. In this chapter, you will learn how to go a step beyond these commands by creating your own.

Define a Command The key skill of the computational designer is to express long, tedious tasks as succinct descriptions of process. From the computer's perspective, a compact programming form does not usually imply that the described task is any simpler than its non-compact form. The number of internal operations does not change; the only difference lies in the designer's perspective. A small, elegant program is conceptually easier to understand than one that is clumsily written.

The mechanisms of computation are designed to scale in a way that let you make intellectual investments that can be successively built upon in a concrete manner. The key to realizing these opportunities is rising one step above recognizing patterns of numbers, to recognizing patterns of process. An example best illustrates this point. Consider drawing a Manhattan skyline as a series of 29 filled rectangles.

```
Paper 0
// reinterpreted
// manhattan skyline
Repeat A 0 100
{
  Line A 10 A 0
}
Repeat A 1 15
{
  Line A 25 A 10
}
Repeat A 4 12
{
  Line A 28 A 25
}
Repeat A 17 31
{
  Line A 40 A 10
}
Repeat A 20 28
{
  Line A 50 A 40
}
Repeat A 21 27
{
  Line A 53 A 50
}
Repeat A 22 26
{
  Line A 56 A 53
}
Repeat A 23 25
{
  Line A 58 A 56
}
Repeat A 24 24
{
  Line A 64 A 58
}
Repeat A 35 45
{
  Line A 72 A 10
}
Repeat A 47 57
{
  Line A 72 A 10
}
Repeat A 38 38
{
  Line A 76 A 72
}
Repeat A 62 76
{
  Line A 50 A 10
}
Repeat A 63 75
{
  Line A 55 A 50
}
Repeat A 65 73
{
  Line A 61 A 55
}
Repeat A 68 70
{
  Line A 70 A 61
}
Repeat A 69 69
{
  Line A 79 A 70
}
Repeat A 80 98
{
  Line A 30 A 10
}
Repeat A 82 96
{
  Line A 35 A 30
}
Repeat A 86 92
{
  Line A 38 A 35
}
Repeat A 89 89
{
  Line A 42 A 38
}
Repeat A 16 17
{
  Line A 20 A 10
}
Repeat A 33 33
{
  Line A 20 A 10
}
Repeat A 34 35
{
  Line A 15 A 10
}
Repeat A 45 46
{
  Line A 17 A 10
}
Repeat A 57 59
{
  Line A 22 A 10
}
Repeat A 59 61
{
  Line A 24 A 10
}
Repeat A 79 81
{
  Line A 15 A 10
}
Repeat A 100 100
{
  Line A 16 A 10
}
```

Each rectangle corresponds to four lines of code, which differ across rectangles only in the actual numbers used. A total of four numbers are used per rectangle, corresponding to the left and right and to top and bottom bounds. Rewriting the program with variables to emphasize the similarities, using L and R for the left and right, and T and B for top and bottom, produces a significantly longer program.

```
Paper 0
// some minor
// construction
// to the
// infrastructure
Set L 0
Set R 100
Set T 10
Set B 0
Repeat A L R
{
  Line A T A B
}
Set L 1
Set R 15
Set T 25
Set B 10
Repeat A L R
{
  Line A T A B
}
Set L 4
Set R 12
Set T 28
Set B 25
Repeat A L R
{
  Line A T A B
}
Set L 17
Set R 31
Set T 40
Set B 10
Repeat A L R
{
  Line A T A B
}
Set L 20
Set R 28
Set T 50
Set B 40
Repeat A L R
{
  Line A T A B
}
Set L 21
Set R 27
Set T 53
Set B 50
Repeat A L R
{
  Line A T A B
}
Set L 22
Set R 26
Set T 56
Set B 53
Repeat A L R
{
  Line A T A B
}
Set L 23
Set R 25
Set T 58
Set B 56
Repeat A L R
{
  Line A T A B
}
Set L 24
Set R 24
Set T 64
Set B 58
Repeat A L R
{
  Line A T A B
}
Set L 35
Set R 45
Set T 72
Set B 10
Repeat A L R
{
  Line A T A B
}
Set L 47
Set R 57
Set T 72
Set B 10
Repeat A L R
{
  Line A T A B
}
Set L 38
Set R 38
Set T 76
Set B 72
Repeat A L R
{
  Line A T A B
}
Set L 62
Set R 76
Set T 50
Set B 10
Repeat A L R
{
  Line A T A B
}
Set L 63
Set R 75
Set T 55
Set B 50
Repeat A L R
{
  Line A T A B
}
Set L 65
Set R 73
Set T 61
Set B 55
Repeat A L R
{
  Line A T A B
}
Set L 68
Set R 70
Set T 70
Set B 61
Repeat A L R
{
  Line A T A B
}
Set L 69
Set R 69
Set T 79
Set B 70
Repeat A L R
{
  Line A T A B
}
Set L 80
Set R 98
Set T 30
Set B 10
Repeat A L R
{
  Line A T A B
}
Set L 82
Set R 96
Set T 35
Set B 30
Repeat A L R
{
  Line A T A B
}
Set L 86
Set R 92
Set T 38
Set B 35
Repeat A L R
{
  Line A T A B
}
Set L 89
Set R 89
Set T 42
Set B 38
Repeat A L R
{
  Line A T A B
}
Set L 16
Set R 17
Set T 20
Set B 10
Repeat A L R
{
  Line A T A B
}
Set L 33
Set R 33
Set T 20
Set B 10
Repeat A L R
{
  Line A T A B
}
Set L 34
Set R 35
Set T 15
Set B 10
Repeat A L R
{
  Line A T A B
}
Set L 45
Set R 46
Set T 17
Set B 10
Repeat A L R
{
  Line A T A B
}
Set L 57
Set R 59
Set T 22
Set B 10
Repeat A L R
{
  Line A T A B
}
Set L 59
Set R 61
Set T 24
Set B 10
Repeat A L R
{
  Line A T A B
}
Set L 79
Set R 81
Set T 15
Set B 10
Repeat A L R
{
  Line A T A B
}
Set L 100
Set R 100
Set T 16
Set B 10
Repeat A L R
{
  Line A T A B
}
```

In a situation where a process is reused in the manner of the rectangles in the skyline, there is an opportunity to name the process, similar to labeling a number with a variable name. Once a name is attached to the process, or more specifically a block of code, the corresponding block of code is run whenever the name is invoked. The name of the block is thus a reference to a brand new command, which is created with **Command**, followed by the name of the command. The block of code that corresponds to the command must follow immediately. In the example of the skyline, the process of creating a filled rectangle can be defined as a simple command **Box**

```
Command Box
{
  Repeat A L R
  {
    Line A T A B
  }
}
```

The Box command will repeat over the variable A from L to R and execute Line with descriptors A, T, A, and B, which is the same sequence used to create each filled rectangle. Now, instead of explicitly Repeating a Line, you can simply use the command Box.

```
//
// define a Box command
//
Command Box
{
  Repeat A L R
  {
    Line A T A B
  }
}
// now use it ...
Paper 0
Set L 0
Set R 100
Set T 10
Set B 0
Box
Set L 1
Set R 15
Set T 25
Set B 10
Box
Set L 4
Set R 12
Set T 28
Set B 25
Box
Set L 17
Set R 32
Set T 40
Set B 10
Box
Set L 20
Set R 29
Set T 50
Set B 40
Box
Set L 21
Set R 28
Set T 53
Set B 50
Box
Set L 22
Set R 27
Set T 56
Set B 53
Box
Set L 23
Set R 26
Set T 58
Set B 56
Box
Set L 24
Set R 25
Set T 64
Set B 58
Box
Set L 35
Set R 45
Set T 68
Set B 10
Box
Set L 47
Set R 57
Set T 68
Set B 10
Box
Set L 38
Set R 38
Set T 72
Set B 68
Box
Set L 62
Set R 76
Set T 50
Set B 10
Box
Set L 63
Set R 76
Set T 55
Set B 50
Box
Set L 65
Set R 74
Set T 61
Set B 55
Box
Set L 68
Set R 71
Set T 70
Set B 61
Box
Set L 69
Set R 70
Set T 79
Set B 70
Box
Set L 80
Set R 98
Set T 30
Set B 10
Box
Set L 82
Set R 96
Set T 35
Set B 30
Box
Set L 86
Set R 92
Set T 38
Set B 35
Box
Set L 89
Set R 89
Set T 42
Set B 38
Box
Set L 16
Set R 17
Set T 20
Set B 10
Box
Set L 33
Set R 33
Set T 20
Set B 10
Box
Set L 34
Set R 35
Set T 15
Set B 10
Box
Set L 45
Set R 46
Set T 17
Set B 10
Box
Set L 57
Set R 59
Set T 22
Set B 10
Box
Set L 59
Set R 61
Set T 24
Set B 10
Box
Set L 79
Set R 81
Set T 15
Set B 10
Box
Set L 100
Set R 100
Set T 16
Set B 10
Box
```

The program is now significantly shorter in length but yields the identical result. The process is also much easier to understand because the Box, or filled rectangle, is clearly visible as the higher level activity actually performed. The command invocation does not make the computer's job any easier because the Box only hides the Repeat of the Line behind a more descriptive command name. You may have noticed that Box does not require any descriptors the way Paper, Pen, and Line do. This is because you have not specified a need for them. Currently, all parameters of Repeat and Line are set as variables L, R, T, and B before the Box command is invoked. Since these parameters are essentially those that would be used as qualifiers for Box, all that remains is to declare them as such.

Descriptors can be declared as names of variables used in the command's block declared directly after the name of the command. For example, Box can be modified to accommodate descriptors L, R, T, and B.

```
Command Box L R T B
{
  Repeat A L R
  {
    Line A T A B
  }
}
```

Declaring Box in this form means that the variables will be automatically set from the qualifier list when Box is invoked. Instead of Set-ing the variables before running the Box command, the values are assigned to Box as descriptors.

```
//
// define Box command again,
// this time with descriptors
//
Command Box l R T B
{
  Repeat A L R
  {
    Line A T A B
  }
}
// code goes on a diet
Box 0 100 10 0
Box 1 15 25 10
Box 4 12 28 25
Box 17 31 40 10
Box 20 28 50 40
Box 21 27 53 50
Box 22 26 56 53
Box 23 25 58 56
Box 24 24 64 58
Box 35 45 72 10
Box 47 57 72 10
Box 38 38 76 72
Box 62 76 50 10
Box 63 75 55 50
Box 65 73 61 55
Box 68 70 70 61
Box 69 69 79 70
Box 80 98 30 10
Box 82 96 35 30
Box 86 92 38 35
Box 89 89 42 38
Box 16 17 20 10
Box 33 33 20 10
Box 34 35 15 10
Box 45 46 17 10
Box 57 59 22 10
Box 59 61 24 10
Box 79 81 15 10
Box 100 100 16 10
```

In comparison to the way the skyline was originally drawn, the new version using a command you created is significantly shorter because of the initial investment made in defining what a Box is and then immediately using the command. The new program is also easier to read and more intuitive to modify.

Pay close attention to the order in which the descriptor names appear in the Command declaration because when invoking a new command, you must enter each descriptor value as defined in the order of declaration. As with all commands you have used until now, the number of descriptors given when the command is invoked must equal the number of descriptors in the Command definition.

Commands From Commands A command represents a named process that can be built out of other named processes. Any command can be the point of departure to explore this scalable aspect of computation. Consider the definition of a framed rectangle where the qualifiers describe the horizontal and vertical position of the left bottom corner and the right top corner.

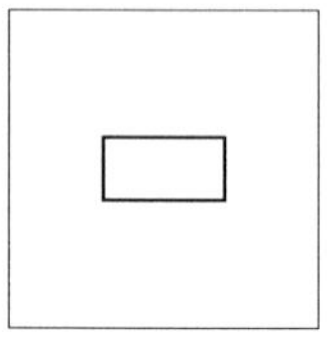

```
// make a rectangle command
Command Rectangle L B R T
{
  Line L B R B
  Line R B R T
  Line R T L T
  Line L T L B
}
// use it
Paper 0
Pen 100
Rectangle 30 40 70 60
```

With the **Rectangle** command defined, you can draw a simple figure of a person.

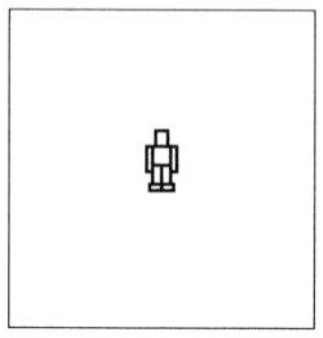

```
// this time use the Rectangle
// in a creative manner
Command Rectangle L B R T
{
  Line L B R B
  Line R B R T
  Line R T L T
  Line L T L B
}
Paper 0
Pen 100
Set PH 50
Set PV 43
// feet
Rectangle (PH-4) PV PH (PV+2)
Rectangle (PH+4) PV PH (PV+2)
// legs
Rectangle (PH-3) (PV+2) PH (PV+8)
Rectangle (PH+3) (PV+2) PH (PV+8)
// arms
Rectangle (PH-5) (PV+6) (PH-3) (PV+14)
Rectangle (PH+5) (PV+6) (PH+3) (PV+14)
// head
Rectangle (PH-2) (PV+14) (PH+2) (PV+19)
// body is implicit
```

You can define a block of code to draw a person using a command and then invoke the command several times to draw a group of people.

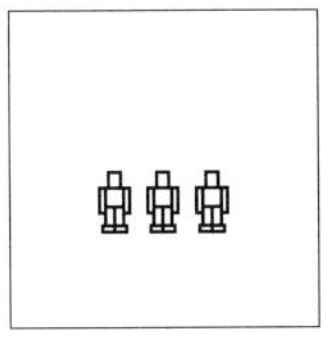

```
Command Rectangle L B R T
{
  Line L B R B
  Line R B R T
  Line R T L T
  Line L T L B
}
// go one step further and play God
// by *defining* a person ...
Command Person PH PV
{
  Rectangle (PH-4) PV PH (PV+2)
  Rectangle (PH+4) PV PH (PV+2)
  Rectangle (PH-3) (PV+2) PH (PV+8)
  Rectangle (PH+3) (PV+2) PH (PV+8)
  Rectangle (PH-5) (PV+6) (PH-3) (PV+14)
  Rectangle (PH+5) (PV+6) (PH+3) (PV+14)
  Rectangle (PH-2) (PV+14) (PH+2) (PV+19)
}
Paper 0
Pen 100
// there is strength in numbers
Person 34 30
Person 50 30
Person 66 30
```

You can then expand your creativity with a special configuration of people.

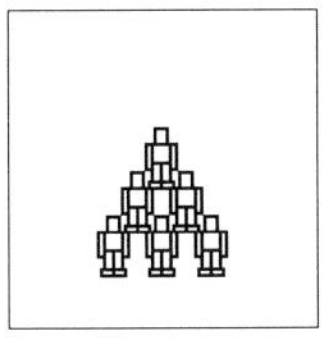

```
Command Rectangle L B R T
{
  Line L B R B
  Line R B R T
  Line R T L T
  Line L T L B
}
Command Person PH PV
{
  Rectangle (PH-4) PV PH (PV+2)
  Rectangle (PH+4) PV PH (PV+2)
  Rectangle (PH-3) (PV+2) PH (PV+8)
  Rectangle (PH+3) (PV+2) PH (PV+8)
  Rectangle (PH-5) (PV+6) (PH-3) (PV+14)
  Rectangle (PH+5) (PV+6) (PH+3) (PV+14)
  Rectangle (PH-2) (PV+14) (PH+2) (PV+19)
}
Command Pyramid U V
{
  Person U V
  Person (U+16) V
  Person (U-16) V
  Person (U-8) (V+14)
  Person (U+8) (V+14)
  Person U (V+28)
}
Paper 0
Pen 100
// play cheer squad
Pyramid 50 16
```

And take it to its limits.

```
Command Rectangle L B R T
{
  Line L B R B
  Line R B R T
  Line R T L T
  Line L T L B
}
Command Person PH PV
{
  Rectangle (PH-4) PV PH (PV+2)
  Rectangle (PH+4) PV PH (PV+2)
  Rectangle (PH-3) (PV+2) PH (PV+8)
  Rectangle (PH+3) (PV+2) PH (PV+8)
  Rectangle (PH-5) (PV+6) (PH-3) (PV+14)
  Rectangle (PH+5) (PV+6) (PH+3) (PV+14)
  Rectangle (PH-2) (PV+14) (PH+2) (PV+19)
}
Command PyramidMany H V N
{
  // init vertical position
  Set PY V
  // repeat over levels
  Repeat Y 0 N
  {
    Set Y2 (Y)
    Set DN (Y2*16)
    Set DM (DN/2)
    // center horizontal position
    Set PX (H-DM)
    // repeat over a level
    Repeat X 0 Y
    {
      Person PX PY
      // advance horizontal
      Set PX (PX+16)
    }
    // advance vertical
    Set PY (PY+14)
  }
}
Paper 0
Pen 100
// superhuman strength
PyramidMany 50 0 7
```

A single command leads you back to the abstract.

```
Command Rectangle L B R T
{
  Line L B R B
  Line R B R T
  Line R T L T
  Line L T L B
}
Paper 0
// ode to gerstner
Repeat B 0 25
{
  Set A (B*2)
  Pen A
  Rectangle (50-A) (50-A) (A+50) (A+50)
}
```

The expression can be varied.

```
Command Rectangle L B R T
{
  Line L B R B
  Line R B R T
  Line R T L T
  Line L T L B
}
// the power of abstraction
Command RectInRect H V N S
{
  Repeat B 0 N
  {
    Set A (B*S)
    Rectangle (H-A) (V-A) (A+H) (A+V)
  }
}
Paper 0
RectInRect 50 50 25 2
```

And applied to different interactions.

```
Command Rectangle L B R T
{
  Line L B R B
  Line R B R T
  Line R T L T
  Line L T L B

}
Command RectInRect H V N S
{
  Repeat B 0 N
  {
    Set A (B*S)
    Rectangle (H-A) (V-A) (A+H) (A+V)
  }
}
Paper 0
// quad expansion
RectInRect 26 26 12 2
RectInRect 74 26 12 2
RectInRect 26 74 12 2
RectInRect 74 74 12 2
```

Because it has been coded with flexibility, it is easily modified in a significant manner.

```
Command Rectangle L B R T
{
  Line L B R B
  Line R B R T
  Line R T L T
  Line L T L B
}
Command RectInRect H V N S
{
  Repeat B 0 N
  {
    Set A (B*S)
    Rectangle (H-A) (V-A) (A+H) (A+V)
  }
}
Paper 0
// larger step-size
RectInRect 26 26 6 4
RectInRect 74 26 6 4
RectInRect 26 74 6 4
RectInRect 74 74 6 4
```

It also surprises.

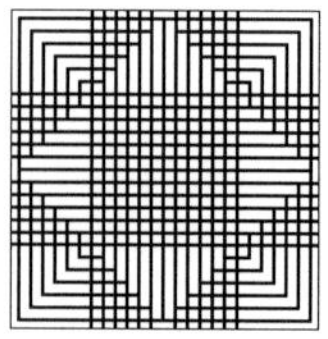

```
Command Rectangle L B R T
{
  Line L B R B
  Line R B R T
  Line R T L T
  Line L T L B
}
Command RectInRect H V N S
{
  Repeat B 0 N
  {
    Set A (B*S)
    Rectangle (H-A) (V-A) (A+H) (A+V)
  }
}
Paper 0
// increase rectangle count
RectInRect 26 26 12 4
RectInRect 74 26 12 4
RectInRect 26 74 12 4
RectInRect 74 74 12 4
```

The experience can be built upon using more layers of generalization.

```
Command Rectangle L B R T
{
  Line L B R B
  Line R B R T
  Line R T L T
  Line L T L B
}
Command RectInRect H V N S
{
  Repeat B 0 N
  {
    Set A (B*S)
    Rectangle (H-A) (V-A) (A+H) (A+V)
  }
}
// even more abstraction
Command RectInRectInRect H V N S
{
  RectInRect (H-N*S) (V-N*S) N S
  RectInRect (H+N*S) (V-N*S) N S
  RectInRect (H+N*S) (V+N*S) N S
  RectInRect (H-N*S) (V+N*S) N S
}
Paper 0
RectInRectInRect 50 50 12 2
```

You can go one step further.

```
Command Rectangle L B R T
{
  Line L B R B
  Line R B R T
  Line R T L T
  Line L T L B
}
Command RectInRect H V N S
{
  Repeat B 0 N
  {
    Set A (B*S)
    Rectangle (H-A) (V-A) (A+H) (A+V)
  }
}
Command RectInRectInRect H V N S
{
  RectInRect (H-N*S) (V-N*S) N S
  RectInRect (H+N*S) (V-N*S) N S
  RectInRect (H+N*S) (V+N*S) N S
  RectInRect (H-N*S) (V+N*S) N S
}
Paper 0
// quad expansion
RectInRectInRect 25 25 6 2
RectInRectInRect 75 25 6 2
RectInRectInRect 25 75 6 2
RectInRectInRect 75 75 6 2
```

And again take it to the limits.

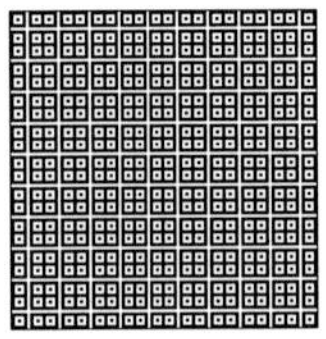

```
Command Rectangle L B R T
{
  Line L B R B
  Line R B R T
  Line R T L T
  Line L T L B
}
Command RectInRect H V N S
{
  Repeat B 0 N
  {
    Set A (B*S)
    Rectangle (H-A) (V-A) (A+H) (A+V)
  }
}
Command RectInRectInRect H V N S
{
  RectInRect (H-N*S) (V-N*S) N S
  RectInRect (H+N*S) (V-N*S) N S
  RectInRect (H+N*S) (V+N*S) N S
  RectInRect (H-N*S) (V+N*S) N S
}
Paper 0
// do it the old fashioned way
Repeat H 0 10
{
  Repeat V 0 10
  {
    RectInRectInRect (10*H) (10*V) 1 2
  }
}
```

In this manner, commands can be built from commands, which can be built from commands, and so forth until the only commands used are the primitive set of commands such as Repeat and Set. There is no limit to how many levels you can define commands out of commands, but that is not the goal. The challenge is to discover the right set of commands to use as the building blocks for your future experiments in computational media design.

Libraries of Commands When designing this system for learning basic computational media design, I intentionally limited the set of commands and constructs to a minimal number of possibilities. If I had given you drawing capability beyond a line or setting a dot, the examples could have been more exciting, but the point could not be made clearly because your attention would be drawn to the picture and not to the code. Now that you can define your own commands, you are free to extend the system to suit your own tastes. To get you started, as sort of a sendoff gift, I present you with a set of basic primitives that will serve you well.

First, in order to gain a sense of appreciation for the Line command, examine the following.

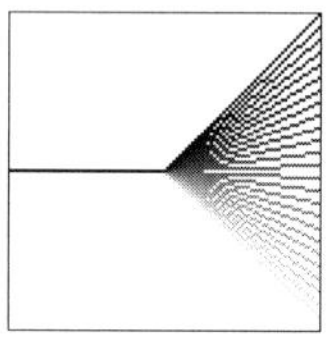

```
// a line command a la Bresenham
Command Line AX AY BX BY GVAL
{
  Set CX AX
  Set CY AY
  // get absolute distances
  Set BAX (BX-AX)
  Set BAY (BY-AY)
  Smaller? BAX 0
  {
    Set DX (0-BAX)
  }
  NotSmaller? BAX 0
  {
    Set DX BAX
  }
  Smaller? BAY 0
  {
    Set DY (0-BAY)
  }
  NotSmaller? BAY 0
  {
    Set DY BAY
  }
  // get increment
  Smaller? BX AX
  {
    Set XINC (0-1)
  }
  NotSmaller? BX AX
  {
    Set XINC 1
  }
  Smaller? BY AY
  {
    Set YINC (0-1)
  }
  NotSmaller? BY AY
  {
    Set YINC 1
  }
  NotSmaller? DX DY
  {
    Set DGR (DY*2)
    Set DGRU (DGR-DX*2)
    Set G (DGR-DX)
    Repeat DDX 0 DX
    {
      Set [CX CY] GVAL
      Smaller? 0 G
      {
        Set CY (CY+YINC)
        Set NEWG (G+DGRU)
      }
      NotSmaller? 0 G
      {
        Set NEWG (G+DGR)
      }
      Set CX (CX+XINC)
      Set G NEWG
    }
  }
  Smaller? DX DY
  {
    Set DGR (DX*2)
    Set DGRU (DGR-DY*2)
    Set G (DGR-DY)
    Repeat DDY 0 DY
    {
      Set [CX CY] GVAL
      Smaller? 0 G
      {
        Set CX (CX+XINC)
        Set G (G+DGRU)
      }
      NotSmaller? 0 G
      {
        Set G (G+DGR)
      }
      Set CY (CY+YINC)
    }
  }
}
Paper 0
// a test pattern
Line 0 50 50 50 100
Repeat A 0 25
{
  Line 50 50 100 (A*4) (A*4)
}
```

A **Triangle** primitive is always useful.

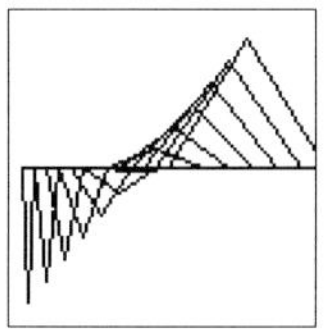

```
// triangle is simple to code
Command Triangle H1 V1 H2 V2 H3 V3
{
  Line H1 V1 H2 V2
  Line H2 V2 H3 V3
  Line H3 V3 H1 V1
}
Paper 0
Pen 100
// a test pattern
Repeat A 1 13
{
  Triangle (A*4) 50 (A*6) (A*7) (A*8) 50
}
```

And also a solid gray **Field** will be handy.

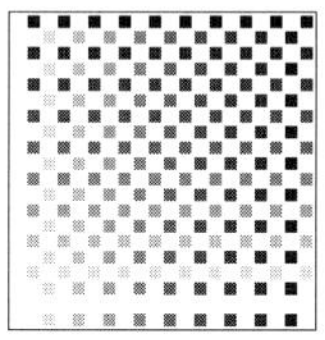

```
//  a field of gray tone
// (also called a filled rectangle
//  but that is too long to type)
Command Field L B R T G
{
  Pen G
  Repeat H L R
  {
    Line H T H B
  }
}
Paper 0
// a test pattern
Repeat A 0 10
{
  Repeat B 0 10
  {
    Set A1 (A*10)
    Set B1 (B*10)
    Set A1 (A1+1)
    Set B1 (B1+1)
    Field A1 B1 (A1+3) (B1+3) (A*10)
    Set B1 (B1+5)
    Set A1 (A1+5)
    Field A1 B1 (A1+3) (B1+3) (B*10)
  }
}
```

And finally, the warmth of a real circle.

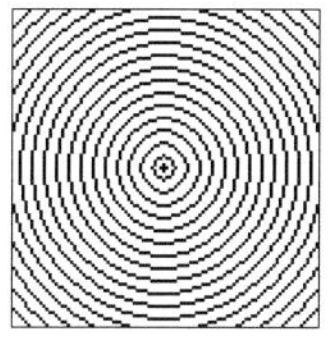

```
// circle maker is easier than i thought
Command CirclePixels CX CY DX DY V
{
  Set [(CX+DX) (CY+DY)] V
  Set [(CX+DX) (CY-DY)] V
  Set [(CX-DX) (CY+DY)] V
  Set [(CX-DX) (CY-DY)] V
  Set [(CX+DY) (CY+DX)] V
  Set [(CX+DY) (CY-DX)] V
  Set [(CX-DY) (CY+DX)] V
  Set [(CX-DY) (CY-DX)] V
}
Command Circle CX CY Radius V
{
  Set X 0
  Set Y Radius
  Set D (1-Radius)
  CirclePixels CX CY X Y V
  // 707/1000 approximates
  // square root of 0.5 = cos(45)
  Repeat X 0 (Radius*707/1000)
  {
    Set tempD D
    Smaller? tempD 0
    {
      Set D (D+(2*X)+3)
    }
    NotSmaller? tempD 0
    {
      Set D (D+(2*(X-Y))+5)
      Set Y (Y-1)
    }
    CirclePixels CX CY X Y V
  }
}
Paper 0
// a test pattern
Repeat A 0 20
{
  Circle 50 50 (A*4) 100
}
```

Defining all of these commands in your program will make the preamble annoyingly long and thus may discourage you from using them.

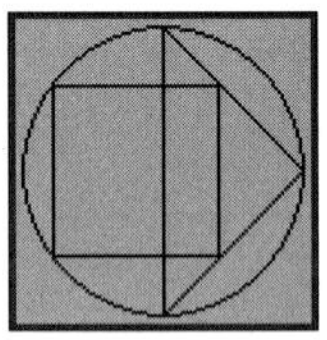

```
// a lengthy warming up, followed
// by putting all that exercise to
// good use ...
Command Triangle H1 V1 H2 V2 H3 V3
{
  Line H1 V1 H2 V2
  Line H2 V2 H3 V3
  Line H3 V3 H1 V1
}
Command Rectangle L B R T
{
  Line L B R B
  Line R B R T
  Line R T L T
  Line L T L B
}
Command Field L B R T G
{
  Pen G
  Repeat H L R
  {
    Line H T H B
  }
}
Command CirclePixels CX CY DX DY V
{
  Set [(CX+DX) (CY+DY)] V
  Set [(CX+DX) (CY-DY)] V
  Set [(CX-DX) (CY+DY)] V
  Set [(CX-DX) (CY-DY)] V
  Set [(CX+DY) (CY+DX)] V
  Set [(CX+DY) (CY-DX)] V
  Set [(CX-DY) (CY+DX)] V
  Set [(CX-DY) (CY-DX)] V
}
Command Circle CX CY RADIUS V
{
  Set X 0
  Set Y RADIUS
  Set D (1-RADIUS)
  CirclePixels CX CY X Y V
  Repeat X 0 (RADIUS*707/1000)
  {
    Set TEMPD D
    Smaller? TEMPD 0
    {
      Set D (D+(2*X)+3)
    }
    NotSmaller? TEMPD 0
    {
      Set D (D+(2*(X-Y))+5)
      Set Y (Y-1)
    }
    CirclePixels CX CY X Y V
  }
}
Paper 75
Field 2 2 98 98 25
Pen 100
Triangle 50 96 50 4 96 50
Circle 50 50 46 100
Rectangle 14 23 68 77
```

In your journey through computation, you have seen programs of many lines reduced to a single line, and you may find it unfathomable that a program like this cannot be reduced just one last time for the sake of clarity. This brings us to the final complexity reduction technique: the **Load** command. By placing your commands into a separate file, called a *library file,* you can simply instruct the program to load the library when it runs. When instructed to load, the computer visits the library file to look up the code corresponding to a command you requested in your main program.

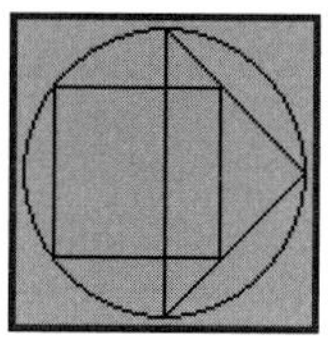

```
// the art of concealment
Load dbngraphics.dbn
Paper 75
Field 2 2 98 98 25
Pen 100
Triangle 50 96 50 4 96 50
Circle 50 50 46 100
Rectangle 14 23 68 77
```

Summary Taking a process and assigning a relevant name to it is the basis of computer programming. A program embodies a process that is either defined as a long sequence of primitive commands, a set of streamlined processes that involve Repeats, or a preamble of command definitions followed by references to the commands.

As you define each new command, your vocabulary of expression is gradually increased in a concrete, quantitative sense. Regardless of how general or specific the process defined by the command may be, its status in your vocabulary will be determined by how often it is used. If you glance through any book on graphics programming, you will see countless commands that you can incorporate into your work. Most of these commands are rarely used, however, because they represent the intent of the graphics toolkit builder, and not necessarily of the artist.

Working with many premade options is not necessarily the best way to build a vocabulary of expression although it certainly is the easiest. Ideally, you will find satisfaction in actively building and refining your own set of commands. Each command embodies a concrete insight. The collection of these insights may be called your *style.* Style was once something demonstrated over many examples. In computation, style can be defined with a single command. For that reason, if you give away your commands, you are actually giving away your own style, which is why you should closely guard your intimate set of commands and not publish them in a book as I have done here.

This chapter concludes your introduction to programming. I do not mean to suggest that there is nothing left for you to learn, but there is much to practice from the chapters presented thus far. When you feel ready, proceed to Chapter 13 and begin studying advanced topics in computational expression that illustrate the relevance of the skills that you have just begun to master, and that preview the challenges that lie ahead.

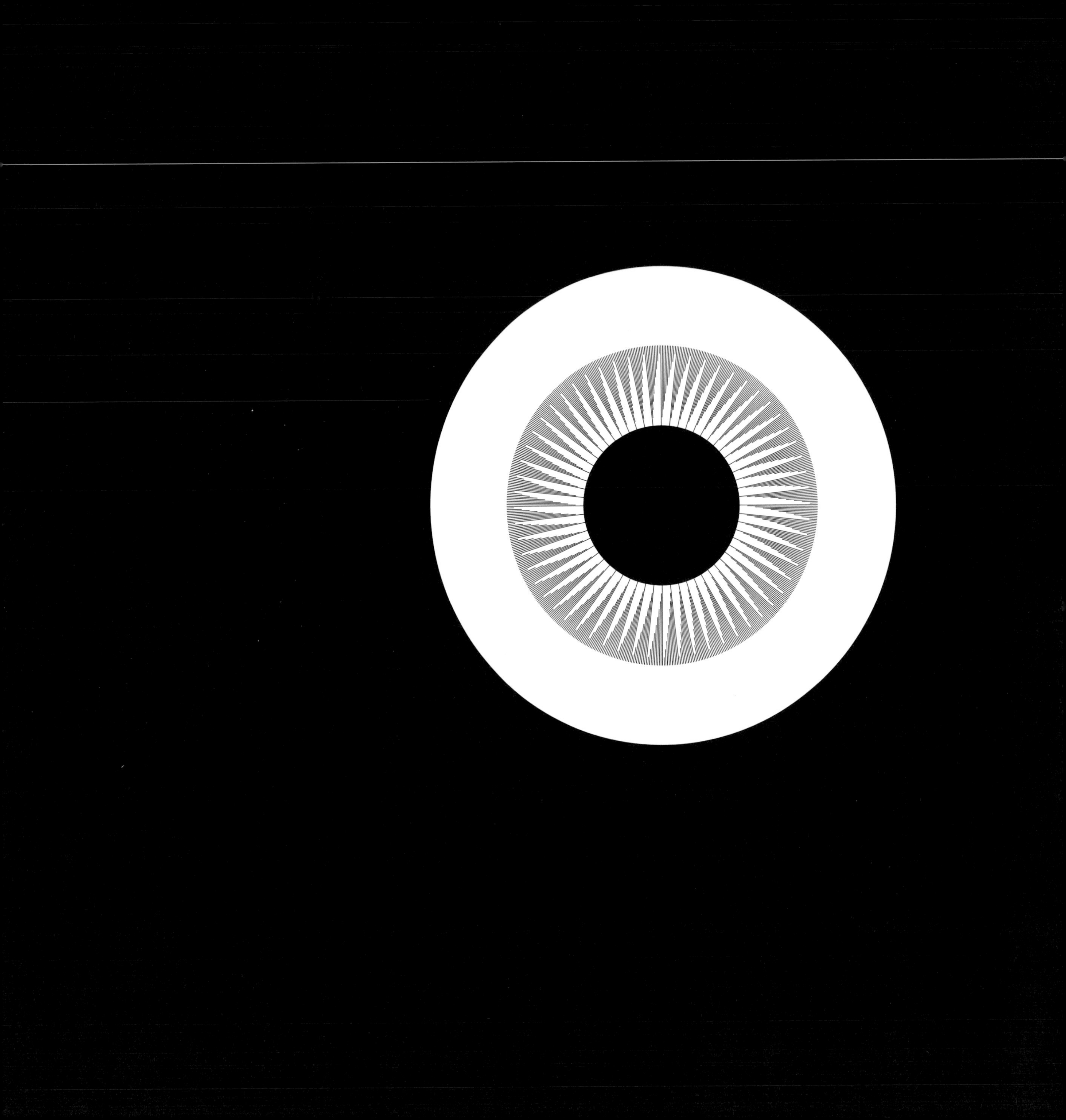

13 TIME Computation enables a dialogue with the process of creation. Precise statements of how a form is drawn, coupled with a sense of what the computer is best at drawing, result in a rare synergy between artist and computer. Using variables, Repeats, and other assorted programming constructs lets you draw in a manner that would be considered tedious if done by hand. As a result, the practice of encoding a graphical form as a program can easily turn into an experiment in visual complexity.

A computer will always execute any task you present to it, whether it is drawing circles for a week or arranging several thousand images in collage. Encode the task as a program, however complex it may be, and the computer diligently proceeds to render precisely your every wish. The computer never complains. As long as you are patient and can precisely instruct it, you can easily create artwork in a matter of minutes that would normally take a staff of hundreds several years to complete by hand.

There was a time when I created various monstrosities of lines, type, tone, and image out of the misguided notion that I wanted to glorify the computer's role in the graphic arts. But I began to feel a conflict between my training to design with economy and my youthful will to overpower visually by applying computation. I chose to seek simplicity in a forced regime of complexity; after much searching, I discovered my peace along the axis of time.

This chapter begins a series of discussions, which will continue until Chapter 18, concerning the expressive capability of the computational medium in the time domain. Various temporal phenomena are constructed. As we progress, you will most likely find it increasingly difficult to appreciate the textual descriptions and graphics of this book because the static medium of paper does not communicate rapid visual change. Dynamic forms are best understood in their natural habitat. You can save yourself from unnecessary confusion by typing the short examples into the computer and viewing the results in realtime.

Paper Animation A straightforward expression of time in a program is to control the generation of various sheets of Paper, which you may have already discovered by accident. Two Paper commands run in succession illustrate this property.

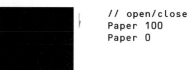

```
// open/close
Paper 100
Paper 0
```

This visual transition is displayed as two consecutive frames. Considering that you may not have a computer available to test these programs, all time-based examples are displayed as sequences of consecutive images and are reduced in scale whenever necessary. In this example, the two events of "Paper 100" and "Paper 0" are visible as a two-frame sequence. The sequence is easily extended to three frames.

```
// blink
Paper 100
Paper 0
Paper 100
```

The sheet should have changed from black to white, and then back to black. Depending upon the speed of the computer, you may not even see the white sheet in-between.

This transition can be made more pleasing with the addition of gray sheets to create a sequence of five sheets.

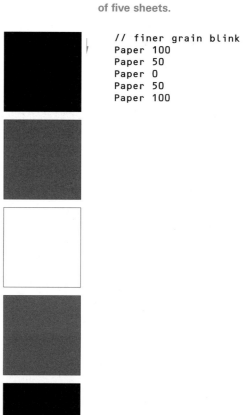

```
// finer grain blink
Paper 100
Paper 50
Paper 0
Paper 50
Paper 100
```

Generating more sheets can greatly smooth the temporal progression. A single Repeat models a hundred progressions from black to white, listed out in their entirety for just this once.

```
// even finer grain blink
Repeat T 100 0
{
  Paper T
}
```

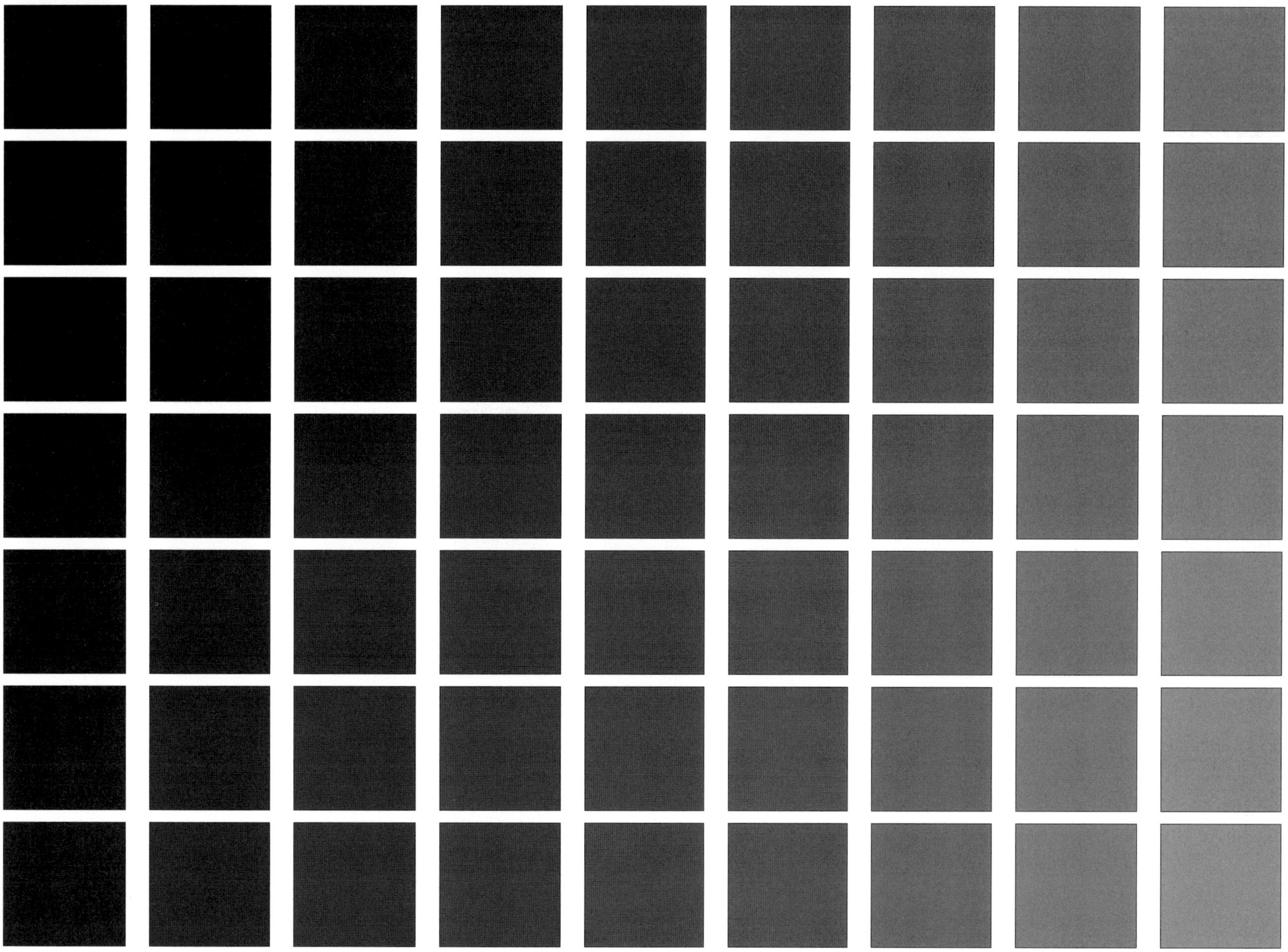

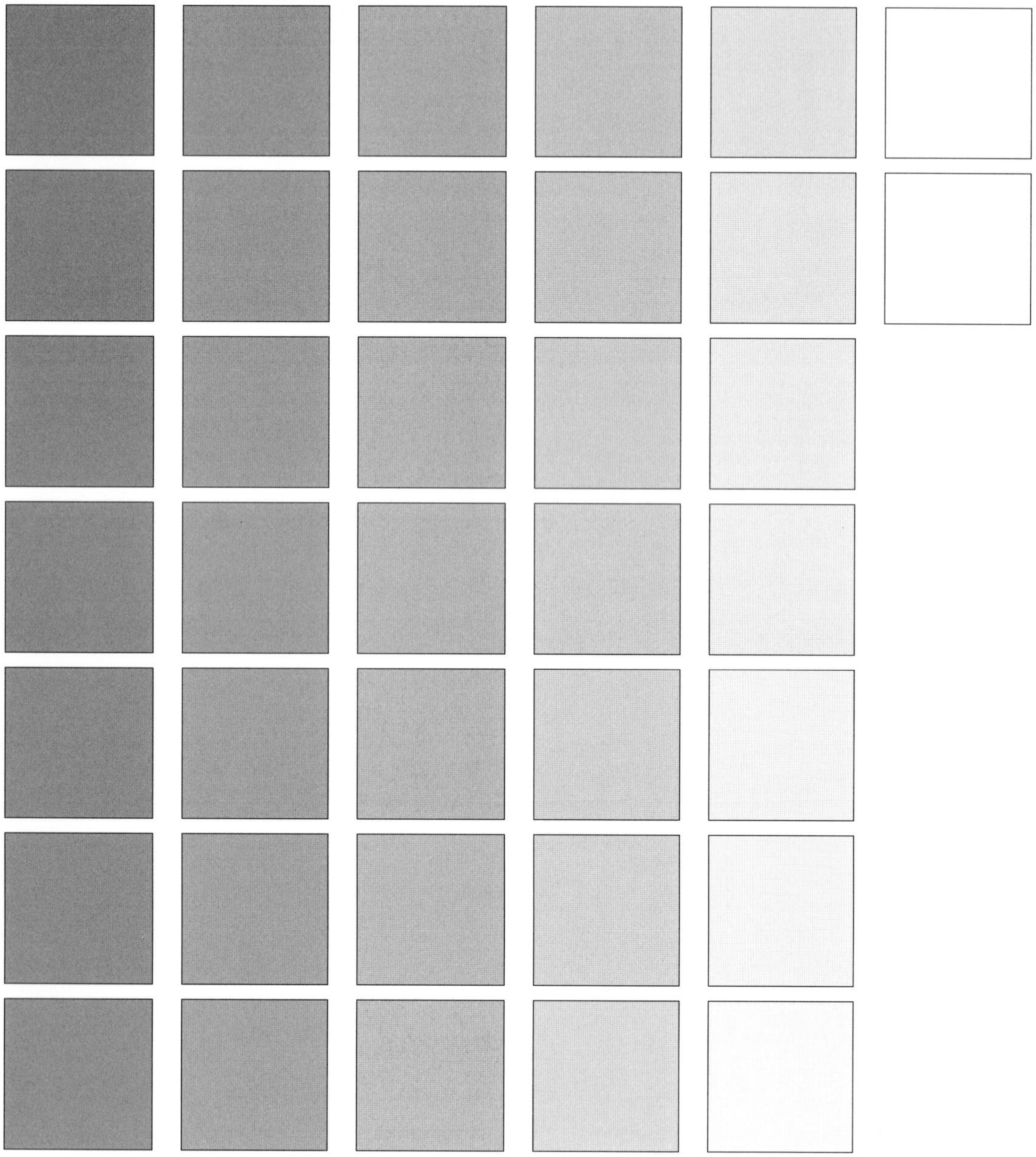

The large quantity of images that can be generated by a small program form is dramatized in this manner, illustrating a fundamental property of temporal expression. While viewing this form on the computer screen, you probably did not see all individual 101 squares as they appeared. You are more likely to think that this single square rapidly changes in gray value. Although the computer has performed a moderately complex task by generating 101 sheets of paper, the complexity of the task is not perceived because the task is mapped onto the dimension of time. Furthermore, it may be perceived as a *simple* temporal phenomenon.

Maintaining the illusion of simplicity in a temporal expression is a conscious effort. Generally you want to avoid sudden tonal changes in a subject because they are generally perceived in a negative light, as in the example of an annoying composition that blinks rapidly.

```
// incessantly blink
Repeat T 0 100
{
  Paper 0
  Paper 100
}
```

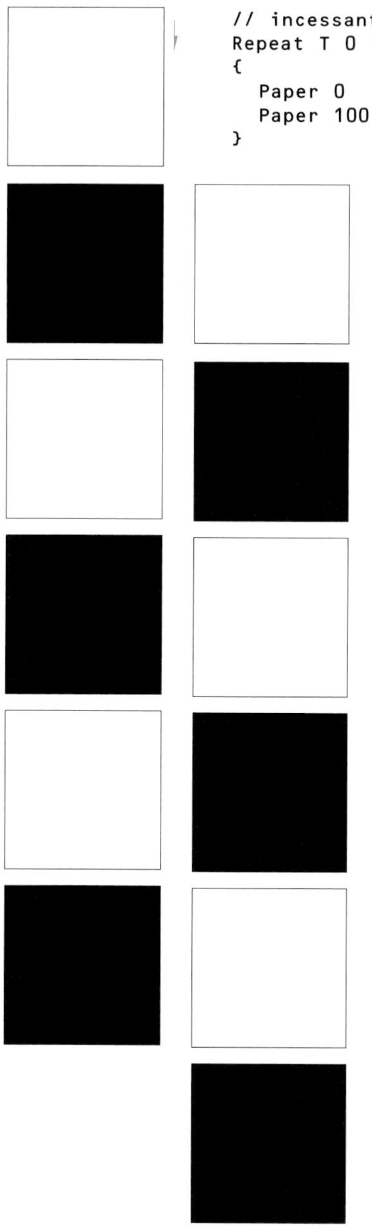

Such a square can be tamed by awareness of the progression of time. This effect is achieved by relating the tonal changes to the varying quantity of the Repeat, in this case, T.

```
// fade while blinking
Repeat T 0 100
{
  Paper 0
  Paper T
}
```

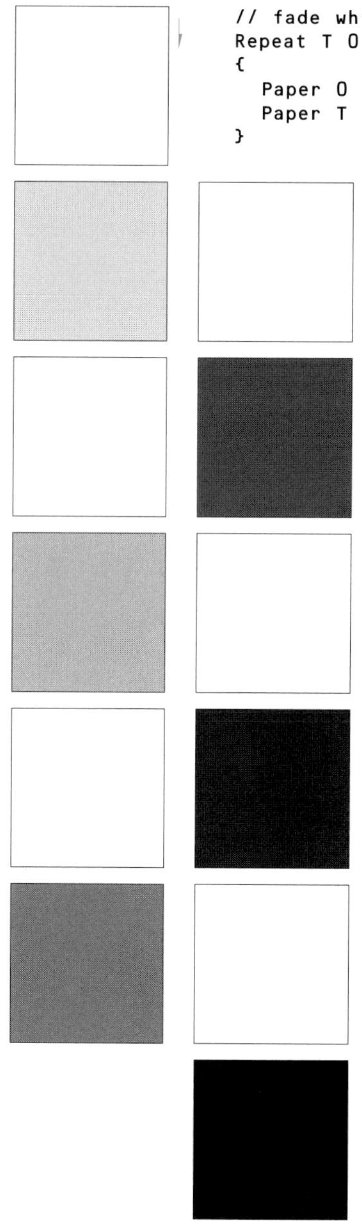

When the blinking effect is gradually introduced, the result is less offensive. In general, a "Paper T," where T varies in a Repeat, has this soothing effect. However, the monotonous character of a "Paper T" can quickly lose its appeal, in which case the speed of transition becomes an important element. The speed is adjusted through calculations that involve either division or multiplication, where divide can decrease the speed and multiply can increase it.

```
// slow fade to white
Repeat A 200 0
{
  Paper (A/2)
}
// fast fade to black
Repeat A 0 50
{
  Paper (A*2)
}
```

A variety of speeds can be displayed in a single composition or program by using a nested Repeat, where with each outer cycle, the speed of the inner transitions increase by reducing the limits of the inner variable.

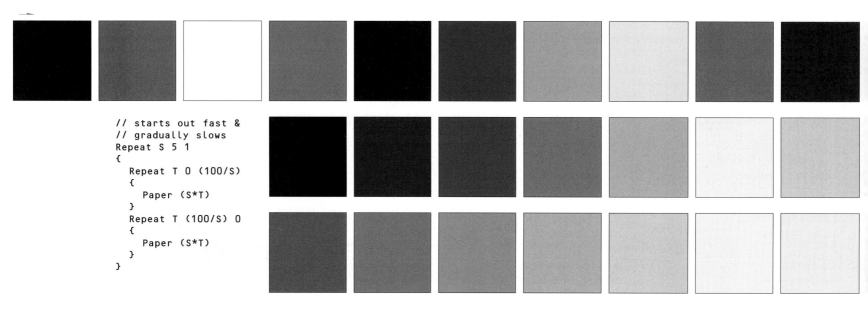

```
// starts out fast &
// gradually slows
Repeat S 5 1
{
  Repeat T 0 (100/S)
  {
    Paper (S*T)
  }
  Repeat T (100/S) 0
  {
    Paper (S*T)
  }
}
```

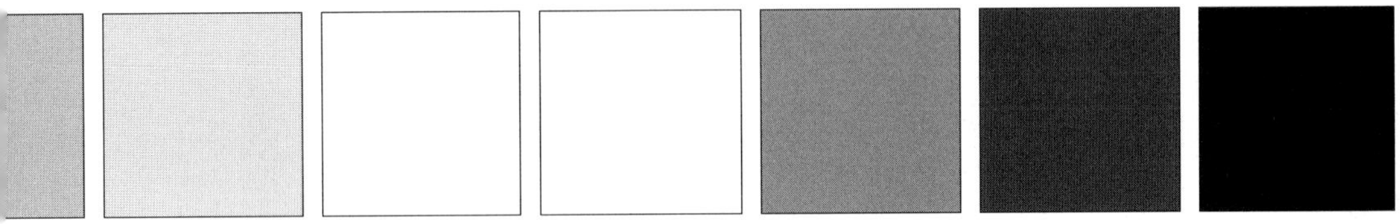

The subtleties of display speed are especially meaningless when rendered on paper, so I again encourage you to view these examples in the digital medium, which best befits the expression.

Flying Lines Variation of tone is an effective temporal design technique not only when applied to an entire field of view, but also when used in a subarea of the page. i have seen a beginning student enter the following program by accident when attempting to draw a gradated rectangle. Imagine her surprise when she inadvertently made a line appear out of nowhere.

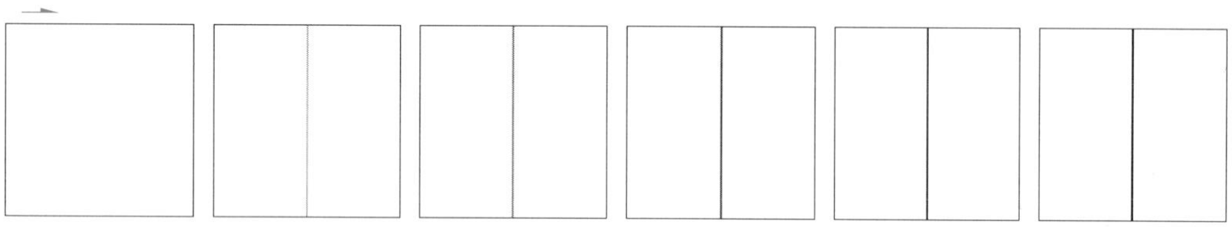

```
Paper 0
// line fades into view
Repeat T 0 100
{
  Pen T
  Line 50 0 50 100
}
```

The perception is quite different from the entire Paper changing tone because there is the tonal reference of the white Paper in the background, which accentuates the contrast with the fading line in the foreground. This contrast is enhanced on top of a black background.

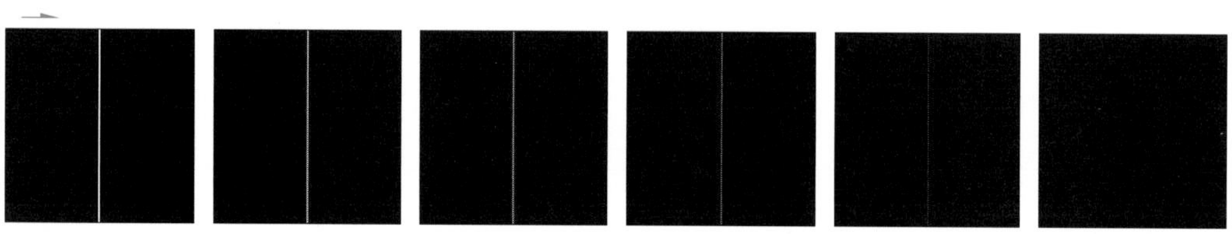

```
Paper 100
// line fades out now
Repeat T 0 100
{
  Pen T
  Line 50 0 50 100
}
```

Rather than varying in tone when the line is freed to vary in position, temporal expression graduates to what we associate with actual motion. Until now, we have thought of a moving line as a technique for filling a rectangle. For example, white lines drawn in succession across a black sheet of paper result in a completely white drawing area.

```
Paper 100
Pen 0
// your garden variety filled area
Repeat T 0 100
{
  Line T 0 T 100
}
```

But when viewed over time, each individual Line in the Repeat can be seen as enacting a behavior of flying through space. We can see this effect by focusing on the individual lines that are drawn, generating a new sheet of paper with each cycle.

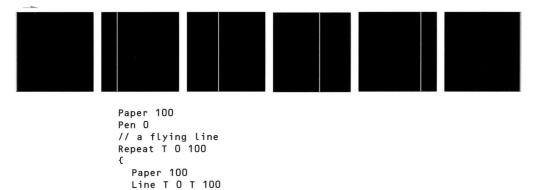

```
Paper 100
Pen 0
// a flying line
Repeat T 0 100
{
  Paper 100
  Line T 0 T 100
}
```

Each cycle of the Repeat creates a fresh new drawing and, in this case, results in a short animation of a traveling line. If you were to slow the process of drawing the filled rectangle without generating a Paper each cycle, the result would still be an animation, but one quite different in character.

```
Paper 100
Pen 0
// a gradual wipe from black to white
Repeat T 0 100
{
  Line T 0 T 100
}
```

Both animated forms share the same process at their roots, but they are perceived differently through slight modification in the relationship between the way the drawing actions are presented as either cumulative or independent.

Adding another line to the scene improves this basic animated study by establishing a motion reference, in the same way that the background Paper shade provides a tonal reference. For example, breaking our line in half, one half can fly twice as fast as the other.

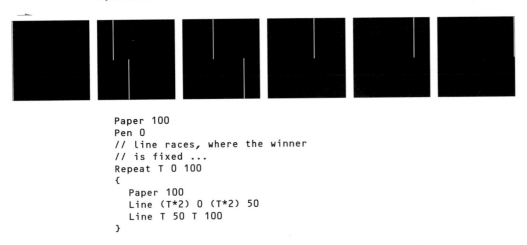

```
Paper 100
Pen 0
// line races, where the winner
// is fixed ...
Repeat T 0 100
{
  Paper 100
  Line (T*2) 0 (T*2) 50
  Line T 50 T 100
}
```

There can also be a comparative change in scale.

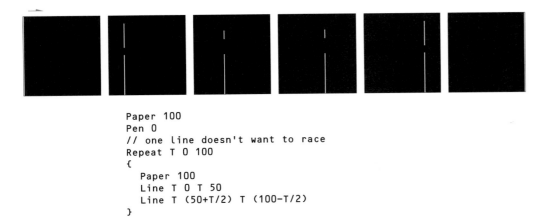

```
Paper 100
Pen 0
// one line doesn't want to race
Repeat T 0 100
{
  Paper 100
  Line T 0 T 50
  Line T (50+T/2) T (100-T/2)
}
```

Or there can be a change in the shape; in this case, a vertical line to a horizontal line, which is qualitatively a different shape but would be described more as a change in orientation.

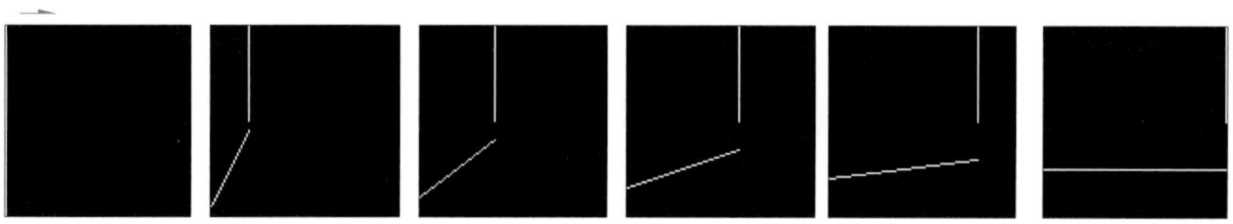

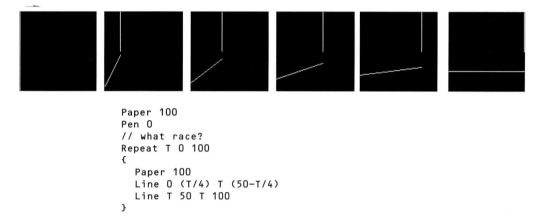

```
Paper 100
Pen 0
// what race?
Repeat T 0 100
{
  Paper 100
  Line 0 (T/4) T (50-T/4)
  Line T 50 T 100
}
```

By adding a few more lines, there is a connection, and a change in shape.

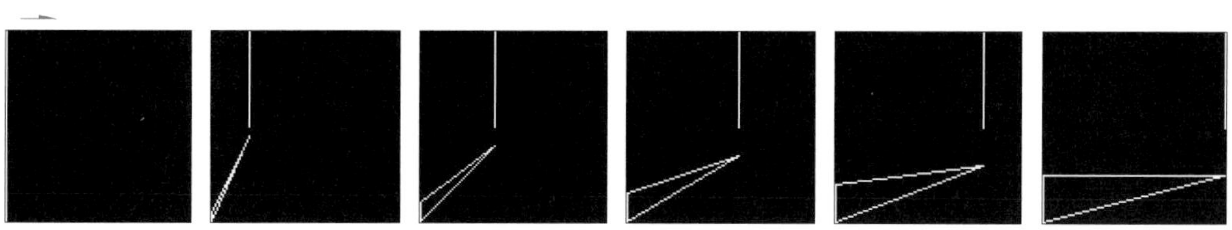

```
Paper 100
Pen 0
// playing architect
Repeat T 0 100
{
  Paper 100
  Line 0 (T/4) T (50-T/4)
  Line 0 0 T (50-T/4)
  Line 0 (T/4) 0 0
  Line T 50 T 100
}
```

Thus tone, position, scale, orientation, and shape are some of the ways that a form can numerically reorganize over time. Each class of change can be combined to build more complex transformations in form. Addressing the parameters of change individually will lead to better understanding of their respective strengths.

Defy Reality When designing an animated expression, the activity in the foreground usually governs the show. The background, which in this case is usually just the shade of the Paper, serves an unobtrusive role—upholding the context for the foreground. Although I first introduced animation by varying the background, you now know that manipulating the foreground generally produces the more inspired results. The background usually dominates most of the visual field; it is our natural human tendency to prefer that it stay constant because we are more accustomed to seeing objects moving around than having the surrounding environment rapidly change. The analogy would be to watch the sky quickly turn from day to night, which is experienced in the rare occurrence of an eclipse. To see this effect continuously, however, can be disconcerting.

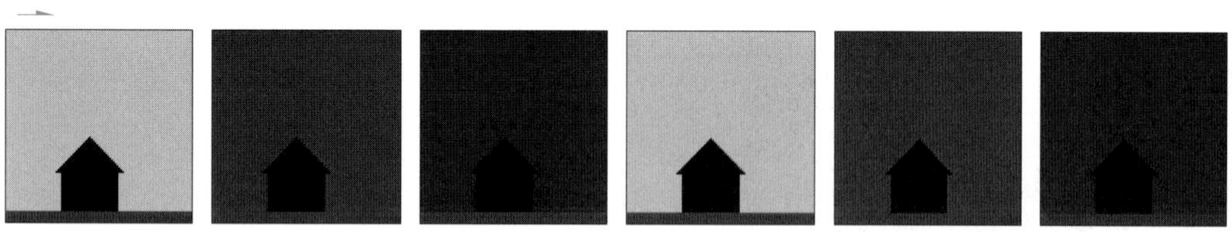

```
// house day to nite
// 2 times consecutively
Paper 0
Repeat DAY 0 1
{
  Repeat T 20 80
  {
    Paper T
    Pen 100
    Field 0 0 100 5 70
    Field 30 6 60 26 100
    Repeat A 27 63
    {
      Line A 26 45 44
    }
  }
}
```

In the same manner, if the background exhibits continual, erratic change, there is even more of an element of the visually abnormal. We tolerate lightning storms but do not welcome their insistence to remain.

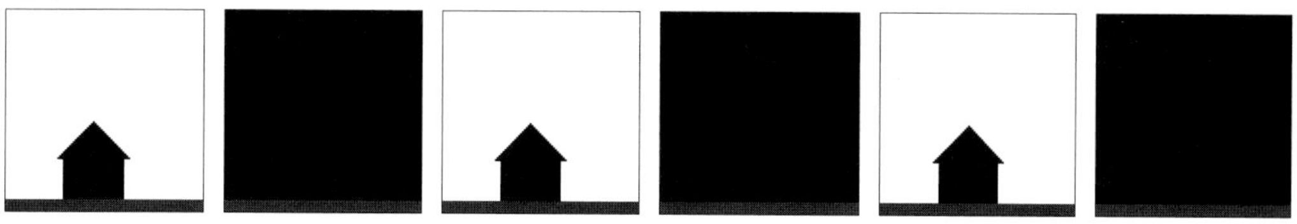

```
// house flashing
Command Drawhouse
{
  Field 0 0 100 5 70
  Field 30 6 60 26 100
  Repeat A 27 63
  {
    Line A 26 45 44
  }
}
Repeat T 0 100
{
  Paper 0
  Drawhouse
  Paper 100
  Drawhouse
}
```

Trying to cope with the demands of reality while manipulating a medium that can easily defy our established visual conventions of the world around us illustrates the creative challenges of working in a medium that has absolutely no physical constraints.

Anything can be created, but creating what appears natural to our senses is difficult because we have to limit ourselves to existing visual phenomena. Choosing to work in the abstract rather than the representative is a powerful method for overcoming self-imposed prejudices. A system where a line travels on a backdrop that changes does not threaten or confuse because it is only an imaginary occurrence. We can overcome what is considered traditionally bad to our senses by reprogramming our senses to make the imaginary seem perfectly *real.*

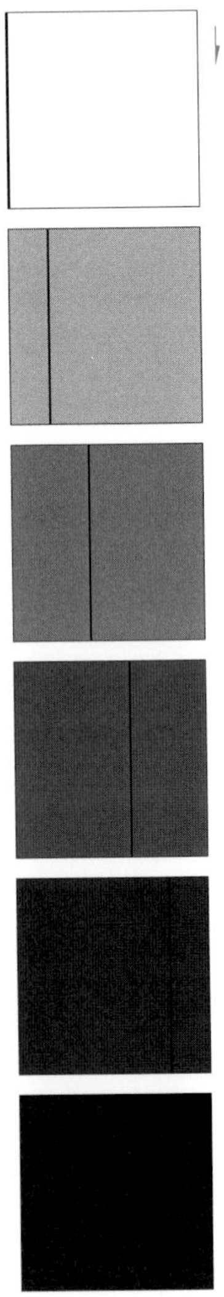

```
Pen 100
// paper fade in sync with
// line position
Repeat T 0 100
{
  Paper T
  Line T 0 T 100
}
```

The line can even defy the imaginary context where it exists.

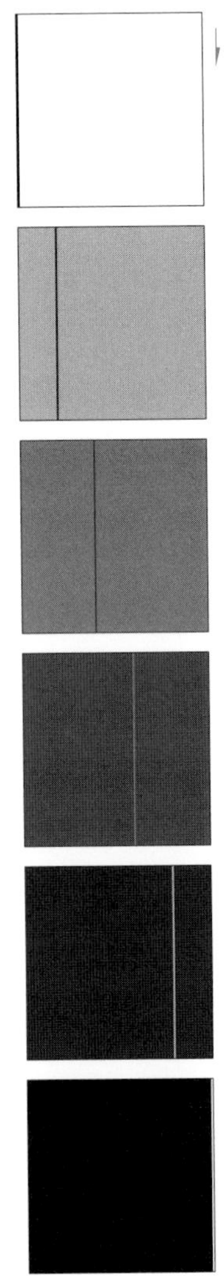

```
// paper fade in opposition to
// line position
Repeat T 0 100
{
  Paper T
  Pen (100-T)
  Line T 0 T 100
}
```

Or the line and the context can cooperate in defying each other.

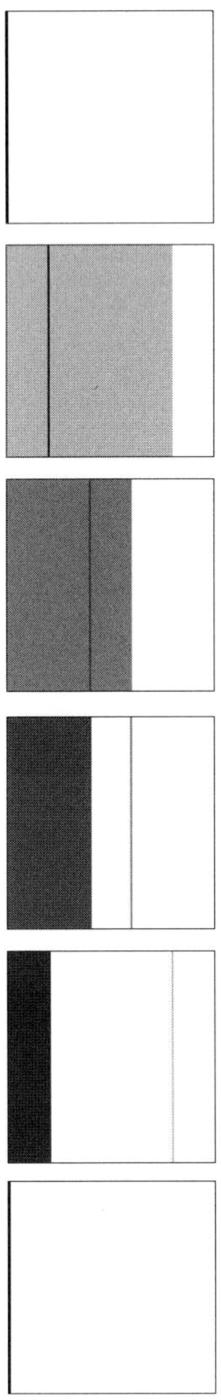

```
// struggle between background
// and foreground
Repeat B 0 100
{
  Paper 0
  Pen B
  Repeat A 0 (100-B)
  {
    Line A 0 A 100
  }
  Pen (100-B)
  Line B 0 B 100
}
```

Working in the abstract allows you to explore computational media to its fullest, especially when trying to make sense of a medium that redefines what is real.

Summary Any drawing created in this book can be considered a type of time-based expression due to the step-by-step processing of each command in a program. Usually we are more eager to see the computer complete a drawing process than to see each command painstakingly rendered, because we seek the final result. Watching the computer draw in your stead, much like supervising an entire group of illustrators carrying out your instructions, is a powerful feeling.

The fact that the computer allows your form to exist in a state of continual flux should be the starting point for your temporal explorations. The goal is not to salvage a static atrocity by extending its existence over time, but to find forms most relevant to dynamic computational expression.

The method of computation is hands-off, but at the same time you are in absolute control. The medium is manipulated indirectly, but it is more direct than if you were to use your hands. The medium is always in perfect accord with your will, because your will must be wholly stated as a set of instructions.

14 PAINT Before you started writing programs, the thought of digital painting may have invoked an image of drawing on the computer screen with your mouse. Because it is infinitely more pleasurable to use a real pen and paper, you may have secretly desired to scribble in the program's drawing area with your mouse while doing the exercises in this book. In the program domain, you type in a few numbers and commands, see a resulting change in the form, change the numbers, see a slight change, change the numbers or commands, and perhaps see more significant changes. But you never get to use the refined eye-to-hand reflexes that are the hallmark of a skilled visual creator. When the computer first emerged on the art scene in the 1960s, the foreign nature of this method of indirect expression built a natural barrier between natural media-based expression and expression that existed as abstractions of mathematics, or computation.

In the 1970s, there was a gradual change in the perception of the role of computers in design and the arts. Digital painting systems had emerged as a means for the non-numerically inclined people to engage in expressive activity on the computer. Input devices that mimicked the qualities of a writing instrument allowed the traditional artist to use the computer just as if it were a paintbrush and set of paints. This revolution enabled hardware and software companies to find new applications for computers in the graphical world, and companies like Apple and Adobe found a community eager to express in the new medium.

Today we take digital paint for granted and pay great attention to the result of the process, a digital image file, but pay very little attention to the tool that got the paint into the file in the first place. Because so little about these systems is understood by the average digital designer, the user is rarely aware of the abuse they receive from the tool. In this chapter, you will look at the basic mechanics that underlie the systems used in digital art creation as a first step towards true creative freedom.

A Paintbrush In order to paint, you need to know the position of the cursor relative to the sheet of paper. A quick glance can reveal the whereabouts of the cursor position, but you should not have to manually input this value into the computer. There must be some way that a running program can determine the instantaneous position of the cursor. Such information is external to the program and is referred to as *external data.* There are various types of external data besides the cursor position, such as the state of the keyboard and information on the network, which will be covered in Chapters 15 through 18. Each variety of external data has a name associated with it and a requisite numeric descriptor. Since external data is a special type of information used in a program, there is a typographic convention of enclosing the specifier within the symbols < and >.

In the case of the cursor position, the command is **Mouse** and the numeric qualifier is 1, 2, or 3. More specifically, <Mouse 1> refers to the horizontal position, <Mouse 2> refers to the vertical position, and <Mouse 3> refers to the state of the main button, pressed or not pressed. To paint the dot that is directly under the cursor, the dot position can be determined by mapping the mouse values to a dot to be Set.

```
Paper 0
Set [<Mouse 1> <Mouse 2>] 100
```

This program will Set a black dot at the current location of the cursor which could be anywhere, even off the Paper so no dot may be Set.

You can remedy this situation by repeating this process over many cycles. The result is the appearance of ink flowing from the cursor while the mouse is moved.

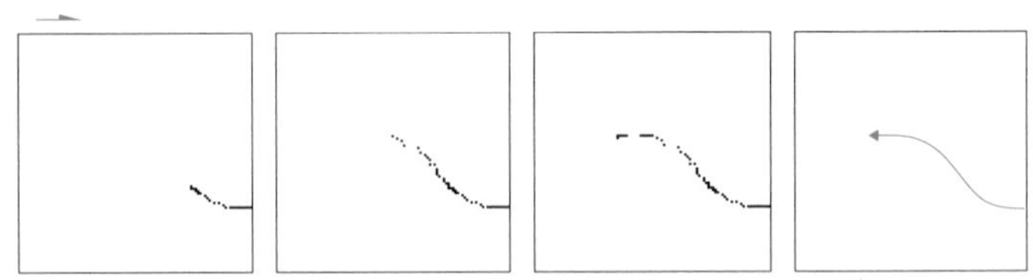

```
Paper 0
// set the current dot under
// the mouse to 100% black
// for 10 thousand cycles of T
Repeat T 0 10000
{
  Set [<Mouse 1> <Mouse 2>] 100
}
```

However, like a windup toy, the program eventually ends and the cursor pen appears to run out of ink. You can keep the ink flowing forever with the **Forever** command.

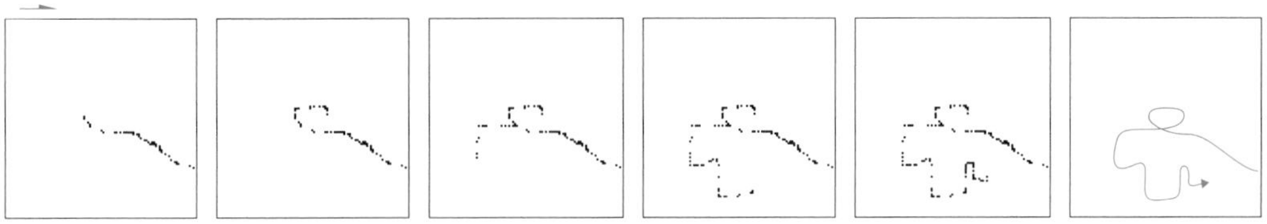

```
Paper 0
// set the current dot under
// the mouse to 100% black *forever*
Forever
{
  Set [<Mouse 1> <Mouse 2>] 100
}
```

Forever is similar to Repeat, except there are no qualifiers and the block repeats forever. On the actual computer system you are using, you will have to explicitly stop a program that runs forever before being able to run another program.

The state of the mouse's main button is accessed through <Mouse 3> and is 0 when not pressed and 100 when pressed. A simple program illustrates this convention.

```
// map mouse button to paper shade
Forever
{
  Paper <Mouse 3>
}
```

When the button is pressed, you see a black sheet of paper; when released (not pressed), you see a white sheet of paper.

Testing the state of the mouse while monitoring the position of the device can result in depositing paint only when the button is pressed.

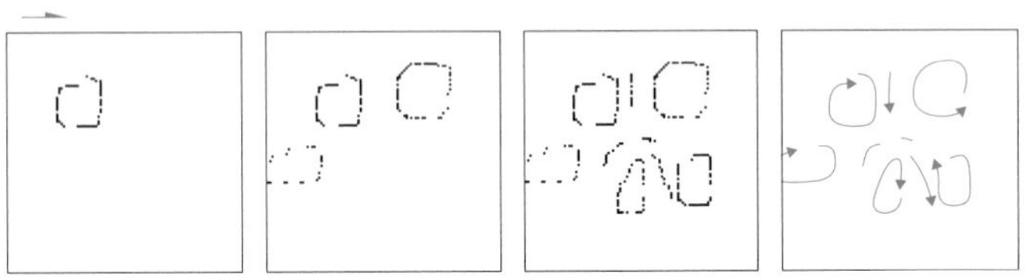

```
Paper 0
// set dot under mouse position to
// either 0 or 100, which is determined
// by mouse button state
Forever
{
   Set [<Mouse 1> <Mouse 2>] <Mouse 3>
}
```

While the mouse is dragged with its button pressed, black ink is deposited. Notice that white ink is deposited when the mouse is dragged and its button is not pressed. Thus the pen either writes or erases depending on the state of the button. To remove the erasing action, a question is necessary.

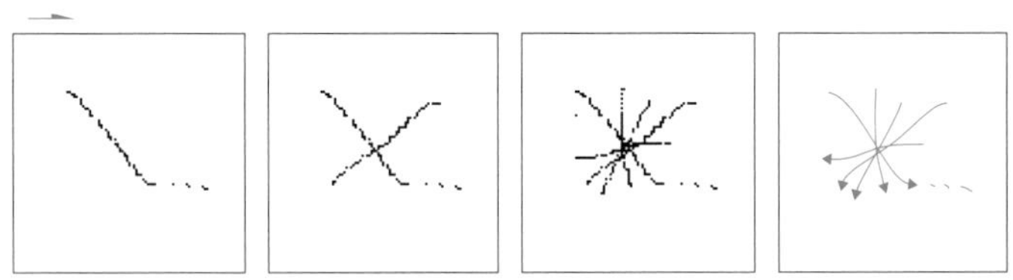

```
Paper 0
// only if the mouse button is down
// will the dot under mouse be set
// to 100 percent black
Forever
{
   Same? <Mouse 3> 100
   {
      Set [<Mouse 1> <Mouse 2>] 100
   }
}
```

Special Brushes Perhaps the most entertaining exercise in studying digital paint is the process of designing your own special paintbrush. There really is no limit to the kind of brush you can create, ranging from the most straightforward to the completely nonsensical. How you approach this creative endeavor is up to you, but I present here a range of examples from conservative to expressive styles of brush.

In the original example of setting the dot directly under the cursor, you may have found that it is difficult to draw a continuous stroke unless you move very slowly. A superior method is to connect the space between dots with lines. This technique requires you to keep track of the previous position of the cursor while acquiring the new position. In the following example, the current position is stored in the variables H1 and V1 while the previous position is stored in H0 and V0. Each cycle H0 and V0 are updated to reflect the most recent position of the mouse.

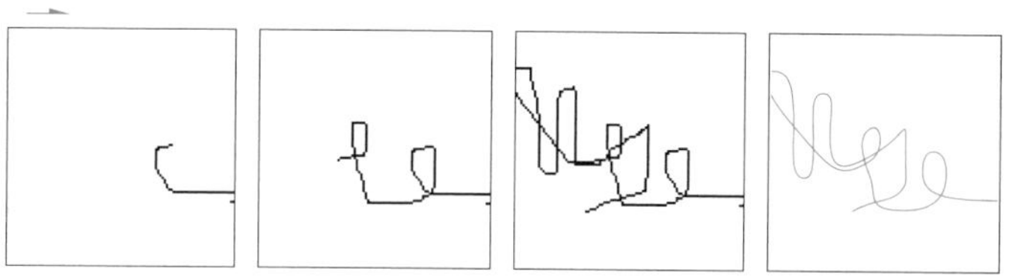

```
Paper 0
Pen 100
Set H0 <Mouse 1>
Set V0 <Mouse 2>
Forever
{
  Set H1 <Mouse 1>
  Set V1 <Mouse 2>
  Line H0 V0 H1 V1
  // update the position
  Set H0 H1
  Set V0 V1
}
```

The points are now connected, and the pen seems to behave in a much more conventional fashion, less like a cheap ballpoint pen and more like a fine writing instrument.

With the classical pen established, deviating from the norm is quite simple. For example, consider a pen with multishaded ink.

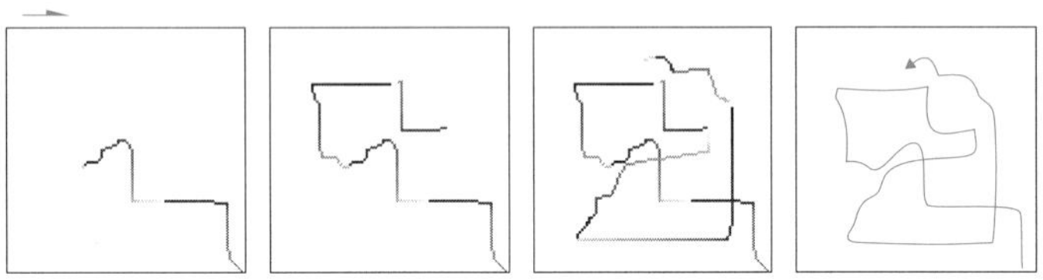

```
Paper 0
Pen 100
// this pen leaks grayscale,
// rainbow-style ink
Set H0 <Mouse 1>
Set V0 <Mouse 2>
Set G 0
Forever
{
  Pen G
  Set H1 <Mouse 1>
  Set V1 <Mouse 2>
  Line H0 V0 H1 V1
  // update the position
  Set H0 H1
  Set V0 V1
  Set G (G + 1)
  Same? G 101
  {
    Set G 0
  }
}
```

Or, returning to the functional, a basic calligraphy pen is constructed by increasing the pen's width by adding an extra set of parallel lines.

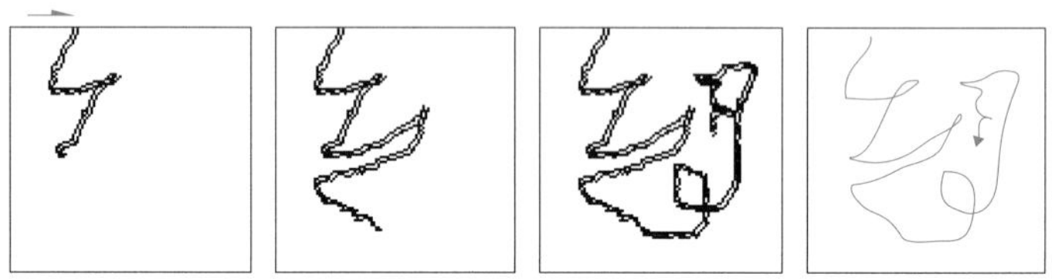

```
Paper 0
Pen 100
// a line is drawn in parallel
// at a small offset
Set H0 <Mouse 1>
Set V0 <Mouse 2>
Forever
{
  Set H1 <Mouse 1>
  Set V1 <Mouse 2>
  Line H0 V0 H1 V1
  Line (H0+1) (V0-2) (H1+2) (V1-1)
  // update the position
  Set H0 H1
  Set V0 V1
}
```

You should recognize this as an opportunity for a generalization in a Repeat, where a variable W can represent the width of the brush tip.

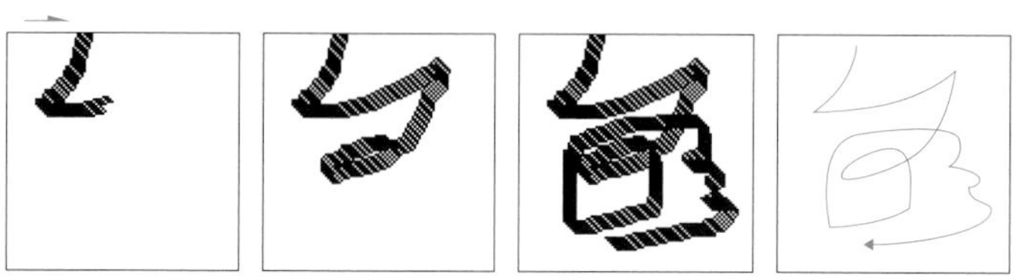

```
Paper 0
Pen 100
// a variable number of lines, W,
// are drawn parallel to the current line
Set H0 <Mouse 1>
Set V0 <Mouse 2>
Set W 5
Forever
{
  Set H1 <Mouse 1>
  Set V1 <Mouse 2>
  Repeat B 0 W
  {
    Line (H0+B) (V0-B) (H1+B) (V1-B)
  }
  // update the position
  Set H0 H1
  Set V0 V1
```

To complete the utility of the system, an erase command is useful, activated by pressing the mouse button.

```
Paper 0
Pen 100
// to clear screen, just hold down
// the mouse button a bit
Set H0 <Mouse 1>
Set V0 <Mouse 2>
Set W 5
Forever
{
  Set H1 <Mouse 1>
  Set V1 <Mouse 2>
  Repeat B 0 W
  {
    Line (H0+B) (V0-B) (H1+B) (V1-B)
  }
  // update the position
  Set H0 H1
  Set V0 V1
  // if Mouse down, erase screen
  Same? <Mouse 3> 100
  {
    Paper 0
  }
}
```

Now that you have the basic idea behind digital paintbrushes, you should experiment and discover the many pens that you cannot find on the average digital paint system. Experience the power of creating your own possibilities versus being forced to buy them from the creativity-limiting digital paint industry.

Vector Drawings If you are fairly experienced with digital design tools, you know that in addition to paint systems, there are draw systems that use vectors to represent drawings. The latter refers to systems using graphical primitives that are placed onto a canvas and are freely transformable in terms of position, scale, and so forth. Draw systems maintain a list of the objects that have been entered instead of the dot-based image that is the rendered result. Unfortunately, the system described in this book is not well suited for creating so-called *object-oriented* systems; however, with a little imagination, certain aspects of draw systems can be realized.

Consider the bottom row of the sheet of paper to represent a series of horizontal and vertical positions in space stored in a sequence. In other words, the gray value of [0 0] stores the horizontal position and [1 0] stores the corresponding vertical position; [2 0] is the next horizontal position; [3 0] is the vertical position, and so forth all the way across the row. A line is represented by four pairs of positions. Therefore, if the entire bottom row of 101 dots is used in this manner, a total of 25 distinct lines can be stored.

This method can be illustrated by encoding a few lines into the bottom row. If there are two lines, one line starts from 20 20 and ends at 20 100; the other starts at 40 20 and ends at 80 60. These values can be encoded as described above and subsequently rendered in a figure of eight dots in the bottom row that are simultaneously used to represent two lines.

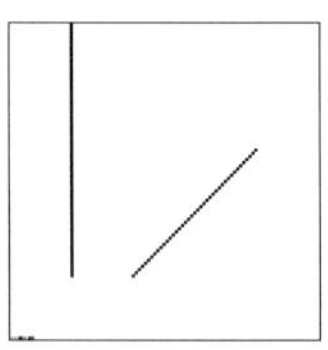

3x mag

```
Paper 0
// there are 2 Lines
Set [0 0] 20
Set [1 0] 20
Set [2 0] 20
Set [3 0] 100
// points for the second Line
Set [4 0] 40
Set [5 0] 20
Set [6 0] 80
Set [7 0] 60
// render Lines
Pen 100
Repeat A 0 1
{
  Line [(A*4) 0] [(A*4+1) 0] [(A*4+2) 0] [(A*4+3) 0]
}
```

The bottom row can be used as a general storage device for Line information. A maximum of 25 lines can be stored in this row. You can either numerically enter Lines or incrementally add to the list using information input via the mouse.

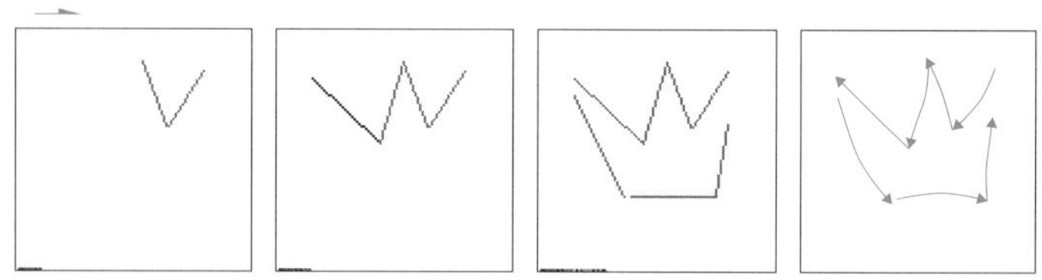

```
// an advanced code that is provided
// for those that are curious...
Paper 0
Set N 0
Set B <Mouse 3>
Set LX <Mouse 1>
Set Ly <Mouse 2>
Set LC 0
Forever
{
  Field 0 1 100 100 0
  Set MX <Mouse 1>
  Set MY <Mouse 2>
  Set MB <Mouse 3>
  NotSame? B MB
  {
    Same? LC 25
    {
      Set LC 0
    }
    Set P (LC*4+1N)
    Set [P 0] MX
    Set P (P+1)
    Set [P 0] MY
    Set N (N+2)
    Same? N 4
    {
      Set LC (LC+1)
      Set N 0
    }
    Set LX MX
    Set Ly MY
    Set B MB
  }
  Same? N 2
  {
    Pen 100
    Line LX Ly MX MY
  }
  NotSame? LC 0
  {
    Pen 50
    Repeat A 0 (LC-1)
    {
      Set P (A*4+1)
      Set P1 (P+1)
      Set P2 (P+2)
      Set P3 (P+3)
      Line [P 0] [P1 0] [P2 0] [P3 0]
    }
  }
}
```

Note that strokes entered are straightened on-the-fly. The row of dots on the bottom grows as each line is added, shown here magnified.

3x mag

This example is fairly advanced and is not the usual way you might do this on the computer. Otherwise, all the draw systems you use would have an array of gray dots that litter the edges of the screen. But the general process performed in drawing systems is represented in this example program. The program essentially adds points to the structure at the bottom row. Each time four components are added, the structure acknowledges the new line. As you add lines, the row at the bottom will quickly fill up. Once completely filled with 25 lines, storage will start over again from zero and write over data as necessary. For each cycle, the lines stored as dots at the bottom will be converted to the lines that are visible on the screen. The careful reader will recognize that if any of the lines are drawn into the bottom row, the storage structure will no longer be valid but will be corrupted in a way you don't often see today. I encourage you to try this yourself.

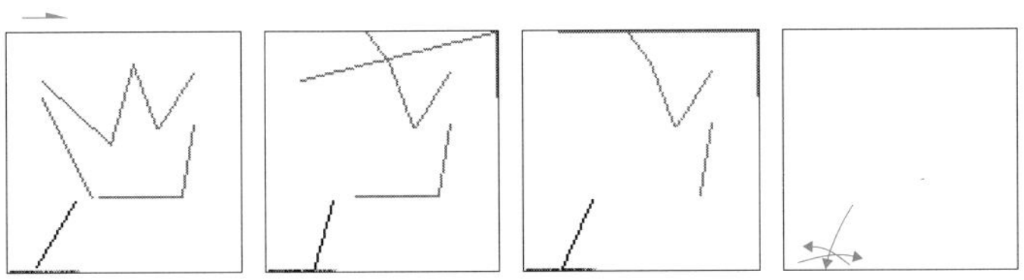

Usually, when you corrupt memory on the computer, a program crashes or causes visual havoc. This program safely accomplishes the latter.

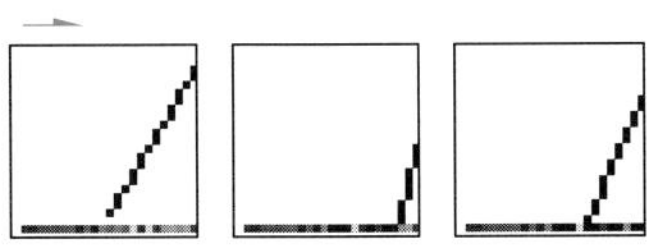

3x mag

Summary Digital painting depends upon the ability to retrieve the position of the mouse as a set of numbers that specify the horizontal and vertical position and to whether the mouse button is pressed. This information is monitored by the program as external data, denoted by the symbols < and >. There are various types of external data; Mouse is the first one that you have learned to use. By tracking the mouse, you realize a one-to-one correspondence between gesture and graphic in a digital simulation of painting. With the Forever command, this simulation can run for as long as you like, or until the machine is unplugged.

I am not a big fan of digital painting tools, but like many designers, I need to use them regularly and am subject to all of their annoying idiosyncracies. I often want to do something that the tool cannot support because of limitations involved in programming a commercial tool. When that occurs, I write a tool to best suit my intentions and then throw it away after I am done. I guess if I didn't throw away my tools I could have my name on the box of some shrink-wrapped software tool—but that is a fate I choose to avoid.

As you noticed in the transition from Chapter 13 to this chapter, what once was an animation has been trivially reshaped into a drawing tool. The computational medium has this odd property of becoming anything you desire. In terms of program length, there is not a significant difference between the animation or drawing tool examples; however, when the Forever command was slipped in, a conceptual distinction was made. An animation starts and stops. It is finite. A digital tool, if not intentionally turned off, will run forever. It is infinite. Both expressions share the same heritage of time, so it might be useful to understand the finite case of an animated sequence before setting out to study the infinite. Another perspective to the problem of designing for infinite time is to accept it *as is*—without carrying the prejudices inherent to animation. Such is the joy and responsibility when interpreting a new medium.

15 REACT Painting with a mouse on the computer screen has a high entertainment value, but it is a novelty that should be put into proper perspective. Artists and designers of all ages who are already skilled with pencil and paper have recently approached the computer with expectations of being pioneers. What is the allure? It is the challenge of mastering a new medium. But drawing a stroke with a pen is no different from drawing a stroke with a mouse. The real challenge is to discover the intrinsic properties of the new medium and to find out how the stroke you "draw" via computation is one you could never draw, or even imagine, without computation.

Computation allows you to create digital forms, in the finest level of detail, that react or respond to their environment. For many years I have been fascinated with the design of what I call *reactive graphics*, which are programmed to respond directly to actions of the user. There are reactions that are concise, can cooperate, or can gracefully flow into other reactions in a breathtaking manner appropriate to the digital medium. In this basic area of visual inquiry, I have focused primarily on the mouse as the interface for eliciting reactions from the computer by directly relating movement of the cursor to elicit graphical reactions.

Tonal Reactions Because I felt that the broader concept of interactivity was too difficult to comprehend, a few years ago I tried to focus less on high-level communicative interactions and more on the most basic level of a simple reaction to stimuli that does not necessarily communicate. Inspired by the pure compositions by the Russian Suprematist Kasimir Malevich (1878-1935), I began to create compositions that removed the context of meaning from the computer and sought to find the most minimal of expressions for an interactive system. For my first experiment, I wrote a program to relate the motion of the mouse directly to the color of the entire screen, creating a unique visual effect while the mouse was vigorously moved. In the spirit of designing a reaction, nothing would happen without movement of the mouse. This little experiment can be recreated in spirit with a simpler code that uses grayscale instead of color.

```
// map paper shade to horizontal
// mouse position
Forever
{
  Paper <Mouse 1>
}
```

As the mouse is moved in the horizontal direction, a new sheet of paper with a tone specified by the numeric value of the horizontal position is created.

Both the horizontal and vertical dimensions of the mouse can be incorporated by combining them in a calculation, such as averaging the two components by taking their sum and dividing by 2.

```
// compute the average
Forever
{
  Set H <Mouse 1>
  Set V <Mouse 2>
  Paper ((H+V)/2)
}
```

There can be different variations on this theme, with each one being impossible to describe in pictures alone. You can piece short animations together in your imagination fairly well by simply looking at sequences of images, but interaction is not so easily visualized. Although the series of images may appear to be the same, the gesture that elicits the reaction can be very different. You are strongly encouraged to experience the subtle differences of each piece. For instance, a multiplicative combination results in more profound changes as you move the mouse.

```
// more sensitive to changes
Forever
{
  Set H <Mouse 1>
  Set V <Mouse 2>
  Paper ((H*V)/2)
}
```

A combination of the two dimensions weighted unevenly can also surprise you.

```
// horizontal and vertical are
// weighted unevenly
Forever
{
  Set H <Mouse 1>
  Set V <Mouse 2>
  Paper (H/3+V*2/3)
}
```

Finally, instead of referencing from the lower left corner, the center can become the graphical reference for white. The result is perceived as more pleasing because our natural tendency is to touch an object, even a virtual one, from the center rather than from the edges.

```
// measure from the center
Forever
{
  Set H <Mouse 1>
  Set V <Mouse 2>
  Smaller? H 50
  {
    Set HADJ (50-H)
  }
  NotSmaller? H 50
  {
    Set HADJ (H-50)
  }
  Smaller? V 50
  {
    Set VADJ (50-V)
  }
  NotSmaller? V 50
  {
    Set VADJ (V-50)
  }
  Paper (HADJ+VADJ)
}
```

As an alternative to shading the entire display area, the paper can be divided into two halves. Each side can display a separate reaction, such as both dimensions displayed at the same time.

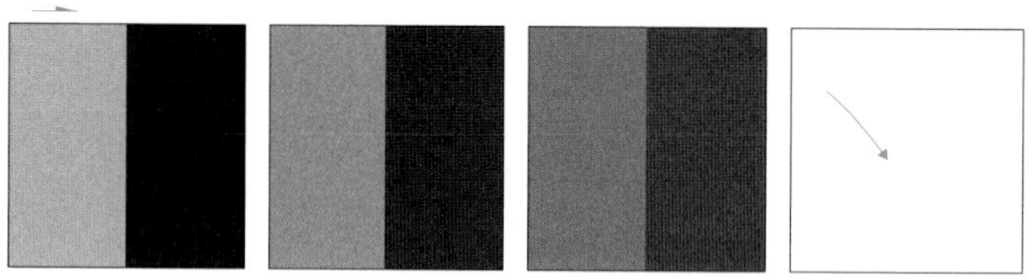

```
// shade left and right halves
// according to horizontal and
// vertical positions
Forever
{
  Set H <Mouse 1>
  Set V <Mouse 2>
  Field 0 0 49 100 H
  Field 50 0 100 100 V
}
```

Since a visual experience is perceived over time, creating an awareness of a short time interval that precedes the present time tempers the reaction in a positive, subtle manner. This can be demonstrated by maintaining a short history of the most recent events, such as the two most recent mouse positions visualized in this paper divided into halves.

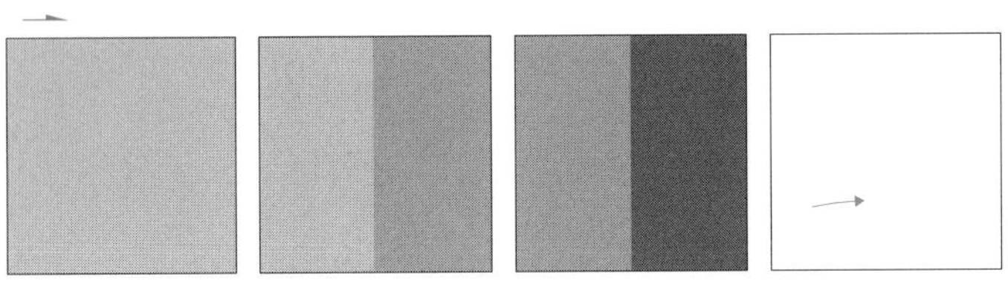

```
// maintain history of horizontal
// and shade based uponthat
Set OLDH <Mouse 1>
Forever
{
  Set H <Mouse 1>
  Field 0 0 49 100 OLDH
  Field 50 0 100 100 H
  Set OLDH H
}
```

Maintaining and displaying a longer history provides more context, as in dividing the area into three separate display elements.

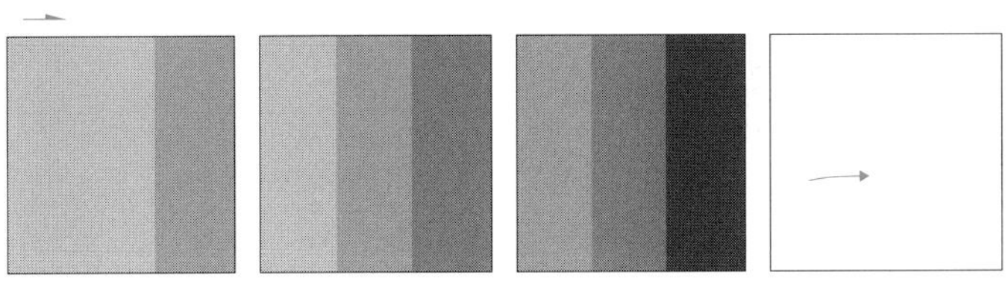

```
Set OLDOLDH <Mouse 1>
Set OLDH OLDOLDH
Forever
{
  Set H <Mouse 1>
  Field 0 0 32 100 OLDOLDH
  Field 33 0 65 100 OLDH
  Field 66 0 100 100 H
  Set OLDOLDH OLDH
  Set OLDH H
}
```

Successive partitioning reveals more of the context and reduces to a denser graph of motion.

Follow the Cursor Another experiment in coding a response to changes in the mouse position is to relate the position of the cursor to a graphical representation. The most common instance of a visual form with this property is the cursor graphic itself.

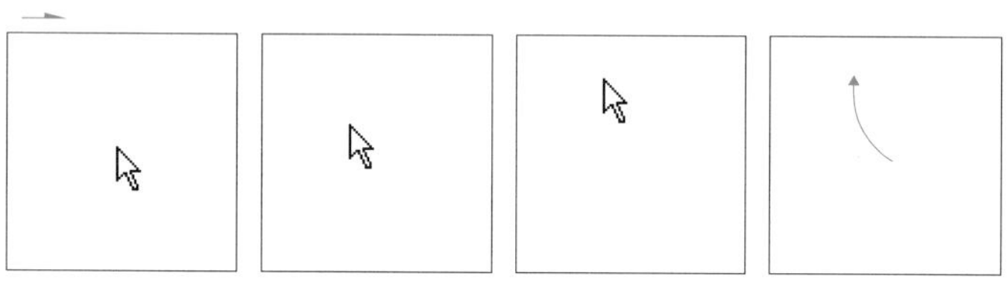

```
Pen 100
// connect the dots that form
// the omnipresent arrow cursor
Forever
{
  Paper 0
  Set H <Mouse 1>
  Set V <Mouse 2>
  Line (H-2) (V+2) (H+8) (V-8)
  Line (H-2) (V+2) (H-2) (V-12)
  Line (H-2) (V-12) (H+1) (V-9)
  Line (H+2) (V-9) (H+5) (V-16)
  Line (H+8) (V-8) (H+4) (V-8)
  Line (H+4) (V-8) (H+7) (V-15)
  Line (H+6) (V-16) (H+7) (V-16)
}
```

Although the direct response of the cursor graphic represents the quintessential example of interactive design, daily exposure to the arrow pointer usually prevents you from realizing this subtlety. The drama of linking the cursor to its surrounding space provides a better context for appreciating this basic mechanism of relating graphic to position.

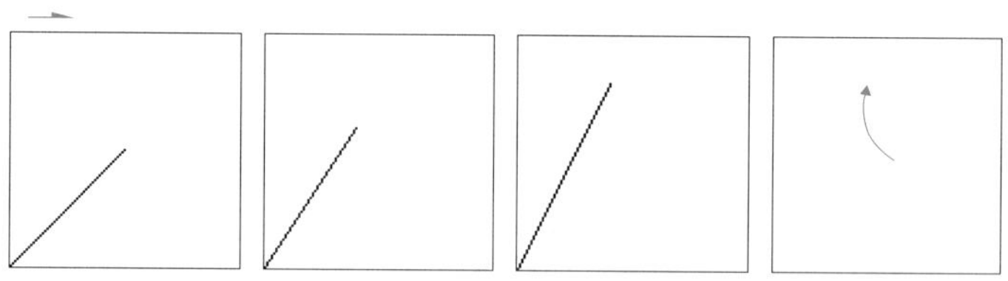

```
Pen 100
// line that follows you
Forever
{
  Paper 0
  Line 0 0 <Mouse 1> <Mouse 2>
}
```

Whenever the cursor is moved, a new line is drawn from the cursor's position to the lower left corner, referred to as a *rubberband* line for its stretchy characteristics. The tension felt in relation to the corner can be further emphasized with lines from all corners.

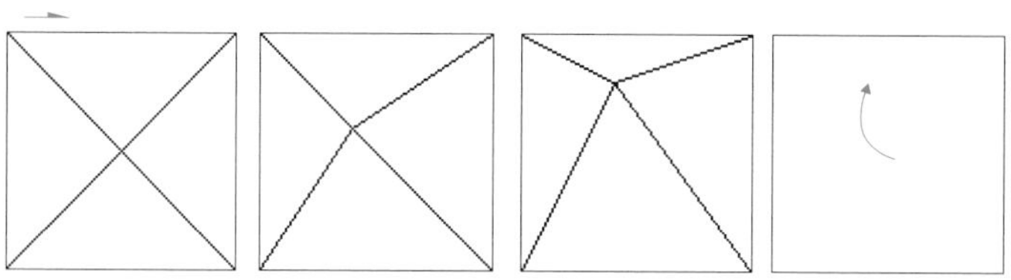

```
Pen 100
// lines emanating from four corners
// that follow you
Forever
{
  Paper 0
  Set H <Mouse 1>
  Set V <Mouse 2>
  Line H V 0 0
  Line H V 100 0
  Line H V 100 100
  Line H V 0 100
}
```

Keeping some parts of the graphic stationary and some parts directly linked to the pointer yields the benefits of contrast between mixture of reactive and nonreactive components.

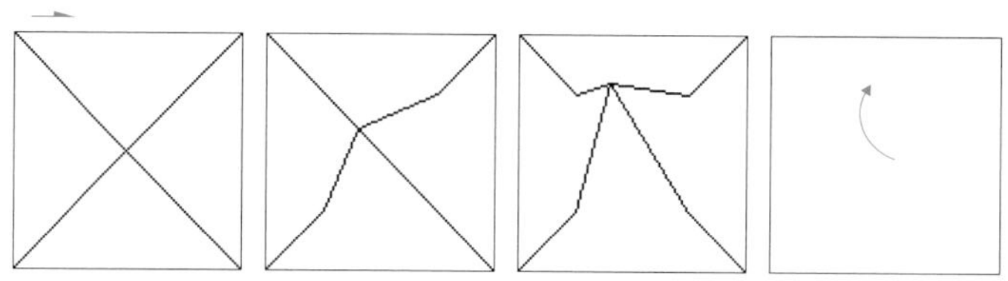

```
Pen 100
// some lines follow you, some don't
Forever
{
  Paper 0
  // stationery part
  Line 0 0 25 25
  Line 100 0 75 25
  Line 0 100 25 75
  Line 100 100 75 75
  // reactive part
  Set H <Mouse 1>
  Set V <Mouse 2>
  Line 25 25 H V
  Line 75 25 H V
  Line 25 75 H V
  Line 75 75 H V
}
```

A different effect is achieved by making the transitions less fluid and more discrete, as illustrated in this example, where the screen is divided into a discrete grid of 10 dots per grid unit.

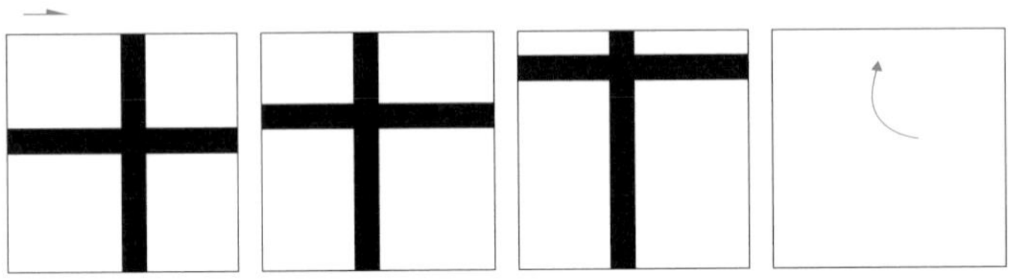

```
// thick crosshairs that follow you
Forever
{
  Set H <Mouse 1>
  Set V <Mouse 2>
  Paper 0
  Repeat A 0 10
  {
    Smaller? H (A*10)
    {
      Set A1 (A-1)
      NotSmaller? H (A1*10)
      {
        Field (A1*10) 0 (A*10) 100 100
      }
    }
  }
  Repeat B 0 10
  {
    Smaller? V (B*10)
    {
      Set B1 (B-1)
      NotSmaller? V (B1*10)
      {
        Field 0 (B1*10) 100 (B*10) 100
      }
    }
  }
}
```

Lastly, the element of history, as discussed earlier, relates the current instant of time with its previous context. Using the technique demonstrated at the end of Chapter 14, a maximum of 50 of the most recent mouse positions can be stored in the bottom row of dots. In this example only five positions are used and displayed in successively faded grays.

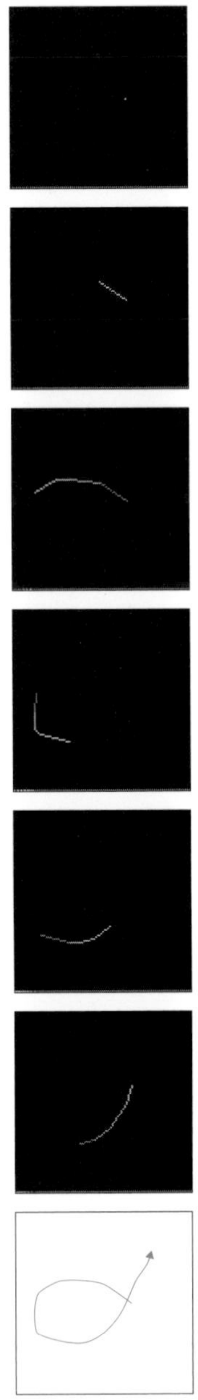

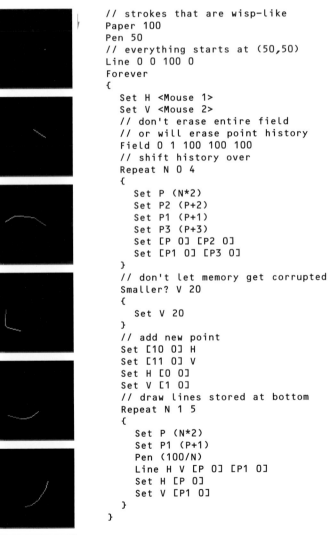

```
// strokes that are wisp-like
Paper 100
Pen 50
// everything starts at (50,50)
Line 0 0 100 0
Forever
{
  Set H <Mouse 1>
  Set V <Mouse 2>
  // don't erase entire field
  // or will erase point history
  Field 0 1 100 100 100
  // shift history over
  Repeat N 0 4
  {
    Set P (N*2)
    Set P2 (P+2)
    Set P1 (P+1)
    Set P3 (P+3)
    Set [P 0] [P2 0]
    Set [P1 0] [P3 0]
  }
  // don't let memory get corrupted
  Smaller? V 20
  {
    Set V 20
  }
  // add new point
  Set [10 0] H
  Set [11 0] V
  Set H [0 0]
  Set V [1 0]
  // draw lines stored at bottom
  Repeat N 1 5
  {
    Set P (N*2)
    Set P1 (P+1)
    Pen (100/N)
    Line H V [P 0] [P1 0]
    Set H [P 0]
    Set V [P1 0]
  }
}
```

By displaying the history of positions, a gesture of the hand is made visible in an emphemeral manner. For a brief moment the computer captures the essence of your action, and sets it free.

Reactive Collage Until now, each reaction to the cursor was related in a continuous manner that corresponded to changes in form. You can also consider cases where, depending upon the position of the cursor, a significantly different response is triggered. For instance, depending upon the horizontal position of the cursor, you can issue a contrasting graphical response.

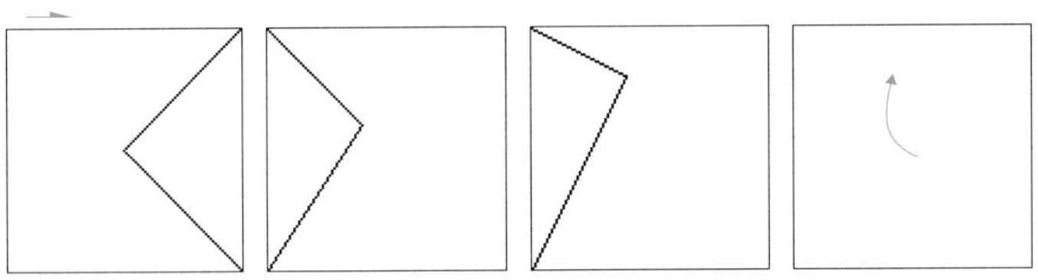

```
// do something different as
// cross boundary of halves
Forever
{
  Paper 0
  Set H <Mouse 1>
  Set V <Mouse 2>
  Smaller? H 50
  {
    Line 0 0 H V
    Line 0 100 H V
  }
  NotSmaller? H 50
  {
    Line 100 0 H V
    Line 100 100 H V
  }
}
```

A discontinuous response results from moving across the middle of the sheet of paper. You can build an accented response by changing the Paper and Pen shade accordingly.

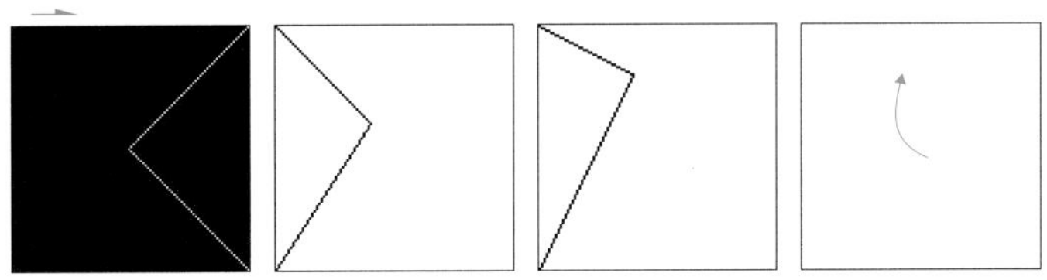

```
// one half is white on black,
// the other is black on white
Forever
{
  Set H <Mouse 1>
  Set V <Mouse 2>
  Smaller? H 50
  {
    Paper 0
    Pen 100
    Line 0 0 H V
    Line 0 100 H V
  }
  NotSmaller? H 50
  {
    Paper 100
    Pen 0
    Line 100 0 H V
    Line 100 100 H V
  }
}
```

Returning to the initial example, to smooth the transition across the center, you can add an overlapping area that ties the halves together.

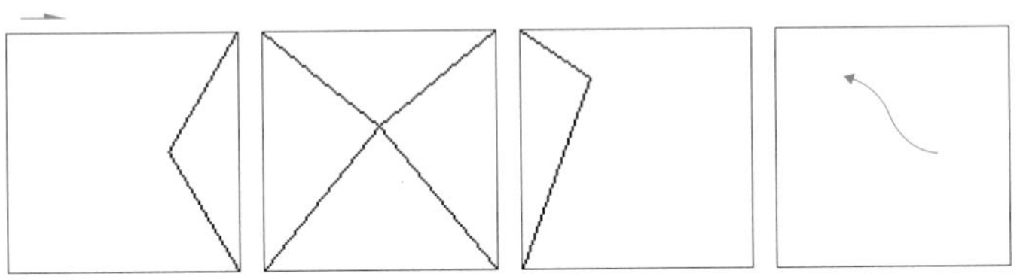

```
Pen 100
Forever
{
  Paper 0
  Set H <Mouse 1>
  Set V <Mouse 2>
  Smaller? H 66
  {
    Line 0 0 H V
    Line 0 100 H V
  }
  NotSmaller? H 33
  {
    Line 100 0 H V
    Line 100 100 H V
  }
}
```

A finer division of the input area can result in greater responsive detail. For instance, both the vertical and the horizontal can be divided into four distinct quadrants.

```
Pen 100
Forever
{
  Paper 0
  Set H <Mouse 1>
  Set V <Mouse 2>
  Smaller? H 50
  {
    Smaller? V 50
    {
      Line 0 0 H V
    }
    NotSmaller? V 50
    {
      Line 0 100 H V
    }
  }
  NotSmaller? H 50
  {
    Smaller? V 50
    {
      Line 100 0 H V
    }
    NotSmaller? V 50
    {
      Line 100 100 H V
    }
  }
}
```

The four separate responses can appear united in the middle by defining a central area of overlap.

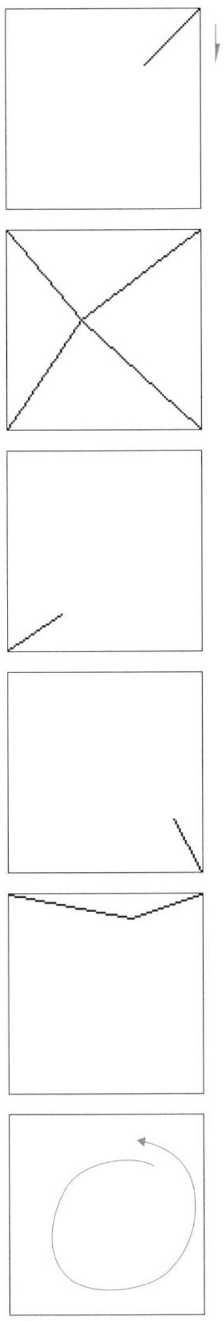

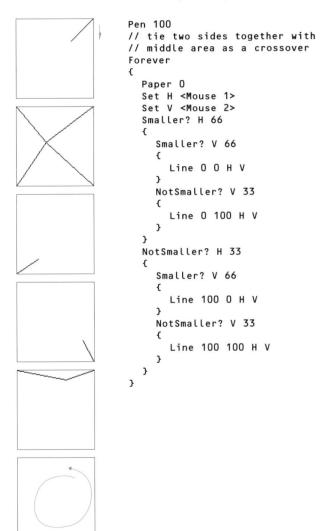

```
Pen 100
// tie two sides together with
// middle area as a crossover
Forever
{
  Paper 0
  Set H <Mouse 1>
  Set V <Mouse 2>
  Smaller? H 66
  {
    Smaller? V 66
    {
      Line 0 0 H V
    }
    NotSmaller? V 33
    {
      Line 0 100 H V
    }
  }
  NotSmaller? H 33
  {
    Smaller? V 66
    {
      Line 100 0 H V
    }
    NotSmaller? V 33
    {
      Line 100 100 H V
    }
  }
}
```

The subtlety of this technique of partitioning interactive space is demonstrated through variation. For example, consider the previous example rendered as a set of subtly shaded Fields.

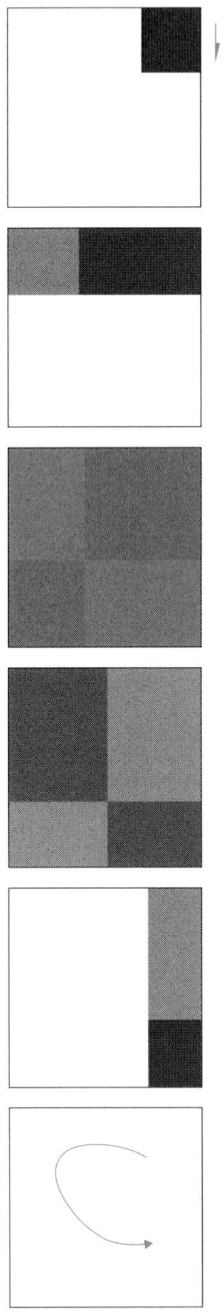

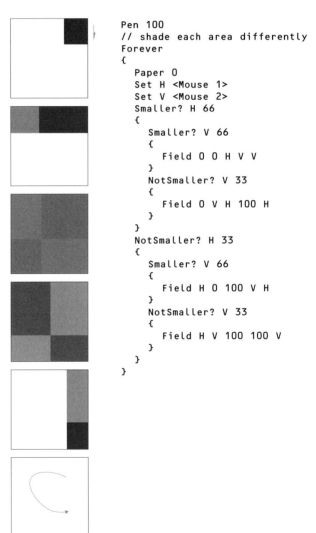

```
Pen 100
// shade each area differently
Forever
{
  Paper 0
  Set H <Mouse 1>
  Set V <Mouse 2>
  Smaller? H 66
  {
    Smaller? V 66
    {
      Field 0 0 H V V
    }
    NotSmaller? V 33
    {
      Field 0 V H 100 H
    }
  }
  NotSmaller? H 33
  {
    Smaller? V 66
    {
      Field H 0 100 V H
    }
    NotSmaller? V 33
    {
      Field H V 100 100 V
    }
  }
}
```

A variety of visual experiences can be blended into a single structure.

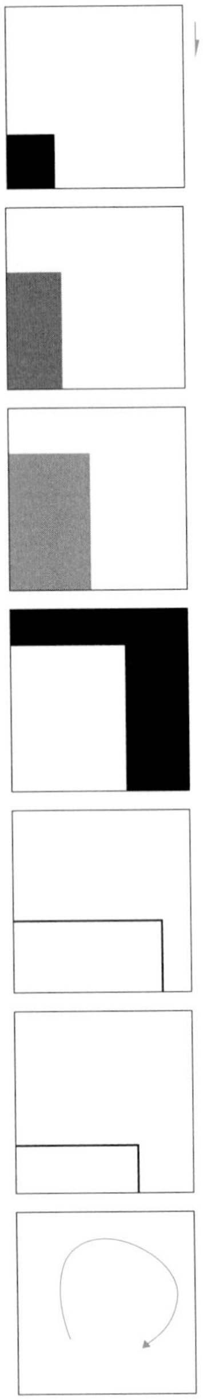

```
Pen 100
Set G 0
Forever
{
   Set H <Mouse 1>
   Set V <Mouse 2>
   Pen 100
   Paper 0
   // count G faster depending upon
   // which quadrant the cursor is in
   Smaller? H 50
   {
      Smaller? V 50
      {
         Field 0 0 H V 100
      }
      NotSmaller? V 50
      {
         Field 0 0 H V (100-V)
      }
   }
   NotSmaller? H 50
   {
      Smaller? V 50
      {
         Line H 0 H V
         Line 0 V H V
      }
      NotSmaller? V 50
      {
         Field 0 V 100 100 100
         Field H 0 100 V 100
      }
   }
   // reset G to 0
   Smaller? 100 G
   {
      Set G 0
   }
}
```

When several responses are layered in this manner, the effect is similar to *collage*. Collage is usually thought of as a completed set of layers to be enjoyed visually. However, in a reactive graphic the viewer has to interact physically with the graphic in order to truly appreciate the experience, unless the form has been declared to react simply to the progression of time.

As in all expressions, the simplest example speaks for all of the potentials.

```
Pen 100
Set G 0
Forever
{
   Set H <Mouse 1>
   Set V <Mouse 2>
   // circle around the center
   // to blink
   Smaller? H 50
   {
      Smaller? V 50
      {
         Paper 0
      }
      NotSmaller? V 50
      {
         Paper 100
      }
   }
   NotSmaller? H 50
   {
      Smaller? V 50
      {
         Paper 100
      }
      NotSmaller? V 50
      {
         Paper 0
      }
   }
}
```

Finally, the perception of collage can be felt in a purely temporal fashion, such as adjusting the rate of blinking for a subtle form of texture.

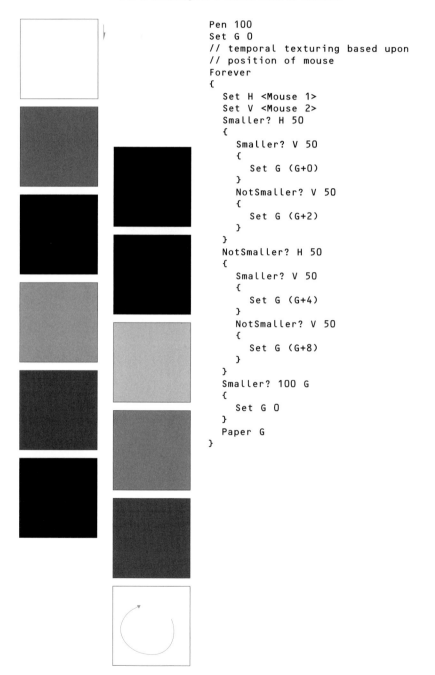

```
Pen 100
Set G 0
// temporal texturing based upon
// position of mouse
Forever
{
   Set H <Mouse 1>
   Set V <Mouse 2>
   Smaller? H 50
   {
      Smaller? V 50
      {
         Set G (G+0)
      }
      NotSmaller? V 50
      {
         Set G (G+2)
      }
   }
   NotSmaller? H 50
   {
      Smaller? V 50
      {
         Set G (G+4)
      }
      NotSmaller? V 50
      {
         Set G (G+8)
      }
   }
   Smaller? 100 G
   {
      Set G 0
   }
   Paper G
}
```

Summary Graphic reactions will become an important topic of study over the next few years as more designers and artists become involved in their creation. You can already see many examples on the Web, and we can expect these to grow in sophistication with earnest research and study. Reactive graphics are especially relevant today because the effect of tying an animation in direct relation to an input device requires the computational paradigm to achieve a fluent degree of interactive control.

In the spring of 1994, I had the opportunity to teach computation to third-year design students at Tama Art University in Japan. As an experiment in studying reactivity, I created a small language called *G*. Initially, the language could only accept 50 lines of program code. My students insisted on increasing the limit to 100. I increased it to 100, then 1000, and finally 5000 lines. One student actually wrote a 2000 line program! By the end of the term, the students realized an important concept about designing in computation. It is neither the size of the program nor the technological sophistication that determines the reactive form's degree of effectiveness. Rather, it is the clear statement of one's concept of reaction, even if it is embodied in a simple, 10-line program. Seek clear, original solutions in the computational medium that are not just appropriate to the technology, but are expressions of yourself. A combination of your own talents together with your own practical intentions, shall result in meaningful expressions of reaction.

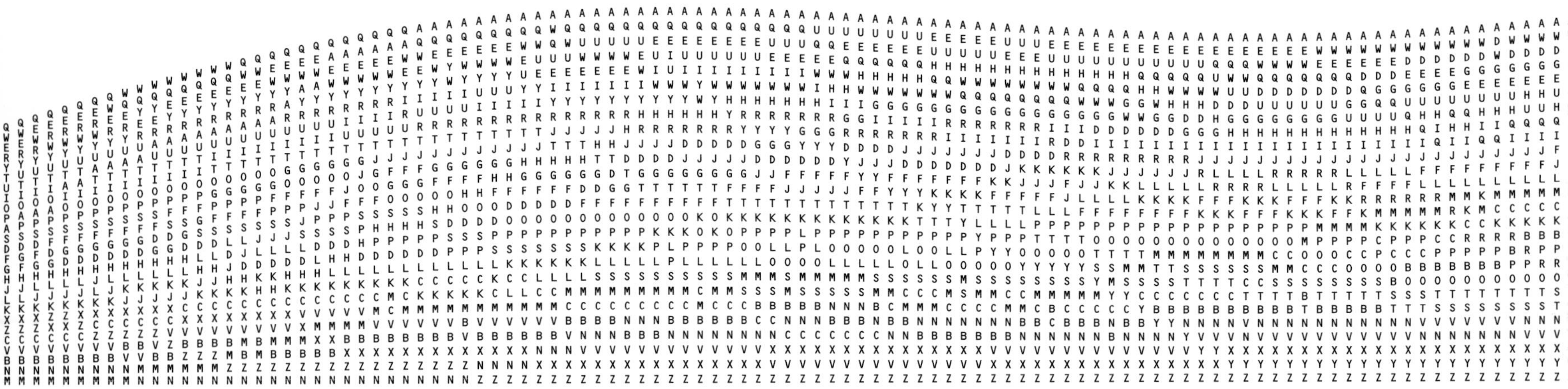

16 TOUCH The mouse is generally considered to be the primary input device used to "drive" on the information superhighway. Manufacturers of these devices have recently expanded this car metaphor to the extreme, and now heavily stylize their mice into sleek objects reminiscent of the streamlined automobiles popular in the 1950s.

I, like many over 30, did not grow up with a mouse and still feel most secure with my keyboard. The standard keyboard has 105 buttons, compared to three buttons on a mouse. Although there are many operations that are more easily performed with a mouse, there are many activities, such as typing, for which the keyboard is superior.

A great deal of my childhood was spent training to become a maniacally efficient typist. I developed a natural association that my left pinkie was either *A, Q, Z, 1,* or *Shift,* my thumb was *Space,* and all the rest of my fingers had some alphanumeric significance. It was not until after my first daughter was born that I began to view the keyboard in a different light. I would sometimes sit her on my lap as I tried to work at the computer, which proved to be a futile effort. She was enthralled by the feel of the keys and their clicking sounds, and it became impossible to prevent her joyful spontaneous pounding on the keyboard. At first I considered this a nuisance, but then realized that perhaps this was a message. I had always viewed the keyboard as a practical tool for entering textual information; my daughter taught me to see it as a unique vehicle for play.

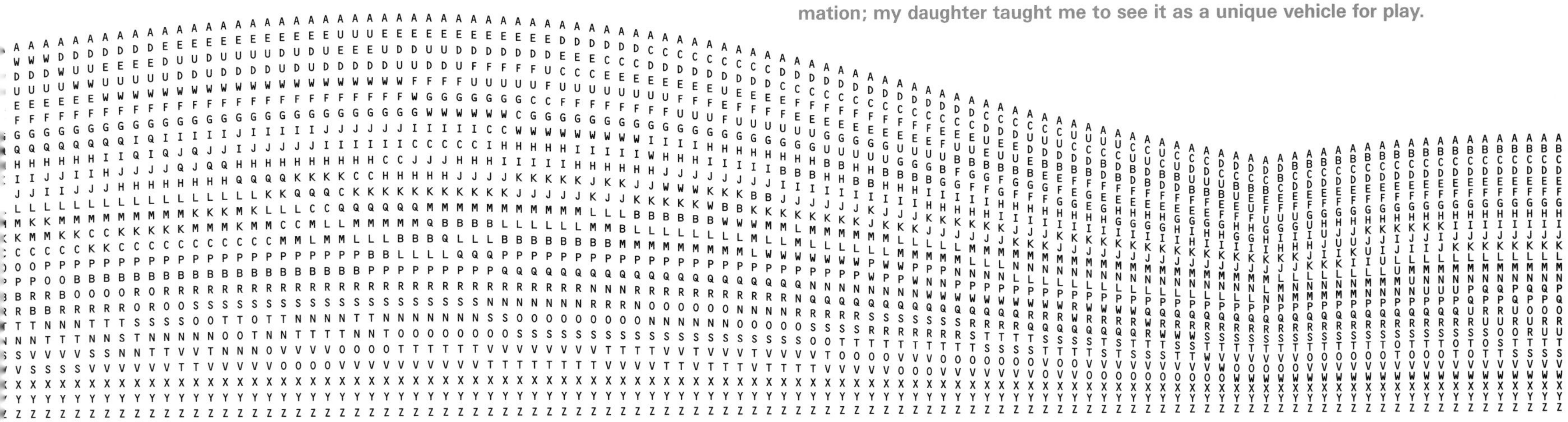

Watching the Keys In the DBN system, a total of 26 keys from the standard keyboard are available to sense the presence of pressure from a finger, pencil, or whatever can come into physical contact with the keyboard. The 26 keys correspond to the letters *A* through *Z.* The state of each key can be accessed through the external data interface **< >** with the keyword **Key** followed by a numeric descriptor ranging from 1 to 26. For example, when the *A* key is pressed, <Key 1> is 100; when it is released, <Key 1> is 0. Recall that the mouse button, identified by <Mouse 3>, behaves in an identical manner.

The keys on the keyboard are not arranged in a logical order. On a standard QWERTY layout keyboard, there are three rows of keys with ten keys in the first row, nine keys in the second row, and seven keys in the third row. You can visualize the state of the first three keys *A, B,* and *C* with a simple program that draws a line corresponding to the press of a key.

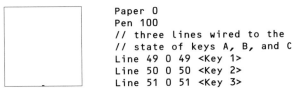

```
Paper 0
Pen 100
// three lines wired to the
// state of keys A, B, and C
Line 49 0 49 <Key 1>
Line 50 0 50 <Key 2>
Line 51 0 51 <Key 3>
```

But unless the keys are down immediately when the program is run, all that is displayed is three dots at the bottom of the screen.

Checking the state of the keys Forever is more meaningful and is enhanced by monitoring all 26 keys at once in a Repeat.

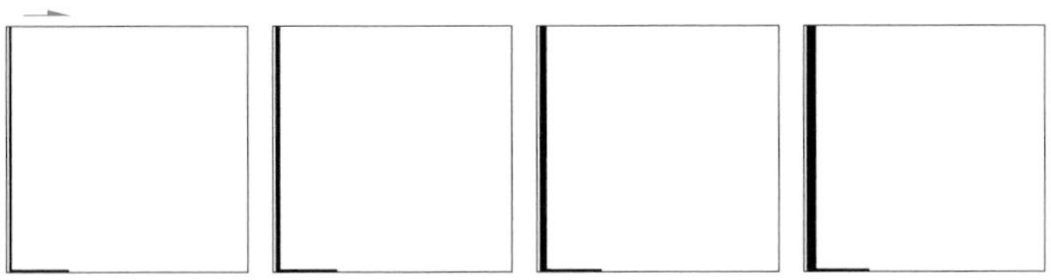

A, B, C, D

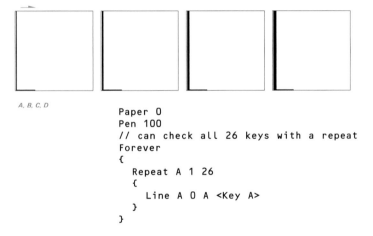

```
Paper 0
Pen 100
// can check all 26 keys with a repeat
Forever
{
  Repeat A 1 26
  {
    Line A 0 A <Key A>
  }
}
```

In this sequence, the 26 keys are continuously visualized as 26 corresponding vertical lines.
If the *A* key is down, then the Line from 1 0 to 1 100 will be drawn. If the *B* key is down, then the Line from 2 0 to 2 100 will be drawn, and so forth. If no keys are down, then by default there will be Lines that start and end at the same point that litter the bottom as an array of black dots.

Once a key is pressed, its corresponding line is drawn and stays there because the image is never refreshed. An alternative is to refresh each cycle with a new Paper.

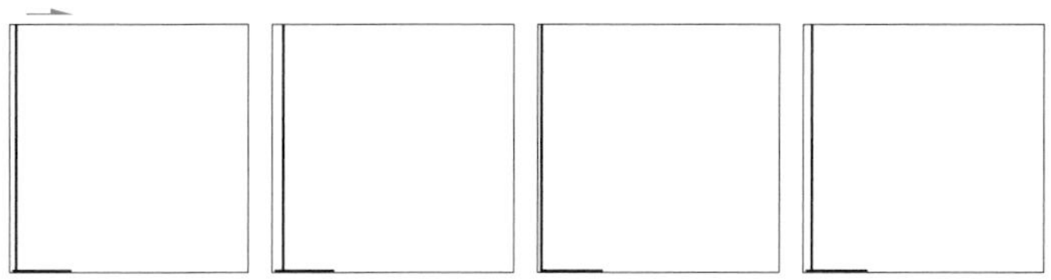

B, D, A, C

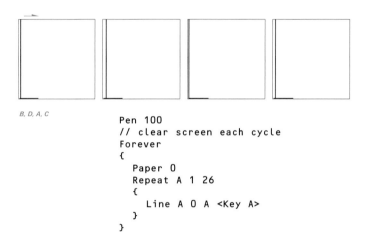

```
Pen 100
// clear screen each cycle
Forever
{
  Paper 0
  Repeat A 1 26
  {
    Line A 0 A <Key A>
  }
}
```

Now the only lines that you will see are those that correspond to keys being pressed at that specific instant in time. Note that results may differ depending on your computer because some key-boards become confused when more than one key is simultaneously pressed.

The cumulative effects of holding a key down are also interesting to visualize. For each cycle that a key is held down, a corresponding dot on the bottom row is darkened. This tally is updated each cycle and a dot is drawn at a raised position for each registered increase.

```
Paper 0
// use bottom row as state
Forever
{
  Repeat A 1 26
  {
    Same? <Key A> 100
    {
      Set [A 0] ([A 0]+1)
      Set [A [A 0]] 100
    }
  }
}
```

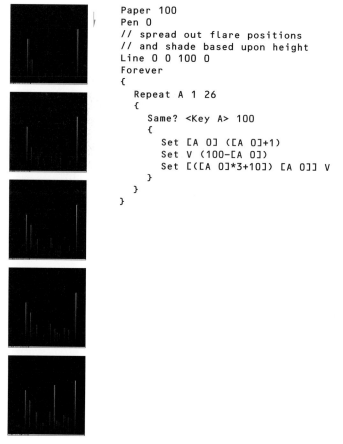

A, A, A, D, D, D, D, D, F, F, F, S, ...

Setting the background to black, increasing the spacing between the lines, and setting the dots to gray values instead of a constant 100 presents an opportunity to launch virtual flares.

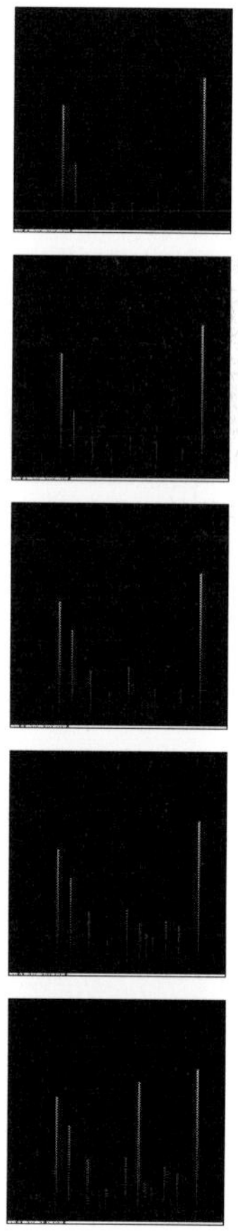

```
Paper 100
Pen 0
// spread out flare positions
// and shade based upon height
Line 0 0 100 0
Forever
{
  Repeat A 1 26
  {
    Same? <Key A> 100
    {
      Set [A 0] ([A 0]+1)
      Set V (100-[A 0])
      Set [([A 0]*3+10]) [A 0]] V
    }
  }
}
```

A, A, C, D, D, D, D, D, D, F, F, F, I, I, K, L, L, ...

The two-dimensional nature of the key arrangements can also be illustrated by appropriate subdivision of the square into three rows where each row is divided into 10, 9, and 7 units respectively. This non-uniform grid is arranged in the classic QWERTY keyboard layout.

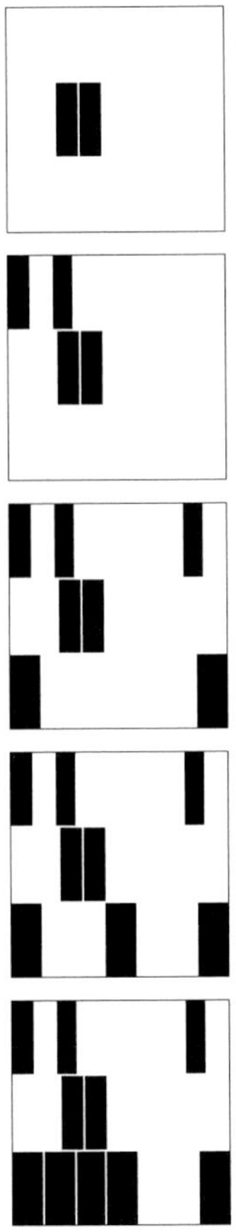

D, F, Q, E, O, Z, M, V, ...

```
Paper 0
// type to draw ...
Forever
{
  Same? <Key 1> 100
  {
    Field 0 34 10 66 100
  }
  Same? <Key 2> 100
  {
    Field 59 0 71 32 100
  }
  Same? <Key 3> 100
  {
    Field 30 0 42 32 100
  }
  Same? <Key 4> 100
  {
    Field 23 34 32 66 100
  }
  Same? <Key 5> 100
  {
    Field 21 68 29 100 100
  }
  Same? <Key 6> 100
  {
    Field 34 34 43 66 100
  }
  Same? <Key 7> 100
  {
    Field 45 34 54 66 100
  }
  Same? <Key 8> 100
  {
    Field 56 34 65 66 100
  }
  Same? <Key 9> 100
  {
    Field 71 68 79 100 100
  }
  Same? <Key 10> 100
  {
    Field 67 34 76 66 100
  }
  Same? <Key 11> 100
  {
    Field 78 34 87 66 100
  }
  Same? <Key 12> 100
  {
    Field 89 34 100 66 100
  }
  Same? <Key 13> 100
  {
    Field 87 0 100 32 100
  }
  Same? <Key 14> 100
  {
    Field 73 0 85 32 100
  }
  Same? <Key 15> 100
  {
    Field 81 68 89 100 100
  }
  Same? <Key 16> 100
  {
    Field 91 68 100 100 100
  }
  Same? <Key 17> 100
  {
    Field 0 68 9 100 100
  }
  Same? <Key 18> 100
  {
    Field 31 68 39 100 100
  }
  Same? <Key 19> 100
  {
    Field 12 34 21 66 100
  }
  Same? <Key 20> 100
  {
    Field 41 68 49 100 100
  }
  Same? <Key 21> 100
  {
    Field 61 68 69 100 100
  }
  Same? <Key 22> 100
  {
    Field 44 0 57 32 100
  }
  Same? <Key 23> 100
  {
    Field 11 68 19 100 100
  }
  Same? <Key 24> 100
  {
    Field 15 0 28 32 100
  }
  Same? <Key 25> 100
  {
    Field 51 68 59 100 100
  }
  Same? <Key 26> 100
  {
    Field 0 0 13 32 100
  }
}
```

In this form, the keyboard can become a tactile scanner that shows the impression left by an object placed on the keyboard. Alternatively it can become a tactile tool for doodling.

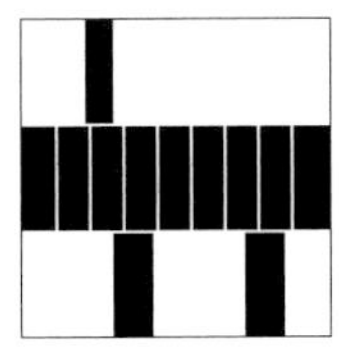

Digital Typewriter The keyboard is not just a sensing device, but also a means to map letters of the alphabet to virtual impressions of those symbols onto the computer. Press *A,* and an "A" will usually appear on the screen. The first step in creating this behavior is that the computer must have an idea about how to draw the letters *A* to *Z.*

There is a set of digital letters that are known by the system, which are in the file *dbnletters.dbn.* Inside this file are the definitions for 26 letters encoded as individual commands that draw a specified letter within an area of 11 by 11 dots. The commands are named **LetterA** for *A,* **LetterB** for *B,* and so forth, where each command takes two descriptors for the horizontal and vertical position of where to draw the letter.

```
Load dbnletters.dbn
Paper 0
Pen 100
// draw dbn letters A through Z
Set X 17
Set Y 73
Set DX 12
Set DY 12
LetterA X Y
LetterB (X+DX) Y
LetterC (X+2*DX) Y
LetterD (X+3*DX) Y
LetterE (X+4*DX) Y
Set Y (Y-DY)
LetterF X Y
LetterG (X+DX) Y
LetterH (X+2*DX) Y
LetterI (X+3*DX) Y
LetterJ (X+4*DX) Y
Set Y (Y-DY)
LetterK X Y
LetterL (X+DX) Y
LetterM (X+2*DX) Y
LetterN (X+3*DX) Y
LetterO (X+4*DX) Y
Set Y (Y-DY)
LetterP x Y
LetterQ (X+DX) Y
LetterR (X+2*DX) Y
LetterS (X+3*DX) Y
LetterT (X+4*DX) Y
Set Y (Y-DY)
LetterU X Y
LetterV (X+DX) Y
LetterW (X+2*DX) Y
LetterX (X+3*DX) Y
LetterY (X+4*dX) Y
Set Y (Y-DY)
LetterZ (X+5*DX) Y
```

You can also draw a letter with the more general **Letter** command, where the first descriptor is the number of the letter, 1 to 26 as used in <Key>, and the second and third descriptors are the horizontal and vertical positions to draw the letter. The advantage is that Letter has been designed to be easily used in a Repeat.

```
load dbnletters.dbn
// display all letteres using repeat
Paper 0
Pen 100
Set X 17
Set Y 73
Set DX 12
Set DY 12
Set N 0
Repeat A 1 25
{
  Letter A X Y
  Set X (X+DX)
  Set N (N+1)
  Same? N 5
  {
    // do a linewrap at 5 chars
    Set X 17
    Set Y (Y-DY)
    Set N 0
  }
}
Set X (X+DX*5)
Letter 26 X Y
```

With the 26 letters available in this manner, rather than representing a keypress in an abstract manner with rectangle or line, the Letter currently pressed can be literally displayed.

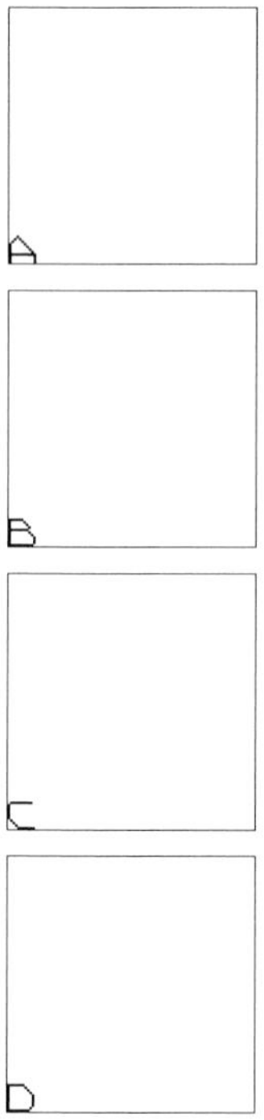

A, B, C, D

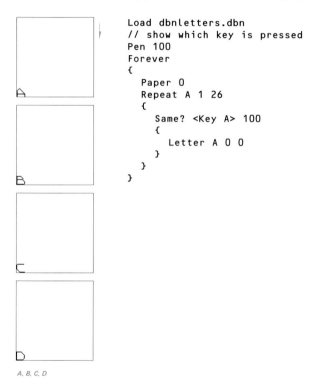

```
Load dbnletters.dbn
// show which key is pressed
Pen 100
Forever
{
  Paper 0
  Repeat A 1 26
  {
    Same? <Key A> 100
    {
      Letter A 0 0
    }
  }
}
```

You can keep track of the sequence of keys entered and emulate the behavior of a digital typewriter with a simple Repeat, which displays the corresponding Letter that is pressed. When the letters get to the edge, the starting point is moved back to the left edge and down a row so that more text can be added.

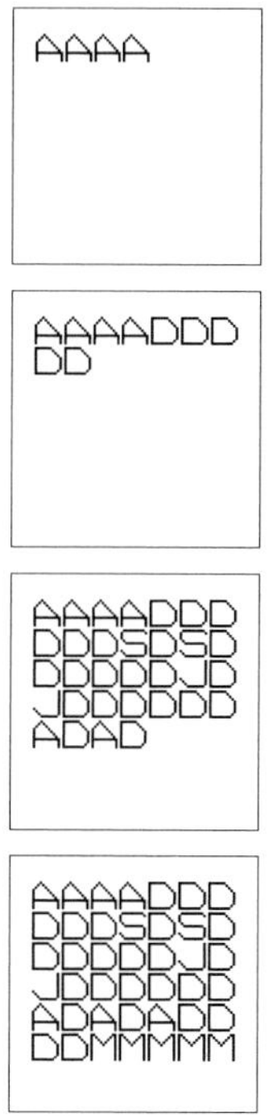

A, A, A, A, D, D, D, ...

```
Load dbnletters.dbn
// write a letter ...
Paper 0
Pen 100
Set X 9
Set Y 80
Set DX 12
Set DY 12
Forever
{
  Repeat A 1 26
  {
    Same? <Key A> 100
    {
      NotSmaller? X 92
      {
        Set X 9
        Set Y (Y-DY)
      }
      Smaller? Y 5
      {
        Set Y 80
        Paper 0
        Set X 9
      }
      Letter A X Y
      Set X (X+DX)
    }
  }
}
```

Note that this typewriter will behave a little differently than its conventional counterpart because each key is checked cyclically if it is pressed. This distinction is difficult to describe in text and most easily recognized when you run the program. There may be the case where you hit a key so briefly that the program does not detect it and so will not display your intent; on the other hand you might hold a key down so long that the key appears on the computer more than once.

The complete letter definitions follow, but they should not prevent you from building your own.

```
//
// dbnletters.dbn
//
Command LetterA H V
{
  Line H V H (V+7)
  Line (H) (V+7) (H+3) (V+10)
  Line (H+3) (V+10) (H+10) (V+3)
  Line (H+10) (V+3) (H+10) V
  Line H (V+3) (H+10) (V+3)
}
Command LetterB H V
{
  Line H V H (V+10)
  Line H (V+10) (H+5) (V+10)
  Line (H+5) (V+10) (H+8) (V+7)
  Line H (V+6) (H+7) (V+6)
  Line (H+7) (V+6) (H+10) (V+3)
  Line (H+10) (V+3) (H+10) (V+1)
  Line H V (H+9) V
}
Command LetterC H V
{
  Line (H+4) V (H+10) V
  Line (H+4) V H (V+4)
  Line H (V+4) H (V+9)
  Line (H+1) (V+10) (H+9) (V+10)
}
Command LetterD H V
{
  Line H V H (V+10)
  Line H V (H+8) V
  Line (H+8) V (H+10) (V+2)
  Line (H+10) (V+2) (H+10) (V+6)
  Line (H+10) (V+6) (H+6) (V+10)
  Line (H+6) (V+10) H (V+10)
}
Command LetterE H V
{
  Line H (V+3) H (V+10)
  Line H (V+3) (H+3) V
  Line (H+3) V (H+10) V
  Line H (V+6) (H+9) (V+6)
  Line H (V+10) (H+9) (V+10)
}
Command LetterF H V
{
  Line H V H (V+10)
  Line H (V+6) (H+8) (V+6)
  Line H (V+10) (H+10) (V+10)
}
Command LetterG H V
{
  Line (H+4) V (H+9) V
  Line (H+4) V H (V+4)
  Line H (V+4) H (V+9)
  Line (H+1) (V+10) (H+9) (V+10)
  Line (H+10) (V+1) (H+10) (V+5)
  Line (H+10) (V+5) (H+6) (V+5)
}
Command LetterH H V
{
  Line H V H (V+10)
  Line H (V+4) (H+10) (V+4)
  Line (H+10) V (H+10) (V+10)
}
Command LetterI H V
{
  Line H V (H+10) V
  Line (H+5) V (H+5) (V+10)
  Line H (V+10) (H+9) (V+10)
}
Command LetterJ H V
{
  Line H (V+3) (H+3) V
  Line (H+3) V (H+9) V
  Line (H+10) (V+1) (H+10) (V+10)
}
Command LetterK H V
{
  Line H V H (V+10)
  Line H (V+1) (H+9) (V+10)
  Line (H+5) (V+5) (H+10) V
}
Command LetterL H V
{
  Line H V H (V+10)
  Line H V (H+10) V
}
Command LetterM H V
{
  Line H V H (V+10)
  //Line H (V+10) (H+2) (V+10)
  Line (H+1) (V+10) (H+5) (V+6)
  Line (H+5) (V+6) (H+9) (V+10)
  Line (H+10) (V+10) (H+10) V
}
Command LetterN H V
{
  Line H V H (V+10)
  Line H (V+10) (H+3) (V+10)
  Line (H+3) (V+10) (H+10) (V+3)
  Line (H+10) (V+10) (H+10) V
}
Command LetterO H V
{
  Line (H+4) V (H+9) V
  Line (H+4) V H (V+4)
  Line H (V+4) H (V+9)
  Line (H+1) (V+10) (H+7) (V+10)
  Line (H+7) (V+10) (H+10) (V+7)
  Line (H+10) (V+7) (H+10) (V+1)
}
Command LetterP H V
{
  Line H V H (V+10)
  Line H (V+10) (H+7) (V+10)
  Line (H+7) (V+10) (H+10) (V+7)
  Line (H+10) (V+6) (H+8) (V+4)
  Line H (V+4) (H+8) (V+4)
}
Command LetterQ H V
{
  Line (H+4) V (H+8) V
  Line (H+4) V H (V+4)
  Line H (V+4) H (V+9)
  Line (H+1) (V+10) (H+7) (V+10)
  Line (H+7) (V+10) (H+10) (V+7)
  Line (H+10) (V+7) (H+10) (V+2)
  Line (H+6) (V+4) (H+10) V
}
```

```
Command LetterR H V
{
  Line H V H (V+10)
  Line H (V+10) (H+7) (V+10)
  Line (H+7) (V+10) (H+10) (V+7)
  Line (H+10) (V+6) (H+8) (V+4)
  Line H (V+4) (H+8) (V+4)
  Line (H+6) (V+4) (H+10) V
}
Command LetterS H V
{
  Line H (V+2) (H+2) V
  Line (H+2) V (H+9) V
  Line (H+10) (V+1) (H+10) (V+4)
  Line (H+9) (V+5) (H+2) (V+5)
  Line (H+2) (V+5) H (V+7)
  Line H (V+7) H (V+9)
  Line (H+1) (V+10) (H+9) (V+10)
  Line (H+9) (V+10) (H+10) (V+9)
}
Command LetterT H V
{
  Line H (V+10) (H+10) (V+10)
  Line (H+5) (V+10) (H+5) V
}
Command LetterU H V
{
  Line H (V+10) H (V+3)
  Line H (V+3) (H+3) V
  Line (H+3) V (H+9) V
  Line (H+10) (V+1) (H+10) (V+10)
}
Command LetterV H V
{
  Line H (V+10) H (V+5)
  Line H (V+5) (H+5) V
  Line (H+5) V (H+10) (V+5)
  Line (H+10) (V+5) (H+10) (V+10)
}
Command LetterW H V
{
  Line H (V+10) H (V+3)
  Line H (V+3) (H+3) V
  Line (H+3) V (H+6) (V+3)
  Line (H+6) (V+3) (H+9) V
  Line (H+10) (V+1) (H+10) (V+10)
}
Command LetterX H V
{
  Line H (V+10) H (V+9)
  Line H (V+9) (H+4) (V+5)
  Line (H+4) (V+5) (H+6) (V+5)
  Line (H+6) (V+5) (H+10) (V+9)
  Line (H+10) (V+9) (H+10) (V+10)
  Line H V H (V+1)
  Line H (V+1) (H+4) (V+5)
  Line (H+6) (V+5) (H+10) (V+1)
  Line (H+10) (V+1) (H+10) V
}
Command LetterY H V
{
  Line H (V+10) H (V+7)
  Line H (V+7) (H+3) (V+4)
  Line (H+3) (V+4) (H+10) (V+4)
  Line (H+10) (V+10) (H+10) (V+1)
  Line (H+9) V (H+2) V
  Line (H+2) V H (V+2)
}
Command LetterZ H V
{
  Line H (V+10) (H+10) (V+10)
  Line (H+10) (V+10) H V
  Line H V (H+10) V
}
Command Letter L H V
{
  Same? L 1
  {
    LetterA H V
  }
  Same? L 2
  {
    LetterB H V
  }
  Same? L 3
  {
    LetterC H V
  }
  Same? L 4
  {
    LetterD H V
  }
  Same? L 5
  {
    LetterE H V
  }
  Same? L 6
  {
    LetterF H V
  }
  Same? L 7
  {
    LetterG H V
  }
  Same? L 8
  {
    LetterH H V
  }
  Same? L 9
  {
    LetterI H V
  }
  Same? L 10
  {
    LetterJ H V
  }
  Same? L 11
  {
    LetterK H V
  }
  Same? L 12
  {
    LetterL H V
  }
  Same? L 13
  {
    LetterM H V
  }
  Same? L 14
  {
    LetterN H V
  }
  Same? L 15
  {
    LetterO H V
  }
  Same? L 16
  {
    LetterP H V
  }
  Same? L 17
  {
    LetterQ H V
  }
  Same? L 18
  {
    LetterR H V
  }
  Same? L 19
  {
    LetterS H V
  }
  Same? L 20
  {
    LetterT H V
  }
  Same? L 21
  {
    LetterU H V
  }
  Same? L 22
  {
    LetterV H V
  }
  Same? L 23
  {
    LetterW H V
  }
  Same? L 24
  {
    LetterX H V
  }
  Same? L 25
  {
    LetterY H V
  }
  Same? L 26
  {
    LetterZ H V
  }
}
```

Atypical Typewriting When I first began to explore the use of the keyboard in expression, I created a piece called *Color Typewriter,* which translated the input letters into tokens of color. By emulating the behavior of a word processor, but not actually writing words, the system simply records your touch as a stream of colors. A similar effect can be coded in grayscale.

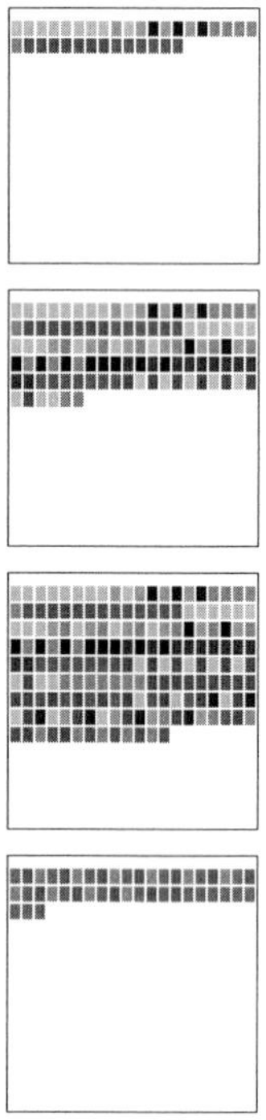

A, A, A, A, A, B, A, B, S, ...

```
Paper 0
// remake of color typewriter
Set X 1
Set Y 90
Set DX 5
Set DY 7
Forever
{
   Repeat A 1 26
   {
      Same? <Key A> 100
      {
         Same? X 101
         {
            Set X 1
            Set Y (Y-DY)
         }
         Smaller? Y 5
         {
            Paper 0
            Set X 1
            Set Y 90
         }
         Field X Y (X+DX-2) (Y+DY-2) (A*3+11)
         Set X (X+DX)
      }
   }
}
```

As you press each key, a corresponding gray rectangle is added to the line of abstracted type. *A* corresponds to a light shade of gray, and as you work your way to *Z* the rectangle increasingly darkens. You can map the time history of the keyboard input into tokens of gray, which, if the input is planned, results in another quick doodle.

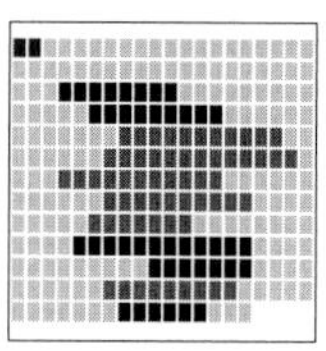

The experience is enhanced with a blinking text cursor and partial erasure of the previous page. The blinking cursor invites the user to interact.

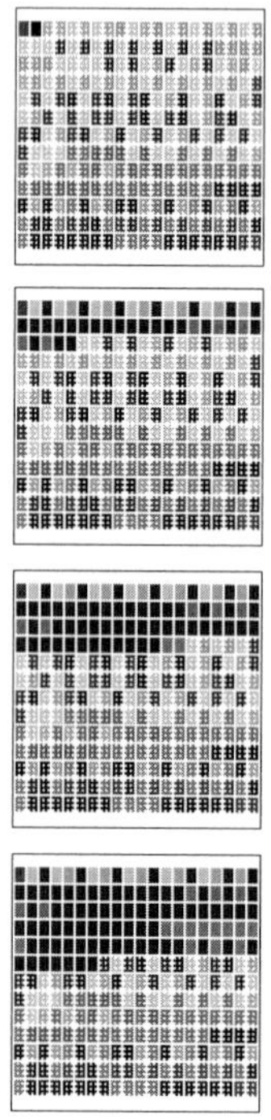

S, A, S, A, A, S, S, A, A, A, ...

```
Paper 0
// enhanced remake of color typewriter
Set X 1
Set Y 90
Set DX 5
Set DY 7
Forever
{
   Set B (100-B)
   Pen B
   Field X Y (X+DX-2) (Y+DY-2) B
   Repeat A 1 26
   {
      Same? <Key A> 100
      {
         Same? X 101
         {
            Set X 1
            Set Y (Y-DY)
         }
         Smaller? Y 5
         {
            Repeat H 0 50
            {
               Repeat V 0 50
               {
                  Set H2 (H*2)
                  Set V2 (V*2)
                  Set [H2 V2] 0
               }
            }
            Set X 1
            Set Y 90
         }
         Field X Y (X+DX-2) (Y+DY-2) (A*3+11)
         Set X (X+DX)
      }
   }
}
```

Type and key input can relate in an abstract sense as simple, dynamic typography, such as type falling from the sky when a key is pressed.

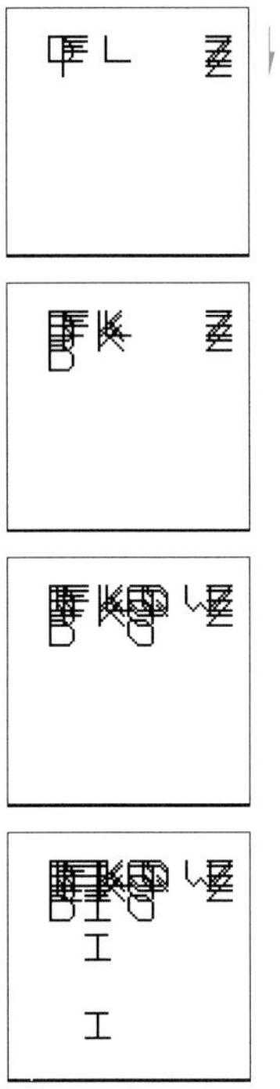

D, F, F, F, L, Z, Z, Z, Z, K, K, ...

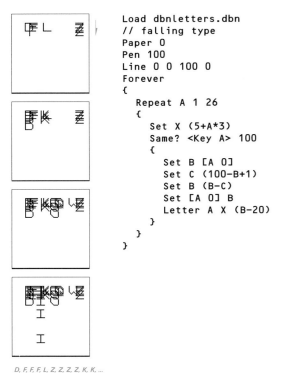

```
Load dbnletters.dbn
// falling type
Paper 0
Pen 100
Line 0 0 100 0
Forever
{
  Repeat A 1 26
  {
    Set X (5+A*3)
    Same? <Key A> 100
    {
      Set B [A 0]
      Set C (100-B+1)
      Set B (B-C)
      Set [A 0] B
      Letter A X (B-20)
    }
  }
}
```

Or it can be a remote controlled letter that moves within the confines of the paper, nudged gently by pressing the *A* or *B* keys.

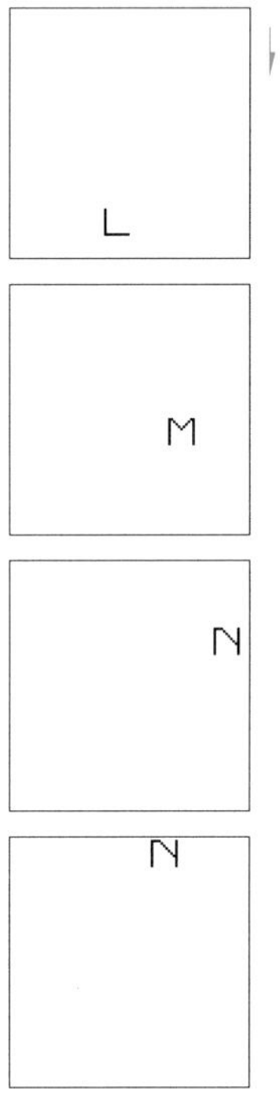

A, A, A, B, A, B, ...

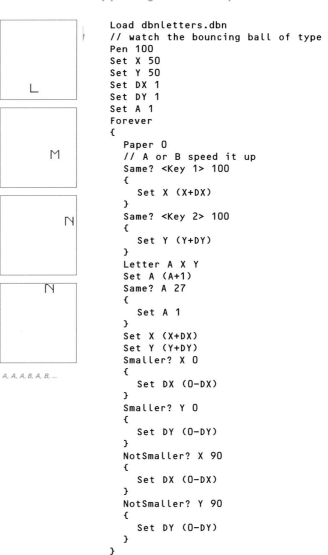

```
Load dbnletters.dbn
// watch the bouncing ball of type
Pen 100
Set X 50
Set Y 50
Set DX 1
Set DY 1
Set A 1
Forever
{
  Paper 0
  // A or B speed it up
  Same? <Key 1> 100
  {
    Set X (X+DX)
  }
  Same? <Key 2> 100
  {
    Set Y (Y+DY)
  }
  Letter A X Y
  Set A (A+1)
  Same? A 27
  {
    Set A 1
  }
  Set X (X+DX)
  Set Y (Y+DY)
  Smaller? X 0
  {
    Set DX (0-DX)
  }
  Smaller? Y 0
  {
    Set DY (0-DY)
  }
  NotSmaller? X 90
  {
    Set DX (0-DX)
  }
  NotSmaller? Y 90
  {
    Set DY (0-DY)
  }
}
```

Each letter can correspond to a particular rhythm of display, ranging from *A* as slow, to *Z* as fast. The speed can be displayed as well.

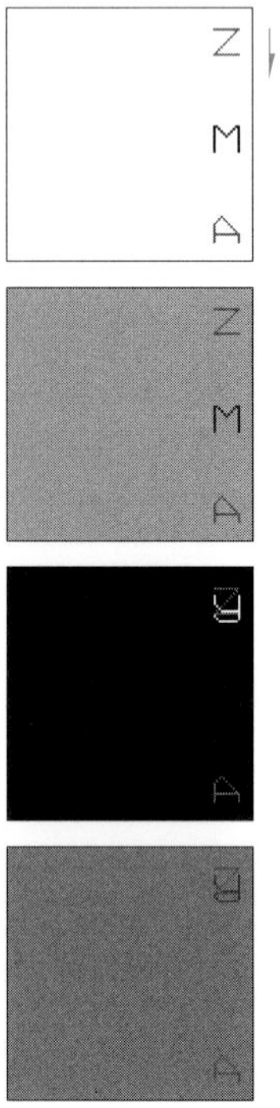

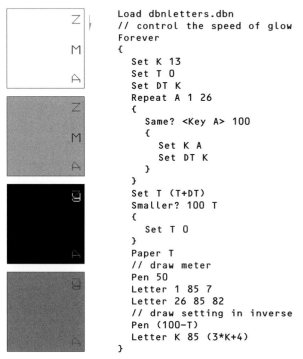

```
Load dbnletters.dbn
// control the speed of glow
Forever
{
  Set K 13
  Set T 0
  Set DT K
  Repeat A 1 26
  {
    Same? <Key A> 100
    {
      Set K A
      Set DT K
    }
  }
  Set T (T+DT)
  Smaller? 100 T
  {
    Set T 0
  }
  Paper T
  // draw meter
  Pen 50
  Letter 1 85 7
  Letter 26 85 82
  // draw setting in inverse
  Pen (100-T)
  Letter K 85 (3*K+4)
}
```

A, A, O, O, O, U, U, U, F, F, D, I, I, ...

And finally it can be a basic composition of overlapping, gray type placed at an angle in opposing diagonal directions.

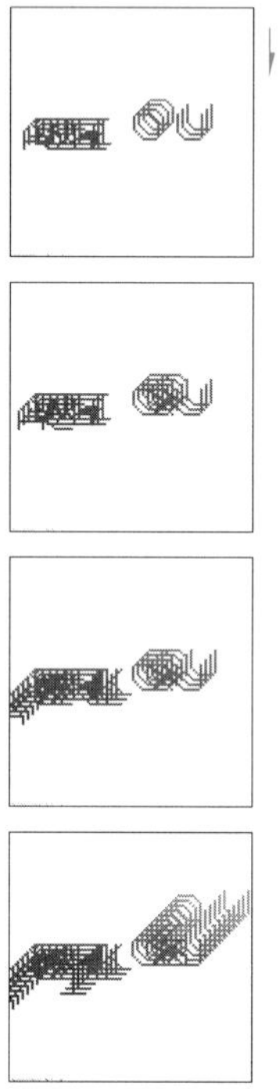

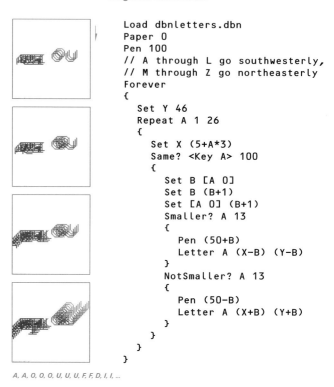

```
Load dbnletters.dbn
Paper 0
Pen 100
// A through L go southwesterly,
// M through Z go northeasterly
Forever
{
  Set Y 46
  Repeat A 1 26
  {
    Set X (5+A*3)
    Same? <Key A> 100
    {
      Set B [A 0]
      Set B (B+1)
      Set [A 0] (B+1)
      Smaller? A 13
      {
        Pen (50+B)
        Letter A (X-B) (Y-B)
      }
      NotSmaller? A 13
      {
        Pen (50-B)
        Letter A (X+B) (Y+B)
      }
    }
  }
}
```

A, A, O, O, O, U, U, U, F, F, D, I, I, ...

An important question to ask is if having type involved in these compositions makes them any better, but that discussion is left for a future work.

The keyboard differs from the mouse in that there are actual symbols stamped on all the keys while the mouse has a completely unlabeled surface. You can choose either to ignore the labels on the keys, or to be aware of them. But in either case, the keyboard can add visual surprise and delight to your digital design experience.

Summary Using the computer can be an unsatisfying experience. But to say that the computer is devoid of sensorial sophistication is more a statement of its general use than its actual capabilities. The average computer has a monitor, keyboard, and mouse—a minimal configuration for word processing and home computing needs. Said differently, the average computer has 300,000 independent light-emitting units, is capable of acquiring high-precision measurements of changes in two-dimensional position, and includes a tactile pad capable of sensing over a hundred independent changes in pressure. In this light, it seems unfair to label a computer as unsophisticated, and more accurate to blame uninspired humans for their lack of creativity and inspiration in applying the available technology.

In addition to the keyboard, mouse, and monitor, there are many other emerging input and output technologies which, through creative reinterpretation, can reveal their hidden potential. The ability to imagine in a medium deeply rests upon the extent of one's ability to create in the medium. Never blindly accept a new technology and naively apply it without studying its intrinsic behavior and properties. To transcend mere industrial expectations, explore the medium for its intrinsic set of potentials rather than its commercially imposed limitations.

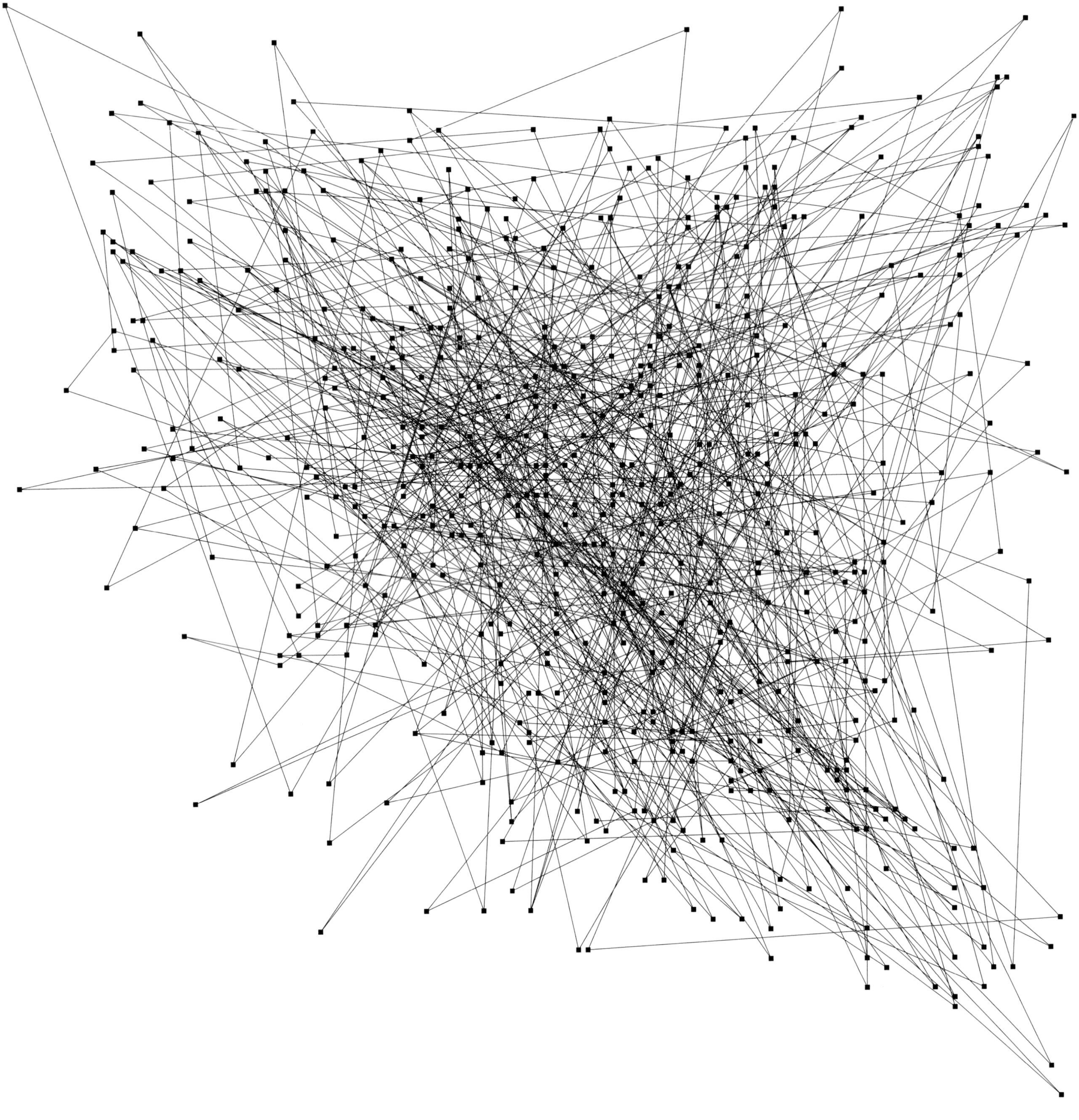

17 NETWORK Accessing the Internet from a computer program used to be a difficult task for the amateur, but now it is easy. Just as the introduction of the mouse made computer graphics easily accessible in the 1980s, today's flood of network extensions has spurred an explosion of artistic exploration on the Internet. The outcome is hundreds of specialized communication systems of varying degrees of complexity, ranging from simple person-to-person systems to those that enable vast communities of people to connect online.

On the network, communication can be manipulated in its raw state to be interpreted in various themes of artistic inquiry. Since the scope is worldwide and the Internet is now a common household word, many traditional art institutions across the world are finally attempting to forge deeper bonds with technology. Many young artists want to create art on the Internet. But they are confused when they find that the only works they can create are things that they have already seen. Chat systems, video portals, and hypertexts all have certain well-tested limitations to their respective abilities to entertain and challenge the mind.

As an area for visual exploration, the Internet by itself provides nothing new. Methods for input such as the mouse or keyboard also do not provide anything new in a visual sense, but they do provide a context to relate our physical selves to the computer. The ability to project one's existence, either physically or through an intermediary, into a space with some form of visual or other sensorial feedback is a prerequisite for any experience to occur, so input and output become important considerations. But you must remember that the Internet is merely a powerless intermediary, a communication channel that is given more attention than it deserves.

Shared Paper A subset of the global aspect of the Internet is modeled in this programming system as a shared bank of memory which can be freely accessed by all computers connected to the Internet and running the DBN system. In other words, there is a computer on the Net that is dedicated to managing a set of numbered locations. There are a total of 1000 such locations, or *addresses* as they are called, accessed through the external data specifier **Net**. More specifically, <Net 1> through <Net 1000> refer to the values that are stored on a central computer. In the same way that you can retrieve the value of <Net 1>, so can a user in Africa, Europe, or Asia. Depending upon how many people are using network memory, there can be unpredictable results because multiple users can change memory in the time it takes your computer to update the screen. Paper <Net 1> could result in a 50 percent gray paper.

```
//
// the paper is set by accessing
// net memory location '1'
//
Paper <Net 1>
```

Or perhaps an 82 percent black paper.

```
//
// there is no guarantee as to
// what this expression may yield
//
Paper <Net 1>
```

The result depends upon the instantaneous value of <Net 1>, which could be anything.

You can specifically set the value at a location on the Net by using the usual **Set** command; for instance, as "Set <Net 1> 100." The value on the central server at address 1 is set to 100. You might do this with intent of accessing <Net 1> as the descriptor for Paper to get a black page. Someone else could have "Set <Net 1> 33" immediately after you, and then "Paper <Net 1>" would yield 33 percent gray.

```
//
// net memory 1 is set to 100
//
Set <Net 1> 100
// but the value is not guaranteed...
Paper <Net 1>
```

For the sake of getting through this chapter smoothly, assume that there are not many people accessing the Net memory, so we have a relatively high probability of getting what we want.

There are two actions performed: Setting the value on the Net, and looking at the value on the Net. The key fact to consider is that a single machine does not necessarily have to both Set and retrieve; one can Set, the other can retrieve. In other words, one computer can be sending out changes to <Net 1> in a Forever statement.

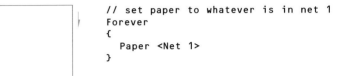

```
Paper 100
// store 0 through 100 into net 1
Forever
{
  Repeat A 0 100
  {
    Set <Net 1> A
  }
}
```

Meanwhile, another computer, or computers, can be updating themselves based upon the value stored at <Net 1>.

```
// set paper to whatever is in net 1
Forever
{
  Paper <Net 1>
}
```

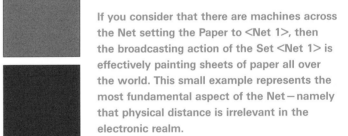

If you consider that there are machines across the Net setting the Paper to <Net 1>, then the broadcasting action of the Set <Net 1> is effectively painting sheets of paper all over the world. This small example represents the most fundamental aspect of the Net—namely that physical distance is irrelevant in the electronic realm.

The user at the computer that Sets the value of <Net 1> can become a part of the entire process by simply transferring the instantaneous position of one of the mouse's dimensions. Moving the mouse serves as a remote control device to change Papers that are listening in to <Net 1>.

```
// this is the SERVER
Paper 0
Forever
{
  Set H <Mouse 1>
  Set <Net 1> H
}
```

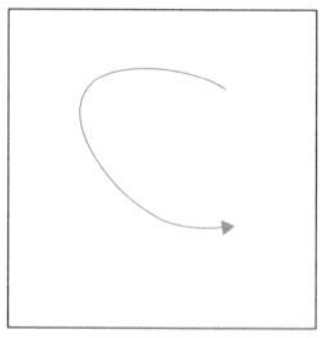

There is no change to the display area because the mouse position is only broadcasted, and not incorporated locally.

The other computers, which run the simple program of listening in, reflect the remote user's mouse position accordingly.

```
// this is the CLIENT
Forever
{
  Paper <Net 1>
}
```

Here the value of one user's mouse position is visualized as another user's paper. By directly connecting your mouse to the Net in this manner, you expand your presence and let people all over the world get a sense of your hand motions. This theme is further developed in the next section.

Collaborative Drawing Information is easily shared between parties using the Net memory mechanism. But to facilitate true communication, there must be a mutual understanding of the nature of the information being stored and retrieved. Unless all parties involved understand that <Net 1> holds the shade of a sheet of paper, then <Net 1> can easily be used for a variety of unintentional purposes. It can be mistakenly used as a gray value, or the state of the keyboard, etc. Therefore, compliance to a set of standards specified by involved parties is crucial in establishing meaningful Net data transfer.

Assume that you have a partner with whom you wish to communicate. Both of you have agreed to use <Net 100> and <Net 101> to hold the respective horizontal and vertical positions of your pointer, and <Net 102> and <Net 103> hold your partner's pointer information. There are two programs to consider, yours and your partner's.

```
// your program
Paper 0
Forever
{
  // broadcast your position
  Set <Net 100> <Mouse 1>
  Set <Net 101> <Mouse 2>
}
```

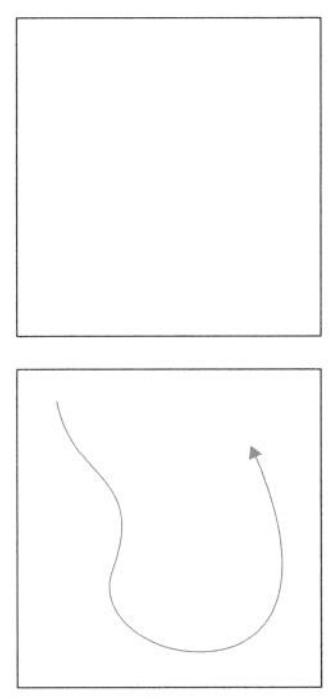

```
// your partner's program
Paper 0
Forever
{
  // partner broadcasts his/her position
  Set <Net 102> <Mouse 1>
  Set <Net 103> <Mouse 2>
}
```

An indirect communication link has been established. This link is valid as long as no other parties interfere with Net memory 100 to 103.

Each party can see the other party's pointer position by accessing the partner's Net memory. The effect is painting on each other's screen.

```
// your program
Forever
{
  // broadcast your position
  Set <Net 100> <Mouse 1>
  Set <Net 101> <Mouse 2>
  // get partner's position
  Set [<Net 102> <Net 103>] 100
}
```

```
// your partner's program
Forever
{
  // partner broadcasts their position
  Set <Net 102> <Mouse 1>
  Set <Net 103> <Mouse 2>
  // partner gets your position
  Set [<Net 100> <Net 101>] 100
}
```

A person can see only his or her partner's scribbles; thus the motion that you make does not correspond to the drawing that you see.

You can improve this system by visualizing both people's motions on the same screen. It is further enhanced by connecting the dots with lines.

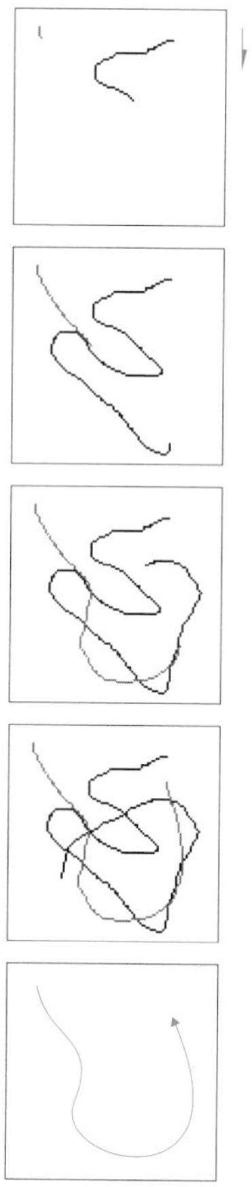

```
// your program
Paper 0
Set HP <Mouse 1>
Set VP <Mouse 2>
Set HHP <Net 102>
Set VVP <Net 103>
Forever
{
  // broadcast your position
  Set H <Mouse 1>
  Set V <Mouse 2>
  Set <Net 100> H
  Set <Net 101> V
  Set HH <Net 102>
  Set VV <Net 103>
  // draw your stroke in gray;
  // your partner's in black
  Pen 100
  Line HHP VVP HH VV
  Pen 50
  Line HP VP H V
  Set HHP HH
  Set VVP VV
  Set HP H
  Set VP V
}
```

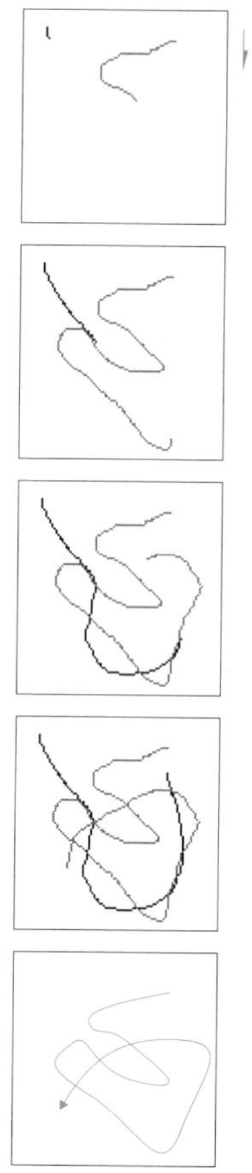

```
// your partner's program
Paper 0
Set HP <Mouse 1>
Set VP <Mouse 2>
Set HHP <Net 100>
Set VVP <Net 101>
Forever
{
  // broadcast your position
  Set H <Mouse 1>
  Set V <Mouse 2>
  Set <Net 102> H
  Set <Net 103> V
  Set HH <Net 100>
  Set VV <Net 101>
  // partner is now gray;
  // 'you' are in black
  Pen 100
  Line HHP VVP HH VV
  Pen 50
  Line HP VP H V
  Set HHP HH
  Set VVP VV
  Set HP H
  Set VP V
}
```

The result is a simple collaborative drawing system that can be easily extended.

For example, a third party can be added by declaring <Net 104> and <Net 105> as another set of mouse positions, and then defining three different programs to run on each computer.

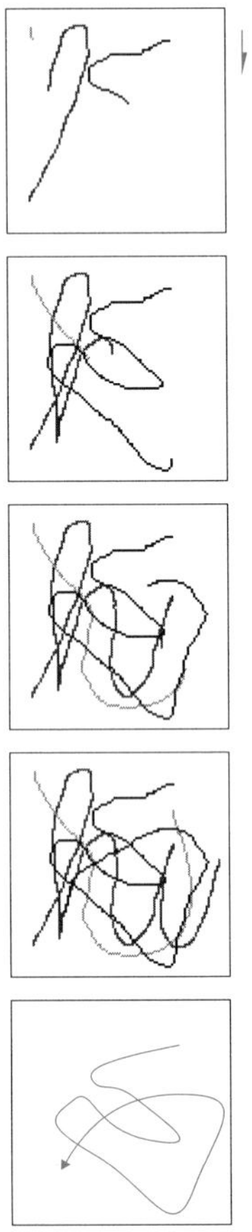

```
// your program
Paper 0
Set HP <Mouse 1>
Set VP <Mouse 2>
Set HHP <Net 102>
Set VVP <Net 103>
Set HHHP <Net 104>
Set VVVP <Net 105>
Forever
{
  // broadcast your position @100,101
  Set H <Mouse 1>
  Set V <Mouse 2>
  Set <Net 100> H
  Set <Net 101> V
  Set HH <Net 102>
  Set VV <Net 103>
  Set HHH <Net 104>
  Set VVV <Net 105>
  // you are always 100% black;
  // partner 1 is always 66%;
  // partner 2 is always 33%
  Pen 33
  Line HHHP VVVP HH VV
  Pen 66
  Line HHP VVP HH VV
  Pen 100
  Line HP VP H V
  Set HHHP HH
  Set VVVP VV
  Set HHP HH
  Set VVP VV
  Set HP H
  Set VP V
}
```

```
// partner 1's program
Paper 0
Set HP <Mouse 1>
Set VP <Mouse 2>
Set HHP <Net 100>
Set VVP <Net 101>
Set HHHP <Net 104>
Set VVVP <Net 105>
Forever
{
  // broadcast your Position @102,103
  Set H <Mouse 1>
  Set V <Mouse 2>
  Set <Net 102> H
  Set <Net 103> V
  Set HH <Net 100>
  Set VV <Net 101>
  Set HHH <Net 104>
  Set VVV <Net 105>
  // you are always 100% black;
  // Partner 1 is always 66%;
  // Partner 2 is always 33%
  Pen 33
  Line HHHP VVVP HH VV
  Pen 100
  Line HHP VVP HH VV
  Pen 66
  Line HP VP H V
  Set HHHP HH
  Set VVVP VV
  Set HHP HH
  Set VVP VV
  Set HP H
  Set VP V
}
```

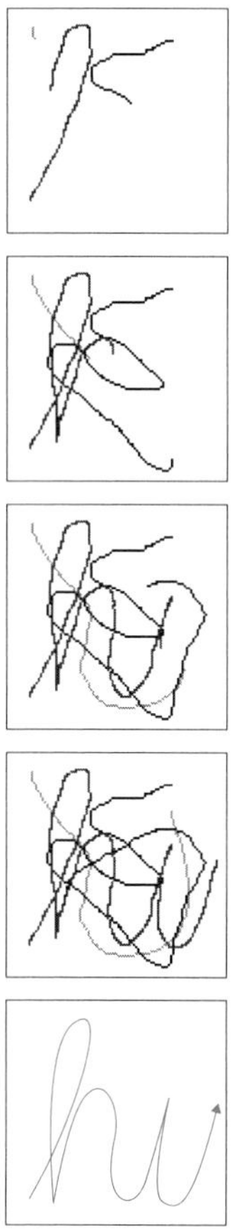

```
// partner 2's program
Paper 0
Set HP <Mouse 1>
Set VP <Mouse 2>
Set HHP <Net 102>
Set VVP <Net 103>
Set HHHP <Net 100>
Set VVVP <Net 101>
Forever
{
  // broadcast your position @104,105
  Set H <Mouse 1>
  Set V <Mouse 2>
  Set <Net 104> H
  Set <Net 105> V
  Set HH <Net 102>
  Set VV <Net 103>
  Set HHH <Net 100>
  Set VVV <Net 101>
  // you are always 100% black;
  // partner 1 is always 66%;
  // partner 2 is always 33%
  Pen 100
  Line HHHP VVVP HH VV
  Pen 66
  Line HHP VVP HH VV
  Pen 33
  Line HP VP H V
  Set HHHP HH
  Set VVVP VV
  Set HHP HH
  Set VVP VV
  Set HP H
  Set VP V
}
```

Each party is assigned a specific shading of the brush to distinguish their identities. The brush could be redesigned to be more expressive, as demonstrated in Chapter 14. However, rather than concentrate on the visual details, consider the odd simplicity of defining a canvas that can span the entire globe.

On a technical note, there are two major methods for drawing on the Internet, where the technique just discussed is generally superior to the other. Broadcasting the position of the mouse requires a minimum of two slots of network memory, versus the alternative method of broadcasting the entire image as 101 by 101 dots, totaling 10,201 slots of network memory needed. Since this exceeds the limits of Net memory, the broadcast area is limited to a 16-by-16 dot area in the lower left corner.

```
Paper 0
Pen 100
// draw border
Line 0 0 15 0
Line 15 0 15 15
Line 15 15 0 15
Line 0 15 0 0
// track mouse for 10000 cycles
Set G 0
Repeat T 0 10000
{
  Set H <Mouse 1>
  Set V <Mouse 2>
  Smaller? H 16
  {
    Smaller? V 16
    {
      Set [H V] G
    }
  }
  Set G (G+1)
  Same? G 101
  {
    Set G 0
  }
}
// send image in lower left corner
Set C 0
Repeat A 0 15
{
  Repeat B 0 15
  {
    Set <Net C> [A B]
    Set C (C+1)
  }
}
```

Once the time T has expired, the image in the lower left corner is broadcast and can be displayed by the following simple program.

```
Paper 0
// receive image in lower left corner
Set C 0
Repeat A 0 15
{
  Repeat B 0 15
  {
    Set [A B] <Net C>
    Set C (C+1)
  }
}
```

Sending the entire 16-by-16 image requires a total of 256 slots of network memory and is thus somewhat wasteful in terms of requisite communication traffic. In more sophisticated language systems like C, there are ways to compact the image such as to use fewer slots, but it is difficult to improve upon a system that uses only two slots to send the mouse coordinates. Of course this system has its share of disadvantages, which are quickly revealed through experimentation.

Primitive Chat In the same manner that stroke information can be shared, you can also share the keyboard state. You see this phenomenon quite often as *chat* facilities on the Internet, where messages are passed between users in real time. A similar sort of experience can be realized in a minimal sense by declaring <Net 1> and <Net 2> to hold the number of the key being depressed on keyboards of separate computers.

```
// Computer 1
Paper 100
Forever
{
  // look through all keys
  // and Set <Net 1> to that key
  Repeat A 1 26
  {
    Same? <Key A> 100
    {
      Set <Net 1> A
    }
  }
}
```

```
// Computer 2
Paper 100
Forever
{
  // look through all keys
  // and Set <Net 2> to that key
  Repeat A 1 26
  {
    Same? <Key A> 100
    {
      Set <Net 2> A
    }
  }
}
```

When both programs are running, <Net 1> and <Net 2> will each hold a number between 1 and 26 that represents the last keypress registered on a computer. Closer inspection of the Repeat reveals that if two keys are pressed at the same time on a single keyboard, there will be slight confusion during the Repeat because <Net 1> or <Net 2> will oscillate between values. This can be construed as a feature, not a problem.

All that remains is to display the respective state of the keyboard using the letters introduced in Chapter 16. The difference between the two users is displayed when one user's screen has a white background and the other's is the opposite.

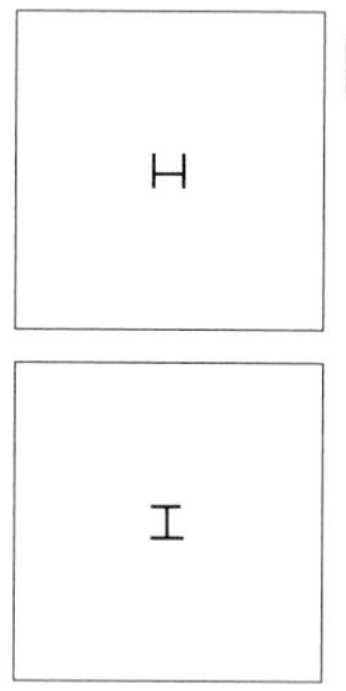

H, H, H, O, O, O ...

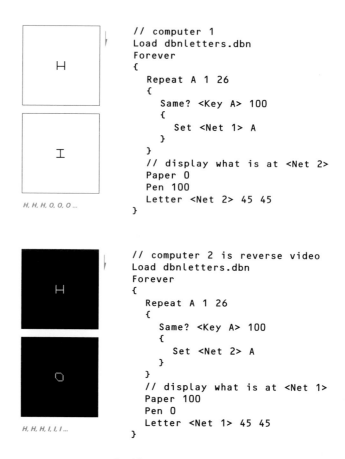

```
// computer 1
Load dbnletters.dbn
Forever
{
   Repeat A 1 26
   {
      Same? <Key A> 100
      {
         Set <Net 1> A
      }
   }
   // display what is at <Net 2>
   Paper 0
   Pen 100
   Letter <Net 2> 45 45
}
```

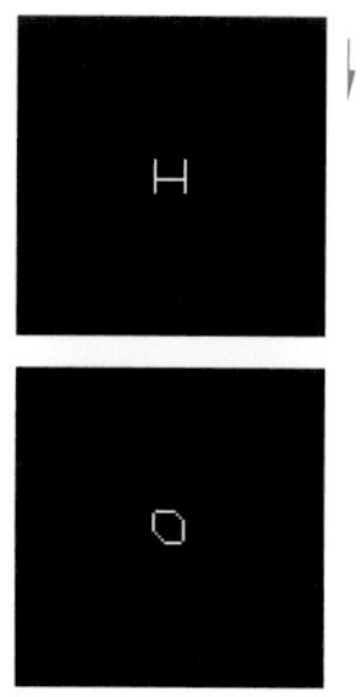

H, H, H, I, I, I ...

```
// computer 2 is reverse video
Load dbnletters.dbn
Forever
{
   Repeat A 1 26
   {
      Same? <Key A> 100
      {
         Set <Net 2> A
      }
   }
   // display what is at <Net 1>
   Paper 100
   Pen 0
   Letter <Net 1> 45 45
}
```

In this current state, a message would be difficult to reliably transmit between parties. You can imagine more sophisticated ways to place the letters using the typewriter example in Chapter 16.

There are better uses for the network than the transfer of literal messages. For instance to create a spirited game of tug-of-war.

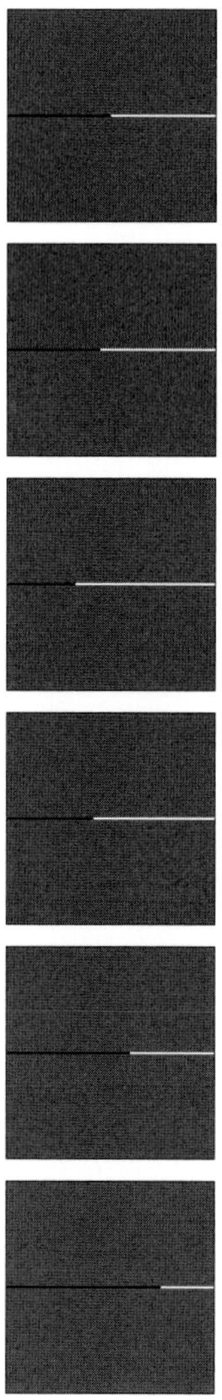

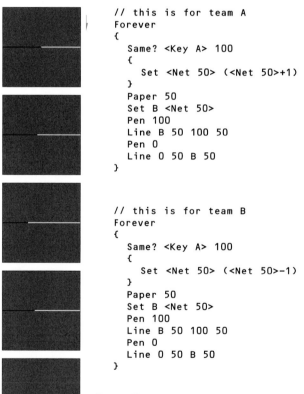

```
// this is for team A
Forever
{
  Same? <Key A> 100
  {
    Set <Net 50> (<Net 50>+1)
  }
  Paper 50
  Set B <Net 50>
  Pen 100
  Line B 50 100 50
  Pen 0
  Line 0 50 B 50
}


// this is for team B
Forever
{
  Same? <Key A> 100
  {
    Set <Net 50> (<Net 50>-1)
  }
  Paper 50
  Set B <Net 50>
  Pen 100
  Line B 50 100 50
  Pen 0
  Line 0 50 B 50
}
```

Depending upon how many keys are registered as pressed, the “rope” will move to the left or right. As in real life, if there are more people on a particular team, that team shall win, unless their network conditions are particularly poor.

Summary The mouse and keyboard were introduced as mechanisms for acquiring external information. Now the Net has been presented as another means for getting input. Notice that the Internet was nothing more than a communication channel. This is an important point: There really is nothing particularly special about the Net from the viewpoint of computational design. Although distances indeed become irrelevant, the actual problems of designing high-quality content remain the same.

Communicating numbers is quite a boring endeavor when you are simply passing values to each other to reconstruct an original image or gestural state at a distant location. The true power is realized by sending computation itself, that is, sending entire programs to different computers, to be run on those computers. This difference can be seen on the Internet today. Some designers create GIF images or complex hypertexts. Others write Java programs that synthesize the texts and images appropriately upon receipt at the destination computer.
The Internet is the ideal delivery vehicle for true computational art because the viewing mechanism is always some form of a computer. As more people explore the expressive boundaries of computation, the quality of information will be improved to a level appropriate to the attention that the Internet has received.

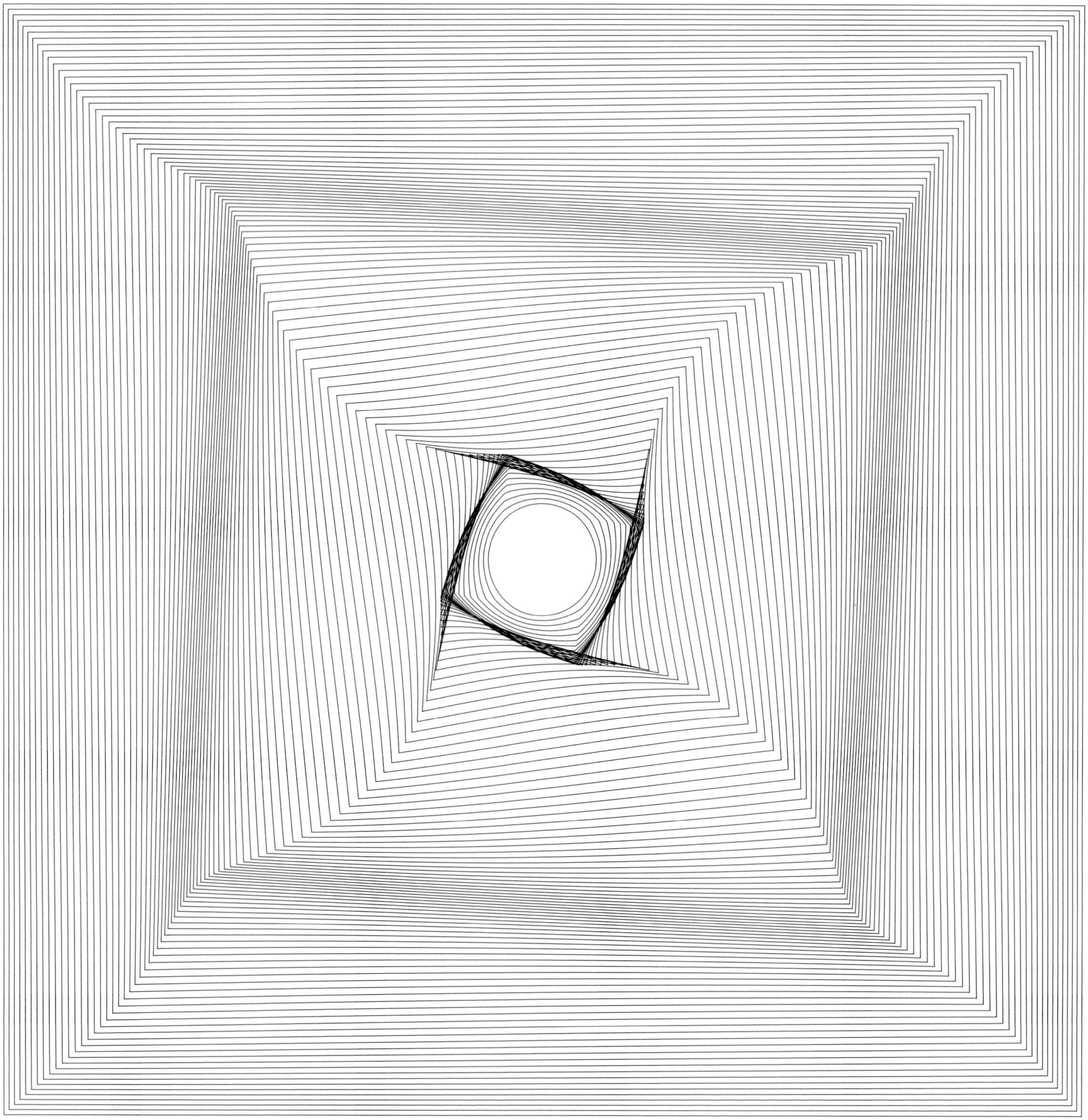

18 CHANGE Computation is a means for defining systems of change—change in response to a direct stimulus, change in response to an indirect stimulus, or change just for the sake of change. Nature continually inflicts change upon its subjects, perhaps because the ever-present catalyst for change is *time.* A computer is a pure abstraction of time, and thus it is the ideal agent for change. Even when you are designing computational forms that transform in ways beyond your control, never forget that it is you, and not the computer, who is affecting the change. Left alone, a computer would never initiate change because it does not have intent.

A program is a strict codification of some basic intent, manifested as an action that does not occur until the program is processed. When a defined action is not influenced by any unpredictable occurrences, such as external data fluctuation, a single form or multiple set of forms is synthesized for display purposes only. On the other hand, when external data is involved, the input either directly modulates the action while it occurs, or else the input elicits a discrete change in action. In both cases, the intent reflected is the design of an experience that changes in a dynamic manner that only the computational medium can realize.

Spatial Lenses The simplest form of transformation is an identity transform, where a form is identically reproduced. Such a transform is used when copying numbers verbatim, like copying a portion of the paper to be repeated at a different position on the sheet.

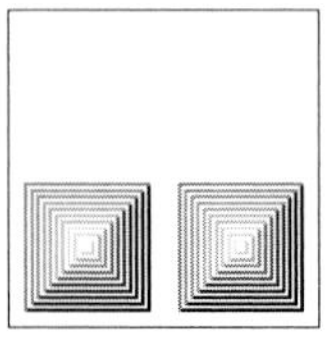

```
Paper 0
// draw test pattern
Repeat A 0 10
{
  Pen (A*10)
  Set B (A*2)
  Line (25-B) (25-B) (25+B) (25-B)
  Line (25+B) (25-B) (25+B) (25+B)
  Pen (A*3)
  Line (25+B) (25+B) (25-B) (25+B)
  Line (25-B) (25+B) (25-B) (25-B)
}
// copy the lower left
// quadrant to the right
Repeat A 0 49
{
  Repeat B 0 49
  {
    // transfer dot over
    Set [(A+50) B] [A B]
  }
}
```

A more interesting process of transfer can be described by introducing different numerical handicraft during the transfer. Using various calculations, you can manipulate either the positions or the actual values of the dots. Operating on the position values results in changes in the position and orientation of the original image. For instance, inverting the horizontal copy order results in a mirror image.

```
Paper 0
// draw test pattern
Repeat A 0 10
{
  Pen (A*10)
  Set B (A*2)
  Line (25-B) (25-B) (25+B) (25-B)
  Line (25+B) (25-B) (25+B) (25+B)
  Pen (A*3)
  Line (25+B) (25+B) (25-B) (25+B)
  Line (25-B) (25+B) (25-B) (25-B)
}
// transform the lower left
// quadrant to the right
Repeat A 0 49
{
   Repeat B 0 49
   {
      // transfer dot over as
      // flipped in horizontal
      Set [(A+50) B] [(50-A) B]
   }
}
```

Simply reversing the positions of A and B results in a straightforward rotation.

```
Paper 0
// draw test pattern
Repeat A 0 10
{
  Pen (A*10)
  Set B (A*2)
  Line (25-B) (25-B) (25+B) (25-B)
  Line (25+B) (25-B) (25+B) (25+B)
  Pen (A*3)
  Line (25+B) (25+B) (25-B) (25+B)
  Line (25-B) (25+B) (25-B) (25-B)
}
// transform the lower left
// quadrant to the right
Repeat A 0 49
{
   Repeat B 0 49
   {
      // transfer dot over
      // reflected across diagonal
      Set [(A+50) B] [B A]
   }
}
```

The second means for introducing change is to modify the values of the respective dots. For example, by adding an offset to the value transferred, the copy becomes darker than the original.

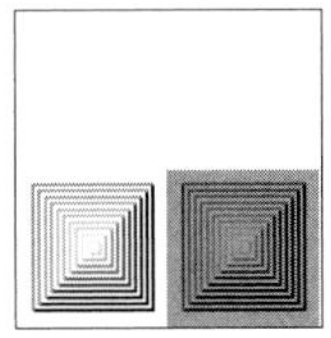

```
Paper 0
// draw test pattern
Repeat A 0 10
{
  Pen (A*10)
  Set B (A*2)
  Line (25-B) (25-B) (25+B) (25-B)
  Line (25+B) (25-B) (25+B) (25+B)
  Pen (A*3)
  Line (25+B) (25+B) (25-B) (25+B)
  Line (25-B) (25+B) (25-B) (25-B)
}
// transform the lower left
// quadrant to the right
Repeat A 0 49
{
  Repeat B 0 49
  {
    // transfer dot over as darkened
    Set [(A+50) B] ([A B]+25)
  }
}
```

It follows that by subtracting an offset from the original values, the image is lightened.

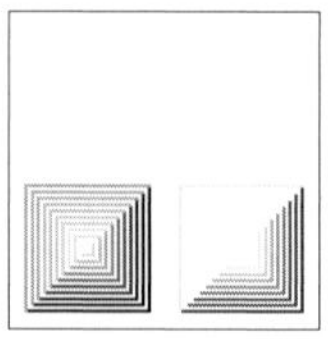

```
Paper 0
// draw test pattern
Repeat A 0 10
{
  Pen (A*10)
  Set B (A*2)
  Line (25-B) (25-B) (25+B) (25-B)
  Line (25+B) (25-B) (25+B) (25+B)
  Pen (A*3)
  Line (25+B) (25+B) (25-B) (25+B)
  Line (25-B) (25+B) (25-B) (25-B)
}
// transform the lower left
// quadrant to the right
Repeat A 0 49
{
  Repeat B 0 49
  {
    // transfer dot over as lightened
    Set [(A+50) B] ([A B]-25)
  }
}
```

By inverting the value relative to 100, the image becomes the negative copy.

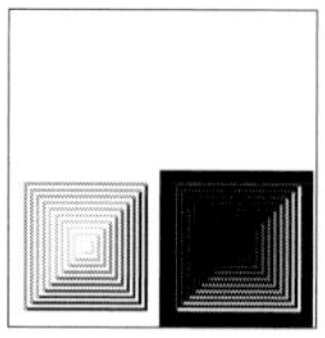

```
Paper 0
// draw test pattern
Repeat A 0 10
{
  Pen (A*10)
  Set B (A*2)
  Line (25-B) (25-B) (25+B) (25-B)
  Line (25+B) (25-B) (25+B) (25+B)
  Pen (A*3)
  Line (25+B) (25+B) (25-B) (25+B)
  Line (25-B) (25+B) (25-B) (25-B)
}
// transform the lower left
// quadrant to the right
Repeat A 0 49
{
  Repeat B 0 49
  {
    // transfer dot over as negative
    Set [(A+50) B] (100-[A B])
  }
}
```

You may recognize this general activity from any previous experience with a digital photo manipulation package. Playing with the transfer step by introducing different varieties of calculation will reveal all the commonly known *plug-in filters* that are usually seen in a pulldown menu. Several types of these filters are demonstrated here, starting with *blur.* Blur is simply an averaging of the dot values surrounding a respective Dot. Four neighboring values are added to every spot on the grid, and that sum is then divided by 5.

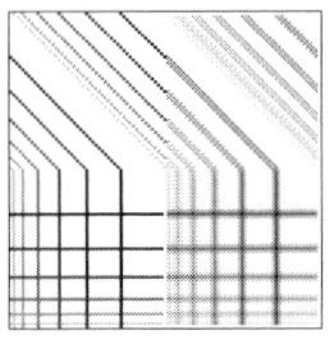

```
Paper 0
// draw test pattern
Repeat A 0 6
{
  Pen (A*16)
  Line (A*A) 0 (A*A) 49
  Line 0 (A*A) 49 (A*A)
  Line 0 (50+A*A) (A*A) 50
  Line (A*A) 100 50 (50+A*A)
}
// transform the lower left
// quadrant to the right
Repeat A 1 49
{
  Repeat B 1 99
  {
    // transfer dot over as blurred
    Set C [A B]
    Set A1 (A+1)
    Set D [A1 B]
    Set E (C+D)
    Set A1 (A-1)
    Set D [A1 B]
    Set E (E+D)
    Set B1 (B-1)
    Set D [A B1]
    Set E (E+D)
    Set B1 (B+1)
    Set D [A B1]
    Set E (E+D)
    Set E (E/5)
    Set [(A+50) B] E
  }
}
```

Thickening the original is performed by simply drawing a larger dot when a dot is detected in the original; in this instance, a Field is used at each dot to fatten it by a factor of 3.

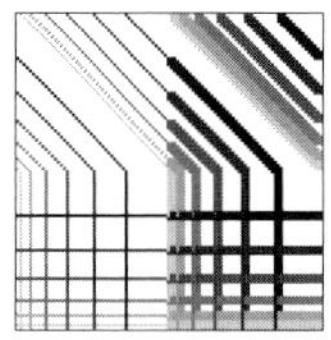

```
Paper 0
// draw test pattern
Repeat A 0 6
{
  Pen (A*16)
  Line (A*A) 0 (A*A) 49
  Line 0 (A*A) 49 (A*A)
  Line 0 (50+A*A) (A*A) 50
  Line (A*A) 100 50 (50+A*A)
}
// transform the lower left
// quadrant to the right
Repeat A 1 49
{
  Repeat B 1 99
  {
    // transfer dot over as fattened dot
    NotSame? [A B] 0
    {
      Set C (A+50)
      Set V [A B]
      Field (C-1) (B-1) (C+1) (B+1) V
    }
  }
}
```

Taking every other dot has the effect of thinning the image.

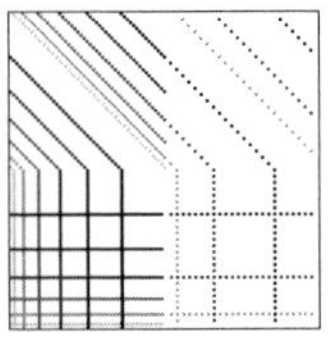

```
Paper 0
// draw test pattern
Repeat A 0 6
{
  Pen (A*16)
  Line (A*A) 0 (A*A) 49
  Line 0 (A*A) 49 (A*A)
  Line 0 (50+A*A) (A*A) 50
  Line (A*A) 100 50 (50+A*A)
}
// transform the lower left
// quadrant to the right
Repeat A 1 49
{
  Repeat B 1 99
  {
    // if numbers are even then
    // exactly divisible by 2
    Set C (2*(A/2))
    Set D (2*(B/2))
    same? C A
    {
      same? D B
      {
        Set E (A+50)
        Set [E B] [A B]
      }
    }
  }
}
```

An example of the simple kind of magic attainable with this process is a nonsense filter.

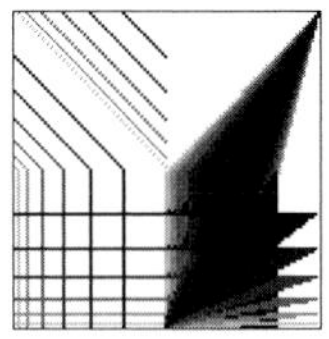

```
Paper 0
// draw test pattern
Repeat A 0 6
{
  Pen (A*16)
  Line (A*A) 0 (A*A) 49
  Line 0 (A*A) 49 (A*A)
  Line 0 (50+A*A) (A*A) 50
  Line (A*A) 100 50 (50+A*A)
}
// transform the lower left
// quadrant to the right
Repeat A 0 49
{
  Repeat B 0 49
  {
    // transfer dot over as
    // an extended wild line
    NotSame? [A B] 0
    {
      Pen [A B]
      Line 50 0 (A+50) B
      Line 100 100 (50+B/2) A
    }
  }
}
```

Creating irrelevant visual effects is so easy with computation that you must always remind yourself to think before you code. Otherwise you can suddenly find yourself immersed in an unnatural stew of undigested mathematics that shall overcome and pollute your senses.

The Art of Clockmaking I began designing clocks when I realized that time is the most relevant subject to depict by means of a dynamically changing form. The clock of the computer can be accessed with the external data tag **Time** with one descriptor. <Time 1> is the hour 0 to 23, <Time 2> is the minutes 0 to 59, and <Time 3> is the number of seconds 0 to 59. Given the ability to computationally observe the progress of time, a form that can reflect the time is easily constructed as three lines, where each line shall represents the respective hour, minute, and second reading.

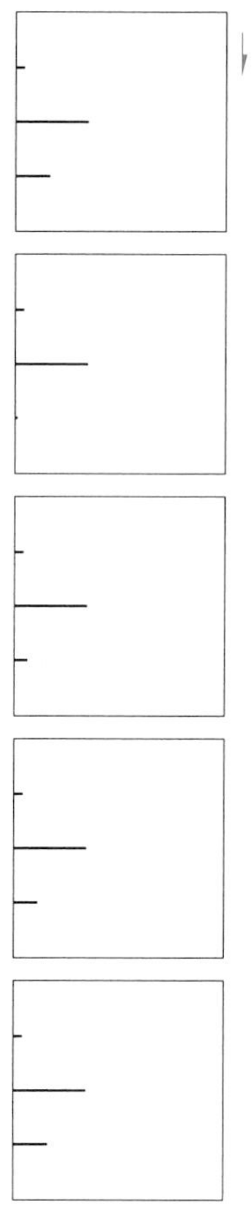

```
// display the time as lines
Forever
{
  Paper 0
  Pen 100
  Line 0 75 <Time 1> 75
  Line 0 50 <Time 2> 50
  Line 0 25 <Time 3> 25
}
```

Using this as a clock is somewhat challenging but is easily improved with some additional thought. The first problem is recognizing the hour, which is remedied by adding some useful division marks and expanding the range from 0 to 23, to 0 to 92 by multiplying by 4. Tickmarks make the hour clearly visible, revealing the current time at which I am writing this section.

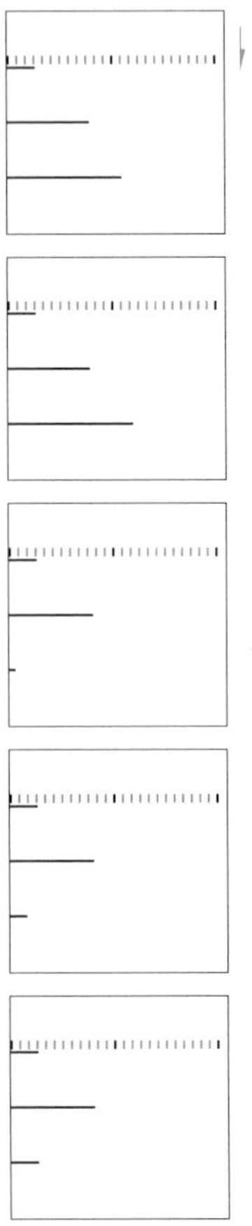

```
// expand hour resolution
Forever
{
  Paper 0
  // tick marks for hours
  Repeat A 0 24
  {
    Pen 33
    Same? A 0
    {
      Pen 100
    }
    Same? A 12
    {
      Pen 100
    }
    Same? A 24
    {
      Pen 100
    }
    Line (A*4) 77 (A*4) 80
  }
  Pen 100
  Line 0 75 (<Time 1>*4) 75
  Line 0 50 <Time 2> 50
  Line 0 25 <Time 3> 25
}
```

Minutes and seconds are easily clarified by visualizing the termination of the lines.

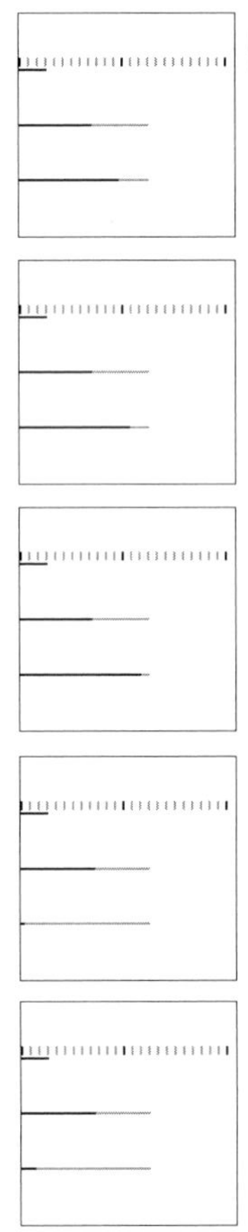

```
// add some info-rich decoration
Forever
{
  Paper 0
  // tick marks for hours
  Repeat A 0 24
  {
    Pen 33
    Same? A 0
    {
      Pen 100
    }
    Same? A 12
    {
      Pen 100
    }
    Same? A 24
    {
      Pen 100
    }
    Line (A*4) 77 (A*4) 80
  }
  Pen 100
  Line 0 75 (<Time 1>*4) 75
  Line 0 50 <Time 2> 50
  Line 0 25 <Time 3> 25
  // continuation for mins and secs
  Pen 33
  Line 60 50 <Time 2> 50
  Line 60 25 <Time 3> 25
}
```

Designing a clock is an excellent exercise for the computational designer because the context is numeric and, most importantly, always changing. As a beginning exercise, you can interpret the flow of seconds.

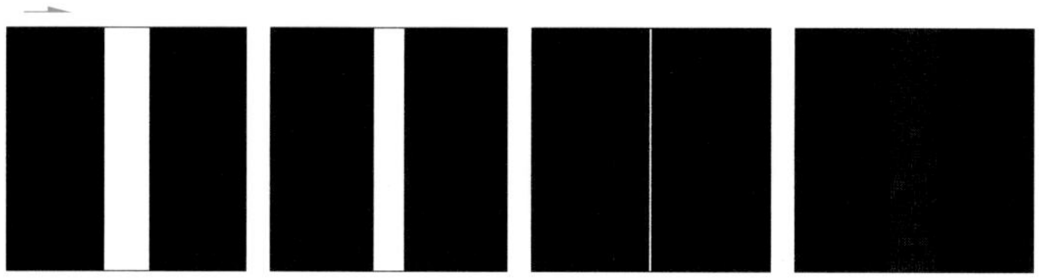

```
// end the minute with panache
Forever
{
  Paper 0
  Set S <Time 3>
  Field 0 0 S 100 100
  Field (100-S) 0 100 100 100
  Smaller? 50 S
  {
    Set L (S-50)
    Set L (L*5)
    Set V (100-L*2)
    Field (50-L) 0 (50+L) 100 V
  }
}
```

As the transition is made from 50 seconds to the end of a minute, in the last ten seconds a subtle overlap is introduced to surprise the viewer.

At the mid-minute mark, the two lines walking together across the screen switch behaviors.

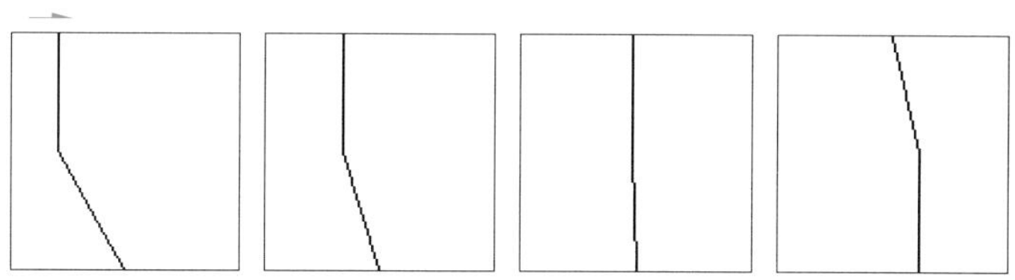

```
// sophisticate the walk across
Forever
{
  Set S <Time 3>
  Paper 0
  Set X (S*2-10)
  Smaller? X 50
  {
    Line 50 0 X 50
    Line X 50 X 100
  }
  NotSmaller? X 50
  {
    Line 50 100 X 50
    Line X 50 X 0
  }
}
```

Many lines drawn against all sides accentuate the close of a minute with almost complete darkness.

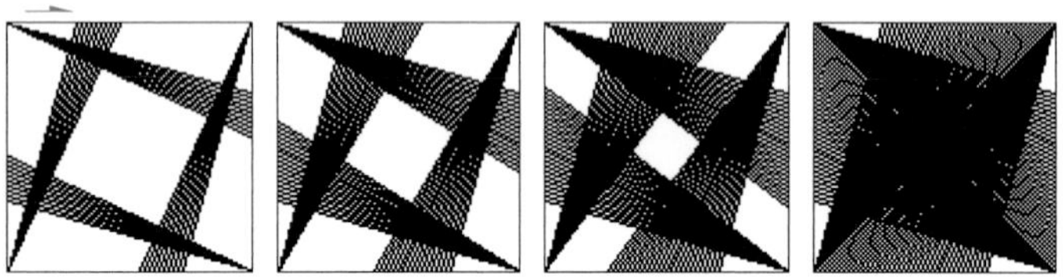

```
// line it all up
Forever
{
  Set S <Time 3>
  Set S (S*2)
  Line 0 0 S 100
  Line 0 100 100 (100-S)
  Line 100 100 (100-S) 0
  Line 100 0 0 S
}
```

When running these examples, you might wish that they went a little faster, as a minute is quite long. Incidentally, the computer operates at extremely high speeds so a second really is a long time from the computer's perspective. There is a smaller unit of time, hundredths of seconds, that is accessed through <Time 4>, where the value ranges from 0 to 100. Monitoring this smaller unit of time produces results that better illustrate the extraordinary processing ability of the computer. In this example of two lines that race across the screen, the hundredths second mark seems to flaunt its superiority quite well.

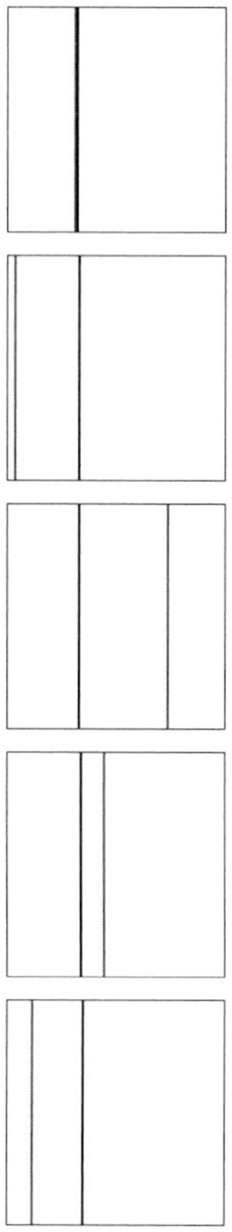

```
// illustrating finer Time
Forever
{
  Paper 0
  Pen 50
  Line <Time 4> 0 <Time 4> 100
  Pen 100
  Line <Time 3> 0 <Time 3> 100
}
```

These studies of time are visibly lacking the ability to draw circular forms, which we traditionally associate with the display of time. Such forms require an understanding of mathematics beyond addition, subtraction, multiplication, and division and are addressed in Chapter 19.

Living Numbers Change is a transformation of state, and in a figurative sense, time imparts life upon change. If real life is simply the transformation of state over a period of time, then you should be able to synthesize a state of life on the computer. Such experiments have been performed under the collective title of *artificial life,* where themes from biology and sociology are mixed with mathematics. The results of this potent mixture are synthetic entities that emulate living systems as numbers. These systems go beyond the scope of this book, but it is useful to look at a couple of seminal examples to fuel your future thought. Both examples are formally known as *cellular automata,* which can be an intimidating term. The concepts used are very simple, but their implications are not.

A cellular automaton is defined by an initial set of states, which is transformed by a set of rules into a new set of states. In this case, consider the dots of the bottom row of the paper as the initial set of states, and the row immediately above as the place for the new set of states. A simple rule would be to transfer the set of initial states to the new set of states.

```
Paper 0
// draw an initial pattern
Repeat A 0 50
{
  Set A2 (A*2)
  Set [A2 0] 100
}
Set B 1
// copy the pattern below
Repeat A 0 100
{
  Same? [A (B-1)] 100
  {
    Set [A B] 100
  }
  NotSame? [A (B-1)] 100
  {
    Set [A B] 0
  }
}
```

This process can be continued over many cycles by enclosing the general transform in a Repeat.

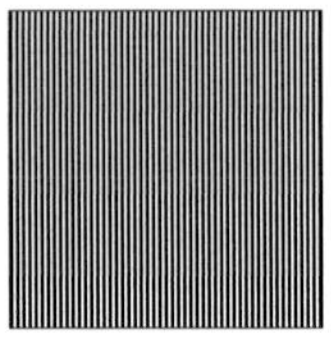

```
Paper 0
// draw an initial pattern
Repeat A 0 50
{
  Set A2 (A*2)
  Set [A2 0] 100
}
// copy the pattern below
Repeat B 1 100
{
  Repeat A 0 100
  {
    Same? [A (B-1)] 100
    {
      Set [A B] 100
    }
    NotSame? [A (B-1)] 100
    {
      Set [A B] 0
    }
  }
}
```

In this manner, the states in the bottom row are copied to the row above and continually copied verbatim from above. A slight modification in the rules for relating successive changes results in a less monotonous outcome. For example, the value from a row above is inverted.

```
Paper 0
// draw an initial pattern
Repeat A 0 50
{
  Set A2 (A*2)
  Set [A2 0] 100
}
// copy the pattern below
Repeat B 1 100
{
  Repeat A 0 100
  {
    Set [A B] (100-[A (B-1)])
  }
}
```

Another slightly more complex method of transfer, discovered by the mathematician Stephen Wolfram, results in a surprising outcome.

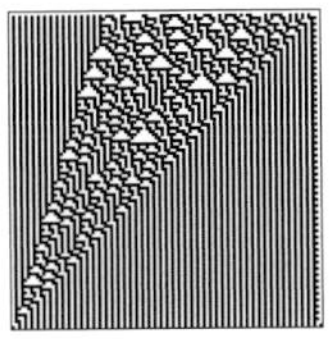

```
// draw an initial pattern
Repeat T 0 50
{
  Set [(T*2) 0] 100
}
// apply wolfram 1-d ca
Repeat B 1 99
{
  Repeat A 1 99
  {
    Set AA (A-1)
    Set AB (A+1)
    Set BB (B-1)
    Same? [AA BB] 100
    {
      Same? [A BB] 100
      {
        Same? [AB BB] 100
        {
          Set [A B] 0
        }
        NotSame? [AB BB] 100
        {
          Set [A B] 0
        }
      }
      NotSame? [A BB] 100
      {
        Same? [AB BB] 100
        {
          Set [A B] 0
        }
        NotSame? [AB BB] 100
        {
          Set [A B] 100
        }
      }
    }
    NotSame? [AA BB] 100
    {
      Same? [A BB] 100
      {
        Same? [AB BB] 100
        {
          Set [A B] 100
        }
        NotSame? [AB BB] 100
        {
          Set [A B] 100
        }
      }
      NotSame? [A BB] 100
      {
        Same? [AB BB] 100
        {
          Set [A B] 100
        }
        NotSame? [AB BB] 100
        {
          Set [A B] 0
        }
      }
    }
  }
}
```

Starting from a simpler state of just one black dot in the bottom row emphasizes the generative aspect of this process, strikingly different from the original example of a simple copy.

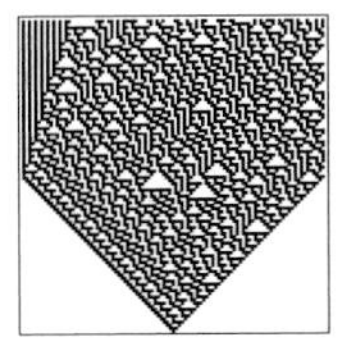

Such an example of a simple process that appears to "give birth" in this manner is said to support the notion of an artificial lifeform. Nothing in this example is really alive per se; however, a transformation process that exhibits complex properties without any obvious visible repetition is plainly seen. The process is only 15 lines of code, yet nothing you have written thus far has produced such a seemingly organic outcome. Artificial life researchers argue that these type of processes are indicative of an almost biological process at work in the numerical domain.

Another key example to consider is the two-dimensional cellular automaton known as Conway's *Life,* which is attributed to the mathematician John Conway. Instead of a single row of states as in the first automaton example, Life applies to a two-dimensional grid of states, where each state is considered to be a cell that is either alive or dead. Each cell has a total of eight neighboring cells, and whether these neighbors are dead or alive determines the next state.

In Life, there are a few simple rules that govern whether a living cell on the grid will live to the next generation or whether a new cell will be born in place of a dead cell. If there are two or three living neighbors, then a living cell will continue to live. If there are no living neighbors or only one, the living cell will die. Having four or more neighbors will also cause a living cell to die. When there is a dead cell with exactly three live neighbors, a new cell is born.

Conway's rules make sense from a biological perspective because the two situations for death are akin to being either isolated (less than two) or overcrowded (more than three). Continuation of life is a function of having enough company (two or three) and birth is determined by the right situation for mating (exactly three, which obviously differs from human reproduction). These rules are applied to the left half of the grid, where the next generation is transplanted to the right half of the paper, copied back to the original location, and run for a few cycles.

```
Paper 0
Set W 48
Set H 99
// initial pattern is a single dot
Set [25 50] 100
// do it forever
Forever
{
  Field 51 1 (51+W) H 20
  Repeat B2 1 H
  {
    Set B1 (B2-1)
    Set B3 (B2+1)
    Repeat A2 1 W
    {
      Set A1 (A2-1)
      Set A3 (A2+1)
      Set A4 (A2+50)
      // count neighbors
      Set N [A1 B1]
      Set N (N+[A2 B1])
      Set N (N+[A3 B1])
      Set N (N+[A1 B2])
      Set N (N+[A3 B2])
      Set N (N+[A1 B3])
      Set N (N+[A2 B3])
      Set N (N+[A3 B3])
      Set N (N/100)
      // when alive this generation
      Same? [A2 B2] 100
      {
        // two or three neighbors is comfortable
        Same? N 2
        {
          Set [A4 B2] 100
        }
        Same? N 3
        {
          Set [A4 B2] 100
        }
        // overcrowding results in death
        Smaller? 3 N
        {
          Set [A4 B2] 0
        }
        // loneliness also
        Smaller? N 2
        {
          Set [A4 B2] 0
        }
      }
      // when dead this generation
      NotSame? [A2 B2] 100
      {
        // takes three to cause a birth
        Same? N 3
        {
          Set [A4 B2] 100
        }
        // no hope for life
        NotSame? N 3
        {
          Set [A4 B2] 0
        }
      }
    }
  }
  // transfer buffer over to left side
  Repeat B2 1 H
  {
    Repeat A2 1 W
    {
      Set A4 (A2+50)
      Set [A2 B2] [A4 B2]
    }
  }
}
```

Nothing really interesting happens because the single dot dies from isolation.

A more festive initial pattern restores your faith.

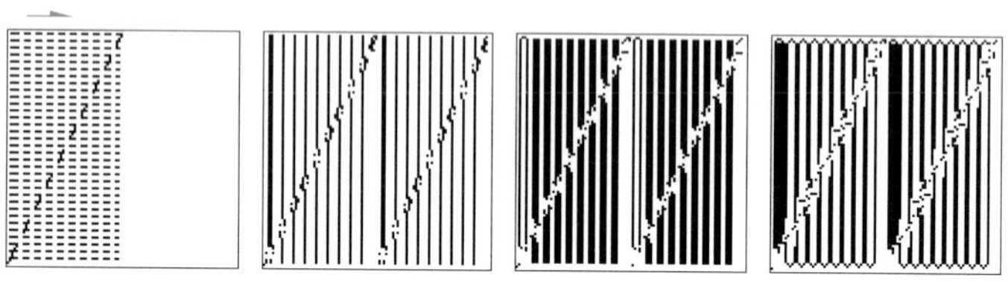

```
Paper 0
// initial pattern
Set W 48
Set H 99
Repeat A 1 H
{
  Set A2 (A/2)
  Set [A2 A] 100
}
Repeat A 1 W
{
  Repeat B 1 (H/3)
  {
    Set B2 (B*3)
    Set [A B2] 100
  }
}
Repeat B 1 (W/5)
{
  Set B2 (B*5)
  Set B3 (B2+1)
  Pen 0
  Line B2 1 B2 h
  Line B3 1 B3 h
}
// do it forever
Forever
...
```

I recall first seeing these thriving patterns 15 years ago as a freshman at MIT, thinking that the patterns were quite beautiful but at the same time wondering, "What does this have to do with life?" While it turns out that there really is no resemblance to life, there are certain patterns that seem to exhibit lifelike characteristics. The most compelling example is a five-cell figure called the *glider.*

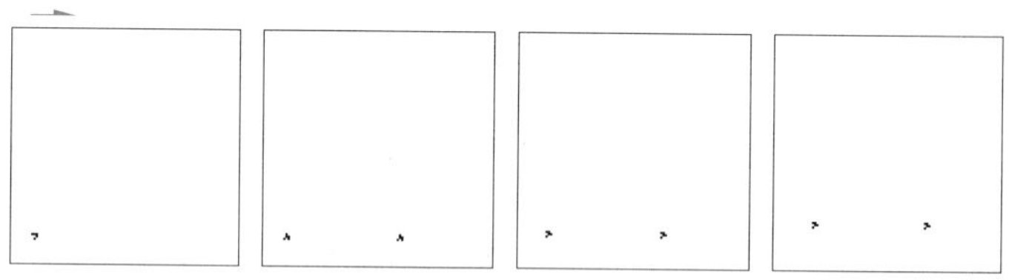

```
Paper 0
Set W 48
Set H 99
// initial pattern is a glider
Set [10 10] 100
Set [11 11] 100
Set [11 12] 100
Set [10 12] 100
Set [9 12] 100
// do it forever
Forever
...
```

The five cells of the glider appear to move around the grid as a single entity even though there are no specific rules that suggest such a phenomenon would occur. Such an occurrence is referred to as an *emergent* characteristic of the system because of the way an unexpected concept seems to emerge from a simple set of rules. There are many other *A-Life* systems, as they are called, visible on the Web today. These systems deserve special attention because they represent the ideal method for composing a computational form. However their use is still somewhat exotic and overinterpreted, and will require efforts by more artists and designers to tame this paradigm.

Summary Change in the world is usually beyond our control. The computer is the only machine that allows you to have total control of a changing situation. For change to occur, there must be a state that exists before the event of change and a state after the event. The changed state is related to its original state through a computational transfer process of varying complexity. There are meaningful transfer processes that perform a useful function, such as the telling of time or simulating numerical forms of life. There are also meaningless transformation processes, such as a nonsense filter applied to an image. In response to all needs for defining change, the computational medium will comply.

A computationally motivated transformation is irrelevant in the computational medium when the transformed state is terminal because the result could easily be printed on paper. A series of transformations, no matter how complex and colorful, is also not especially relevant to the computational medium because the result could easily be recorded on video. Only when the process of transformation continues without end and exhibits the characteristics of absolute control can you fully engage the true potential of the computational medium.

0, 1, 2, 3, 4, 5, 6, 7, 8, 9, 10, 11, 12, 13, 14, 15, 16, 17, 18, 19, 20, 21, 22, 23, 24, 25, 26, 27, 28, 29, 30, 31, 32, 33, 34, 35, 36, 37, 38, 39, 40, 41, 42, 43, 44, 45, 46, 47, 48, 49, 50, 51, 52, 53, 54, 55, 56, 57, 58, 59, 60, 61, 62, 63, 64, 65, 66, 67, 68, 69, 70, 71, 72, 73, 74, 75
1, 2, 3, 4, 5, 6, 7, 8, 9, 10, 11, 12, 13, 14, 15, 16, 17, 18, 19, 20, 21, 22, 23, 24, 25, 26, 27, 28, 29, 30, 31, 32, 33, 34, 35, 36, 37, 38, 39, 40, 41, 42, 43, 44, 45, 46, 47, 48, 49, 50, 51, 52, 53, 54, 55, 56, 57, 58, 59, 60, 61, 62, 63, 64, 65, 66, 67, 68, 69, 70, 71, 72, 73, 74, 75,
2, 3, 4, 5, 6, 7, 8, 9, 10, 11, 12, 13, 14, 15, 16, 17, 18, 19, 20, 21, 22, 23, 24, 25, 26, 27, 28, 29, 30, 31, 32, 33, 34, 35, 36, 37, 38, 39, 40, 41, 42, 43, 44, 45, 46, 47, 48, 49, 50, 51, 52, 53, 54, 55, 56, 57, 58, 59, 60, 61, 62, 63, 64, 65, 66, 67, 68, 69, 70, 71, 72, 73, 74, 75, 76,
3, 4, 5, 6, 7, 8, 9, 10, 11, 12, 13, 14, 15, 16, 17, 18, 19, 20, 21, 22, 23, 24, 25, 26, 27, 28, 29, 30, 31, 32, 33, 34, 35, 36, 37, 38, 39, 40, 41, 42, 43, 44, 45, 46, 47, 48, 49, 50, 51, 52, 53, 54, 55, 56, 57, 58, 59, 60, 61, 62, 63, 64, 65, 66, 67, 68, 69, 70, 71, 72, 73, 74, 75, 76, 77
4, 5, 6, 7, 8, 9, 10, 11, 12, 13, 14, 15, 16, 17, 18, 19, 20, 21, 22, 23, 24, 25, 26, 27, 28, 29, 30, 31, 32, 33, 34, 35, 36, 37, 38, 39, 40, 41, 42, 43, 44, 45, 46, 47, 48, 49, 50, 51, 52, 53, 54, 55, 56, 57, 58, 59, 60, 61, 62, 63, 64, 65, 66, 67, 68, 69, 70, 71, 72, 73, 74, 75, 76, 77,
5, 6, 7, 8, 9, 10, 11, 12, 13, 14, 15, 16, 17, 18, 19, 20, 21, 22, 23, 24, 25, 26, 27, 28, 29, 30, 31, 32, 33, 34, 35, 36, 37, 38, 39, 40, 41, 42, 43, 44, 45, 46, 47, 48, 49, 50, 51, 52, 53, 54, 55, 56, 57, 58, 59, 60, 61, 62, 63, 64, 65, 66, 67, 68, 69, 70, 71, 72, 73, 74, 75, 76, 77, 78,
6, 7, 8, 9, 10, 11, 12, 13, 14, 15, 16, 17, 18, 19, 20, 21, 22, 23, 24, 25, 26, 27, 28, 29, 30, 31, 32, 33, 34, 35, 36, 37, 38, 39, 40, 41, 42, 43, 44, 45, 46, 47, 48, 49, 50, 51, 52, 53, 54, 55, 56, 57, 58, 59, 60, 61, 62, 63, 64, 65, 66, 67, 68, 69, 70, 71, 72, 73, 74, 75, 76, 77, 78, 79
7, 8, 9, 10, 11, 12, 13, 14, 15, 16, 17, 18, 19, 20, 21, 22, 23, 24, 25, 26, 27, 28, 29, 30, 31, 32, 33, 34, 35, 36, 37, 38, 39, 40, 41, 42, 43, 44, 45, 46, 47, 48, 49, 50, 51, 52, 53, 54, 55, 56, 57, 58, 59, 60, 61, 62, 63, 64, 65, 66, 67, 68, 69, 70, 71, 72, 73, 74, 75, 76, 77, 78, 79,
8, 9, 10, 11, 12, 13, 14, 15, 16, 17, 18, 19, 20, 21, 22, 23, 24, 25, 26, 27, 28, 29, 30, 31, 32, 33, 34, 35, 36, 37, 38, 39, 40, 41, 42, 43, 44, 45, 46, 47, 48, 49, 50, 51, 52, 53, 54, 55, 56, 57, 58, 59, 60, 61, 62, 63, 64, 65, 66, 67, 68, 69, 70, 71, 72, 73, 74, 75, 76, 77, 78, 79, 80,
9, 10, 11, 12, 13, 14, 15, 16, 17, 18, 19, 20, 21, 22, 23, 24, 25, 26, 27, 28, 29, 30, 31, 32, 33, 34, 35, 36, 37, 38, 39, 40, 41, 42, 43, 44, 45, 46, 47, 48, 49, 50, 51, 52, 53, 54, 55, 56, 57, 58, 59, 60, 61, 62, 63, 64, 65, 66, 67, 68, 69, 70, 71, 72, 73, 74, 75, 76, 77, 78, 79, 80, 81
10, 11, 12, 13, 14, 15, 16, 17, 18, 19, 20, 21, 22, 23, 24, 25, 26, 27, 28, 29, 30, 31, 32, 33, 34, 35, 36, 37, 38, 39, 40, 41, 42, 43, 44, 45, 46, 47, 48, 49, 50, 51, 52, 53, 54, 55, 56, 57, 58, 59, 60, 61, 62, 63, 64, 65, 66, 67, 68, 69, 70, 71, 72, 73, 74, 75, 76, 77, 78, 79, 80, 81,
11, 12, 13, 14, 15, 16, 17, 18, 19, 20, 21, 22, 23, 24, 25, 26, 27, 28, 29, 30, 31, 32, 33, 34, 35, 36, 37, 38, 39, 40, 41, 42, 43, 44, 45, 46, 47, 48, 49, 50, 51, 52, 53, 54, 55, 56, 57, 58, 59, 60, 61, 62, 63, 64, 65, 66, 67, 68, 69, 70, 71, 72, 73, 74, 75, 76, 77, 78, 79, 80, 81, 82,
12, 13, 14, 15, 16, 17, 18, 19, 20, 21, 22, 23, 24, 25, 26, 27, 28, 29, 30, 31, 32, 33, 34, 35, 36, 37, 38, 39, 40, 41, 42, 43, 44, 45, 46, 47, 48, 49, 50, 51, 52, 53, 54, 55, 56, 57, 58, 59, 60, 61, 62, 63, 64, 65, 66, 67, 68, 69, 70, 71, 72, 73, 74, 75, 76, 77, 78, 79, 80, 81, 82, 83,
13, 14, 15, 16, 17, 18, 19, 20, 21, 22, 23, 24, 25, 26, 27, 28, 29, 30, 31, 32, 33, 34, 35, 36, 37, 38, 39, 40, 41, 42, 43, 44, 45, 46, 47, 48, 49, 50, 51, 52, 53, 54, 55, 56, 57, 58, 59, 60, 61, 62, 63, 64, 65, 66, 67, 68, 69, 70, 71, 72, 73, 74, 75, 76, 77, 78, 79, 80, 81, 82, 83, 84,
14, 15, 16, 17, 18, 19, 20, 21, 22, 23, 24, 25, 26, 27, 28, 29, 30, 31, 32, 33, 34, 35, 36, 37, 38, 39, 40, 41, 42, 43, 44, 45, 46, 47, 48, 49, 50, 51, 52, 53, 54, 55, 56, 57, 58, 59, 60, 61, 62, 63, 64, 65, 66, 67, 68, 69, 70, 71, 72, 73, 74, 75, 76, 77, 78, 79, 80, 81, 82, 83, 84, 85,
15, 16, 17, 18, 19, 20, 21, 22, 23, 24, 25, 26, 27, 28, 29, 30, 31, 32, 33, 34, 35, 36, 37, 38, 39, 40, 41, 42, 43, 44, 45, 46, 47, 48, 49, 50, 51, 52, 53, 54, 55, 56, 57, 58, 59, 60, 61, 62, 63, 64, 65, 66, 67, 68, 69, 70, 71, 72, 73, 74, 75, 76, 77, 78, 79, 80, 81, 82, 83, 84, 85, 86,
16, 17, 18, 19, 20, 21, 22, 23, 24, 25, 26, 27, 28, 29, 30, 31, 32, 33, 34, 35, 36, 37, 38, 39, 40, 41, 42, 43, 44, 45, 46, 47, 48, 49, 50, 51, 52, 53, 54, 55, 56, 57, 58, 59, 60, 61, 62, 63, 64, 65, 66, 67, 68, 69, 70, 71, 72, 73, 74, 75, 76, 77, 78, 79, 80, 81, 82, 83, 84, 85, 86, 87,
17, 18, 19, 20, 21, 22, 23, 24, 25, 26, 27, 28, 29, 30, 31, 32, 33, 34, 35, 36, 37, 38, 39, 40, 41, 42, 43, 44, 45, 46, 47, 48, 49, 50, 51, 52, 53, 54, 55, 56, 57, 58, 59, 60, 61, 62, 63, 64, 65, 66, 67, 68, 69, 70, 71, 72, 73, 74, 75, 76, 77, 78, 79, 80, 81, 82, 83, 84, 85, 86, 87, 88,
18, 19, 20, 21, 22, 23, 24, 25, 26, 27, 28, 29, 30, 31, 32, 33, 34, 35, 36, 37, 38, 39, 40, 41, 42, 43, 44, 45, 46, 47, 48, 49, 50, 51, 52, 53, 54, 55, 56, 57, 58, 59, 60, 61, 62, 63, 64, 65, 66, 67, 68, 69, 70, 71, 72, 73, 74, 75, 76, 77, 78, 79, 80, 81, 82, 83, 84, 85, 86, 87, 88, 89,
19, 20, 21, 22, 23, 24, 25, 26, 27, 28, 29, 30, 31, 32, 33, 34, 35, 36, 37, 38, 39, 40, 41, 42, 43, 44, 45, 46, 47, 48, 49, 50, 51, 52, 53, 54, 55, 56, 57, 58, 59, 60, 61, 62, 63, 64, 65, 66, 67, 68, 69, 70, 71, 72, 73, 74, 75, 76, 77, 78, 79, 80, 81, 82, 83, 84, 85, 86, 87, 88, 89, 90,
20, 21, 22, 23, 24, 25, 26, 27, 28, 29, 30, 31, 32, 33, 34, 35, 36, 37, 38, 39, 40, 41, 42, 43, 44, 45, 46, 47, 48, 49, 50, 51, 52, 53, 54, 55, 56, 57, 58, 59, 60, 61, 62, 63, 64, 65, 66, 67, 68, 69, 70, 71, 72, 73, 74, 75, 76, 77, 78, 79, 80, 81, 82, 83, 84, 85, 86, 87, 88, 89, 90, 91,
21, 22, 23, 24, 25, 26, 27, 28, 29, 30, 31, 32, 33, 34, 35, 36, 37, 38, 39, 40, 41, 42, 43, 44, 45, 46, 47, 48, 49, 50, 51, 52, 53, 54, 55, 56, 57, 58, 59, 60, 61, 62, 63, 64, 65, 66, 67, 68, 69, 70, 71, 72, 73, 74, 75, 76, 77, 78, 79, 80, 81, 82, 83, 84, 85, 86, 87, 88, 89, 90, 91, 92,
22, 23, 24, 25, 26, 27, 28, 29, 30, 31, 32, 33, 34, 35, 36, 37, 38, 39, 40, 41, 42, 43, 44, 45, 46, 47, 48, 49, 50, 51, 52, 53, 54, 55, 56, 57, 58, 59, 60, 61, 62, 63, 64, 65, 66, 67, 68, 69, 70, 71, 72, 73, 74, 75, 76, 77, 78, 79, 80, 81, 82, 83, 84, 85, 86, 87, 88, 89, 90, 91, 92, 93,
23, 24, 25, 26, 27, 28, 29, 30, 31, 32, 33, 34, 35, 36, 37, 38, 39, 40, 41, 42, 43, 44, 45, 46, 47, 48, 49, 50, 51, 52, 53, 54, 55, 56, 57, 58, 59, 60, 61, 62, 63, 64, 65, 66, 67, 68, 69, 70, 71, 72, 73, 74, 75, 76, 77, 78, 79, 80, 81, 82, 83, 84, 85, 86, 87, 88, 89, 90, 91, 92, 93, 94,
24, 25, 26, 27, 28, 29, 30, 31, 32, 33, 34, 35, 36, 37, 38, 39, 40, 41, 42, 43, 44, 45, 46, 47, 48, 49, 50, 51, 52, 53, 54, 55, 56, 57, 58, 59, 60, 61, 62, 63, 64, 65, 66, 67, 68, 69, 70, 71, 72, 73, 74, 75, 76, 77, 78, 79, 80, 81, 82, 83, 84, 85, 86, 87, 88, 89, 90, 91, 92, 93, 94, 95,
25, 26, 27, 28, 29, 30, 31, 32, 33, 34, 35, 36, 37, 38, 39, 40, 41, 42, 43, 44, 45, 46, 47, 48, 49, 50, 51, 52, 53, 54, 55, 56, 57, 58, 59, 60, 61, 62, 63, 64, 65, 66, 67, 68, 69, 70, 71, 72, 73, 74, 75, 76, 77, 78, 79, 80, 81, 82, 83, 84, 85, 86, 87, 88, 89, 90, 91, 92, 93, 94, 95, 96,
26, 27, 28, 29, 30, 31, 32, 33, 34, 35, 36, 37, 38, 39, 40, 41, 42, 43, 44, 45, 46, 47, 48, 49, 50, 51, 52, 53, 54, 55, 56, 57, 58, 59, 60, 61, 62, 63, 64, 65, 66, 67, 68, 69, 70, 71, 72, 73, 74, 75, 76, 77, 78, 79, 80, 81, 82, 83, 84, 85, 86, 87, 88, 89, 90, 91, 92, 93, 94, 95, 96, 97,
27, 28, 29, 30, 31, 32, 33, 34, 35, 36, 37, 38, 39, 40, 41, 42, 43, 44, 45, 46, 47, 48, 49, 50, 51, 52, 53, 54, 55, 56, 57, 58, 59, 60, 61, 62, 63, 64, 65, 66, 67, 68, 69, 70, 71, 72, 73, 74, 75, 76, 77, 78, 79, 80, 81, 82, 83, 84, 85, 86, 87, 88, 89, 90, 91, 92, 93, 94, 95, 96, 97, 98,
28, 29, 30, 31, 32, 33, 34, 35, 36, 37, 38, 39, 40, 41, 42, 43, 44, 45, 46, 47, 48, 49, 50, 51, 52, 53, 54, 55, 56, 57, 58, 59, 60, 61, 62, 63, 64, 65, 66, 67, 68, 69, 70, 71, 72, 73, 74, 75, 76, 77, 78, 79, 80, 81, 82, 83, 84, 85, 86, 87, 88, 89, 90, 91, 92, 93, 94, 95, 96, 97, 98, 99,
29, 30, 31, 32, 33, 34, 35, 36, 37, 38, 39, 40, 41, 42, 43, 44, 45, 46, 47, 48, 49, 50, 51, 52, 53, 54, 55, 56, 57, 58, 59, 60, 61, 62, 63, 64, 65, 66, 67, 68, 69, 70, 71, 72, 73, 74, 75, 76, 77, 78, 79, 80, 81, 82, 83, 84, 85, 86, 87, 88, 89, 90, 91, 92, 93, 94, 95, 96, 97, 98, 99, 100,
30, 31, 32, 33, 34, 35, 36, 37, 38, 39, 40, 41, 42, 43, 44, 45, 46, 47, 48, 49, 50, 51, 52, 53, 54, 55, 56, 57, 58, 59, 60, 61, 62, 63, 64, 65, 66, 67, 68, 69, 70, 71, 72, 73, 74, 75, 76, 77, 78, 79, 80, 81, 82, 83, 84, 85, 86, 87, 88, 89, 90, 91, 92, 93, 94, 95, 96, 97, 98, 99, 100, 0, 1
31, 32, 33, 34, 35, 36, 37, 38, 39, 40, 41, 42, 43, 44, 45, 46, 47, 48, 49, 50, 51, 52, 53, 54, 55, 56, 57, 58, 59, 60, 61, 62, 63, 64, 65, 66, 67, 68, 69, 70, 71, 72, 73, 74, 75, 76, 77, 78, 79, 80, 81, 82, 83, 84, 85, 86, 87, 88, 89, 90, 91, 92, 93, 94, 95, 96, 97, 98, 99, 100, 0, 1, 2,
32, 33, 34, 35, 36, 37, 38, 39, 40, 41, 42, 43, 44, 45, 46, 47, 48, 49, 50, 51, 52, 53, 54, 55, 56, 57, 58, 59, 60, 61, 62, 63, 64, 65, 66, 67, 68, 69, 70, 71, 72, 73, 74, 75, 76, 77, 78, 79, 80, 81, 82, 83, 84, 85, 86, 87, 88, 89, 90, 91, 92, 93, 94, 95, 96, 97, 98, 99, 100, 0, 1, 2, 3,
33, 34, 35, 36, 37, 38, 39, 40, 41, 42, 43, 44, 45, 46, 47, 48, 49, 50, 51, 52, 53, 54, 55, 56, 57, 58, 59, 60, 61, 62, 63, 64, 65, 66, 67, 68, 69, 70, 71, 72, 73, 74, 75, 76, 77, 78, 79, 80, 81, 82, 83, 84, 85, 86, 87, 88, 89, 90, 91, 92, 93, 94, 95, 96, 97, 98, 99, 100, 0, 1, 2, 3, 4, 5,
34, 35, 36, 37, 38, 39, 40, 41, 42, 43, 44, 45, 46, 47, 48, 49, 50, 51, 52, 53, 54, 55, 56, 57, 58, 59, 60, 61, 62, 63, 64, 65, 66, 67, 68, 69, 70, 71, 72, 73, 74, 75, 76, 77, 78, 79, 80, 81, 82, 83, 84, 85, 86, 87, 88, 89, 90, 91, 92, 93, 94, 95, 96, 97, 98, 99, 100, 0, 1, 2, 3, 4, 5, 6,
35, 36, 37, 38, 39, 40, 41, 42, 43, 44, 45, 46, 47, 48, 49, 50, 51, 52, 53, 54, 55, 56, 57, 58, 59, 60, 61, 62, 63, 64, 65, 66, 67, 68, 69, 70, 71, 72, 73, 74, 75, 76, 77, 78, 79, 80, 81, 82, 83, 84, 85, 86, 87, 88, 89, 90, 91, 92, 93, 94, 95, 96, 97, 98, 99, 100, 0, 1, 2, 3, 4, 5, 6, 7, 8,
36, 37, 38, 39, 40, 41, 42, 43, 44, 45, 46, 47, 48, 49, 50, 51, 52, 53, 54, 55, 56, 57, 58, 59, 60, 61, 62, 63, 64, 65, 66, 67, 68, 69, 70, 71, 72, 73, 74, 75, 76, 77, 78, 79, 80, 81, 82, 83, 84, 85, 86, 87, 88, 89, 90, 91, 92, 93, 94, 95, 96, 97, 98, 99, 100, 0, 1, 2, 3, 4, 5, 6, 7, 8, 9,
37, 38, 39, 40, 41, 42, 43, 44, 45, 46, 47, 48, 49, 50, 51, 52, 53, 54, 55, 56, 57, 58, 59, 60, 61, 62, 63, 64, 65, 66, 67, 68, 69, 70, 71, 72, 73, 74, 75, 76, 77, 78, 79, 80, 81, 82, 83, 84, 85, 86, 87, 88, 89, 90, 91, 92, 93, 94, 95, 96, 97, 98, 99, 100, 0, 1, 2, 3, 4, 5, 6, 7, 8, 9, 10,
38, 39, 40, 41, 42, 43, 44, 45, 46, 47, 48, 49, 50, 51, 52, 53, 54, 55, 56, 57, 58, 59, 60, 61, 62, 63, 64, 65, 66, 67, 68, 69, 70, 71, 72, 73, 74, 75, 76, 77, 78, 79, 80, 81, 82, 83, 84, 85, 86, 87, 88, 89, 90, 91, 92, 93, 94, 95, 96, 97, 98, 99, 100, 0, 1, 2, 3, 4, 5, 6, 7, 8, 9, 10, 11,
39, 40, 41, 42, 43, 44, 45, 46, 47, 48, 49, 50, 51, 52, 53, 54, 55, 56, 57, 58, 59, 60, 61, 62, 63, 64, 65, 66, 67, 68, 69, 70, 71, 72, 73, 74, 75, 76, 77, 78, 79, 80, 81, 82, 83, 84, 85, 86, 87, 88, 89, 90, 91, 92, 93, 94, 95, 96, 97, 98, 99, 100, 0, 1, 2, 3, 4, 5, 6, 7, 8, 9, 10, 11, 12,
40, 41, 42, 43, 44, 45, 46, 47, 48, 49, 50, 51, 52, 53, 54, 55, 56, 57, 58, 59, 60, 61, 62, 63, 64, 65, 66, 67, 68, 69, 70, 71, 72, 73, 74, 75, 76, 77, 78, 79, 80, 81, 82, 83, 84, 85, 86, 87, 88, 89, 90, 91, 92, 93, 94, 95, 96, 97, 98, 99, 100, 0, 1, 2, 3, 4, 5, 6, 7, 8, 9, 10, 11, 12, 13,
41, 42, 43, 44, 45, 46, 47, 48, 49, 50, 51, 52, 53, 54, 55, 56, 57, 58, 59, 60, 61, 62, 63, 64, 65, 66, 67, 68, 69, 70, 71, 72, 73, 74, 75, 76, 77, 78, 79, 80, 81, 82, 83, 84, 85, 86, 87, 88, 89, 90, 91, 92, 93, 94, 95, 96, 97, 98, 99, 100, 0, 1, 2, 3, 4, 5, 6, 7, 8, 9, 10, 11, 12, 13, 14,
42, 43, 44, 45, 46, 47, 48, 49, 50, 51, 52, 53, 54, 55, 56, 57, 58, 59, 60, 61, 62, 63, 64, 65, 66, 67, 68, 69, 70, 71, 72, 73, 74, 75, 76, 77, 78, 79, 80, 81, 82, 83, 84, 85, 86, 87, 88, 89, 90, 91, 92, 93, 94, 95, 96, 97, 98, 99, 100, 0, 1, 2, 3, 4, 5, 6, 7, 8, 9, 10, 11, 12, 13, 14, 15,
43, 44, 45, 46, 47, 48, 49, 50, 51, 52, 53, 54, 55, 56, 57, 58, 59, 60, 61, 62, 63, 64, 65, 66, 67, 68, 69, 70, 71, 72, 73, 74, 75, 76, 77, 78, 79, 80, 81, 82, 83, 84, 85, 86, 87, 88, 89, 90, 91, 92, 93, 94, 95, 96, 97, 98, 99, 100, 0, 1, 2, 3, 4, 5, 6, 7, 8, 9, 10, 11, 12, 13, 14, 15, 16,
44, 45, 46, 47, 48, 49, 50, 51, 52, 53, 54, 55, 56, 57, 58, 59, 60, 61, 62, 63, 64, 65, 66, 67, 68, 69, 70, 71, 72, 73, 74, 75, 76, 77, 78, 79, 80, 81, 82, 83, 84, 85, 86, 87, 88, 89, 90, 91, 92, 93, 94, 95, 96, 97, 98, 99, 100, 0, 1, 2, 3, 4, 5, 6, 7, 8, 9, 10, 11, 12, 13, 14, 15, 16, 17,
45, 46, 47, 48, 49, 50, 51, 52, 53, 54, 55, 56, 57, 58, 59, 60, 61, 62, 63, 64, 65, 66, 67, 68, 69, 70, 71, 72, 73, 74, 75, 76, 77, 78, 79, 80, 81, 82, 83, 84, 85, 86, 87, 88, 89, 90, 91, 92, 93, 94, 95, 96, 97, 98, 99, 100, 0, 1, 2, 3, 4, 5, 6, 7, 8, 9, 10, 11, 12, 13, 14, 15, 16, 17, 18,
46, 47, 48, 49, 50, 51, 52, 53, 54, 55, 56, 57, 58, 59, 60, 61, 62, 63, 64, 65, 66, 67, 68, 69, 70, 71, 72, 73, 74, 75, 76, 77, 78, 79, 80, 81, 82, 83, 84, 85, 86, 87, 88, 89, 90, 91, 92, 93, 94, 95, 96, 97, 98, 99, 100, 0, 1, 2, 3, 4, 5, 6, 7, 8, 9, 10, 11, 12, 13, 14, 15, 16, 17, 18, 19,
47, 48, 49, 50, 51, 52, 53, 54, 55, 56, 57, 58, 59, 60, 61, 62, 63, 64, 65, 66, 67, 68, 69, 70, 71, 72, 73, 74, 75, 76, 77, 78, 79, 80, 81, 82, 83, 84, 85, 86, 87, 88, 89, 90, 91, 92, 93, 94, 95, 96, 97, 98, 99, 100, 0, 1, 2, 3, 4, 5, 6, 7, 8, 9, 10, 11, 12, 13, 14, 15, 16, 17, 18, 19, 20,
48, 49, 50, 51, 52, 53, 54, 55, 56, 57, 58, 59, 60, 61, 62, 63, 64, 65, 66, 67, 68, 69, 70, 71, 72, 73, 74, 75, 76, 77, 78, 79, 80, 81, 82, 83, 84, 85, 86, 87, 88, 89, 90, 91, 92, 93, 94, 95, 96, 97, 98, 99, 100, 0, 1, 2, 3, 4, 5, 6, 7, 8, 9, 10, 11, 12, 13, 14, 15, 16, 17, 18, 19, 20, 21,
49, 50, 51, 52, 53, 54, 55, 56, 57, 58, 59, 60, 61, 62, 63, 64, 65, 66, 67, 68, 69, 70, 71, 72, 73, 74, 75, 76, 77, 78, 79, 80, 81, 82, 83, 84, 85, 86, 87, 88, 89, 90, 91, 92, 93, 94, 95, 96, 97, 98, 99, 100, 0, 1, 2, 3, 4, 5, 6, 7, 8, 9, 10, 11, 12, 13, 14, 15, 16, 17, 18, 19, 20, 21, 22,
50, 51, 52, 53, 54, 55, 56, 57, 58, 59, 60, 61, 62, 63, 64, 65, 66, 67, 68, 69, 70, 71, 72, 73, 74, 75, 76, 77, 78, 79, 80, 81, 82, 83, 84, 85, 86, 87, 88, 89, 90, 91, 92, 93, 94, 95, 96, 97, 98, 99, 100, 0, 1, 2, 3, 4, 5, 6, 7, 8, 9, 10, 11, 12, 13, 14, 15, 16, 17, 18, 19, 20, 21, 22, 23,
51, 52, 53, 54, 55, 56, 57, 58, 59, 60, 61, 62, 63, 64, 65, 66, 67, 68, 69, 70, 71, 72, 73, 74, 75, 76, 77, 78, 79, 80, 81, 82, 83, 84, 85, 86, 87, 88, 89, 90, 91, 92, 93, 94, 95, 96, 97, 98, 99, 100, 0, 1, 2, 3, 4, 5, 6, 7, 8, 9, 10, 11, 12, 13, 14, 15, 16, 17, 18, 19, 20, 21, 22, 23, 24,
52, 53, 54, 55, 56, 57, 58, 59, 60, 61, 62, 63, 64, 65, 66, 67, 68, 69, 70, 71, 72, 73, 74, 75, 76, 77, 78, 79, 80, 81, 82, 83, 84, 85, 86, 87, 88, 89, 90, 91, 92, 93, 94, 95, 96, 97, 98, 99, 100, 0, 1, 2, 3, 4, 5, 6, 7, 8, 9, 10, 11, 12, 13, 14, 15, 16, 17, 18, 19, 20, 21, 22, 23, 24, 25,
53, 54, 55, 56, 57, 58, 59, 60, 61, 62, 63, 64, 65, 66, 67, 68, 69, 70, 71, 72, 73, 74, 75, 76, 77, 78, 79, 80, 81, 82, 83, 84, 85, 86, 87, 88, 89, 90, 91, 92, 93, 94, 95, 96, 97, 98, 99, 100, 0, 1, 2, 3, 4, 5, 6, 7, 8, 9, 10, 11, 12, 13, 14, 15, 16, 17, 18, 19, 20, 21, 22, 23, 24, 25, 26,
54, 55, 56, 57, 58, 59, 60, 61, 62, 63, 64, 65, 66, 67, 68, 69, 70, 71, 72, 73, 74, 75, 76, 77, 78, 79, 80, 81, 82, 83, 84, 85, 86, 87, 88, 89, 90, 91, 92, 93, 94, 95, 96, 97, 98, 99, 100, 0, 1, 2, 3, 4, 5, 6, 7, 8, 9, 10, 11, 12, 13, 14, 15, 16, 17, 18, 19, 20, 21, 22, 23, 24, 25, 26, 27,
55, 56, 57, 58, 59, 60, 61, 62, 63, 64, 65, 66, 67, 68, 69, 70, 71, 72, 73, 74, 75, 76, 77, 78, 79, 80, 81, 82, 83, 84, 85, 86, 87, 88, 89, 90, 91, 92, 93, 94, 95, 96, 97, 98, 99, 100, 0, 1, 2, 3, 4, 5, 6, 7, 8, 9, 10, 11, 12, 13, 14, 15, 16, 17, 18, 19, 20, 21, 22, 23, 24, 25, 26, 27, 28,
56, 57, 58, 59, 60, 61, 62, 63, 64, 65, 66, 67, 68, 69, 70, 71, 72, 73, 74, 75, 76, 77, 78, 79, 80, 81, 82, 83, 84, 85, 86, 87, 88, 89, 90, 91, 92, 93, 94, 95, 96, 97, 98, 99, 100, 0, 1, 2, 3, 4, 5, 6, 7, 8, 9, 10, 11, 12, 13, 14, 15, 16, 17, 18, 19, 20, 21, 22, 23, 24, 25, 26, 27, 28, 29,
57, 58, 59, 60, 61, 62, 63, 64, 65, 66, 67, 68, 69, 70, 71, 72, 73, 74, 75, 76, 77, 78, 79, 80, 81, 82, 83, 84, 85, 86, 87, 88, 89, 90, 91, 92, 93, 94, 95, 96, 97, 98, 99, 100, 0, 1, 2, 3, 4, 5, 6, 7, 8, 9, 10, 11, 12, 13, 14, 15, 16, 17, 18, 19, 20, 21, 22, 23, 24, 25, 26, 27, 28, 29, 30,
58, 59, 60, 61, 62, 63, 64, 65, 66, 67, 68, 69, 70, 71, 72, 73, 74, 75, 76, 77, 78, 79, 80, 81, 82, 83, 84, 85, 86, 87, 88, 89, 90, 91, 92, 93, 94, 95, 96, 97, 98, 99, 100, 0, 1, 2, 3, 4, 5, 6, 7, 8, 9, 10, 11, 12, 13, 14, 15, 16, 17, 18, 19, 20, 21, 22, 23, 24, 25, 26, 27, 28, 29, 30, 31,
59, 60, 61, 62, 63, 64, 65, 66, 67, 68, 69, 70, 71, 72, 73, 74, 75, 76, 77, 78, 79, 80, 81, 82, 83, 84, 85, 86, 87, 88, 89, 90, 91, 92, 93, 94, 95, 96, 97, 98, 99, 100, 0, 1, 2, 3, 4, 5, 6, 7, 8, 9, 10, 11, 12, 13, 14, 15, 16, 17, 18, 19, 20, 21, 22, 23, 24, 25, 26, 27, 28, 29, 30, 31, 32,
60, 61, 62, 63, 64, 65, 66, 67, 68, 69, 70, 71, 72, 73, 74, 75, 76, 77, 78, 79, 80, 81, 82, 83, 84, 85, 86, 87, 88, 89, 90, 91, 92, 93, 94, 95, 96, 97, 98, 99, 100, 0, 1, 2, 3, 4, 5, 6, 7, 8, 9, 10, 11, 12, 13, 14, 15, 16, 17, 18, 19, 20, 21, 22, 23, 24, 25, 26, 27, 28, 29, 30, 31, 32, 33,
61, 62, 63, 64, 65, 66, 67, 68, 69, 70, 71, 72, 73, 74, 75, 76, 77, 78, 79, 80, 81, 82, 83, 84, 85, 86, 87, 88, 89, 90, 91, 92, 93, 94, 95, 96, 97, 98, 99, 100, 0, 1, 2, 3, 4, 5, 6, 7, 8, 9, 10, 11, 12, 13, 14, 15, 16, 17, 18, 19, 20, 21, 22, 23, 24, 25, 26, 27, 28, 29, 30, 31, 32, 33, 34,
62, 63, 64, 65, 66, 67, 68, 69, 70, 71, 72, 73, 74, 75, 76, 77, 78, 79, 80, 81, 82, 83, 84, 85, 86, 87, 88, 89, 90, 91, 92, 93, 94, 95, 96, 97, 98, 99, 100, 0, 1, 2, 3, 4, 5, 6, 7, 8, 9, 10, 11, 12, 13, 14, 15, 16, 17, 18, 19, 20, 21, 22, 23, 24, 25, 26, 27, 28, 29, 30, 31, 32, 33, 34, 35,
63, 64, 65, 66, 67, 68, 69, 70, 71, 72, 73, 74, 75, 76, 77, 78, 79, 80, 81, 82, 83, 84, 85, 86, 87, 88, 89, 90, 91, 92, 93, 94, 95, 96, 97, 98, 99, 100, 0, 1, 2, 3, 4, 5, 6, 7, 8, 9, 10, 11, 12, 13, 14, 15, 16, 17, 18, 19, 20, 21, 22, 23, 24, 25, 26, 27, 28, 29, 30, 31, 32, 33, 34, 35, 36,
64, 65, 66, 67, 68, 69, 70, 71, 72, 73, 74, 75, 76, 77, 78, 79, 80, 81, 82, 83, 84, 85, 86, 87, 88, 89, 90, 91, 92, 93, 94, 95, 96, 97, 98, 99, 100, 0, 1, 2, 3, 4, 5, 6, 7, 8, 9, 10, 11, 12, 13, 14, 15, 16, 17, 18, 19, 20, 21, 22, 23, 24, 25, 26, 27, 28, 29, 30, 31, 32, 33, 34, 35, 36, 37,
65, 66, 67, 68, 69, 70, 71, 72, 73, 74, 75, 76, 77, 78, 79, 80, 81, 82, 83, 84, 85, 86, 87, 88, 89, 90, 91, 92, 93, 94, 95, 96, 97, 98, 99, 100, 0, 1, 2, 3, 4, 5, 6, 7, 8, 9, 10, 11, 12, 13, 14, 15, 16, 17, 18, 19, 20, 21, 22, 23, 24, 25, 26, 27, 28, 29, 30, 31, 32, 33, 34, 35, 36, 37, 38,
66, 67, 68, 69, 70, 71, 72, 73, 74, 75, 76, 77, 78, 79, 80, 81, 82, 83, 84, 85, 86, 87, 88, 89, 90, 91, 92, 93, 94, 95, 96, 97, 98, 99, 100, 0, 1, 2, 3, 4, 5, 6, 7, 8, 9, 10, 11, 12, 13, 14, 15, 16, 17, 18, 19, 20, 21, 22, 23, 24, 25, 26, 27, 28, 29, 30, 31, 32, 33, 34, 35, 36, 37, 38, 39,
67, 68, 69, 70, 71, 72, 73, 74, 75, 76, 77, 78, 79, 80, 81, 82, 83, 84, 85, 86, 87, 88, 89, 90, 91, 92, 93, 94, 95, 96, 97, 98, 99, 100, 0, 1, 2, 3, 4, 5, 6, 7, 8, 9, 10, 11, 12, 13, 14, 15, 16, 17, 18, 19, 20, 21, 22, 23, 24, 25, 26, 27, 28, 29, 30, 31, 32, 33, 34, 35, 36, 37, 38, 39, 40,
68, 69, 70, 71, 72, 73, 74, 75, 76, 77, 78, 79, 80, 81, 82, 83, 84, 85, 86, 87, 88, 89, 90, 91, 92, 93, 94, 95, 96, 97, 98, 99, 100, 0, 1, 2, 3, 4, 5, 6, 7, 8, 9, 10, 11, 12, 13, 14, 15, 16, 17, 18, 19, 20, 21, 22, 23, 24, 25, 26, 27, 28, 29, 30, 31, 32, 33, 34, 35, 36, 37, 38, 39, 40, 41,
69, 70, 71, 72, 73, 74, 75, 76, 77, 78, 79, 80, 81, 82, 83, 84, 85, 86, 87, 88, 89, 90, 91, 92, 93, 94, 95, 96, 97, 98, 99, 100, 0, 1, 2, 3, 4, 5, 6, 7, 8, 9, 10, 11, 12, 13, 14, 15, 16, 17, 18, 19, 20, 21, 22, 23, 24, 25, 26, 27, 28, 29, 30, 31, 32, 33, 34, 35, 36, 37, 38, 39, 40, 41, 42,
70, 71, 72, 73, 74, 75, 76, 77, 78, 79, 80, 81, 82, 83, 84, 85, 86, 87, 88, 89, 90, 91, 92, 93, 94, 95, 96, 97, 98, 99, 100, 0, 1, 2, 3, 4, 5, 6, 7, 8, 9, 10, 11, 12, 13, 14, 15, 16, 17, 18, 19, 20, 21, 22, 23, 24, 25, 26, 27, 28, 29, 30, 31, 32, 33, 34, 35, 36, 37, 38, 39, 40, 41, 42, 43,
71, 72, 73, 74, 75, 76, 77, 78, 79, 80, 81, 82, 83, 84, 85, 86, 87, 88, 89, 90, 91, 92, 93, 94, 95, 96, 97, 98, 99, 100, 0, 1, 2, 3, 4, 5, 6, 7, 8, 9, 10, 11, 12, 13, 14, 15, 16, 17, 18, 19, 20, 21, 22, 23, 24, 25, 26, 27, 28, 29, 30, 31, 32, 33, 34, 35, 36, 37, 38, 39, 40, 41, 42, 43, 44,
72, 73, 74, 75, 76, 77, 78, 79, 80, 81, 82, 83, 84, 85, 86, 87, 88, 89, 90, 91, 92, 93, 94, 95, 96, 97, 98, 99, 100, 0, 1, 2, 3, 4, 5, 6, 7, 8, 9, 10, 11, 12, 13, 14, 15, 16, 17, 18, 19, 20, 21, 22, 23, 24, 25, 26, 27, 28, 29, 30, 31, 32, 33, 34, 35, 36, 37, 38, 39, 40, 41, 42, 43, 44, 45,
73, 74, 75, 76, 77, 78, 79, 80, 81, 82, 83, 84, 85, 86, 87, 88, 89, 90, 91, 92, 93, 94, 95, 96, 97, 98, 99, 100, 0, 1, 2, 3, 4, 5, 6, 7, 8, 9, 10, 11, 12, 13, 14, 15, 16, 17, 18, 19, 20, 21, 22, 23, 24, 25, 26, 27, 28, 29, 30, 31, 32, 33, 34, 35, 36, 37, 38, 39, 40, 41, 42, 43, 44, 45, 46,
74, 75, 76, 77, 78, 79, 80, 81, 82, 83, 84, 85, 86, 87, 88, 89, 90, 91, 92, 93, 94, 95, 96, 97, 98, 99, 100, 0, 1, 2, 3, 4, 5, 6, 7, 8, 9, 10, 11, 12, 13, 14, 15, 16, 17, 18, 19, 20, 21, 22, 23, 24, 25, 26, 27, 28, 29, 30, 31, 32, 33, 34, 35, 36, 37, 38, 39, 40, 41, 42, 43, 44, 45, 46, 47,
75, 76, 77, 78, 79, 80, 81, 82, 83, 84, 85, 86, 87, 88, 89, 90, 91, 92, 93, 94, 95, 96, 97, 98, 99, 100, 0, 1, 2, 3, 4, 5, 6, 7, 8, 9, 10, 11, 12, 13, 14, 15, 16, 17, 18, 19, 20, 21, 22, 23, 24, 25, 26, 27, 28, 29, 30, 31, 32, 33, 34, 35, 36, 37, 38, 39, 40, 41, 42, 43, 44, 45, 46, 47, 48,
76, 77, 78, 79, 80, 81, 82, 83, 84, 85, 86, 87, 88, 89, 90, 91, 92, 93, 94, 95, 96, 97, 98, 99, 100, 0, 1, 2, 3, 4, 5, 6, 7, 8, 9, 10, 11, 12, 13, 14, 15, 16, 17, 18, 19, 20, 21, 22, 23, 24, 25, 26, 27, 28, 29, 30, 31, 32, 33, 34, 35, 36, 37, 38, 39, 40, 41, 42, 43, 44, 45, 46, 47, 48, 49,
77, 78, 79, 80, 81, 82, 83, 84, 85, 86, 87, 88, 89, 90, 91, 92, 93, 94, 95, 96, 97, 98, 99, 100, 0, 1, 2, 3, 4, 5, 6, 7, 8, 9, 10, 11, 12, 13, 14, 15, 16, 17, 18, 19, 20, 21, 22, 23, 24, 25, 26, 27, 28, 29, 30, 31, 32, 33, 34, 35, 36, 37, 38, 39, 40, 41, 42, 43, 44, 45, 46, 47, 48, 49, 50,
78, 79, 80, 81, 82, 83, 84, 85, 86, 87, 88, 89, 90, 91, 92, 93, 94, 95, 96, 97, 98, 99, 100, 0, 1, 2, 3, 4, 5, 6, 7, 8, 9, 10, 11, 12, 13, 14, 15, 16, 17, 18, 19, 20, 21, 22, 23, 24, 25, 26, 27, 28, 29, 30, 31, 32, 33, 34, 35, 36, 37, 38, 39, 40, 41, 42, 43, 44, 45, 46, 47, 48, 49, 50, 51,
79, 80, 81, 82, 83, 84, 85, 86, 87, 88, 89, 90, 91, 92, 93, 94, 95, 96, 97, 98, 99, 100, 0, 1, 2, 3, 4, 5, 6, 7, 8, 9, 10, 11, 12, 13, 14, 15, 16, 17, 18, 19, 20, 21, 22, 23, 24, 25, 26, 27, 28, 29, 30, 31, 32, 33, 34, 35, 36, 37, 38, 39, 40, 41, 42, 43, 44, 45, 46, 47, 48, 49, 50, 51, 52,
80, 81, 82, 83, 84, 85, 86, 87, 88, 89, 90, 91, 92, 93, 94, 95, 96, 97, 98, 99, 100, 0, 1, 2, 3, 4, 5, 6, 7, 8, 9, 10, 11, 12, 13, 14, 15, 16, 17, 18, 19, 20, 21, 22, 23, 24, 25, 26, 27, 28, 29, 30, 31, 32, 33, 34, 35, 36, 37, 38, 39, 40, 41, 42, 43, 44, 45, 46, 47, 48, 49, 50, 51, 52, 53,
81, 82, 83, 84, 85, 86, 87, 88, 89, 90, 91, 92, 93, 94, 95, 96, 97, 98, 99, 100, 0, 1, 2, 3, 4, 5, 6, 7, 8, 9, 10, 11, 12, 13, 14, 15, 16, 17, 18, 19, 20, 21, 22, 23, 24, 25, 26, 27, 28, 29, 30, 31, 32, 33, 34, 35, 36, 37, 38, 39, 40, 41, 42, 43, 44, 45, 46, 47, 48, 49, 50, 51, 52, 53, 54,
82, 83, 84, 85, 86, 87, 88, 89, 90, 91, 92, 93, 94, 95, 96, 97, 98, 99, 100, 0, 1, 2, 3, 4, 5, 6, 7, 8, 9, 10, 11, 12, 13, 14, 15, 16, 17, 18, 19, 20, 21, 22, 23, 24, 25, 26, 27, 28, 29, 30, 31, 32, 33, 34, 35, 36, 37, 38, 39, 40, 41, 42, 43, 44, 45, 46, 47, 48, 49, 50, 51, 52, 53, 54, 55,
83, 84, 85, 86, 87, 88, 89, 90, 91, 92, 93, 94, 95, 96, 97, 98, 99, 100, 0, 1, 2, 3, 4, 5, 6, 7, 8, 9, 10, 11, 12, 13, 14, 15, 16, 17, 18, 19, 20, 21, 22, 23, 24, 25, 26, 27, 28, 29, 30, 31, 32, 33, 34, 35, 36, 37, 38, 39, 40, 41, 42, 43, 44, 45, 46, 47, 48, 49, 50, 51, 52, 53, 54, 55, 56,
84, 85, 86, 87, 88, 89, 90, 91, 92, 93, 94, 95, 96, 97, 98, 99, 100, 0, 1, 2, 3, 4, 5, 6, 7, 8, 9, 10, 11, 12, 13, 14, 15, 16, 17, 18, 19, 20, 21, 22, 23, 24, 25, 26, 27, 28, 29, 30, 31, 32, 33, 34, 35, 36, 37, 38, 39, 40, 41, 42, 43, 44, 45, 46, 47, 48, 49, 50, 51, 52, 53, 54, 55, 56, 57,
85, 86, 87, 88, 89, 90, 91, 92, 93, 94, 95, 96, 97, 98, 99, 100, 0, 1, 2, 3, 4, 5, 6, 7, 8, 9, 10, 11, 12, 13, 14, 15, 16, 17, 18, 19, 20, 21, 22, 23, 24, 25, 26, 27, 28, 29, 30, 31, 32, 33, 34, 35, 36, 37, 38, 39, 40, 41, 42, 43, 44, 45, 46, 47, 48, 49, 50, 51, 52, 53, 54, 55, 56, 57, 58,
86, 87, 88, 89, 90, 91, 92, 93, 94, 95, 96, 97, 98, 99, 100, 0, 1, 2, 3, 4, 5, 6, 7, 8, 9, 10, 11, 12, 13, 14, 15, 16, 17, 18, 19, 20, 21, 22, 23, 24, 25, 26, 27, 28, 29, 30, 31, 32, 33, 34, 35, 36, 37, 38, 39, 40, 41, 42, 43, 44, 45, 46, 47, 48, 49, 50, 51, 52, 53, 54, 55, 56, 57, 58, 59,
87, 88, 89, 90, 91, 92, 93, 94, 95, 96, 97, 98, 99, 100, 0, 1, 2, 3, 4, 5, 6, 7, 8, 9, 10, 11, 12, 13, 14, 15, 16, 17, 18, 19, 20, 21, 22, 23, 24, 25, 26, 27, 28, 29, 30, 31, 32, 33, 34, 35, 36, 37, 38, 39, 40, 41, 42, 43, 44, 45, 46, 47, 48, 49, 50, 51, 52, 53, 54, 55, 56, 57, 58, 59, 60,
88, 89, 90, 91, 92, 93, 94, 95, 96, 97, 98, 99, 100, 0, 1, 2, 3, 4, 5, 6, 7, 8, 9, 10, 11, 12, 13, 14, 15, 16, 17, 18, 19, 20, 21, 22, 23, 24, 25, 26, 27, 28, 29, 30, 31, 32, 33, 34, 35, 36, 37, 38, 39, 40, 41, 42, 43, 44, 45, 46, 47, 48, 49, 50, 51, 52, 53, 54, 55, 56, 57, 58, 59, 60, 61,
89, 90, 91, 92, 93, 94, 95, 96, 97, 98, 99, 100, 0, 1, 2, 3, 4, 5, 6, 7, 8, 9, 10, 11, 12, 13, 14, 15, 16, 17, 18, 19, 20, 21, 22, 23, 24, 25, 26, 27, 28, 29, 30, 31, 32, 33, 34, 35, 36, 37, 38, 39, 40, 41, 42, 43, 44, 45, 46, 47, 48, 49, 50, 51, 52, 53, 54, 55, 56, 57, 58, 59, 60, 61, 62,
90, 91, 92, 93, 94, 95, 96, 97, 98, 99, 100, 0, 1, 2, 3, 4, 5, 6, 7, 8, 9, 10, 11, 12, 13, 14, 15, 16, 17, 18, 19, 20, 21, 22, 23, 24, 25, 26, 27, 28, 29, 30, 31, 32, 33, 34, 35, 36, 37, 38, 39, 40, 41, 42, 43, 44, 45, 46, 47, 48, 49, 50, 51, 52, 53, 54, 55, 56, 57, 58, 59, 60, 61, 62, 63,
91, 92, 93, 94, 95, 96, 97, 98, 99, 100, 0, 1, 2, 3, 4, 5, 6, 7, 8, 9, 10, 11, 12, 13, 14, 15, 16, 17, 18, 19, 20, 21, 22, 23, 24, 25, 26, 27, 28, 29, 30, 31, 32, 33, 34, 35, 36, 37, 38, 39, 40, 41, 42, 43, 44, 45, 46, 47, 48, 49, 50, 51, 52, 53, 54, 55, 56, 57, 58, 59, 60, 61, 62, 63, 64,
92, 93, 94, 95, 96, 97, 98, 99, 100, 0, 1, 2, 3, 4, 5, 6, 7, 8, 9, 10, 11, 12, 13, 14, 15, 16, 17, 18, 19, 20, 21, 22, 23, 24, 25, 26, 27, 28, 29, 30, 31, 32, 33, 34, 35, 36, 37, 38, 39, 40, 41, 42, 43, 44, 45, 46, 47, 48, 49, 50, 51, 52, 53, 54, 55, 56, 57, 58, 59, 60, 61, 62, 63, 64, 65,
93, 94, 95, 96, 97, 98, 99, 100, 0, 1, 2, 3, 4, 5, 6, 7, 8, 9, 10, 11, 12, 13, 14, 15, 16, 17, 18, 19, 20, 21, 22, 23, 24, 25, 26, 27, 28, 29, 30, 31, 32, 33, 34, 35, 36, 37, 38, 39, 40, 41, 42, 43, 44, 45, 46, 47, 48, 49, 50, 51, 52, 53, 54, 55, 56, 57, 58, 59, 60, 61, 62, 63, 64, 65, 66,
94, 95, 96, 97, 98, 99, 100, 0, 1, 2, 3, 4, 5, 6, 7, 8, 9, 10, 11, 12, 13, 14, 15, 16, 17, 18, 19, 20, 21, 22, 23, 24, 25, 26, 27, 28, 29, 30, 31, 32, 33, 34, 35, 36, 37, 38, 39, 40, 41, 42, 43, 44, 45, 46, 47, 48, 49, 50, 51, 52, 53, 54, 55, 56, 57, 58, 59, 60, 61, 62, 63, 64, 65, 66, 67,
95, 96, 97, 98, 99, 100, 0, 1, 2, 3, 4, 5, 6, 7, 8, 9, 10, 11, 12, 13, 14, 15, 16, 17, 18, 19, 20, 21, 22, 23, 24, 25, 26, 27, 28, 29, 30, 31, 32, 33, 34, 35, 36, 37, 38, 39, 40, 41, 42, 43, 44, 45, 46, 47, 48, 49, 50, 51, 52, 53, 54, 55, 56, 57, 58, 59, 60, 61, 62, 63, 64, 65, 66, 67, 68,
96, 97, 98, 99, 100, 0, 1, 2, 3, 4, 5, 6, 7, 8, 9, 10, 11, 12, 13, 14, 15, 16, 17, 18, 19, 20, 21, 22, 23, 24, 25, 26, 27, 28, 29, 30, 31, 32, 33, 34, 35, 36, 37, 38, 39, 40, 41, 42, 43, 44, 45, 46, 47, 48, 49, 50, 51, 52, 53, 54, 55, 56, 57, 58, 59, 60, 61, 62, 63, 64, 65, 66, 67, 68, 69,
97, 98, 99, 100, 0, 1, 2, 3, 4, 5, 6, 7, 8, 9, 10, 11, 12, 13, 14, 15, 16, 17, 18, 19, 20, 21, 22, 23, 24, 25, 26, 27, 28, 29, 30, 31, 32, 33, 34, 35, 36, 37, 38, 39, 40, 41, 42, 43, 44, 45, 46, 47, 48, 49, 50, 51, 52, 53, 54, 55, 56, 57, 58, 59, 60, 61, 62, 63, 64, 65, 66, 67, 68, 69, 70,
98, 99, 100, 0, 1, 2, 3, 4, 5, 6, 7, 8, 9, 10, 11, 12, 13, 14, 15, 16, 17, 18, 19, 20, 21, 22, 23, 24, 25, 26, 27, 28, 29, 30, 31, 32, 33, 34, 35, 36, 37, 38, 39, 40, 41, 42, 43, 44, 45, 46, 47, 48, 49, 50, 51, 52, 53, 54, 55, 56, 57, 58, 59, 60, 61, 62, 63, 64, 65, 66, 67, 68, 69, 70, 71,
99, 100, 0, 1, 2, 3, 4, 5, 6, 7, 8, 9, 10, 11, 12, 13, 14, 15, 16, 17, 18, 19, 20, 21, 22, 23, 24, 25, 26, 27, 28, 29, 30, 31, 32, 33, 34, 35, 36, 37, 38, 39, 40, 41, 42, 43, 44, 45, 46, 47, 48, 49, 50, 51, 52, 53, 54, 55, 56, 57, 58, 59, 60, 61, 62, 63, 64, 65, 66, 67, 68, 69, 70, 71, 72,
100, 0, 1, 2, 3, 4, 5, 6, 7, 8, 9, 10, 11, 12, 13, 14, 15, 16, 17, 18, 19, 20, 21, 22, 23, 24, 25, 26, 27, 28, 29, 30, 31, 32, 33, 34, 35, 36, 37, 38, 39, 40, 41, 42, 43, 44, 45, 46, 47, 48, 49, 50, 51, 52, 53, 54, 55, 56, 57, 58, 59, 60, 61, 62, 63, 64, 65, 66, 67, 68, 69, 70, 71, 72, 73,

80, 81, 82, 83, 84, 85, 86, 87, 88, 89, 90, 91, 92, 93, 94, 95, 96, 97, 98, 99, 100.
81, 82, 83, 84, 85, 86, 87, 88, 89, 90, 91, 92, 93, 94, 95, 96, 97, 98, 99, 100, 0.
81, 82, 83, 84, 85, 86, 87, 88, 89, 90, 91, 92, 93, 94, 95, 96, 97, 98, 99, 100, 0, 1.
82, 83, 84, 85, 86, 87, 88, 89, 90, 91, 92, 93, 94, 95, 96, 97, 98, 99, 100, 0, 1, 2.
83, 84, 85, 86, 87, 88, 89, 90, 91, 92, 93, 94, 95, 96, 97, 98, 99, 100, 0, 1, 2, 3.
83, 84, 85, 86, 87, 88, 89, 90, 91, 92, 93, 94, 95, 96, 97, 98, 99, 100, 0, 1, 2, 3, 4.
84, 85, 86, 87, 88, 89, 90, 91, 92, 93, 94, 95, 96, 97, 98, 99, 100, 0, 1, 2, 3, 4, 5.
85, 86, 87, 88, 89, 90, 91, 92, 93, 94, 95, 96, 97, 98, 99, 100, 0, 1, 2, 3, 4, 5, 6.
85, 86, 87, 88, 89, 90, 91, 92, 93, 94, 95, 96, 97, 98, 99, 100, 0, 1, 2, 3, 4, 5, 6, 7.
86, 87, 88, 89, 90, 91, 92, 93, 94, 95, 96, 97, 98, 99, 100, 0, 1, 2, 3, 4, 5, 6, 7, 8.
87, 88, 89, 90, 91, 92, 93, 94, 95, 96, 97, 98, 99, 100, 0, 1, 2, 3, 4, 5, 6, 7, 8, 9.
88, 89, 90, 91, 92, 93, 94, 95, 96, 97, 98, 99, 100, 0, 1, 2, 3, 4, 5, 6, 7, 8, 9, 10.
89, 90, 91, 92, 93, 94, 95, 96, 97, 98, 99, 100, 0, 1, 2, 3, 4, 5, 6, 7, 8, 9, 10, 11.
90, 91, 92, 93, 94, 95, 96, 97, 98, 99, 100, 0, 1, 2, 3, 4, 5, 6, 7, 8, 9, 10, 11, 12.
91, 92, 93, 94, 95, 96, 97, 98, 99, 100, 0, 1, 2, 3, 4, 5, 6, 7, 8, 9, 10, 11, 12, 13.
92, 93, 94, 95, 96, 97, 98, 99, 100, 0, 1, 2, 3, 4, 5, 6, 7, 8, 9, 10, 11, 12, 13, 14.
93, 94, 95, 96, 97, 98, 99, 100, 0, 1, 2, 3, 4, 5, 6, 7, 8, 9, 10, 11, 12, 13, 14, 15.
94, 95, 96, 97, 98, 99, 100, 0, 1, 2, 3, 4, 5, 6, 7, 8, 9, 10, 11, 12, 13, 14, 15, 16.
95, 96, 97, 98, 99, 100, 0, 1, 2, 3, 4, 5, 6, 7, 8, 9, 10, 11, 12, 13, 14, 15, 16, 17.
96, 97, 98, 99, 100, 0, 1, 2, 3, 4, 5, 6, 7, 8, 9, 10, 11, 12, 13, 14, 15, 16, 17, 18.
97, 98, 99, 100, 0, 1, 2, 3, 4, 5, 6, 7, 8, 9, 10, 11, 12, 13, 14, 15, 16, 17, 18, 19.
98, 99, 100, 0, 1, 2, 3, 4, 5, 6, 7, 8, 9, 10, 11, 12, 13, 14, 15, 16, 17, 18, 19, 20.
99, 100, 0, 1, 2, 3, 4, 5, 6, 7, 8, 9, 10, 11, 12, 13, 14, 15, 16, 17, 18, 19, 20, 21.
100, 0, 1, 2, 3, 4, 5, 6, 7, 8, 9, 10, 11, 12, 13, 14, 15, 16, 17, 18, 19, 20, 21, 22.
0, 1, 2, 3, 4, 5, 6, 7, 8, 9, 10, 11, 12, 13, 14, 15, 16, 17, 18, 19, 20, 21, 22, 23.
1, 2, 3, 4, 5, 6, 7, 8, 9, 10, 11, 12, 13, 14, 15, 16, 17, 18, 19, 20, 21, 22, 23, 24.
2, 3, 4, 5, 6, 7, 8, 9, 10, 11, 12, 13, 14, 15, 16, 17, 18, 19, 20, 21, 22, 23, 24, 25.
3, 4, 5, 6, 7, 8, 9, 10, 11, 12, 13, 14, 15, 16, 17, 18, 19, 20, 21, 22, 23, 24, 25, 26.
5, 6, 7, 8, 9, 10, 11, 12, 13, 14, 15, 16, 17, 18, 19, 20, 21, 22, 23, 24, 25, 26, 27.
6, 7, 8, 9, 10, 11, 12, 13, 14, 15, 16, 17, 18, 19, 20, 21, 22, 23, 24, 25, 26, 27, 28.
8, 9, 10, 11, 12, 13, 14, 15, 16, 17, 18, 19, 20, 21, 22, 23, 24, 25, 26, 27, 28, 29.
9, 10, 11, 12, 13, 14, 15, 16, 17, 18, 19, 20, 21, 22, 23, 24, 25, 26, 27, 28, 29, 30.
11, 12, 13, 14, 15, 16, 17, 18, 19, 20, 21, 22, 23, 24, 25, 26, 27, 28, 29, 30, 31.
12, 13, 14, 15, 16, 17, 18, 19, 20, 21, 22, 23, 24, 25, 26, 27, 28, 29, 30, 31, 32.
13, 14, 15, 16, 17, 18, 19, 20, 21, 22, 23, 24, 25, 26, 27, 28, 29, 30, 31, 32, 33.
14, 15, 16, 17, 18, 19, 20, 21, 22, 23, 24, 25, 26, 27, 28, 29, 30, 31, 32, 33, 34.
15, 16, 17, 18, 19, 20, 21, 22, 23, 24, 25, 26, 27, 28, 29, 30, 31, 32, 33, 34, 35.
16, 17, 18, 19, 20, 21, 22, 23, 24, 25, 26, 27, 28, 29, 30, 31, 32, 33, 34, 35, 36.
17, 18, 19, 20, 21, 22, 23, 24, 25, 26, 27, 28, 29, 30, 31, 32, 33, 34, 35, 36, 37.
18, 19, 20, 21, 22, 23, 24, 25, 26, 27, 28, 29, 30, 31, 32, 33, 34, 35, 36, 37, 38.
19, 20, 21, 22, 23, 24, 25, 26, 27, 28, 29, 30, 31, 32, 33, 34, 35, 36, 37, 38, 39.
20, 21, 22, 23, 24, 25, 26, 27, 28, 29, 30, 31, 32, 33, 34, 35, 36, 37, 38, 39, 40.
21, 22, 23, 24, 25, 26, 27, 28, 29, 30, 31, 32, 33, 34, 35, 36, 37, 38, 39, 40, 41.
22, 23, 24, 25, 26, 27, 28, 29, 30, 31, 32, 33, 34, 35, 36, 37, 38, 39, 40, 41, 42.
23, 24, 25, 26, 27, 28, 29, 30, 31, 32, 33, 34, 35, 36, 37, 38, 39, 40, 41, 42, 43.
24, 25, 26, 27, 28, 29, 30, 31, 32, 33, 34, 35, 36, 37, 38, 39, 40, 41, 42, 43, 44.
25, 26, 27, 28, 29, 30, 31, 32, 33, 34, 35, 36, 37, 38, 39, 40, 41, 42, 43, 44, 45.
26, 27, 28, 29, 30, 31, 32, 33, 34, 35, 36, 37, 38, 39, 40, 41, 42, 43, 44, 45, 46.
27, 28, 29, 30, 31, 32, 33, 34, 35, 36, 37, 38, 39, 40, 41, 42, 43, 44, 45, 46, 47.
28, 29, 30, 31, 32, 33, 34, 35, 36, 37, 38, 39, 40, 41, 42, 43, 44, 45, 46, 47, 48.
29, 30, 31, 32, 33, 34, 35, 36, 37, 38, 39, 40, 41, 42, 43, 44, 45, 46, 47, 48, 49.
30, 31, 32, 33, 34, 35, 36, 37, 38, 39, 40, 41, 42, 43, 44, 45, 46, 47, 48, 49, 50.
31, 32, 33, 34, 35, 36, 37, 38, 39, 40, 41, 42, 43, 44, 45, 46, 47, 48, 49, 50, 51.
32, 33, 34, 35, 36, 37, 38, 39, 40, 41, 42, 43, 44, 45, 46, 47, 48, 49, 50, 51, 52.
33, 34, 35, 36, 37, 38, 39, 40, 41, 42, 43, 44, 45, 46, 47, 48, 49, 50, 51, 52, 53.
34, 35, 36, 37, 38, 39, 40, 41, 42, 43, 44, 45, 46, 47, 48, 49, 50, 51, 52, 53, 54.
35, 36, 37, 38, 39, 40, 41, 42, 43, 44, 45, 46, 47, 48, 49, 50, 51, 52, 53, 54, 55.
36, 37, 38, 39, 40, 41, 42, 43, 44, 45, 46, 47, 48, 49, 50, 51, 52, 53, 54, 55, 56.
37, 38, 39, 40, 41, 42, 43, 44, 45, 46, 47, 48, 49, 50, 51, 52, 53, 54, 55, 56, 57.
38, 39, 40, 41, 42, 43, 44, 45, 46, 47, 48, 49, 50, 51, 52, 53, 54, 55, 56, 57, 58.
39, 40, 41, 42, 43, 44, 45, 46, 47, 48, 49, 50, 51, 52, 53, 54, 55, 56, 57, 58, 59.
40, 41, 42, 43, 44, 45, 46, 47, 48, 49, 50, 51, 52, 53, 54, 55, 56, 57, 58, 59, 60.
41, 42, 43, 44, 45, 46, 47, 48, 49, 50, 51, 52, 53, 54, 55, 56, 57, 58, 59, 60, 61.
42, 43, 44, 45, 46, 47, 48, 49, 50, 51, 52, 53, 54, 55, 56, 57, 58, 59, 60, 61, 62.
43, 44, 45, 46, 47, 48, 49, 50, 51, 52, 53, 54, 55, 56, 57, 58, 59, 60, 61, 62, 63.
44, 45, 46, 47, 48, 49, 50, 51, 52, 53, 54, 55, 56, 57, 58, 59, 60, 61, 62, 63, 64.
45, 46, 47, 48, 49, 50, 51, 52, 53, 54, 55, 56, 57, 58, 59, 60, 61, 62, 63, 64, 65.
46, 47, 48, 49, 50, 51, 52, 53, 54, 55, 56, 57, 58, 59, 60, 61, 62, 63, 64, 65, 66.
47, 48, 49, 50, 51, 52, 53, 54, 55, 56, 57, 58, 59, 60, 61, 62, 63, 64, 65, 66, 67.
48, 49, 50, 51, 52, 53, 54, 55, 56, 57, 58, 59, 60, 61, 62, 63, 64, 65, 66, 67, 68.
49, 50, 51, 52, 53, 54, 55, 56, 57, 58, 59, 60, 61, 62, 63, 64, 65, 66, 67, 68, 69.
50, 51, 52, 53, 54, 55, 56, 57, 58, 59, 60, 61, 62, 63, 64, 65, 66, 67, 68, 69, 70.
51, 52, 53, 54, 55, 56, 57, 58, 59, 60, 61, 62, 63, 64, 65, 66, 67, 68, 69, 70, 71.
52, 53, 54, 55, 56, 57, 58, 59, 60, 61, 62, 63, 64, 65, 66, 67, 68, 69, 70, 71, 72.
53, 54, 55, 56, 57, 58, 59, 60, 61, 62, 63, 64, 65, 66, 67, 68, 69, 70, 71, 72, 73.
54, 55, 56, 57, 58, 59, 60, 61, 62, 63, 64, 65, 66, 67, 68, 69, 70, 71, 72, 73, 74.
55, 56, 57, 58, 59, 60, 61, 62, 63, 64, 65, 66, 67, 68, 69, 70, 71, 72, 73, 74, 75.
56, 57, 58, 59, 60, 61, 62, 63, 64, 65, 66, 67, 68, 69, 70, 71, 72, 73, 74, 75, 76.
57, 58, 59, 60, 61, 62, 63, 64, 65, 66, 67, 68, 69, 70, 71, 72, 73, 74, 75, 76, 77.
58, 59, 60, 61, 62, 63, 64, 65, 66, 67, 68, 69, 70, 71, 72, 73, 74, 75, 76, 77, 78.
59, 60, 61, 62, 63, 64, 65, 66, 67, 68, 69, 70, 71, 72, 73, 74, 75, 76, 77, 78, 79.
60, 61, 62, 63, 64, 65, 66, 67, 68, 69, 70, 71, 72, 73, 74, 75, 76, 77, 78, 79, 80.
61, 62, 63, 64, 65, 66, 67, 68, 69, 70, 71, 72, 73, 74, 75, 76, 77, 78, 79, 80, 81.
62, 63, 64, 65, 66, 67, 68, 69, 70, 71, 72, 73, 74, 75, 76, 77, 78, 79, 80, 81, 82.
63, 64, 65, 66, 67, 68, 69, 70, 71, 72, 73, 74, 75, 76, 77, 78, 79, 80, 81, 82, 83.
64, 65, 66, 67, 68, 69, 70, 71, 72, 73, 74, 75, 76, 77, 78, 79, 80, 81, 82, 83, 84.
65, 66, 67, 68, 69, 70, 71, 72, 73, 74, 75, 76, 77, 78, 79, 80, 81, 82, 83, 84, 85.
66, 67, 68, 69, 70, 71, 72, 73, 74, 75, 76, 77, 78, 79, 80, 81, 82, 83, 84, 85, 86.
67, 68, 69, 70, 71, 72, 73, 74, 75, 76, 77, 78, 79, 80, 81, 82, 83, 84, 85, 86, 87.
68, 69, 70, 71, 72, 73, 74, 75, 76, 77, 78, 79, 80, 81, 82, 83, 84, 85, 86, 87, 88.
69, 70, 71, 72, 73, 74, 75, 76, 77, 78, 79, 80, 81, 82, 83, 84, 85, 86, 87, 88, 89.
70, 71, 72, 73, 74, 75, 76, 77, 78, 79, 80, 81, 82, 83, 84, 85, 86, 87, 88, 89, 90.
71, 72, 73, 74, 75, 76, 77, 78, 79, 80, 81, 82, 83, 84, 85, 86, 87, 88, 89, 90, 91.
72, 73, 74, 75, 76, 77, 78, 79, 80, 81, 82, 83, 84, 85, 86, 87, 88, 89, 90, 91, 92.
73, 74, 75, 76, 77, 78, 79, 80, 81, 82, 83, 84, 85, 86, 87, 88, 89, 90, 91, 92, 93.
74, 75, 76, 77, 78, 79, 80, 81, 82, 83, 84, 85, 86, 87, 88, 89, 90, 91, 92, 93, 94.
75, 76, 77, 78, 79, 80, 81, 82, 83, 84, 85, 86, 87, 88, 89, 90, 91, 92, 93, 94, 95.
76, 77, 78, 79, 80, 81, 82, 83, 84, 85, 86, 87, 88, 89, 90, 91, 92, 93, 94, 95, 96.
77, 78, 79, 80, 81, 82, 83, 84, 85, 86, 87, 88, 89, 90, 91, 92, 93, 94, 95, 96, 97.
78, 79, 80, 81, 82, 83, 84, 85, 86, 87, 88, 89, 90, 91, 92, 93, 94, 95, 96, 97, 98.
79, 80, 81, 82, 83, 84, 85, 86, 87, 88, 89, 90, 91, 92, 93, 94, 95, 96, 97, 98, 99.

19 NUMBERS The title of this book, *Design By Numbers,* may have implied to the reader that the majority of discussion would be about mathematics. My premise is that numbers and mathematics can be quite confusing without some kind of motivation, thus the context has consistently been visual. Although I think that this has been an effective way to introduce the topic, advanced applications require a stronger understanding of mathematics, which can seem overwhelming to many. However, now that you are armed with a basic system that allows you to visualize basic numerical information, the more difficult task of developing an intuitive sense for numbers is completely within your reach.

Traditionally, artistic experiments with mathematics have leaned towards the exotic, most noticeably with the popular fascination with fractals, which has more to do with the selection of psychedelic color palettes than real art. Mathematics by itself is indeed an art, but its direct translation to visual representations does not necessarily result in art of any value.

In the context of computational design, mathematics is a fundamental tool for seeing the world through a numerical lens; it is a method for analyzing a situation. Mathematics can also be used as a tool to interpret an analysis in either a purely abstract manner or in the visual domain. Without ample knowledge of numerical methods to analyze situations and to synthesize relevant results, you will be forced to create only within your limited abilities. Being able to analyze and synthesize numerical information is the key to progress in your study of the computational medium. At the same time, remember that regardless of technical sophistication, no concept can be realized as art without proper tempering by a sensitive, human spirit.

Several simple numerical concepts are discussed in this chapter to demonstrate the basic issues addressed by the analysis and synthesis of numbers. The details of the numerical processing are kept at a minimum in favor of emphasizing their visual implications.

Custom Numbers Interactive design originates with a computational system's ability to respond to requests for interaction through external data readings of the mouse or keyboard. The data acquired from a user of the system can be interpreted in one of two ways: (1) as a single reading, or (2) as a series of readings analyzed over an extended period of activity. The latter is beyond the scope of this book, as well as the capabilities of the language. But you should be experienced with the former as the straightforward incorporation of external data values.

For instance, assume you wish to define a system where when the *A* key is pressed, the Paper transforms to black, otherwise it will be white by default. This is written simply as the Paper command with the descriptor, <Key 1>.

... *A*

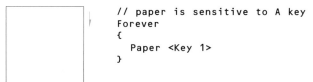

```
// paper is sensitive to A key
Forever
{
  Paper <Key 1>
}
```

But assume that the opposite result is desired, then <Key 1> must be transformed by a calculation that subtracts the value from 100.

... *A*

```
// paper is sensitive in reverse tone
Forever
{
  Paper (100-<Key 1>)
}
```

Imagine an analogous scenario where the value for the hundredths second reading is directly displayed as the Paper shade, which will cycle repeatedly from white to black each second

```
// paper is sensitive to time
Forever
{
  Paper <Time 4>
}
```

If the opposite result is desired, where the Paper changes from black to white, the value can be subtracted from 100.

```
// paper is reverse tone
Forever
{
  Paper (100-<Time 4>)
}
```

In many cases, numerical calculations are reused in this manner because they have a specific function, such as in this example where a value is subtracted from 100, producing a number that is inverted with respect to its original value. Such relationships between numbers can formally be defined so that they can be easily reused, much like a Command is defined. Such a relationship is defined with the **Number** command.

The Number command involves a set of descriptors and produces a numeric response related to the descriptors given. This also describes the general behavior of external data, which we can now reveal as, essentially, instances of Numbers.

Both non-mathematical and mathematical relations can be described by a Number. A Number simply relates one or more numbers to another number, or set of numbers. For a Number that flips, or *inverts,* in value around 100, there is a mapping between a number into its inverted relative that is used as <Invert 5>, with the mapped result being 95. With **Invert** defined, the previous examples can be rewritten.

... A

```
// defining a number
Number Invert A
{
  Value (100-A)
}
// using it
Forever
{
  Set K <Key 1>
  Paper <Invert K>
}
```

```
Number Invert A
{
  Value (100-A)
}
// use it again
Forever
{
  Set T <Time 4>
  Paper <Invert T>
}
```

A Number definition is similar to a Command definition with respect to the name of the Number and descriptor names listed at the beginning followed by the related block of code. The main difference is the use of the command **Value.** Value takes a single descriptor that specifies the final result of the Number processing as a concrete, single numeric quantity. Forgetting to include the Value command will make the value of the Number unclear and, for lack of an alternative, will default to a value of zero.

Distance One of the most useful Number modules is the simple calculation of the distance between two numeric quantities. Roughly defined, the distance is calculated by subtracting one quantity from the other, making sure that the result is not negative. For example, the distance between the numbers 50 and 55 is 5, which can either be arrived upon by our definition of distance as (50-55) or (55-50). But since (50-55) is -5, and thus not acceptable as a distance, the Number **Distance** must be written as (55-50), ensuring a positive result.

```
Number Distance A B
{
  Set D (A-B)
  Smaller? A B
  {
    Set D (B-A)
  }
  Value D
}
```

Distance can be applied in a static setting as a form of spatial calculator—for instance, displaying the horizontal measure from the diagonal of the page as a gray value.

```
Number Distance A B
{
  Set D (A-B)
  Smaller? A B
  {
    Set D (B-A)
  }
  Value D
}
Paper 0
// display distance to diagonal
Repeat B 0 100
{
  Repeat A 0 100
  {
    Set [A B] <Distance A B>
  }
}
```

Dots close to the diagonal are shaded closer to white because the distances are close to zero (recall that zero percent is white). The further away the dots, the closer they are to black.

In an interactive setting, Distance can be used as a measure for the individual horizontal and vertical distances from the cursor to the center of the paper displayed independently.

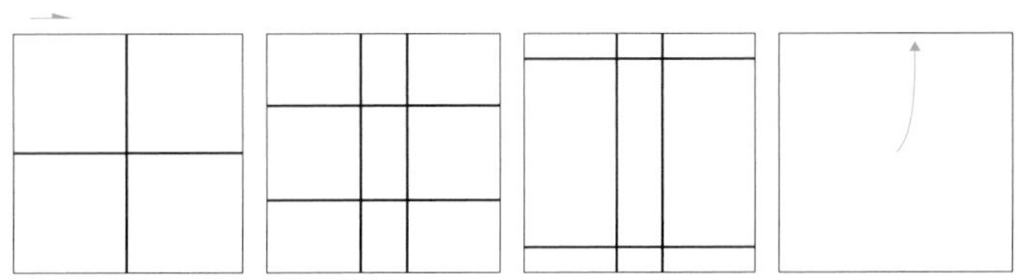

```
Number Distance A B
{
  Set D (A-B)
  Smaller? A B
  {
    Set D (B-A)
  }
  Value D
}
Pen 100
// draw horiz/vert lines
Forever
{
  Paper 0
  Set DH <Distance <Mouse 1> 50>
  Set DV <Distance <Mouse 2> 50>
  Line (50+DH) 0 (50+DH) 100
  Line (50-DH) 0 (50-DH) 100
  Line 0 (50+DV) 100 (50+DV)
  Line 0 (50-DV) 100 (50-DV)
}
```

Since our Paper is two-dimensional, calculating the point-to-point distance makes more sense than using the individual horizontal and vertical distances. There is a proper way, called the *Euclidean* distance, to calculate this quantity as the square root of the sum of the squares of the horizontal and vertical differences. But an approximation suffices for our discussion. The *Manhattan* distance, as it is called, is calculated as if you were measuring the distance you walk from point to point on the grid of streets in downtown Manhattan.

```
Number Distance A B
{
   Set D (A-B)
   Smaller? A B
   {
      Set D (B-A)
   }
   Value D
}
// number defined with a number
Number DistM H1 V1 H2 V2
{
   Set DH <Distance H1 H2>
   Set DV <Distance V1 V2>
   // manhattan distance is the sum
   // of horizontal and vertical
   // distances between 2 points
   Value (DH+DV)
}
```

Note that Numbers can be defined in terms of other Numbers just as Commands can be defined in terms of other Commands.

The newly defined **Distance2** is defined in terms of the previously defined Distance. The best way to test it is to draw a figure that represents all points within a given distance from the center of the Paper, a distance for example of 40.

```
Number Distance A B
{
   Set D (A-B)
   Smaller? A B
   {
      Set D (B-A)
   }
   Value D
}
Number Distance2 H1 V1 H2 V2
{
   Set DH <Distance H1 H2>
   Set DV <Distance V1 V2>
   Value (DH+DV)
}
// plot all dots within 40 units
Repeat B 0 100
{
   Repeat A 0 100
   {
      Smaller? <Distance2 50 50 A B> 40
      {
         Set [A B] 100
      }
   }
}
```

A quick inspection of this figure shows that on the diagonals, the distance measure appears much less than 40. We can do better by modifying the distance with a small adjustment.

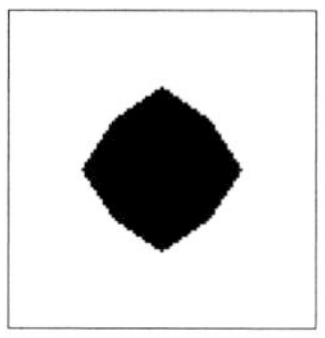

```
Number Distance A B
{
  Set D (A-B)
  Smaller? A B
  {
    Set D (B-A)
  }
  Value D
}
// be more clever with distance
Number Distance3 H1 V1 H2 V2
{
  Set DH <Distance H1 H2>
  Set DV <Distance V1 V2>
  Set SHV (DH+DV)
  Smaller? DH DV
  {
    Set SHV (SHV+DV/2)
  }
  NotSmaller? DH DV
  {
    Set SHV (SHV+DH/2)
  }
  Value SHV
}
Repeat B 0 100
{
  Repeat A 0 100
  {
    Smaller? <Distance3 50 50 A B> 40
    {
      Set [A B] 100
    }
  }
}
```

The diamond appears to have rounded a bit, and thus the distance around the perimeter appears more even. However, it is closer to 30 than 40, which could be amended with a bit of scaling. The perfect solution is the conventional distance calculation, pre-scaled to avoid a square root.

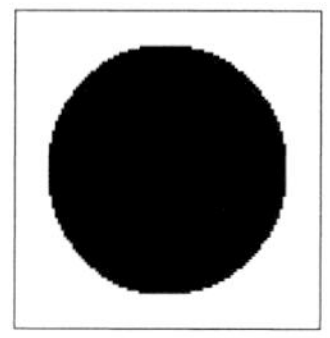

```
Number Distance A B
{
  Set D (A-B)
  Smaller? A B
  {
    Set D (B-A)
  }
  Value D
}
// do even better this time
Number Distance4 H1 V1 H2 V2
{
  Set DH <Distance H1 H2>
  Set DV <Distance V1 V2>
  Set SHV (DH*DH+DV*DV)
  Value (SHV/40)
}
Paper 0
// plot values
Repeat B 0 100
{
  Repeat A 0 100
  {
    Smaller? <Distance4 50 50 A B> 40
    {
      Set [A B] 100
    }
  }
}
```

The distance accuracy is evidenced by the perfectly circular perimeter because a circle is the figure that results when all points are equidistant from a given center point. In general, multiplication is computationally expensive, meaning that it can take longer to do than addition. Thus the approximations are a handy alternative when the program you create is running too slow.

I was once fascinated by the concept of distance and created a series of work that described enclosed spaces as distance. For instance, the distances from the center to the edges can be rendered as mappings to gray.

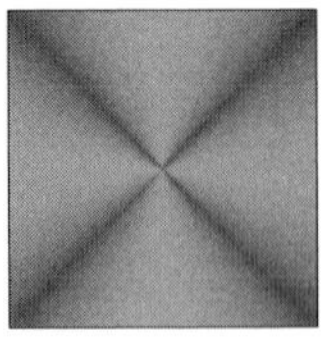

```
Number Distance A B
{
  Set D (A-B)
  Smaller? A B
  {
    Set D (B-A)
  }
  Value D
}
// prescale distance
Number Distance5 h1 V1 h2 V2
{
  Set DH <Distance H1 H2>
  Set DV <Distance V1 V2>
  Set DH (DH*DH)
  Set DV (DV*DV)
  Set SHV (DH+DV)
  Value (SHV/50)
}
Paper 0
// plot line distances from center to edges
Repeat A 0 100
{
  Set G <Distance5 0 A 50 50>
  Pen (G/2)
  Line 100 A 50 50
  Line 0 A 50 50
  Line A 0 50 50
  Line A 100 50 50
}
```

Or the distances from a corner to the edge are also rendered as gray.

```
Number Distance A B
{
  Set D (A-B)
  Smaller? A B
  {
    Set D (B-A)
  }
  Value D
}
Number Distance5 h1 V1 h2 V2
{
  Set DH <Distance H1 H2>
  Set DV <Distance V1 V2>
  Set DH (DH*DH)
  Set DV (DV*DV)
  Set SHV (DH+DV)
  Value (SHV/50)
}
Paper 0
// plot line distances from corners
Repeat A 0 100
{
  Set G <Distance5 0 A 100 0>
  Pen (G/5)
  Line 0 A 100 0
  Line A 100 100 0
}
```

Having the concept of distance easily accessible as a ready-to-use component lends a level of analytical substance to your toolkit for investigating space. There are many sophisticated ways to analyze and measure numerical information. Probability and statistics abound with such methods. Most of those techniques can be realized as Numbers, which will prove to be highly useful.

Trigonometry Sine, cosine, and tangent are the basis of a topic in basic mathematics you may remember as *trigonometry*. Personally, I never understood trigonometry until I needed to draw perfectly circular objects in my work, which sine and cosine allow you to do quite nicely with a simple formula. Unfortunately, there are no methods to do trigonometry in this system, although you could certainly write a fairly good approximation of *sine* or *cosine* as a Number. Here we use **MySine** and **MyCosine**. An approximation can be realized when by recognizing the important characteristics of sine and cosine: they are periodic, meaning they repeat in cycles. To repeat in cycles, there must be a definition of a full period of the descriptor, say 100, and furthermore, the value of the Number at the beginning of the period must be the same as the value at the end.

```
Number MySine X
{
  Value 50
}
```

This Number seems to meet the specified criteria, where <MySine 0> is the same as <MySine 100>, which is 50 in both cases. However, Sine must fluctuate considerably more to qualify. In particular, <MySine 25> should be 100, <MySine 50> should be 50, and <MySine 75> should be 0.

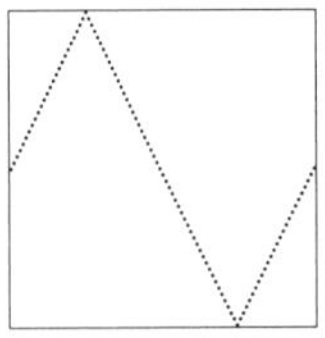

```
// sine masquerade
Number MySine Z
{
  Smaller? Z 75
  {
    Smaller? Z 50
    {
      Smaller? Z 25
      {
        Value (50+(Z*2))
      }
      NotSmaller? Z 25
      {
        Value (50+(2*(50-Z)))
      }
    }
    NotSmaller? Z 50
    {
      Value (2*(75-Z))
    }
  }
  NotSmaller? Z 75
  {
    Value (2*(Z-75))
  }
}
// draw MySine
Paper 0
Repeat A 0 100
{
  Set [A <MySine A>] 100
}
```

The values of MySine are plotted for your viewing convenience and are seen to match the specified values. The final requirement to satisfy is that <MySine 0> to <MySine 100> must repeat over <MySine 100> to <MySine 200>, <MySine 200> to <MySine 300>, and so forth. The commonly used *modulo* operation is perfect for this occasion.

A modulus adjustment ensures that a number varies between 0 and some ceiling value that is never exceeded. **Mod** is equivalent to what is known as the remainder left after division. For example, 115 divided by 100 has a remainder of 15, meaning that 115 with a modulus of 100 is 15. Since MySine works fine from 0 to 100, all that needs to be done is to force the qualifier into the range of 0 to 100 with Mod.

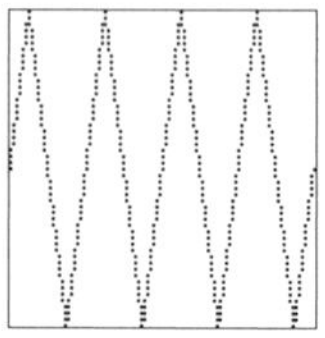

```
// mod is tricky to understand
// and is best used before understood
Number Mod X Y
{
  Value (X-(Y*(X/Y)))
}
Number MySine Z
{
  Set Z <Mod Z 100>
  Smaller? Z 75
  {
    Smaller? Z 50
    {
      Smaller? Z 25
      {
        Value (50+(Z*2))
      }
      NotSmaller? Z 25
      {
        Value (50+(2*(50-Z)))
      }
    }
    NotSmaller? Z 50
    {
      Value (2*(75-Z))
    }
  }
  NotSmaller? Z 75
  {
    Value (2*(Z-75))
  }
}
// show MySine over the
// range 0 to 400
Paper 0
Repeat A 0 400
{
  Set [(A/4) <MySine A>] 100
}
```

The values for MySine are shown over 0 to 100 and you can verify the periodicity. MyCosine is the same as MySine, except it is out of phase by a quarter period. MyCosine is displayed in gray with MySine in black.

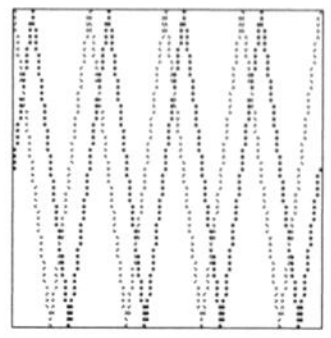

```
Number Mod X Y
{
  ...
}
Number MySine Z
{
  ...
}
// cosine just requires a shift
Number MyCosine Z
{
  Set Z (Z+125)
  Value <MySine Z>
}
Paper 0
Repeat A 0 400
{
  Set [(A/4) <MyCosine A>] 50
  Set [(A/4) <MySine A>] 100
}
```

Finally, the fun part. As you recall from Chapter 18, creating a spinning second hand of a clock was not intuitively obvious. Although sine and cosine are certainly not immediately intuitive quantities, they do enable a splendid spinning effect when the horizontal is mapped to cosine and vertical is mapped to sine.

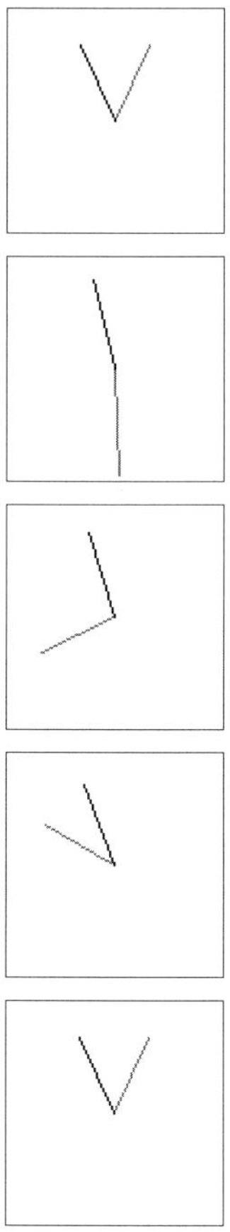

```
Number Mod X Y
{
  ...
}
Number MySine Z
{
  ...
}
Number MyCosine Z
{
  ...
}
Forever
{
  Paper 0
  Pen 50
  // milliseconds in gray, seconds in black
  Set MS <Time 4>
  Line 50 50 <MyCosine MS> <MySine MS>
  Pen 100
  Set MS (<Time 3>*100/60)
  Line 50 50 <MyCosine MS> <MySine MS>
}
```

However, careful scrutiny of the situation reveals that the second hand does not spin a circle, but rather in the shape of a diamond.

```
Number Mod X Y
{
  ...
}
Number MySine Z
{
  ...
}
Number MyCosine Z
{
  ...
}
Paper 0
// plot cos/sin as if it were a circle
Repeat A 0 100
{
  Line 50 50 <MyCosine A> <MySine A>
}
```

Before panicking, don't forget that it is at least spinning. Secondly, you should know that the lack of roundness is due to the fact that MySine bears only a faint resemblance to a real sine.

Consider a better approximation to Sine as constructed from a spline approximation, as pointed out by computer graphics pioneer Jim Blinn.

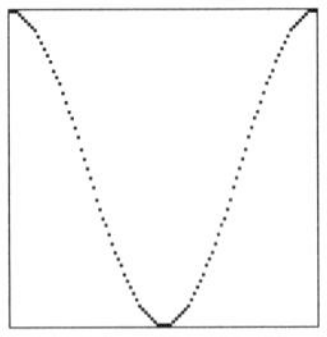

```
// Blinn spline approximation
Paper 0
Number BlSine A
{
  Set B 50
  Smaller? a 50
  {
    Smaller? a 25
    {
      Set T (A*4)
      Set T2 (T*T)
      Set T3 (T*T*T)
      Set B (100-134*T2/10000+34*T3/1000000)
      Set B (B/2+50)
    }
    NotSmaller? A 25
    {
      Set T ((50-A)*4)
      Set T2 (T*T)
      Set T3 (T*T*T)
      Set B (100-134*T2/10000+34*T3/1000000)
      Set B (50-B/2)
    }
  }
  NotSmaller? A 50
  {
    Smaller? A 75
    {
      Set T ((A-50)*4)
      Set T2 (T*T)
      Set T3 (T*T*T)
      Set B (100-134*T2/10000+34*T3/1000000)
      Set B (50-B/2)
    }
    NotSmaller? A 75
    {
      Set T ((100-A)*4)
      Set B (100-134*T2/10000+34*T3/1000000)
      Set B (B/2+50)
    }
  }
  Value B
}
Repeat C 0 100
{
  Set [C <BlSine C>] 100
}
```

This approximation should suit most of your fantasies that involve circular forms and motion.

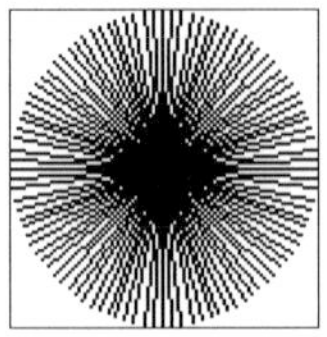

```
Number Mod X Y
{
  ..
}
Number BlSine X
{
  // incorporate mod
  ..
}
Number BlCosine X
{
  // just the shift of sine
  ..
}
// this time get a real circle
Repeat MS 0 100
{
  Line 50 50 <BlCosine MS> <BlSine MS>
}
```

Noise The amateur may be tempted by the cheap thrills of randomness. Random numbers, noise, stochastics, or whatever you want to call the complete lack of control that serves as the roots of techno-styled graphics, is a form of profanity that you should generally avoid. But in many ways, resistance may prove futile because complete control of a complex computational process is still something of a faraway goal and the allure of randomness can be overpowering. My personal philosophy has been that if you are going to use randomness, you should at least know where it comes from. Random number generation is briefly described as the last topic in this book.

The Number **Random** should return a value from 0 to 100. A simple implementation comes to mind: the instantaneous hundredth seconds value.

```
Number Random
{
  Value <Time 4>
}
```

At any given time, the hundredth seconds count is certainly a random number because it is impossible to predict. Unfortunately, this scheme only works when one or, at most, two or three random numbers are necessary because although the first random number is completely unpredictable, you can guess that the random number that follows will be just a few hundredths of a second later.

The formal random number generator used most in conventional computer systems uses the *linear congruential method.* This process requires some initial seed number that is not too small. This number is multiplied by a not-too-large number that is created from an even number with 21 tacked on to the end. One is added, and the total is Mod a number that is one digit smaller than another number ending in 21. This new number is the random number and is used as the seed for the next random number. It should be clear to you that attempting to understand this process might lead you to the hospital. Choose any numbers you like; many will work well, but to shorten your search, I chose a seed of 98, a multiplier of 198621, and a number to mod of 98621. I mod the result with 100 to force the number not to exceed 100.

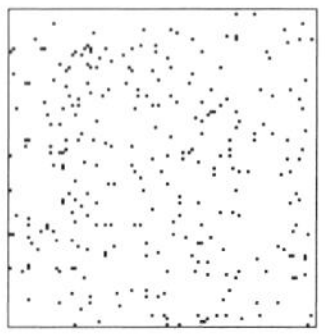

```
Number Mod X Y
{
  Value (X-(Y*(X/Y)))
}
Number Random
{
  Set BB 198621
  Set MM 98621
  Set BL (RSEED*BB+1)
  Set RSEED <Mod BL MM>
  Value <Mod RSEED 100>
}
Set RSEED 98
Paper 0
// plot 1000 random dots
Repeat A 0 1000
{
  Set [<Random> <Random>] 100
}
```

A plot of 1000 random numbers is presented, and you can see that the pattern looks random. But the sequence is not really random because each time you run the program, the result is the same.

To ensure a greater degree of randomness, you should set the initial seed to the instantaneous reading of time so that each time you run the program, there is a good chance that the random numbers used will be different from those of the previous run.

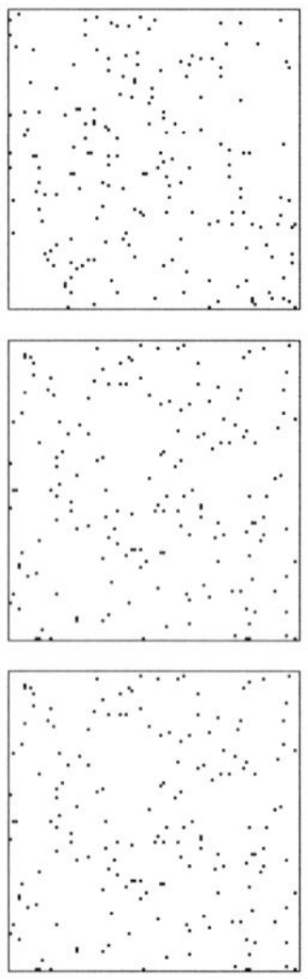

```
Number Mod X Y
{
  Value (X-(Y*(X/Y)))
}
Number Random
{
  Set BB 198621
  Set MM 98621
  Set BL (RSEED*BB+1)
  Set RSEED <Mod BL MM>
  Value <Mod RSEED 100>
}
// randomize the seed
Set RSEED <Time 4>
Paper 0
// plot 1000 random dots
Repeat A 0 1000
{
  Set [<Random> <Random>] 100
}
```

For even greater randomness, introducing time into the seed number ensures a highly unpredictable stream of numbers.

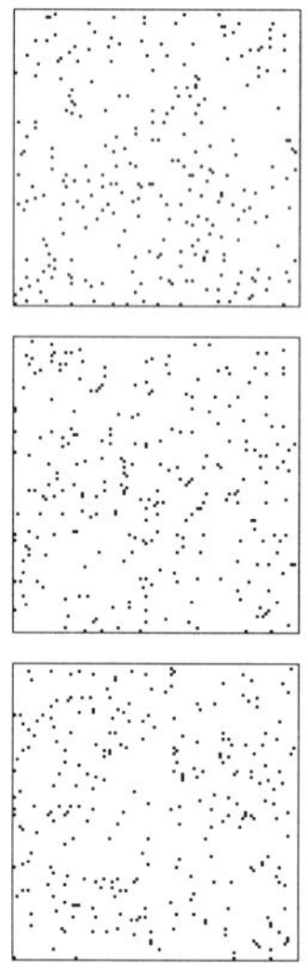

```
Number Mod X Y
{
  Value (X-(Y*(X/Y)))
}
Number Random
{
  Set BB 198621
  Set MM (98621+<Time 4>)
  Set BL (RSEED*BB+1)
  Set RSEED <Mod BL MM>
  Value <Mod RSEED 100>
}
// randomize the seed
Set rseed <Time 4>
Paper 0
// plot 1000 random dots
Repeat A 0 1000
{
  Set [<Random> <Random>] 100
}
```

A random number is a powerful basis for visual expression. If computation can be thought of as a compact means to render complex images, then computation using random numbers is perhaps the single most powerful method to express complex graphics compactly.

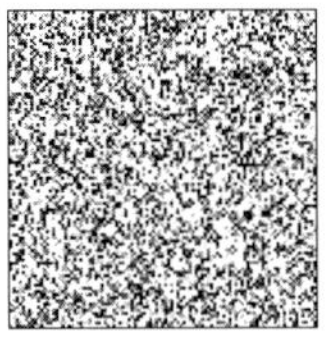

Unfortunately, the outcome is difficult to predict, which seems to be the whole point of using random numbers. There are many better ways to become completely lost in systems of noise, and if this is the path you wish to pursue, then I hope that you get lost in earnest.

Summary In the computational medium, numbers are constantly transformed into other numbers. At any instant, a number can represent a dimension, a tone, or an index that can be transformed into any similar or dissimilar quantity. A number does not necessarily have to represent a visual parameter; it can represent the number itself. The ability to create numerical transformers as command-like entitities of Numbers shows that there are potentially many useful numbers that can be used for visual experimentation. Mouse, Key, and Net were initially introduced as mysterious external data, but are now revealed to simply be translations from numbers into other numbers.

Designing with numbers is primarily about design, not numbers. Numbers are the medium, thus an intimate knowledge of them can aid your design. There are many people who know numbers intimately, but will never have a sense of design. Be proud to be one of the first designers to explore this exciting new domain of computational media design.

20 END Drawing by hand, using pencil on paper, is undisputedly the most natural means for visual expression. When moving on to the world of digital expression, however, the most natural means is not pencil and paper but, rather, computation. Today, many people strive to combine the traditional arts with the computer; and while they may succeed at producing a digitally empowered version of their art, they are not producing true digital art. True digital art embodies the core characteristics of the digital medium, which cannot be replicated in any other.

Computation is intrinsically different from existing media because it is the only medium where the material and the process for shaping the material coexist in the same entity: numbers. The only other medium where a similar phenomenon occurs is pure thought. It naturally follows that computational media could eventually present the rare opportunity to express a conceptual art that is not polluted by textual or other visual representation. This exciting future is still at least a decade or two away. For the moment, we are forced to settle with society's current search for true meaning in an enhanced, *interactive* version of the art that we have always known.

Recently it has become popular to belittle experiments in interactive media. Perhaps it is because the majority of the work is either loud and excessive or minimal and mysterious, projecting the pretense of sophistication in technology and design. In general, interactive media works do not feel natural, which is understandable considering the digital medium's synthetic nature. And yet we do not find it strange that even a book, be it made of plastic or some other synthetic material, can achieve a type of holistic maturity that has yet to be seen in the digital arts.

The reasons for this gap in quality are simple. First of all, our experience in crafting interactive forms is brief compared to the long history of publishing books. Secondly, all attempts at designing for the new media have involved adopting pre-existing notions of the visual narrative without closer consideration of the unique properties of the digital medium. And finally, there has been only minimal emphasis in art and design education on teaching students how to create in the computational medium, profoundly limiting the students' ability to imagine in the digital medium. This book is a first step towards addressing these important concerns.

You may wonder why a programming system for visually inclined people was presented primarily as text instead of some higher-order visual representation. Over the past decade, I have searched extensively for an effective visual language for computational media design and have reached the conclusion that there cannot be such a language because the parameters of computational media design are still undefined. Consider the ubiquitous PostScript language for describing static page layout. PostScript works perfectly because there have been thousands of years of experimentation in two-dimensional depiction of information that can be reduced to a set of language elements. The possibilities are completely known. On the other hand, computational media design has had an extremely short history, spanning about two decades. To declare a definitive visual language, or for that matter, any language to explore the space is simply impossible.

From a computer science perspective, one of my students, Tom White, has pointed out that I have created an "abomination" with DBN because the language cannot compare to refined ones such as Lisp or C. The scope of DBN is extremely narrow and in many respects forces you to do things in the *wrong* way. At the outset of this project, I had debated whether to use an existing language as the basis for instruction. I am glad I chose to introduce this system, even though it may seem like fingernails on a chalkboard to the language purist. My belief in this approach was confirmed when I recently visited a university-level Java class for designers. As I watched the instructor teach the finer points of object-oriented programming and bit masking of 24-bit color values, I quickly became lost in all the gibberish. I asked the instructor why he taught the subject this way. His quick reply was, "I teach it the *right* way, not watered down in any sense." I immediately came to the conclusion that I'd rather teach it the *wrong* way.

The constant goal in programming is to simplify, to generalize, to express compactly and succinctly. This often results in sacrificing legibility for brevity in deference to the non-visual aspects of the aesthetics of programming. Simple codes are as elegant as any modern sculpture. The time has come to understand, appreciate, evaluate, and constructively critique all that shall be made in the powerful medium of computation.

On a final note, I remember meeting the designer Paul Rand for the first time in January 1996. Mr. Rand's work was my inspiration for leaving the field of computer science for graphic design. He was well known for despising the computer's debilitating effect on the field of graphic design, so it was with tremendous trepidation that I showed him my computational work. Surprisingly, the first thing he said was, "How did you do this? Can you show me? You aren't leaving until you do." I, of course, had to leave eventually, but planned to return and explain to Mr. Rand the principles involved. I am glad that I finished this book, but only wish that I had started sooner, so that Mr. Rand could see its completion and perhaps write a few programs whose elegance, I am sure, would put us all to shame.

Bibliography

Aicher, Otl.
The World As Design.
Wissenschaften: Ernst & Sohn, 1991.

Banham, Reyner.
Theory and Design in the First Machine Age.
Cambridge: MIT Press, 1960.

Blinn, Jim.
Jim Blinn's Corner: A Trip Down The Graphics Pipeline.
San Francisco: Morgan-Kaufmann, 1996.

Foley, J.D. and A. Van Dam.
Fundamentals of Interactive Computer Graphics.
Reading: Addison-Wesley, 1982.

Levy, Steven.
Artificial Life: The Quest For A New Creation.
New York: Pantheon Books, 1992.

Rand, Paul.
Paul Rand: A Designer's Art.
New Haven: Yale University Press, 1985.

Sedgewick, Robert.
Algorithms.
Reading: Addison-Wesley, 1988.